ORIGINS OF THE
INDIVIDUALIST SELF

ORIGINS OF THE INDIVIDUALIST SELF

*Autobiography and Self-Identity in
England, 1591–1791*

Michael Mascuch

Stanford University Press
Stanford, California

Stanford University Press
Stanford, California
© 1996 Michael Mascuch
Originating publisher: Polity Press, Cambridge
  in association with Blackwell Publishers Ltd.
First published in the U.S.A. by
  Stanford University Press, 1996
Printed in Great Britain
ISBN 0-8047-2901-8
LC 96-70228

This book is printed on acid-free paper.

To Lianne,
in the prime of life

Contents

Acknowledgments

For permission to consult and quote from manuscripts held in their care I am obligated to the librarian and trustees of Dr Williams's Library, London, the librarian of the Friends' House Library, London, and the master and fellows of Sidney Sussex College, Cambridge. For their assistance I thank the staffs of these institutions; also the staffs of the Cambridge University Library, the Bancroft Library at UC Berkeley, the William Andrews Clark Library of UCLA, and especially the Huntington Library in San Marino, California, where the bulk of my research was done. I am grateful to the British Academy, the University of California, the Center for Seventeenth- and Eighteenth-Century Studies and Clark Memorial Library at UCLA, the Doreen B. Townsend Center for the Humanities at UC Berkeley, and the Huntington Library for grants that enabled the research and writing of this book.

With pleasure, I also acknowledge several more personal obligations. Discussions with colleagues in the Department of Rhetoric, Barbara Shapiro, David Cohen, and Felipe Gutterriez, helped me to think through several conceptual problems. Elizabeth Colwill, Doris McIlwain, and John Sutton, fellow visiting fellows at UCLA's Center for Seventeenth- and Eighteenth-Century Studies in 1994–5, carefully read and commented on the draft of part I. Richard Dienst, friend and colleague since high school, kindly read the entire draft and offered many incisive criticisms. Research assistants Jann Purdy and Peggy Hau provided punctual and meticulous help accessing sources.

My wife's grandmother, Doris McAdoo, made for me a comfortable home away from home during the many months I spent working in the Los Angeles area.

I owe a special debt of gratitude to Keith Wrightson, under whose supervision I first conceived this project; he has generously supported and encouraged its development, and my own as a professional scholar, in ways too numerous to mention. Last, my wife, Lianne Morrison, besides being my most candid critic, has endured the ordeal of the writing of this book with characteristic patience, grace, and – most important of all to me, for they are the elixir of my life – her subtle wit and brilliant humor. To her I owe more than words can express.

A Note on Texts
and Conventions

All quotations retain their original spelling, punctuation, and capitalization. Quotations from books printed in black letter are rendered in roman type. In quotations from prefaces printed predominantly in italic, the roman and italic type are reversed. Dots indicate my omissions; square brackets enclose my additions.

I often give the titles of sixteenth-, seventeenth-, and eighteenth-century printed books in longer than standard "short-titles" form, to indicate their contents more accurately. Titles retain the spelling and capitalization of the original; the type, however, has been standardized.

Dates retain the Old Style, but the year begins on 1 January.

Generic hypothetical personages appearing in these pages, such as authors, autobiographers, readers, writers, Christians, children, prisoners, and so forth, must always be understood to include both genders whether invoked in the context of the early modern period (which tended to deny such equality) or the present. However, for the sake of clarity and economy of style in discussing the persons, practices, and products of a patriarchal society, I use the masculine form throughout.

Prologue
Advertisements for Myself

Promise, large promise, is the soul of an advertisement.
                        Samuel Johnson, *Idler*, No. 40 (1759)

In the *Memoirs of the First Forty-Five Years* of his life, which he composed and first published in 1791, James Lackington recollected how, walking the streets of London one day sometime in or around the year 1776, he was addressed by a stranger who called him aside, and handed him a fly sheet. Anticipating the paper to be, as he put it, "a quack doctor's bill for a certain disease," Lackington, then a 30-year-old journeyman silk- and stuff-shoe-maker who had recently turned to retailing books, expressed surprise at the unconventional manner of its distribution.[1] Evidently even quacks did not accost people in the street with handbills without some introductory statement or gesture. But the representation of this encounter in the *Memoirs* implies an even greater surprise, evoked by the sheet's actual contents. According to Lackington, the bill contained "a particular account of the wonderful conversion of a John Biggs, when he was twenty-one years of age," authored, apparently, by Biggs himself. Lackington reported that in it, "Mr. Biggs says, that ever since that time [of his conversion] he has had *communion with God his father every hour*." Moreover, "He publishes this bill (he says) for the glory of God." "[B]ut," Lackington added, "that the public might have an opportunity of dealing with this wonderful saint and perfectly holy man, he put his address in capitals, JOHN BIGGS, No. 98, STRAND" (1792, p. 260). Thus informed, Lackington's reader finds himself anticipating some revelation of the ultimate significance of Mr Biggs. Yet here, abruptly, Lackington terminated his account of the episode with no further comment save that, "I keep this bill as a curiosity."

Seeking an explanation for this odd anecdotal digression, the reader of the *Memoirs* might recognize the patronizing tone of Lackington's paraphrase as a sign of his imminent renunciation of Methodism, to which he had converted fourteen years before, at age 16. We can infer the critique of both irrationality and hypocrisy, the two principal reasons Lackington offered as grounds for his adult rejection of religious enthusiasm, in his description of Biggs's text. Yet I believe the import of this particular recollection for the overall design of Lackington's work is greater than its function as a trope in the subplot of the memoirist's apostasy. By way of introducing my account of autobiographical practice in England in the seventeenth and eighteenth centuries, I want to propose an alternative meaning for this curious anecdote. It is a meaning Lackington could not have articulated because he lacked the vocabulary which would have enabled him to do so, but one which I believe he nevertheless grasped obscurely: that the "curiosity" of the thing – both the contents of Biggs's handbill and the manner of its distribution – lay in its inventive genius, its deviation from the prevailing practice of spiritual biography and its novelty as a form of self-identification. Furthermore, in that first encounter with Biggs's work Lackington dimly perceived a project he himself would enlarge fifteen years later, by writing and publishing in several editions of his own narrative "self-portrait," the *Memoirs of the First Forty-Five Years of the Life of James Lackington*. For us the publication of this text was a seminal event.

In spite of his contempt for Biggs as a kind of evangelical quack, Lackington admired the self-proclaimed saint's initiative, which mirrored the "dauntless disposition" the *Memoirs* names as the source of Lackington's own "very uncommon success" in trade (1792, pp. 68, 365). Lackington recognized commercial acumen when he saw it, and he found it in the self-representation of Mr Biggs. The idea of a person aggressively developing and directing his own identity through the medium of a printed biographical narrative fascinated Lackington. This fascination made Biggs's publication a curiosity to the memoirist: Lackington was attracted by the fact that, in spite of what it claimed, the bill was obviously a puff for Biggs himself, the person, rather than – as was traditionally the case with sincere narratives of pious persons written in the seventeenth and eighteenth centuries – a testimony to the glory of God. In Lackington's view, the intent of Biggs's handbill was not to adduce the "saint" as an edifying example of grace, but to assert the man claiming sainthood as an end in himself. This meaning is evident in the irony Lackington finds in the bill's discourse, especially in its emphasis on Biggs's address, encouraging public attendance at the living spectacle of "this wonderful saint," no doubt for a fee. Though in such irony Lackington identified yet another instance of his bane, religious hypocrisy, he also discovered something that interested him more: a novel instrument of self-identification. In its printed, circulated form the narrative served a selfish rather than a selfless purpose. Lackington perceived in Biggs's work a new kind of conversion narrative, and a new identity for the convert.

Of course Lackington knew that Biggs's text was not entirely sui generis. As both a bookseller and a voracious reader, Lackington was acquainted with the long tradition of printed hagiography, which included a number of narratives penned by the saints themselves. He counted over a dozen of these "pious lives" in his personal library (1791, p. 137). Yet such lives were typically published posthumously, by editors who valued them as tools for the promotion of godliness. Only in exceptional circumstances did holy people publish their own lives, and then with profuse apologies for their breach of proper practice. Nevertheless, by Lackington's day abuses of the hagiographical tradition for personal rather than spiritual promotion had become so frequent that such texts nearly embodied a genre of their own. In addition to Biggs's bill, the *Memoirs* mentions two other species of this new genus, the hack biography of the public figure, and the hack account of the reformation of the bad man. Each begat a kind of unholy profit.

On the one hand, the "life" as a book commanded a monetary value as a consumable commodity. Lackington recalled how, shortly after the renowned Methodist evangelist John Wesley's death in 1791, "a number of needy bretheren deemed it a fair opportunity of profiting by it," each producing a book containing his own "*Life* of him" (1791, p. 188). He characterized the result as an example of how "the house of prayer is again become a den of thieves":

> for some weeks since the funeral the Chapel-yard and its vicinity has exhibited a truly ludicrous scene, on every night of preaching, owing to the different writers and venders of these hasty performances exerting themselves to secure a good sale; one bawling out, that *his* is the *right* life, a second with a pious shake of the head, declares *his* is the real life, a third protests *he* has got the *only genuine* account; and a fourth calls them all vile cheats and impostors, &c. (1791, pp. 188–9)

Both the hack biographers and Lackington appreciated the reciprocal relationship between the spiritual value of Wesley's activity as an evangelist and the pecuniary value of a textual representation of that activity as a commodity. Lackington estimated that a crowd in number between 40,000 and 50,000 came to pay its last respects to Wesley's corpse before interment. The crush was so great, he said, that "many were glad to get out of the crowd without seeing him at all" (1791, p. 187). At the funeral, thousands more than Wesley's new City Road chapel could hold came and stood in the cold dark, at the godly hour of five on a mid-week morning in March, to observe the funeral procession and hear the physician George Whitehead deliver his eulogy. But while the hacks and their publishers saw in this mass audience only a ready market for a printed souvenir of Wesley, Lackington also observed a profound notoriety that owed itself in part to the aura of a corpus of discourse already in print.[2]

The popularity of Wesley's books was part and parcel of his personal charisma. Lackington noted with respect that the sale of the evangelist's writings were earning annual profits of near £2,000 at the time of Wesley's death (1791, p. 190). Eleven years before, Wesley himself remarked how, as a young man, "I wrote many small tracts, generally a penny apiece; some of these had such a sale as I never thought of, and by this means I became rich."[3] The evangelist was renowned for giving his money away; revenues from the sale of his books enabled a considerable amount of his large charity – a conservative estimate puts the proportion from publishing at about £30,000.[4] Both men witnessed how the commodity value of books constituted a significant dimension of Wesley's public identity.

But the bookseller also noted how print constituted a large part of the charisma of persons less pious than Wesley, such as the "many dreadful offenders against law and justice" sentenced to be hanged, accounts of whose lives and eleventh-hour conversions were likewise written down, hastened into print and laid out for sale (1791, p. 181). As Lackington explained,

> A great number of narratives of these sudden conversions and triumphant exits have been compiled, many of them published, and circulated with the greatest avidity, to the private emolument of the editors, and doubtless to the great edification of all sinners, long habituated to a course of villainous depredation on the lives of the honest part of the community. (1791, p. 182)

The printing and promotion of such narratives, according to Lackington, made bad people eminent, to the scandal of the pious and to the encouragement of the wicked, who might trust that they too would "sooner or later . . . be honoured with a similar degree of notice, and thus by a kind of hocus pocus, be suddenly transformed into saints" (1794, p. 272). It was obvious to him that the polis suffered the consequences of the instant public approbation magically conferred on malefactors by the "honour" of publication. Yet more than the potential social costs of valorizing vice by crowning it with print, the power of the medium itself disturbed Lackington. The notoriety of the London hanged demonstrated to Lackington that print was a potent instrument of publicity even for a person unable to pocket the cash his *Life* might earn. In both cases, of Wesley's *Life* and those of the criminals, Lackington read the bottom line: the richest "emolument" of print was not immediate financial gain but rather an investment in the symbolic capital of public recognition. As Lackington detected in his contact with the textually enhanced Mr Biggs, the printed life helped establish for its subject a public ethos from which a host of other personal advantages might accrue.

No wonder then that the aspiring bookseller, a man who remembered with pride how as a mere child he developed an original marketing strategy to put the local pie-crier out of business (1791, pp. 16–17), should attempt to build up his already considerable personal stock with the public by investing his own experience in a printed narrative. The kinship of the *Memoirs* with Mr Biggs's work is apparent in the full title conceived by Lackington, which includes both his business and address, "the present Bookseller in Chiswell Street, Moorfields, London," and his dedication of the work "To the *public*." Lackington designed his text to compete with Biggs's fly sheet, as an advertisement for the spectacle of his self. But the substance Lackington ascribed to his identity was more akin to that of the weightier printed lives of Wesley and Samuel Johnson, both of which commanded extensive approbation in the *Memoirs*. With firsthand knowledge of biography's capacity to, in Johnson's words, "enchain the heart by irresistible interest,"[5] Lackington consciously fashioned his autobiographical *Memoirs* in the vein of a nascent tradition of self-promotion in biography. In "exhibiting . . . to the public eye" a book-format representation of himself as "a man, well known to have risen from an obscure origin to a degree of notice, and to a participation of the favour of the public, in a particular line of business . . . hitherto unprecedented," Lackington attempted to persuade a vast, anonymous audience to sanction the self-identity manifest in the story of his individual success as a bookseller (1791, pp. 1, 2).

Though I shall explain later, in chapter 2, how the *Memoirs* achieves this intention through figuration at the level of discursive practice, we may here observe how it is manifest at the work's most literal level. Lackington broadcast his desire for personal fame with his rebuke to the compilers of biographies for the second edition of the *Biographia Britannica* – "that truly great and useful work," according to the memoirist (1791, p. 300) – accusing them, as many did, of impoliteness and partiality in their portraits. Addressing the editors through his text, Lackington suggested a balm which made his own intentions transparent:

> I hope that this hint will also induce them in some subsequent edition, when I am gone ... to do justice to my *great and astonishing merits*, by way of compensation for having fallen short in speaking of other *great men*; and should I happen to be *out of print* by the time the editors of the *Biographia Britannica* arrive at letter *L* ... I hope they will not slightly pass *me* over. If they should, let them take the consequence; as I here give them fair and timely notice, and they have not to plead as an excuse, the want of materials. (1791, pp. 300–1)

Lackington obviously had high expectations for the success of his *Memoirs* in establishing his personal reputation among his peers and with posterity.

While this blatant self-interest is not the only purpose the *Memoirs* served, it is arguably the most interesting of the work's intentions to students of the autobiographical genre. Though not absolutely original, Lackington's book survives as one of the earliest examples of popular modern autobiography in English, a work deliberately composed to represent to the public the authoritative ethos of its subject. Thus, the publication of Lackington's *Memoirs* in 1791 marks a unique cultural moment. It constitutes a watershed in the evolution of autobiographical practice, a site whose immediate prehistory this study will explore. It also functions as the point of intersection of the genre with another, tangential, cultural institution this study will consider: "English individualism." In his *Memoirs*, James Lackington realized the generic form of the individualist self.

In a seminal essay in autobiography studies first published in 1956 and now largely disdained by critics of modern culture for its emphasis on the kind of unified, retrospective narrative that is currently considered repressive, George Gusdorf offered a tentative but provocative account of the genre as an object of anthropological interest. Going against the grain of the approaches to discursive texts pursued by his contemporaries – whether literary formalism or historical positivism – Gusdorf argued that autobiography deserved a central place in humanist studies because its appearance marked a unique cultural moment. The moment of autobiography occasioned, in his words, "a new spiritual revolution" in history, in which "the artist and the model coincide, the historian tackles himself as object."[6] For Gusdorf, an autobiography was the product of a historically and geographically contingent practice which he characterized as "the effort of a creator to give the meaning of his own mythic tale" (p. 48). Indeed, throughout his essay Gusdorf stressed the peculiarity of the cultural practice he described; at the start he began by observing that "autobiography seems limited in time and in space: it has not always existed nor has it existed everywhere" (pp. 28–9). However, despite Gusdorf's case for the historical uniqueness of the unified retrospective autobiographical narrative, subsequent study has instead tended to promote its universality, discovering such texts almost everywhere and at nearly all times. Given this overemphasis, it is no surprise that critics now find the form oppressive: we are being smothered by too many autobiographical narratives.

My study therefore promotes a "green" agenda. It aims to clear the air by imposing limits on autobiographical emissions, placing narrative autobiography in a specific and meaningful historical environment. My basic argument, which attempts to build upon the premises originally outlined by Gusdorf, is simply this: that "autobiography" – that is, the unified, retrospective, first-person prose narrative by which the "I" so popular in modernity is identified in discourse – actually has a history differentiating it from other possible forms of autobiographical textuality and personal self-identity. In elaborating this claim, I do not presume to address autobiography's entire history; the "end of autobiography" has already been written in a variety of ways by students of philosophy, psychoanalysis and literary theory.[7] Nor do I attempt to represent either the particular variety of narrative autobiography or the potential diversity of alternative forms; my concern is not to offer a complete anatomy of the genre from antiquity to the future. Rather, from the perspective of the arguments announcing narrative autobiography's end, I offer an account of its origins.

So doing, I discover a secret history of the genre, or at least one which has so far been neglected. For one thing, its beginnings are rather recent. As I write, the narrative form is just over two centuries old; it is therefore a peculiarly modern institution. For another, although modern narrative autobiography has come to be equated with a masculine, middle-class subject of the sort represented by Lackington, the historical agents active in its original production were rather more diverse than the predominance of Lackington look-alikes in its heritage would suggest. While the practical roles of women and paupers were always marginal, I have found that members of both groups contributed to the making of modern narrative autobiography. Also, this history involved neither merely the human agent alone (the "great writer") nor in the opposite view language by itself (the "free play" of signifiers). A complex of technological developments – for example, in writing, in reading, in printing, in marketing, etc. – and institutional pressures – in particular, the requirements of social and religious control – operated together with people and their discourse to produce the modern autobiographical narrative. The sum of these and related discoveries treated in the course of what follows strongly suggests that the emergence of modern autobiography was a broadly cultural phenomenon.

At the same time, to emphasize the anthropological significance of this emergence, I consider autobiography not in literary formalist terms as a genre, but instead as a cultural practice. I read it as evidence of a form of cultural production related to the manifestation in England during the early modern period of the individualist self – the identity of the egocentric person who, like Gusdorf's historiographical "creator" mythifying himself as his own object, regards himself as his own telos. In other words, in contrast to the historical anthropologist Alan Macfarlane, whose controversial book on family ownership of property in land, *The Origins of English Individualism*, implied a kind of universalism by finding that as far back as the thirteenth century (that is, as far as the evidence would reasonably allow) the "ordinary Englishman" was a "rampant individualist," I trace a different genealogical path. Through analysis of personal ownership of a kind of literary property, the written autobiographical text and its referent, the "life" therein, I argue that the ordinary individualist self emerged in London with the appearance of Lackington's unprecedented book, in the final decade of the eighteenth century.

Of course there is more to my account than this, for no persuasive case can be made on the basis of a single text. In what follows I attempt to survey the range of first-person prose narrative produced in Britain between roughly 1550 and 1800 as widely as possible, and to represent what I have learned about it in chronological order.

My focus, and to some extent my method of exposition also, is historical. For reasons that should become clear in the early chapters of my study, the points of transition I have identified are determined largely by hermeneutic imperatives. My interest lies in the function of written utterances as social discourse, as media of particular interpersonal relations, of the encoding of specific cultural knowledge. In my formulation of it as a cultural practice, autobiography is a performance, a public display of self-identity, even when composed secretly for an audience of one. I have represented different autobiographical forms as discrete "traditions" of practice, and attempted to avoid the privileging of individual texts and persons (though it will be apparent that in order to demonstrate a point, some focus of this kind is obligatory). Thus, I have consciously avoided discussion of canonical figures such as Browne, Bunyan, Gibbon, Franklin, et al., to locate instead the cultural context of which they were a part. Works in the literary canon are by definition exceptional; their distinction is not my concern. Instead, I seek to know the practice of ordinary writers who collectively created the cultural standard by which the now canonical texts have been retrospectively valued.

My study has taken me into many areas of inquiry, theoretical, historical, and otherwise, and I can claim expertise in few of them. Undoubtedly, in some places I have failed to appreciate subtleties. I hope that specialists will pardon my oversimplifications and find something to interest or provoke them. As a historical argument, the book is designed as an integral, cumulative structure. However, readers seeking specific information may view its components separately. Those interested strictly in the what and when, who wish to avoid the more speculative why and wherefore, may want to skip part I, for it lays out the theoretical groundwork on which the subsequent analysis is based. Both chapters comprising it draw upon work by other scholars in the fields of linguistics, philosophy, psychology, sociology, anthropology, literary, social and religious history, semiotics, hermeneutics, and bibliography. Chapter 1 situates my argument among existing accounts of individualism and the autobiographical genre, while at the same time offering definitions of key terminology. Chapter 2 looks more closely at Lackington's *Memoirs* in an attempt to illustrate the individualist self, as it were, in performance. It also attempts to offer a justification for my claim that Lackington's text represents the "first" English individualist – a description meant sincerely, but which I hope will not be taken absolutely literally.

Parts II and III return from the scene of Lackington's performance to follow the steps leading up to it, in the fashion of a detective story. They are more strictly historical, and focus exclusively on the texts and contexts of early modern autobiographical practice. Part II looks at authentic first-person written discourse in the seventeenth century, when it can hardly be called autobiographical. Chapter 3 studies Philip Stubbes's *A Christal Glasse for Christian Women*, a prototype of the form and meaning of ordinary "autobiography" as it appeared in the seventeenth century. Chapter 4 looks at manuscript devotional diaries and other unpublished personal religious papers in order to reconsider the historian William Haller's characterization of the "usual practice" of the early modern "Puritan" saint as "spiritual autobiographer." Chapter 5 addresses the importance of printing biographical discourse in the second half of the seventeenth century, and the relation to this practice of diaries and other personal papers written in the first person.

Part III treats developments in the eighteenth century, when discourse which to us appears vaguely autobiographical becomes properly popular. Chapter 6 follows the career of John Dunton, whose publications epitomize some of the innovations occurring in publishing, especially journalism, which affected the cultural value of first-person prose narratives at the beginning of the eighteenth century. Chapter 7 considers the quasi-autobiographical apologetic narratives produced by scandalized gentlewomen in the light of contemporary criminal biographies, to argue that these outlaws and their texts bring autobiographical practice to the brink of modernity. The epilogue ties the scandalous memoirs to Lackington's *Memoirs*, and looks briefly at the latter work's contemporary reception, which heralds the advent in English culture of the genre of autobiography and individualism as we know them.

In all of this I hope to make legible a significant part of the confluence of discourses and practices constituting the genealogy of modern narrative autobiography and its referent, the individualist self.

Part I
The First English Individualist

It is tempting, even if it is only an approximation, to compare the development of modern autobiography with the construction of the middle-class "subject." Autobiography is a human right. Become the owner of your life! Everyone is invited to become the owner of the individual property of one's life, to build a house of writing on one's little plot of existence.

Philippe Lejeune, "Teaching People to Write Their Life Story" (1988)

1

Narrative Subjects
Individualism,
Autobiography, Authority

Individual originally meant indivisible. That now sounds like a paradox. "Individual" stresses a distinction from others; "indivisible" a necessary connection. The development of the modern meaning from the original meaning is a record in language of an extraordinary social and political history.

> Raymond Williams, "Individual," in *Keywords: A Vocabulary of Culture and Society* (1983)

The autobiographical form gives each person the opportunity to believe that he is a complete and responsible subject. . . . [It] is undoubtedly not the instrument of the expression of a subject that preexists it, nor even a "role," but rather that which determines the very existence of "subjects."

> Philippe Lejeune, "The Autobiography of Those Who Do Not Write" (1980)

The present age, if we consider chiefly the state of our own country, may be stiled with great propriety *The Age of Authors*; for, perhaps, there was never a time, in which men of all degrees of ability, of every kind of education, of every profession and employment, were posting with ardour so general to the press.

> Samuel Johnson, *Adventurer*, No. 115 (1753)

What is an individualist self? This is a question of theory in many academic disciplines.

As a culture, "individualism" is a historical phenomenon, owing its existence to a specific combination of factors coalescing at a particular time in a particular place. To identify the precise historical "moment" of individualism would, however, require tracing the development of what the literary historian Ian Watt has correctly called a "vast complex of interdependent factors"[1] – a task too large for any single study. Individualism is a multidimensional phenomenon, an amalgam of practices and values with no discernible center. A variety of forces – social, economic, political, intellectual – contributed to its making, each one of which was paramount at some time or another, either separately or jointly with others.[2] Thus a single account of individualism cannot possibly represent its development, its contours, its functions. The most to be expected of any attempt to do so is the isolation for study of a particular facet of the colossus, by which means we might derive a synecdochic feel for its parameters.

In both the human and social sciences, individualism has come to be epitomized by an (incontestable) emphasis on the individuality of the person. In this view, the "person," understood generically as the human agent in society, is charged with meaning as the "individual" – a person characterized by extreme egocentricity.[3] As one account describes it, "individualism" is consonant with "the view that the individual human subject is a maker of the world we inhabit."[4] Another renders it as essentially the postulation of each person "as an end in himself, as his own telos."[5] Recent comparative social and cultural analysis has highlighted the relative eccentricity of this egocentric personal orientation. The anthropologist Clifford Geertz, for example, explains that the largely Western assumption of the "person as a bounded, unique, more or less integrated motivational and cognitive universe, a dynamic center of awareness, emotion, judgment, and action, organized into a distinctive whole and set contrastively against other such wholes and against a social and natural background, is . . . a rather peculiar idea within the context of the world's cultures."[6] Taking Geertz's point about culture further, others stress the historical contingency of both the individual and the ideology congruent to the individual's point of view. For some, the end of individualism in the West is signaled by the proclaimed death of "the bourgeois subject," more commonly known as "the subject" – a term sometimes deployed as a synonym for the individual. The recent report of the subject's fatality is predicated on the appropriate insight that all concepts of personal identity, individuality among them, are historically constituted in language and society rather than being given by nature.

This claim, on which the critique of the subject is based, originated in the philosopher Friedrich Nietzsche's assertion that "the subject is not something given," in either nature or metaphysics, but is instead "something added and invented and projected behind what there is" in everyday experience. In other words, contrary to the central and essential being attributed to the individual in the modern West, Nietzsche argued for its contingency, for the individual subject's figurative rather than literal presence; as he put it, "The 'subject' is the fiction that many similar states in us are the effect of one substratum: but it is we who first created the 'similarity' of these states; our adjusting them and making them similar is the fact, not their similarity (– which ought rather to be denied –)."[7] In other words, the "substratum," that entity otherwise known as the self, which forms the basis of the concept of personal individuality, is not an object of nature. Rather, it is a product of social and cultural relations. In essence, according to Nietzsche, the self as integral unit is a "fiction," an elaborate metaphor created to organize the process of actually being individuated in personal experience. Nietzsche's critique implies that people deny or mistake their metaphors as facts of nature, thereby rendering the metaphor's referent, the self, an irreducible object tautologically "self-evident" in personal experience. The problem of the self-evident self is deeply rooted in Western experience, traceable back at least to Cartesian dualism if not to primitive Christianity.

Subsequent commentators have refined Nietzsche's seminal insight about the metaphorical nature of subjectivity, enabling us to appreciate even better the individual's cultural and historical contingency as a concept. Of paramount importance is the theory developed by the linguist Emile Benveniste, who followed Nietzsche in claiming that the basis of subjectivity is the exercise of language. For Benveniste, language use – what he calls "discourse" – functions as the medium of subjectivity. In discourse, the "I" upon which so much of our sense of self is based appears as a grammatical form rather than as an elementary phenomenological unit. According to Benveniste,

> Language is . . . the possibility of subjectivity because it always contains the linguistic forms appropriate to the expression of subjectivity, and discourse provokes the emergence of subjectivity because it consists of discrete instances. In some way language puts forth "empty" forms which each speaker, in the exercise of discourse, appropriates to himself and which he relates to his "person," at the same time defining himself as *I* and his partner as *you*. The instance of discourse is thus constitutive of all the coordinates that define the subject.[8]

Adding her own gloss on Benveniste, to highlight in particular the relational quality of discourse, the semiotician Kaja Silverman explains that subjectivity "only comes into play through the principle of difference, by the opposition of the 'other' or the 'you' to the 'I.' In other words, subjectivity is not an essence but a set of relationships."[9] Both Benveniste's and Silverman's accounts treat relations between interlocutors as the media of subjectivity. Speakers identify themselves principally through discursive interaction. Therefore discourse, broadly conceived to include all types of instances of signification (from conversations to watching television and having private thoughts), is the locus of the sense of individuality. And because instances of discourse are themselves discrete events, mediated by local circumstances, it follows that the concept of individuality is historically and culturally contingent. The prevailing cultural and historical conditions determine the limits of what is appropriate or possible to feel and state about personal identity in a given situation. Thus to feel, to think, and to speak as an individual is possible only at a certain time in a certain place, such as the modern West, where so many of the norms and practices governing discursive interaction are structured to privilege individualistic speakers with a firm grasp of their particular "I."

In disciplines less grounded in semiotics such as the social sciences, the concept of the historical and cultural contingency of the individual and individualism – or at least the potential to develop such a concept – has been available to us for an equally long time. The idea that human individuality is in some way enabled or constrained by evolving systems of social, economic, and political organization stands tacitly behind various studies of such structures, back at least to the mid-nineteenth century, with the historian Jacob Burckhardt's account of politologic in Renaissance Italy.[10] But unlike Nietzsche, Burckhardt and his inheritors assumed that subjective individuality was a natural human essence wanting only the proper climate to develop, like a plant. Before the Italian Renaissance, they believed, this quality lay dormant, a seed awaiting the germination ultimately precipitated by the advent of new "political circumstances," characterized in Burckhardt's famous notion of the state as a "work of art."[11] Others, such as Karl Marx, and later the social theorist Max Weber, prioritized social and economic climates over political ones. Marx described the period roughly between 1500 and 1700 as witnessing a revolution from feudalism to capitalism in Europe, which entailed a change in the status of the person in society, from being subject to the collective totality to being individually alienated from it. Among the structural circumstances emerging to cause the dilation of personal individuality at this time were: the invention of private property and the destruction of group ownership; the elimination of the household as the basic unit of production and consumption; the growth of a money economy; the rise of a class of independent wage-laborers; the growing dominance of the profit motive and the psychological drive toward endless accumulation; the rise of modern industrial production; the growth of large urban centers; the suppression of magic and the "irrational;" and the undermining of small, close-knit communities.[12] Perhaps inspired by Weber's treatment of Protestantism as a major factor in the transition to capitalism, the anthropologist Louis Dumont locates the origins of individualism in the laws and rituals of the Western classical and Judeo-Christian heritage. According to Dumont, the transformation of the person from a universal being into the individual was largely complete with the institution of Calvin's theocracy in the sixteenth century. Dumont describes the subjection of human will to providence dictated by Calvin as a "necessary condition for legitimating the decisive shift" to the individual, a transformation which was fully complete by the end of the eighteenth century, with the triumph of the concept of human "rights" over natural law.[13] Still others emphasize the liberation of social space from communal forms of sociability for its contribution to "the triumph of individualism in daily life" in Europe during the sixteenth and seventeenth centuries.[14] And last, in a view which attempts to see all of the structural developments above as interdependent features of a single totalizing system, the historian and social theorist Norbert Elias identified what he called the "process of civilization" as a process of individualization, in which the rise of centralized and urbanized state societies caused the separation and encapsulation of persons in all of their relations to each other, giving rise to the concept of the human subject as the individual.[15]

Each of these views, the semiotic critique and the positivist superstructural account, is by now well known to us. Despite their different assumptions about the nature of subjectivity, both approaches have rendered the notion of the cultural and historical contingency of the individual and individualism a commonplace, at least as a principle of humanistic and social-scientific research, and have thereby laid the foundation upon which my own study attempts to build. Taking the contingency of the individual for granted, then, I shall explore the way some persons reproduce the material conditions of individuality as subjects in their modes of discursive self-identification.

In what follows, I take as my premise that some version of subjectivity or consciousness of self is an indispensable feature of human existential reality, and that, whatever particular form it takes, self-consciousness is therefore a transcultural and transhistorical phenomenon, no matter how much impersonal factors of individuation actually differ in time and space. Thus I assume that in their capacity as persons all humans bear a particular concept of self or, more precisely, a "self-identity." A personal self-identity is an effect of human activity in the landscape of society and culture. It is a tool for negotiation within the web of the world; an imaginary script conceived by each person to underwrite the dramatic interpersonal performances of self described by the sociologist Erving Goffman as an essential feature of everyday life.[16] Although in his formulation Goffman referred to relations in modern Western society, his concept of identity performance applies to human existential reality in general.[17] In its particularity each personal script, like each personal performance, depends heavily upon actual and imagined audience response, and so will be a unique product of the public situation of its bearer. The qualities of individual scripts may therefore vary extensively. However, it is possible also to speak of generic categories or epistemes of self-identity appropriate to epochal social and cultural contexts, in which certain basic types of scripts and interpersonal performances make sense.[18] Epistemes of self-identity will therefore vary in time and place: "the subject" or individual addressed by Nietzsche and Burckhardt is but one generic type of self-identity, arising in the modern West; there are other epistemic possibilities beyond it.[19]

I am interested specifically in the way self-identities take shape in the modern West as objects of representation in "autobiography." My concept of autobiography is not restricted to the conventional parameters of literary genres. Instead, I take it as a practice, which we might imagine as a cultural institution or, in the cultural theorist Pierre Bourdieu's term, a "field" of significance, in which various discursive traditions prevail over time.[20] In the most liberal view, which leaves the *graphe* as open as the *autos,* and *bios,* "autobiography" designates a more generalized practice of self-representation which includes not only conventional "literary" texts, but other – possibly non-verbal as well as non-writerly – texts as well, such as films, photographs, collections of ephemera, wardrobes, gardens, and so forth. In this perspective there are as many potential forms of autobiography as there are conceivable self-identities. However, out of this universe of possibilities, my study is limited to instances of autobiography in written discourse, especially discourse written as narrative prose.

I emphasize the range of possible autobiographical traditions only to suggest the peculiarity of the narrative prose autobiography so familiar to modern readers. As Georges Gusdorf has noted in his seminal essay, "Conditions and Limits of Autobiography," the tradition of first-person, self-reflexive, written narrative, sometimes called "classic" or "modern' autobiography by scholars, is itself a historically contingent phenomenon.[21] Though a handful of unusually precocious examples appeared in the distant history of the West – St Augustine's *Confessions* comes immediately to mind, but there were others even before it – narrative prose autobiography began, at least at the popular level, quite recently, with the advent of the diary and related forms of recording first-person discourse in writing during the seventeenth century, culminating in the "autobiography proper," the retrospective, totalized narrative of personal experience, sometime between the mid-eighteenth and the mid-nineteenth centuries.[22] Precisely where and when modern autobiography emerged is a matter of considerable debate. The term "autobiography" and its synonym "self-biography" appeared in the late eighteenth century in a handful of isolated instances in England and Germany.[23] We should not attach too much significance to these neologisms, however; descriptive terminology usually lags behind practice. But the identification of the first instance of modern autobiographical practice is no simple task either. The usual suspects in the line-up of inaugural practitioners include, among others, St Augustine, St Teresa, Cellini, Cardano, Gibbon, Vico, and Rousseau. On the one hand, identifying the first autobiographer is a merely pedantic activity, a partisan exercise in canon formation which amounts to an ultimately insoluble problem. On the other, though, it is useful, not to say crucial, for an understanding of the present cultural order, to attempt to account for modern autobiography's origins, however problematic making such a record might be. I believe, and I hope my study demonstrates, that our interests in doing so will be better served if we cease to focus on exceptional examples of technical brilliance and look instead at the broader cultural processes out of which such exceptions emerged.

From this more mundane perspective, we can see that the origins of the individualist self lie in the advent of modern autobiographical practice. To comprehend this view, a concept of individualist self-identity is necessary. Like individualism, the individualist self is practically impossible to describe in all of its complexity. Any intelligible description of individualist self-identity – or of any mode of self-identification considered at the general level of culture or ideology – will of necessity be an ideal type to which specific instances may fail to conform precisely. Nevertheless, we can discern its typical features in the diversity of its instantiations. An image of individualist self-identity must be situated within the context of individualism itself; within the web, adduced earlier, of a world in which each person thinks of himself as his own maker, as his own telos. In such a world, according to the political scientist Steven Lukes, four basic values prevail: "the dignity of man," or the person as an end in himself; the autonomy and self-direction of the person; privacy, or personal sovereignty over the domain of self; and self-development, the imperative to allow the self to pursue its own "genius."[24] Therefore, the individualist self is the referent of a person who speaks about and values his own and other persons' identities as independent, autonomous units – "selves" – who have a hand in crafting their separate and therefore individual destinies.

The value – moreover, the paramountcy – for individualism of the autonomous agency of self-determination is inscribed in the concept of individual responsibilities and reciprocal rights, to which all persons who identify themselves as self-creating beings willingly and equally subscribe. Indeed, the tacit act of subscription to such rights and responsibilities, the core of modern citizenship, is understood as a version of self-creation, which is consonant with individualist self-identification. Additionally, as the philosopher Charles Taylor has explained, the enjoyment of the rights of self-creation in modern individualist societies also entails as a correlate a specific personal agentive capacity, that of being, in his formulation, a "respondent."[25] In other words, the individualist self is the identity of a person for whom the question "Who am I?" has subjective value and meaning. More specifically, in Taylor's conception, this person

> is a being who has a sense of self, has a notion of the future and the past, can hold values, make choices; in short, can adopt life-plans. At least, [such] a person must be the kind of person who is in principle capable of all this, however damaged these capacities may be in practice.
>
> Running through all this we can identify a necessary (but not sufficient) condition. A person must be a being with his own point of view on things. The life-plan, the choices, the sense of self must be attributable to him as in some sense their point of origin.[26]

Furthermore, Taylor continues, this personal capacity includes the ability to formulate "peculiarly human ends" above and beyond the more animalistic instinct for mere survival.[27] Elsewhere he has expanded upon this concept, arguing that, in order to formulate human ends, persons must understand their lives as unfolding stories; that as a "basic condition of making sense of ourselves . . . we grasp our lives in a narrative."[28]

With Taylor's account of personality, we can appreciate the culture and ideology of individualism as a virtual space of questions related to self-identity which only an original and coherent narrative can answer. What I call the individualist self is, then, in the first place, the self-identity of a person who feels at home in such a space, a person for whom such questions have a paramount value. Second, the individualist self characterizes that person who is capable of acting on and responding to such questions on his own, and making sense of others' equally autonomous actions and responses to the same questions as well, in narrative. Though Taylor does not address the importance of writing to this mode of self-identification, its influence as a model and an instrument for individualist thought and action should be obvious. However, to suggest that this self-identity is the equivalent of either "self-consciousness" or "historical consciousness" *per se*, as some have done, would be in error – neither of these states of being is peculiar to individualism. Instead, we should view individualist self-identity as a mode of self-consciousness and historical consciousness of a particular sort. The individualist self is, figuratively speaking, a producer and a consumer of stories about himself and other selves which place the self at the center of the system of relations, discursive and otherwise – he is literally a writer and a reader of modern autobiography.

Taylor's account of personality aligns with that of another influential contemporary philosopher, Alasdair MacIntyre. Appealing to our everyday experience of selfhood, MacIntyre argues that we routinely refer to "a concept of a self whose unity resides in the unity of a narrative which links birth to life to death as narrative beginning to middle to end."[29] Where Taylor speaks of the "significance view" used by humans to evaluate action, MacIntyre refers to its moral "intelligibility." Indeed, for MacIntyre as well as for Taylor, narrative is the medium of human agency. In MacIntyre's words, it is "the basic and essential genre for the characterization of human actions."[30] Moreover, MacIntyre maintains, "It is because we all live out narratives in our lives and because we understand our own lives in terms of the narratives that we live out that the form of narrative is appropriate for understanding the actions of others."[31] Both MacIntyre and Taylor argue for narrative as the appropriate form of understanding human life, and highlight narrative competency as the essential characteristic of the person. Thus, their "person" is the subject not merely of discourse, but is more specifically the subject of *narrative* discourse. Though we should challenge the view that this practice characterizes personhood generally in all times and places, we may at least retain the concept of the routine resort to a narrativized script as that which enables (and constrains) the personal agency of the individualist self.

Furthermore, as an agent the individualist self is not merely an actor or, in MacIntyre's terminology, a "character." It is also an originator, a creator; in contemporary terms, an author. The agency of the self as author determines the agency of the self as character. By acting as author, the individualist self becomes its own telos: it constitutes a beginning and an end in itself. MacIntyre, in particular, stresses this process; however, Taylor's discussion implies the same relation.[32] In negotiating the space of identity questions either directly posed or implied in the pursuit of its personal ends, the individualist self functions as an author as well as a character. The self's authority is a central thesis of MacIntyre's concept of agency: "man is in his actions and practice, as well as in his fictions, essentially a story-telling animal."[33] Thus the definitive capacity of the individualist self is that of a "respondent," or a "storyteller" – in short, an author. To be scrupulously precise we ought, as MacIntyre himself acknowledges, to describe this identity as that of co-author, because an agent is never entirely in control of the theater in which he creates and acts out his life. Uniquely, however, the individualist self overlooks this fact and subscribes to the *illusion* of total control, of personal autonomy, over and above mere agency. The individualist self imagines the peculiar fiction of being in total possession of itself in all situations.

Though never actually immanent in the variety of characters the self functions as in the various episodes of a person's lifetime, this total individual authority is nevertheless always implied by the mere fact of role-playing itself. Without acting first and foremost as an author, the individualist self would have no script of life to follow as a character. In this light, reviewing Taylor's formulation of the person as a being able to have "a sense of self . . . a notion of the future and the past . . . values . . . choices; in short . . . life-plans," we can now grasp such a capacity as essentially a unique and largely imaginative degree of individual personal authority. This authoritative stance best epitomizes the generic self-identity of the person under individualism. In its position as the subject of its own life story, the individualist self is a creator/medium/product unified as a single, autonomous totality: the trope of the author as the hero and originator of his heroism.

Hence the importance of modern autobiography to a study of the origins of the individualist self: such texts function as its objective correlate. Among the variety of modes of discourse, the unified, retrospective first-person prose narrative uniquely totalizes its subject as both author and hero. The most celebrated examples of modern autobiography are, with few exceptions, nearly all stories of author-protagonists, from Rousseau and Gibbon to Simone de Beauvoir and Jean-Paul Sartre. But every modern autobiography is actually the account of an author: as the literary critic Karl Weintraub explains it, "the dominant autobiographic truth is . . . the vision of the pattern and meaning of life which the autobiographer has at the moment of writing his autobiography."[34] The "life" represented by the autobiographical narrative represents, figuratively if not literally, a story-teller, a writing subject. This point has been explicated most succinctly by the literary critic Jean Starobinski who, taking Rousseau as his example, argues, "No matter how doubtful the facts related, the text will at least present an 'authentic' image of the man who 'held the pen.'"[35] The modern autobiographer is therefore the prototype of the individualist self, and the modern autobiography is the ideal medium of individualist self-identity. Furthermore, as a form of personal action, modern autobiographical practice constitutes the essential mode of individualist agency. In this light, the prehistory of modern autobiographical practice offered in the pages to follow will serve also as an account of the origins of the individualist self.

It is a commonplace of both history and literary criticism that modern autobiography was first popularized in Protestant countries, and that among them England was especially precocious. Whether or not either of these claims actually stands up to the comparative analysis which has yet to be conducted, it remains true that, beginning in the seventeenth century, Britain produced a widening stream of narrative autobiographical discourse, whose breadth and depth expanded to Mississippian proportions in the course of the eighteenth century. Contemporary to the flood of such practice is the equally precocious acculturation of individualism in England. Following upon the work of Marx and Weber, which identified early modern England as "the cradle and nursery of capitalism," the historian R. H. Tawney outlined the peculiar affinity between what he identified as "the individualism congenial to the world of business," evangelical Protestantism (or "Puritanism"), and politics in England during the

sixteenth and seventeenth centuries, which established its reputation
as the historical locus classicus of individualism.[36] The historian
Christopher Hill saw the English Civil War as the first "bourgeois
revolution," and the political scientist C. B. Macpherson identified it
as the staging ground for the political theory of "possessive individualism."[37] In social relations, England also came first, as the site of
the rise of "affective individualism" in the eighteenth century.[38] In
the light of this remarkable record, we should not be surprised to
find the historical anthropologist Alan Macfarlane claiming that "the
majority of ordinary people in England from at least the thirteenth
century were rampant individualists, highly mobile both geographically and socially, economically 'rational,' market-oriented and
acquisitive, ego-centred in kinship and social life."[39]

It is not my intention to reconfigure the general picture of English
culture and society described in these views. Instead, I seek to contribute another layer of detail, adding definition in areas which have
hitherto appeared blurred. It is certainly appropriate to locate the
origins of the individualist self in early modern Britain, where James
Lackington stands with his *Memoirs* at the nexus of these complementary developments. As the first modern autobiographical practitioner,
he is not a Great Author in a Great Tradition; he is merely a precocious participant in a discursive tradition which was, for better or
worse, to become a cultural institution, tacitly requiring every person
seeking social legitimacy to act as his own "author," whether he ever
actually wrote out his life story or not. In fact, as far as one can tell
from reading his work, Lackington wore his authority fairly lightly.
His work identifies him explicitly as an "author" only in its table of
contents, where Lackington appears in the précis of each letter comprising the *Memoirs* alternately as "the author" and "our hero." One
gathers from reading his text that Lackington was more comfortable
in the role of hero than that of author – which we should expect,
given the newness of authorship as a profession at that time. But the
success represented literally in Lackington's work hardly merited the
attention he claimed for it; unconsciously, Lackington understood the
sum of his performance as something greater than its details. The
Memoirs does not depict him as its author, it exemplifies him as such.
He identified himself, as others identified his contemporaries Wesley
and Johnson, with a commemorative biography. Lackington's hubris,
manifest in his autobiographical practice, marked him in retrospect
as the first "ordinary person" to demonstrate publicly his own authoritative ethos. With this in mind, let us return to his *Memoirs* to
consider its historical singularity.

2

A Novel Self-Identity
The Performance of
Individual Authority in James
Lackington's *Memoirs*

I became in my own eyes a character out of a novel. . . .
One afternoon I was playing croquet with Poupette, Jeanne,
and Madeleine. We were wearing beige pinafores with red
scallops and embroidered with cherries. The clumps of
laurel were shining in the sun, and the earth smelt good.
Suddenly I was struck motionless: I was living through the
first chapter of a novel in which I was the heroine.

I read a novel which seemed to me to translate my spiritual
exile into words. . . . Through the heroine, I identified
myself with the author: one day other adolescents would
bathe with their tears a novel in which I would tell my
own sad story.

If at one time I had dreamed of being a teacher it was
because I wanted to be a law unto myself; I now thought
that literature would allow me to realize this dream. . . .
By writing a work based on my own experience I would
re-create myself and justify my existence.

Simone de Beauvoir, *Memoirs of a Dutiful Daughter* (1959)

How is the individualist self manifested in modern autobiographical
practice? James Lackington's *Memoirs of the First Forty-Five Years
of the Life of James Lackington*, originally published in 1791 and
possibly the earliest English text to accomplish this feat, provides a
fine example of the discursive relations involved. Few readers of
Lackington's *Memoirs* would deny that the ethos of the memoirist
displayed in his text is strongly individualistic. Our image of Lacking-

ton fits Ian Watt's characterization of Daniel Defoe's fictional protagonist, Robinson Crusoe, the ideal-typical *homo economicus* and
eighteenth-century "embodiment" of political, economic, and spiritual individualism, almost to the letter. If, as Watt argues, *Robinson
Crusoe* is the first expression of the diverse elements of individualism
in narrative fiction, then Lackington's *Memoirs* is the first expression
of those elements in a non-fiction narrative.[1] Lackington, a real
person who used a written text to represent his self-identity to the
public, actually performed the act of discursive self-creation essential
to the individualist self. More so than *Crusoe*, the *Memoirs* realizes
individualist self-identity in its totality.

Reading at the most literal level, Watt singles out Crusoe's economic and social habits, in particular his unrelenting pursuit of profit,
his reverence for book-keeping and the law of contracts, his devaluing
of non-economic modes of thought, achievement, pleasure, and social
relations in preference for industry and economic utility, as salient
features of the individualist ethos. A reading of Lackington's *Memoirs*
at the same level finds these traits also embodied in the image of its
author. Lackington's narrative divulged the secrets of its writer's
"uncommon success" in trade, which it ascribed partly to an inborn
native ingenuity but principally to personal discipline and tireless
maintenance of fiscal order. Lackington's chief achievement as a
bookseller, which the *Memoirs* gloatingly recounts, was the invention
of the practice known today as remaindering – the buying and selling
of unsold stock of books at prices below the cover cost.[2] In contrast
to his competitors who sold dear, Lackington explained, "I was for
selling everything cheap, in order to secure those customers already
obtained, as well as increase their numbers" (1794, p. 359). Moreover, Lackington traded nothing on credit. While it enabled him to
sell cheaply, denying credit also put him at odds with a clientele
accustomed to delaying payment for goods. Nonetheless, his unique
"ready-money" policy prevailed:

> I even sometimes thought of relinquishing this my favorite scheme
> altogether, as by it I was obliged to deny credit to my very acquaintance;
> I was also obliged to refuse it to the most respectable characters, as *no
> exception* was, or now is made, not even in favour of Nobility. . . .
> Many unacquainted with my plan of business, were much offended,
> until the advantages accruing to them were duly explained, when they
> very readily acceded to it. (1791, pp. 214–15)

Of course, the advantages accruing to Lackington from his economically rational plan of business were equal to or even greater than

those of his clientele. At the time of writing his *Memoirs*, fifteen years after he began, in an obscure passageway, retailing the contents of a bag of books bought for a guinea, he boasted a catalogue of over 30,000 items, and an annual net income of over £4,000 (1791, p. 263). Lackington's volume of business, allegedly turning over 100,000 books annually, was unrivalled in his day. His purpose-built shop in Finsbury Square, to which he moved in 1793, occupied a block of houses and contained a main floor large enough to drive a coach and six around.[3] As a result of this phenomenal success, Lackington was able to keep a carriage of his own, on the doors of which he had emblazoned the motto "Small profits do great things" – "constantly to remind me," he explained, "to what I am indebted for my prosperity. . . . And I assure you, Sir, that reflecting on the means by which the carriage was procured adds not a little to the pleasure of riding in it" (1791, p. 234). It is difficult to imagine how the bookseller could match the Crusoean prototype of economic individualism more perfectly.

Lackington shared Crusoe's social attitudes as well. Like Crusoe, the bookseller began his career as a kind of castaway – but in the London metropolis rather than on a desert island. According to Lackington, "I was not only poor, but laboured under every other disadvantage; being a stranger in London, and without friends, &c." (1830, p. 28). Hence the "wonder" of his success, out of such inauspicious circumstances. Crusoe, a younger son trapped in a position of mediocrity at home, had exchanged tradition, family, and friends for personal autonomy, which allowed his native commercial talent to thrive. For Lackington, autonomy was a fact of life, not a choice. But as it did for Crusoe, independence proved the key to Lackington's success. He realized early on that he could expect little in the way of capital assistance from others, especially his own family. His father, a journeyman shoemaker, was a drunkard who died both prematurely and penniless, "so that neither myself, my Brothers, or Sisters are indebted to a Father scarcely for any thing that can endear his memory, or cause us to reflect on him with pleasure" (1791, p. 11). His mother, "the daughter of a poor weaver in Wellington," "a woman without a shilling, of a mean family, who supported herself by spinning of wool into yarn" (1794, pp. 38, 39), did her best to support her eleven children, of which James was the eldest, in the same manner; but ultimately she could not even spare the weekly 2*d.* for his tuition, so he was forced to leave school early. Yet what his mother failed to provide in the way of material aid she recouped with moral example.

Lackington remembered his mother as a paragon of industry and sobriety. He recalled, "Never did I know or hear of a woman who worked and lived so hard as she did . . . for many years together, she worked generally nineteen or twenty hours out of every twenty-four." Not even childbearing slowed her: "even when very near her time, sometimes at one hour, she was seen walking backwards and forwards by her Spinning-wheel, and her midwife sent for the next" (1791, p. 12). She reduced her diet to broth, root vegetables, or cabbage so that her children might eat meat. This memory of his mother was shaped, it seems, by Lackington's reading of Confucius and the ancient moralists, especially the Stoics, of whom he said that he "received more real benefit from reading and studying them . . . than from all other Books that I had read before, or have read since. . . . By reading them I was taught to bear the unavoidable evils attending humanity, and to supply all my wants by contracting or restraining my desires" (1792, pp. 175–6). The lesson of industry and sobriety taught by the Stoics and practiced by his mother set a standard by which Lackington measured the worth of himself and others. The *Memoirs* rarely acknowledges the affective ties of family: we never learn the names, let alone the fates, of the memoirist's siblings; we assume that, as a prosperous man thrice married to youthful wives, Lackington would have had a considerable number of offspring, but he never mentioned any children of his own. Though not completely barren of sentiment or affection (a person's humor and wit could elicit his fond remark), Lackington's relations with others were established largely in conformity to his neo-Stoic, almost utilitarian, moral economy.

But beyond the similarities of economic and social relations there remains the more complicated matter of what Watt calls Crusoe's "spiritual individualism." Lackington surpasses his fictional counterpart as an individualist at this "spiritual" or rational level by his attempt to control his self-identity as a discursive totality. Let us consider what happens in *Robinson Crusoe* first, to get a sense of the stakes involved. For Watt, Defoe's novel constitutes the "literary expression" of a general tendency toward individual moral and social authority in England, characteristic first of Calvinism, and later, after the waning of strictly "Puritan" consciousness, of a secular "spiritual individualism." According to Watt, *Robinson Crusoe* asserts the "primacy of individual experience" by its "total subordination of plot to the pattern of the autobiographical memoir."[4] Although he does not describe any essential connection between autobiography and individualism, Watt's reading allows us to see the crucial relationship between a personal autobiographical capacity and individualist self-identity: the meaning of Crusoe's island success story remains incomplete until he can recollect it discursively for the folks back home, whose consumption of his narrative authenticates the tale and thereby sanctions the career it describes. In a moral sense, Crusoe is nothing until his experience is represented to the public in narrative discourse. The unity, substance and autonomy of the written autobiography identify Crusoe as author of the narrative and also, more importantly, of its referent – his own strange, eventful, and triumphant personal experience. Grasped together in a written narrative, Crusoe's actions make his diverse experience a *Life*, which displays the integrity of his individual self.

There is in *Robinson Crusoe* then an almost natural correlation between, on the one hand, the castaway's conquest of circumstance on the island and, on the other, his ability to represent his activity discursively, in a narrative of personal heroism. Left to his own devices on the island, one of Crusoe's first acts is to mark time with crude numerical signs, and then to write a daily journal, by which means, he explains, "I kept things very exact."[5] These practices constitute early efforts to exercise individual control over the aimless drift of personal experience, to make of it something more than, so to speak, "one damn thing after another." As Crusoe's conquest continues, the writing and other actions occur in tandem, as complementary or mutually sustaining endeavors. The total effort culminates in the autobiographical narrative Crusoe produces upon his return to civilization. This text, *The Life and Strange Surprizing Adventures of Robinson Crusoe, of York, Mariner*, constitutes his identity as a respondent. It publicly displays his narrative capacity, and thereby demonstrates his completeness, originality, and purity; in short, his individual personal authority. So able, Crusoe is responsible, in the sense of being respondent to identity questions concerning his person.

The theory of modern autobiographical epistemology advanced by the literary critic Elizabeth Bruss helps us to understand this effect of Crusoe's text. Bruss characterizes autobiographical discourse as a kind of public performance by its author. In her words, autobiography is "an autonomous act with its own peculiar responsibilities." For Bruss autobiography's performative dimension – what she calls "the structural display of the text" – serves as "a demonstration of certain of the capacities and habits of the man about whom we are reading. The way the autobiographer has arranged his text is therefore experienced as a 'sample' of his epistemology and personal skill."[6] In particular, the structural integrity of the narrative – its unity – exemplifies the personal authority of its creator. More specifically, it constitutes the self-identification of its subject as a person with a peculiar consciousness of self; a subject, in the words of Bruss, "with the capacity to know and simultaneously be that which one knows."[7] Bruss's concept of autobiographical practice as personal epistemology fits both our reading of *Crusoe* and the notion of the individualist self to be found in the ethical philosophy of Taylor and MacIntyre. Taken together, they imply that the modern autobiographical narrative is a kind of prosthetic device employed by its author to rationalize the disparate and perhaps conflicting elements of his experience as he negotiates his self-identity in the public realm of discourse. The control demonstrated in the written text's figuration exemplifies the person's grasp of his self; discursively, it represents his moral authority.

The act of autobiographical narration makes a totality of the heterogencity of Crusoe's experience, unifying it in story form as an integral *Life* of adventure, which constitutes its author's moral being, his self-identity. This narrative unification is the definitive feature of the responsibility encoded in Crusoe's text – it displays the level of competence or self-discipline essential to survival in the modern world. In the modern polity the status of every person is comparable to Crusoe's to the extent that each is disembedded and cast away from the institutions of family, church, and other corporations in which pre-modern self-identities were negotiated and delimited.[8] The anomic new world of competitive, urban, industrial capitalism and state bureaucracy necessitated the improvisation of new discourses of self-identity based on aggressive attention to advertisement, appearance, puffery, display, and self-justification.[9] As a consequence, by the eighteenth century individual integrity had become an issue as it had never been before; people increasingly found themselves having to respond individually in public to new challenges regarding their personal status. As these discourses developed, the person came almost to embody a unique case history for which he was individually responsible: to the state and its representatives; to the expanding constellation of professional experts, for example in medicine and the law; and, ultimately, to the fellow citizens with whom he conducted business. Thus an ability to organize experience reflexively in narrative discourse emerged, in the modern world in which *Robinson Crusoe* was produced and consumed, as a critical personal skill. It is but a slight overstatement to say that a narrative capacity became a tacit condition of democratic citizenship. As the author of his own *Life*, Crusoe assumes responsibility for his actions and, by extension, the self-identity to which they refer. The action of survival in the physical environment and the act of autobiographical self-identification in the realm of discourse are complementary capacities, constituting under the sign of "Robinson Crusoe" the authority essential to modern personalities. This, I think, is what Watt was getting at when he identified the form of the autobiographical memoir as the essence of the novel's spiritual individualism.

But how deliberate and complete is *Robinson Crusoe* at this level? Does its author-protagonist truly share the same virtues as, for example, Simone de Beauvoir, passages of whose memoirs serve as epigraphs to this chapter? Beauvoir's statements make explicit the desire for total authority over the self demonstrated by the practice of autobiography in modernity. For her "literature" – in particular, the self-referential discourse of the retrospective autobiographical narrative she produced – enables a person to control her self-identity; or, as she put it, to "realize" the dream of becoming "a law unto myself." Representing herself as the quintessential bourgeois, Beauvoir enacts in her *Memoirs of a Dutiful Daughter* and subsequent volumes of her autobiography a form of self-identification so conventional in her day that even she, a woman, could claim it largely without remark.[10] But this bourgeois lust for individual authority, however routine in the West by the twentieth century, was actually uncommon before the advent of Romanticism. Though the trope of the book commensurate with the self was not unknown to the early modern imagination, the identification of an autonomous, authoritative personality with the source of an autobiographical narrative before the nineteenth century is problematic, at the very least. Moreover the figure of the "author," understood as the referent of a unified narrative text, is itself a historically contingent phenomenon, dependent on the confluence of several independent features of textual structure, of which the notion of "unity" is the sum.[11] In fact, if we bring *Robinson Crusoe* into a more penetrating light, we find that its structural integrity is compromised in several ways.

In the first place, Crusoe is neither the sole originator nor at all the owner of his discourse. He is not, in this literal sense, actually responsible for his *Life*, at least in its published form. Though Crusoe's book was, as its title-page advertises, "written by himself," it is not the same text he began on the island. Despite its usefulness to Crusoe there, the island diary was destined to remain an unfinished, fragmented manuscript had not an anonymous London editor intervened to bring it and the unwritten story behind it to light. It was this editor, not Crusoe, who grasped the potential value of his

Life, and judged it "worth making public," as the book's brief but powerful anonymously written editorial preface explains. The initiative which actually gathered together and recommended the text to the public belonged therefore to an agent other than Crusoe. Whoever actually did the writing of the manuscript published as *Robinson Crusoe*, its editor, rather than its protagonist, deserves credit for the discourse's origination. (Of course the name "Daniel Defoe" appears nowhere in the original edition of *Robinson Crusoe*; the modern convention of placing this sign on the title-page of the text is a function of the very practices of discursive authority under investigation here.) Furthermore, as the imprint on the book's title-page reveals, none of the rights of reproduction and ownership of the *Life* belonged to Crusoe. The work was printed for "W[illiam] Taylor," its publisher, who undertook all the financial and legal risk involved in producing the book for public consumption. Here too, Crusoe deserves (and would have earned) no credit, for he assumed no responsibility in making his discourse public. In short, at the level of textual transmission, which as we shall shortly see is part of the architecture of modern autobiographical authority, Crusoe was merely a cipher, a nonentity.

Second, as a narration Crusoe's discourse lacks the unity of an original plot. This also compromises its structural integrity, and thus the moral integrity of its subject's self-identity. *Robinson Crusoe* is not a story with a precise beginning, middle and end; instead, it is a chronicle of "strange surprizing adventure" defined by the chronology of Crusoe's birth at its beginning, and his "strange delivery" by pirates at its conclusion as well as in the welter of sequels which followed it into print. Therefore, it displays no intentionality attributable to Crusoe. As the account strongly implies, the structure of Crusoe's *Life* is the contiguity "of Providence's chequer-work" rather than the order of an emplotted story disclosing the secret of how a wayward mariner made something of a situation which offered him nothing.[12] Despite the text's explicit depiction of individual physical capacity at its literal level, its figuration, its structure as a narration, fails to complete the promise of authority. Crusoe's tale lacks what Charles Taylor calls a "peculiarly human end" – that is, a decisive conclusion; it defers instead to the wisdom of God, who ultimately determined Crusoe's fate. Had Crusoe found some meaning of his own in his experience and made its discovery the point of its telling, he would have displayed the moral integrity of a modern author. Instead, his story reveals him to be incapable of organizing his personal activity independently from providence's inscrutable machinations. So dependent, Crusoe appears as little more than a medium for recording activity over which he has no control; his success is a miracle to which he merely bears witness, rather than personally creates. As the designated author on the title-page of his *Life*, Crusoe acted as, to borrow a self-descriptive metaphor from the seventeenth-century English divine Richard Baxter, "a pen in God's hand." On this point Crusoe's anonymous editor, whom we can imagine played a part second to providence in determining the structure of Crusoe's tale (to compromise Crusoe's individual authority even further), concurs. The editor's preface explains that the "use" of the work is "to honor the Wisdom of Providence in all the Variety of our Circumstances, let them happen how they will." Crusoe lacks the autonomous moral power of original interpretation which defines authorship in its modern sense and is crucial to individualist self-identity. In sum, then, as a modern autobiographical performance, *Robinson Crusoe* is profoundly compromised.

On the other hand, if we return to our subject, Lackington's *Memoirs*, we find by contrast an integral autobiographical text displaying an authoritative self-identity at both the figurative and literal levels. The *Memoirs* is possibly the first autobiographical narrative in English – fiction or nonfiction – to represent a life of its subject in story form, with a structured plot. To us this may seem odd, because we regard "memoirs" as an alternative to the story form of autobiographical discourse. We expect a memoir to contain an ensemble of forms of personal knowledge: stories, anecdotes, notes, theses, mementos, etc. Unlike a story, which is unified by its focus on the unfolding of a single action by a single protagonist, a memoir is fragmented, heterogeneous, and polyvalent. It resonates with multiple voices and personalities. Lackington, however, apparently did not share our sophisticated concept of the memoir, possibly because it was in his day a relatively new literary form, and lacked the alternative of an emplotted form against which it could be defined. Therefore, the *Memoirs* is a story, of "the first forty-five years of Lackington's life:" the march of his "dauntless disposition" to "uncommon success" in trade. As Lackington explained in his very first letter, setting a focus and direction for what followed, the text will represent "a man, well known to have risen from an obscure origin to a degree of notice, and to a participation of the favor of the Public, in a particular line of business ... hitherto unprecedented" (1791, p. 2). Though Lackington uses "self-portrait" as a metaphor to describe his work, the text presents a character neither static nor fragmentary in form, as a portrait typically does. As the referent of a written artifact, Lackington appears to be a unified, coherent, and dynamic subject. From the very beginning the plot of the *Memoirs* gives his life the flavor of romance, and thereby casts Lackington, its author–protagonist, in the role of the hero.

To be sure, Lackington's plot is primitive. His narrative displays only a minimal grasp of the art of suspense; in later editions the storyline becomes desiccated by digressions – the "humourous stories and droll anecdotes" which he added to the second and subsequent editions of the book, as examples of his style and wit. In this tendency to digress, the form of the *Memoirs* is typical of most early modern biographies and autobiographies, and of memoirs as they came to be established as a literary subgenre. But whereas in other cases of eighteenth-century memoirs such asides constitute the essence of the text, in Lackington's *Memoirs* they are merely temporary excursions from the story Lackington consciously and deliberately attempts to narrate. This is obvious from a reading of the first edition, before the augmentations were made. Moreover there is, from an aesthetic standpoint, a rationale for such digressions: they set up a reciprocal relationship between Lackington's identity as narrator and his identity as protagonist. If the reader should ever doubt the exploits of the hero of the story, all he must do to verify the tale is compare the wit displayed by the narrator in telling it to that of the protagonist acting it out. Rather than cancelling each other out, the two qualities are complementary. In Lackington's case, style operates in the service of plot. We should also note that as biography, the *Memoirs* retains features of traditional early modern historical narrative practice which diminish the novelty of its story. For example, in keeping with the traditional didactic purpose of historiography, the *Memoirs* attempts to justify itself as offering a pattern of conventional morality, rather than an original personality of unique and intrinsic value. In his preface Lackington explains that

> Should my memoirs be attended with no other benefit to society, they will at least tend to show what may be effected by a persevering habit of industry, and an upright conscientious demeanor in trade towards the public, and probably inspire some one of perhaps superior abilities, with a laudable ambition, to emerge from obscurity, by a proper application of those talents with which Providence has favoured him, to his own credit and emolument, as well as the benefit of the community. (1791, p. xvii)

However, Lackington's idiosyncratic and original story subverts the conventional role in which he has cast himself.

The *Memoirs* displays its subject as a product of his own peculiar thought and action, rather than – as is the case of biographical texts lacking plot – a ready-made universal pattern. As a function of his text, Lackington develops into an independent, intentional being, a character who understands that his personal knowledge and skill have rendered him socially mobile. Indeed the genesis of this self-centered and self-initiated action and knowledge constitutes the central structure of his plot. Former exemplary lives, not written by the subjects themselves but rather by a preacher or teacher, conveyed warnings against such rash, autonomous thought and activity, revealing instead the passive example of self-mortification. By contrast Lackington's *Memoirs* incites desire for worldly profit, showing readers how individual effort enabled a nobody to become a somebody. It constitutes the antithesis of personal stasis and disintegration by representing self-direction as the essence of character. The *Memoirs* is a manifestation of what was then an emerging tradition in biographical discourse: the constitution, through narrative configuration accomplished completely by the biographical subject himself, of the unified, autonomous personality. Making himself the protagonist of the story of his life, Lackington enhanced the ethos of his narrational "I" to encompass also the aura of, in his own words, an "original character:" " 'I, great I, the little hero of each tale' " (1791, p. xiv). Lackington fused, in his discourse, the identity of a narrator (or speaker–writer) with that of a protagonist (or actor). So doing, he added to the individual voice manifest in his narration the authority of textual configuration, which made him a complete respondent, or author. Let us consider this authority as an effect of Lackington's discourse. How was it achieved?

The authority of textual configuration derives from the *Memoirs*' "narrativity," its immanent story structure or plot. In narratological terminology, "plot" and "story" are virtually synonymous, each referring to an autonomous layer of meaning beyond the literal surface of the text. According to the hermeneutic theorist Paul Ricœur, "plot" is "the intelligible whole that governs a succession of events in any story."[13] The literary theorist Robert Scholes defines "story" as "a narrative with a certain very specific syntactic shape (beginning–middle–end or situation–transformation–situation) and with a subject matter which allows for or encourages the projection of human values upon this material. . . . When we speak of narrative, we are usually speaking of story, though story is clearly a higher (because more rule-governed) category."[14] For both definitions, the notion of government is paramount.

The narrator who tells stories displays special powers in the realm of interpretation. Ricœur describes emplotment as a "judicatory act of grasping together."[15] In his view, emplotment is "an operation, an integrative process" of "synthesis of heterogeneous elements. . . . [It is] always more than mere enumeration in a simple or serial or successive order of incidents and events."[16] This operation entails two significant forms of discipline or control. First, the organization of time. The storyteller is responsible for the sequencing of events in time, which requires the ability to fix a temporal order other than the relentless drift of the present. The formulation of endings is especially relevant to this task, because endings designate actions marking discrete units of duration. For example, a lifetime designated by an ending other than death or termination by some deus ex machina becomes an individual career, an intentional structure consisting of personal actions and choices independent of atemporal forces such as nature or providence. The temporal career marked by a life story therefore stands as a personal triumph over the chaos of time.[17] Second, emplotment influences the interpretation of the events it comprises. The story form assigns a moral meaning to actions and to the human agents who initiate and carry them out, endowing them with a kind of mythological significance greater than any endowed by a literal or merely sequential representation. As the text critic Hayden White explains it, emplotted history "reveals to us a world that is putatively 'finished,' done with, over, and yet not dissolved, not falling apart. In this world, reality wears the mask of a meaning, the completeness and fullness of which we can only *imagine*, never experience. Insofar as historical stories can be completed, can be given narrative closure, can be shown to have had a *plot* all along, they give to reality the odor of the *ideal*."[18] The ideal proportions attributed by historical narratives to reality, White explains, operate as symbols of value. Stories point to a center, a moral principle for assigning importance to events. They endow their subjects with the formal coherence, unity, and autonomous causal power reality denies them. Thus they ascribe value and meaning. In these two respects, then, the ability to represent reality in story form functions as a kind of supernatural power.

The effect of this power of narrativity transforms a mere speaker or writer of autobiography into a personal authority. In addition to endowing its subject-matter with special meaning, the ordered totality of an emplotted narrative also refers back to its source as equally organized and valuable. According to Ricœur, one of the functions of narrative is to designate retroactively its author. He explains,

"Author says more than speaker: the author is the artisan of a work of language. . . . The singular configuration of the work and the singular configuration of the author are strictly correlative."[19] Therefore the author is a virtual extension of the written work, the consciousness which structured the text. His being is immaterial, a position or a stance enacted, not depicted, by the work.[20] Here the author as textual effect meets up with Bruss's concept of the autobiographical text as a structural display. But although all autobiographical narratives can be described as emplotted in some form or another, not all narratives will display their writers as authors. Authority inheres in the special epistemology and personal skill necessary to formulate the plot of a story with an invented beginning, middle, and end. Only the storied autobiographical narrative displays its writer as a person with the special capacity to know and simultaneously be that which he knows. By configuring his *Memoirs* as a story, Lackington demonstrated this capacity.

The act of producing the *Memoirs* constitutes an extension of the knowledge displayed by the work's hero into the real life of its writer. As a cultural performance by a historical writer–actor, the discourse is entirely consistent with the actions of its protagonist. The fact of this execution of narrative competency, of Lackington's desire and ability to endow his first forty-five years with the coherence and meaning of plot, demonstrates his self-identity as both a "respondent," in Taylor's sense, and as an "author," in MacIntyre's. Lackington literally underwrote his "uncommon success" in trade by making it the substance of a story which displays him as his own telos, the author of his self-identity. In fact, Lackington claimed to have composed the *Memoirs* in response to a desire expressed by acquaintances wanting to know, in his words, the "particulars . . . of my passage through life" (1791, p. xiii). Apparently this desire became an imperative: Lackington mentioned being "repeatedly *threatened*, by a very particular friend and others, that if I declined drawing up a narrative, they were determined to do it for me" (1791, p. xiv). However petty and perhaps even fictitious it may be, this controversy highlights the context in which the *Memoirs* was conceived. Lackington intended his work as a means of responding publicly to the "Who am I?" issue; he authored his story to claim and to control his self-identity as a character in the theater of real life.

Though anxious about his appearance "as an adventurer among the numerous tribe of authors" and aware of "the insignificance of *my* life" in comparison to others', "big with interesting events," Lackington nevertheless asserted at the start of his work that "my performance possessed so much intrinsic merit, as would occasion it to be universally admired by all good judges, as a prodigious effort of human genius" (1791, pp. 2, xvi, x). Thus he understood that the warrant for his claim to the title of "ingenious Author" (1791, p. xlvii) depended upon the effect of his story. Accordingly, he began it first by severing his birth from each of the traditional sources of authority and self-identity: providence, nature (in the form of astrology), family, and guild (1791, pp. 7–8ff), so endowing himself as sole originator and executor of the actions which ensued. This unusual autonomous genesis prefigures the ending of the *Memoirs*, a celebration of its hero's native genius. Having made his name as a bookseller in London, Lackington returned on a visit to Wellington, Somersetshire, the village of his birth, where his former masters and neighbors gazed on him "with surprize and astonishment." "For you must know," he confided, "I had the vanity (I call it humour) to do this in my chariot, attended by my servants" (1791, p. 318). The bells rang merrily all day long, and Lackington "was honored with the attention of many of the most respectable people in and near Wellington and other parts" (1791, p. 319). In the course of his royal progress he encountered one "William Jones, esq., of Foxdowne, near Wellington," who, according to Lackington,

> told me that when I was a boy, about twelve years of age, Mr Paul, then a very considerable wholesale linen-draper, in Friday-street, London, (I believe still living) passing by my father's house, one day stopped at the door, and asked various questions about some guinea pigs which I had in a box. My answers, it seems, pleased and surprised him, and turning towards Mr Jones, said, *"Depend on it, sir, that boy will one day rise far above the situation that his present mean circumstances seem to promise."* So who knows what a great man I may yet be? (1791, pp. 320–1, misprinted as "230")

In the revised version of this story, he answered his rhetorical question thus: " – perhaps 'A double pica in the book of fame!'" (1792, p. 463). With this certification of his personal talent, Lackington closed the circle on his narrative's beginning, unifying his life story and simultaneously alluding to the printed, public text as the grounds of his present and future authoritative self-identity.

Despite the genius he displayed by his idea of emplotting his *Life* as a story, however, Lackington did not invent his plot *ex nihilo*. Rather, he appropriated it from the repertoire of forms available in his culture – a fact which enables us to see that his genius depended as much upon the accident of his nativity as it did upon any imagined biological or genetic advantage. Lackington's story is remarkably similar to the popular English tradition of tradesmen's success stories cast in the mold of the chivalric romance, which runs back at least to the Elizabethan era, with such well-known figures as Dick Whittington, a real merchant, and Jack of Newbury, a fictional one created by Thomas Deloney.[21] The stories of these and other similar figures circulated as chapbooks, and were publicly enacted in plays and puppet shows at fairs and markets throughout Britain well into the nineteenth century. There are significant differences in plot between these tales and Lackington's, however: for example, Dick Whittington's success is attributed to luck brought by his cat, and the heroes of Deloney's stories reject the public honors bestowed on them – neither of which elements would reflect Lackington's aggressive self-interest. But these differences, though revealing in themselves, matter less to us than the similarity of overall design. Lackington's home-coming and distribution of charity mirrors the story of Dick Whittington. We can be reasonably sure Lackington was aware of Lucky Dick's tale; as a young apprentice shoemaker in a shop run by a family of literate religious dissenters, Lackington was exposed to a range of texts read aloud and discussed during work. Among the contents of the master's small library Lackington remembered at least one novel, Deloney's *History of the Gentle Craft* (1791, p. 40). Even if he had no contact with it in the shop, Lackington likely witnessed the Whittington story in performance during his off hours, as did Samuel Pepys, who encountered it on a visit to Southwark Fair one day in 1668, which he recorded in his diary: "saw the puppet show of Whittington which was pretty to see; and how that idle thing do work upon the people that see it and even myself too."[22] We may assume that Lackington knew it, because the traces of its work upon his imagination are embedded in the plot of his *Memoirs*.

Not only are the traces of chapbook romances evident in the narrative structure of the *Memoirs*, a vast range of literature is deliberately woven into the text's surface design as well. Lackington ornamented his prose with tags of verse either copied verbatim or rendered as doggerel; he drew haphazardly upon Herrick, Dryden, Middleton, Shakespeare, old ballads, Horace (in translation), Cowley, Butler, Rowe, Pomfret, Thomson, Pope, Daniel, Gray, Blair, Milton, Prior, Young, and Aaron Hill to adorn his work. The reader rarely finishes more than a page of the *Memoirs*, especially the second and later editions, without finding the trace of another writer besides Lackington there. The cumulative effect of the memoirist's penchant for quotation is the history of him as a reader, even more than as a writer. In fact Lackington turned from shoemaking to bookselling because, he explained, "I loved books," and reasoned "that if I could but be a bookseller, I should then have plenty of books to read, which was the greatest motive I could conceive to induce me to make the attempt" (1791, p. 137). In a very literal sense, then, reading more than any other activity – including writing, since the *Memoirs* and a later sequel were his only published works – informed Lackington's self-identity as an author.

The *Memoirs* is proof of its composer's claim that "everything I read I made my own" (1791, p. 70). For a tradesman, Lackington's reading was quite broad. He first learned to read as an apprentice, in order to participate in the spontaneous debates on religious doctrine arising in the workshop after the master's two boys converted to Methodism. He paid the master's youngest son three-halfpence an hour for spelling lessons, which were given in the dark after bedtime. Only much later did he learn to write. Once he had achieved some competency as a reader, Lackington employed every free minute exercising it: he read by moonlight, and even in "*Cloacina's* Temple" (1791, pp. 47, 103, 50). He began with the Bible, reading ten chapters a day, and then went on to Wesley's hymns, tracts, and sermons, which led to his entrance into Methodist society (1791, p. 50). The *Memoirs* offers proof of how, by the mid-eighteenth century, the privately read book, rather than the orally delivered sermon, was the most ready means of reaching a body of potential converts.[23]

But if reading could beget converts, it could also lead to their apostasy, generating its own secular following of autonomous, enlightened rationalists. Wesley's motto, "Reading Christians will be knowing Christians," contained a double meaning, one pole of which was the antithesis of evangelical religion. The apostate Lackington came to embrace the antithetical extreme. As a journeyman, he and his new co-workers, among them other Methodists, comprised an informal reading society in the shop. "So anxious were we to read a great deal," he recalled

> that we allowed ourselves but about three hours sleep in twenty-four, and for some months together we never were all in bed at the same time; (Sunday nights excepted.) But lest we should oversleep the time allowed, one of us sat up to work until the time appointed for the others to rise, and when all were up, my friend John and your humble servant, took it by turns to read aloud to the rest, while they were at their work. (1791, pp. 93–4)

By this time Lackington's "just taste for literature" brought him in the way of some "proper books" treating subjects other than religion (1791, p. 84). Finding the shops retailing new books too intimidating, he frequented second-hand dealers and stalls at markets and fairs. He remembered one day picking up copies of Hobbes's translations of Homer (he mentioned having "somehow or other heard that Homer was a great poet, but unfortunately ... never heard of Pope's translation of him") and Walker's poetical paraphrase of Epictetus's morals (1791, p. 85). The Epictetus pleased him immensely; Lackington wrote that "I made the book my companion wherever I went, and read it over and over in raptures, thinking that my mind was secured against all the smiles or frowns of fortune" (1791, p. 86).

I have already noted Lackington's affinity for Stoic philosophy, but it was instead the novel which made the greatest impression on his self-identity. He attributed his rejection of Methodism to reading Thomas Amory's *Life of John Buncle*, a novel he described as a "sensible pleasing work." Indeed, he wrote, "I know not of any ... more proper to be put into the hands of a poor ignorant bigotted superstitious methodist." "By the time I had gone through the last volume," Lackington claimed, "my soul had took its freedom up" (1791, p. 166). To all his readers, religious enthusiasts and rationalists alike, Lackington recommended "all the best" novels as a "great source of amusement as well as of knowledge": "by the *best*, I mean those written by Cervantes, Fielding, Smollett, Richardson, Miss Burney, Voltaire, Sterne, Le Sage, Goldsmith, and others. And I have often thought, with Fielding, that some of those publications have given us a more genuine history of Man, in what are called Romances, than is sometimes found under the more respectable titles of History, Biography, &c." (1791, p. 239). He praised these works in the face of the contemporary "sneer against novel-readers" as "excellent productions, [which] tend to polish both the heart and the head" (1830, p. 248). He also observed their influence. Lackington noted that in his day, even

[t]he poorer sort of farmers, and even the poor country people in general, who before ... spent their winter evenings in relating stories of witches, ghosts, hobgoblins, &c. now shorten the nights by hearing their sons and daughters read tales, romances &c. and, on entering their houses, you may see Tom Jones, Roderick Random, and other entertaining books stuck up on their bacon racks, &c. and if *John* goes to town with a load of hay, he is charged to be sure not to forget to bring home "Peregrine Pickle's adventures;" and when *Dolly* is sent to

market to sell her eggs she is commissioned to purchase "The history
of Pamela Andrews." (1791, pp. 254–5)

Though the point of this aside is to praise England because "all ranks
and degrees now READ," it also stands as anecdotal evidence of what
they read: biographical novels. Perhaps the best proof of the impact
of popular novel-reading was the form of the *Memoirs* itself. The
most renowned example of a life in letters in Lackington's day
remained Richardson's *Pamela*, which first appeared in 1740. *Pamela*
was composed entirely of "letters," most of them written by the
protagonist herself, whose writing became the grounds of her individual achievement and self-esteem. The plot struggling to assert itself in
Lackington's work, though it owes something to the chapbook
romances the memoirist likely consumed as a young apprentice, is
largely indebted to the more dignified romances beginning to appear
as novels, like *Pamela*.[24] Lackington apparently read novels as
accounts of personal development and achievement, subject-matter
which the bulk of history and biography available to him, still largely
written in the traditional impersonal and merely chronological mode,
ignored.

The fortune of having been born in an age when the novel was
new accounted as much for the plot of Lackington's *Memoirs* as his
dauntless disposition. Indeed, the practice of reading novels is arguably what enabled Lackington to invent such a peculiar trope in the
first place. If we consider the active experience of reading works like
Pamela or *Tom Jones* in comparison to the relatively passive experience of seeing their stories enacted in a puppet show, or even read
aloud, we find that the hermeneutic effects of plot depend upon the
historically specific situation required of reading modern novels,
where, to achieve their totalizing powers, all other aesthetic effects
are subordinate to the story itself. What kind of autobiographical
work might Pepys have written had he been a reader of Sterne, rather
than a spectator of puppet shows and Restoration comedy? In
comparison to the experience of other narrative genres, the reader of
novels participates actively in what the reader-response theorist
Wolfgang Iser calls a form of "staged play," which enables him to
identify simultaneously with the work's protagonist and its creator.[25]
For Iser, reading novels is an action analogous to writing them. Thus
novels, while they reflect a certain knowledge already shared in the
culture for which they are produced – for example, an interest in
human personality – also add a new dimension to it, by engaging
readers in an active, autonomous process of structuring their know-

ledge as a telos – the telos of the character–author.[26] In this sense, one does not have to be a writer to become an author. Lackington learned to identify himself as his own telos, and therefore to reject religion, and embrace his unique native talent, simply by assimilating the self-identity he assumed in reading novels. The written text he actually authored was the hard copy of a work he, and many other readers like him, had already been composing and revising privately, in his imagination, as a function of novelistic interpretation. In other words, both the literary form of Lackington's *Memoirs* and the authoritative self-identity figured by it were conceivable only after reading, writing, and first-person discourse had coalesced into the peculiar matrix of the novel.[27] Though Lackington's plot was not original, his use of plot to describe his personal history was. The *Memoirs* imitated the form of the novel and, as such, actualized a novel authorial self-identity.

Yet besides this figurative signification we have also to consider the meaning of its publication as a book, for which Lackington himself was also individually responsible. The materiality of a written text is a dimension of its structural display often overlooked by critics attuned to discourse as mere words. In addressing modern autobiographical narratives, invariably we encounter the contents of printed books. But these objects represent just one of many kinds of narrative media. Like emplotment, the book format constitutes a dimension of modern autobiographical authority. It is the result of conscious choices affecting the structure of the work and by extension the self-identity of its producer. It was not until the mid-eighteenth century that the print format entered the mental horizon of a potential autobiographer. The presence and accessibility of print caused an important shift in autobiographical practice, which modern readers now take for granted.

In eighteenth-century England, the culture of print had arrived at a point beyond mere practical utility, so that books were no longer looked upon as the tools and toys of schoolboys, preachers, and tradesmen. The stigma of print so discernible in the Tudor and early Stuart eras had by the end of the seventeenth century largely withered away. In the eighteenth century, print expanded to embrace matter of human interest and curiosity as well as practicality; at the same time, it conferred on its subjects the distinction of being worthy of the discretionary income, leisure time, and attention of a fairly large portion of the public. By the end of the century, therefore, people actually desired to see their names printed, as the emblem of public distinction and personal honor. In 1790, for instance, Tate Wilkinson, an actor and provincial theater-manager, saw published his *Memoirs of His Own Life, By Tate Wilkinson*, in which he frankly declared, "be it known to all men, that there is a secret pride, which, however I would endeavor to conceal, will burst out when I perceive *three volumes* in print – By TATE WILKINSON."[28] Lackington, who knew Wilkinson's work well (the second and later editions of Lackington's *Memoirs* quotes extensively from Wilkinson's), shared the actor's valuation of print. We have already seen Lackington deplore the publication of criminal biographies because such works conferred an honor of which their subjects were unworthy. We have also seen him make his own bid for inclusion in the *Biographia Britannica*, a colossal folio compendium in seven volumes of over 600 pages apiece, whose "first and great motive," according to its editors, was to offer the public "a kind of general MONUMENT erected to the most deserving of all ages ... a BRITISH TEMPLE OF HONOUR, sacred to the piety, learning, valour, publick-spirit, loyalty, and every other glorious virtue of our ancestors, and ready also for the reception of the WORTHIES of our OWN TIME, and the HEROES OF POSTERITY."[29] Last, we have seen him produce a biography of himself which expresses, in its denouement, his wish to be identified by "a double pica in the book of fame." Evidently, the publication of the *Memoirs* marked the conclusion of a line of reasoning which began with the premise that personal worth could be displayed in the typography of a biographical book. What were the values bound up in this premise, and what can they tell us about the self-identity of the subject of a printed autobiography? This will be the last dimension of Lackington's performance I shall consider.

From the perspective of history, writing, as the trace of a practice distinct from speaking, is a radically decontextualizing mechanism.[30] The reception of the spoken word is immediate; moreover, once its sound waves fade, the utterance dissolves without a palpable trace. Writing, on the other hand, remains intact and accessible beyond the space and time of its initial manifestation. It achieves the basic textual effects of what hermeneuticists call "distanciation," or the radical separation of discursive production and consumption, the chief of which is arguably the materiality of the utterance itself. In an era dominated by writing, such as the modern one, the written word "I" will appear as a more substantial signifier than the spoken word "I." Furthermore, as the material word is itself treated as an object by its users, it thereby invests its referents with objectivity; the written word will function as a kind of icon. Not only the signifiers, but also the signifieds, the abstract ideas connoted by words like "I," achieve a degree of objectivity of their own. Obviously, then, the identity of the subject of written autobiographical discourse will be more substantial – that is, more hypostatized and therefore more individualized and autonomous – than the subject of spoken first-person discourse.

Yet if the materiality of writing invests discourse and its referents with objectivity, enabling both to be perceived as possessing their own individual and autonomous structure, print carries this tendency even further. Like the plot, print entails its own peculiar hermeneutic effects. According to the literary theorist Walter Ong, "The objectivity of the text helps impose objectivity on what the text refers to. Eventually writing will create a state of mind in which knowledge itself can be thought of as an object, distinct from the knower. This state of mind, however, is most fully realized only when print intensifies the object-like character of the text."[31] In its printed form, both the text and the knowledge encoded by it embody the effects of what Ong calls "typographical control." A printed work, especially a printed book, arrests the drift and disintegration of the chirographical text, totalizing it and, to a greater degree, also reifying its referents. In comparison to the discourse of the manuscript, which through the process of recopying remains flexible, amenable to the world in which it circulates, the discourse of the printed book imposes an inflexibility, a finality, closure, and completeness which is, Ong claims, "grossly physical."[32] The frontispiece, the title-page, the table of contents, page numbers, and other features of the printed text's graphic organization such as indexes and side- or footnotes help both to label it as an object and to totalize it as the embodiment of a discrete unit of knowledge, set off from other units realized in similar form. Like the closure of plot, the graphic organization of print represents a complex structure of meanings connoting the exercise of judgment and control by the person the text designates as its creator.[33] Ong notes that the advent of print coincided with the emergence in narrative discourse of highly unified plots, culminating in the novel. The totalizing effects of novelistic plot and print are not only compatible, but mutually reinforcing phenomena, almost symbiotic.[34] Print represents another level of configuration superadded to that of narrativity, rendering the structural display of the text even more unified, permanent, and visible.

As the printed text is more substantial than the spoken or handwritten text, so too are the referents of its hermeneutic effects. The materiality of print monumentalizes the narrative competency and self-identity displayed in any given autobiography. This monumentality carries with it an authoritative aura all its own. If plot in narrative points to the authority of its creator as the originator of a hermeneutic action, then print transforms this creator into an author proper, designating the name on the title-page of the printed text as both the originator and the *owner* of the knowledge displayed therein (whether such designation is valid or not). Before the advent of print in the West, according to Ong, words, and the knowledge they encoded, were a common cultural possession. While a person might be designated as the source of a particular text, and perhaps of the knowledge it encoded, neither text nor knowledge was recognized as a product of its source's individual and autonomous effort – texts and knowledge were not personal "intellectual property," as we consider them today. The printed word altered this conception. Largely through processes like the silent reading facilitated by the portable book, print made knowledge the product of individual mental experiences. Knowledge became what was produced secretly rather than what was seen, heard, and shared with others. It became a personal possession, a form of private property. Thus, as a consequence of print, authority designated not only the quality of an originating source, but also the quality of possession of that source. In addition to origination, ownership was ascribed to the figure of the author, as the privilege of individual mental effort. One could claim certain personal rights and responsibilities by virtue of having created or recreated an authentic hermeneutic action, an individual mental experience, encoded by print.[35] As the distillation of this experience, the printed book symbolized the privileges of authorship. Books were the essences of a new form of personal value and a new kind of self-identity, that of the authentic and autonomous author.[36]

Authority in this abstract sense was made more palpable by the function of the printed word as a commodity whose value depended upon rights and responsibilities protected by law. Not only did the published author's work command a figurative value as a display of epistemological control, it also commanded a price in the market for books. Recall how both Lackington and Wesley tallied the profits earned by the evangelist's publications. By the eighteenth century, such profits enabled the purchase of an unprecedented degree of social and economic self-sufficiency for some best-selling writers like Wesley, a material autonomy and authenticity which complemented the writers' internal worth as masters of printed discourse. The symbolic capital of an author rose with the real capital gains made by the sale of his books. As Lackington explained, "every book that is sold tends to spread the fame of the author" (1791, p. 410).

Celebrity became possible, not just for a few, but for writers of any social class who could command the purse-strings of a significant portion of the public. The social type of the "ingenious author," who with his pen honorably serves, and earns the approbation of, a vast unknown public by the production of original works of his imagination, was born.[37] This was the cultural paradigm to which Lackington laid claim with his *Memoirs*. Few contemporaries were better placed to witness the new aura of authority surrounding individual writers than Lackington, who evaluated their books not only as a discerning reader, but also as a seller. Lackington saw the double value of authorship in both its symbolic and economic senses. In his eyes, the writer was a kind of cultural hero, an authorial persona whose monumental status was hewn, literally, out of a bedrock of books.[38]

The emergence of this authorial ideal depended, on the one hand, on the development of bibliographic production and the market for print itself. A host of factors, including the rise of literacy, the increase in wealth among a large portion of the population, the availability of cheaper paper, and an efficient means of provincial distribution, enabled this development. Equally instrumental were the creation of legal measures and trade practices protecting intellectual property. The history of copyright in Britain is difficult to discern because actual practice sometimes contradicted the sense implied by the letter of the law. Although a wide variety of relations between publishers and writers existed from the sixteenth century forward, it seems that generally, prior to the eighteenth century, the rights of an author to his creation were dimly perceived.[39] Emphasis was placed on rights in copies rather than rights in original compositions, which protected publishers but not authors. The reasons for this are complicated, having to do with the state's need for a mechanism of censorship of texts which could be widely disseminated and the publisher's need for a means of protecting the considerable economic investment behind the production and distribution of a book. The implications of these dual requirements for writers were their lack of legal entitlements as owners, and the absence of real autonomy and authority as creators. But by the end of the eighteenth century the writer's legal situation had changed considerably, and with it the recognition of his genius. As the literary historian Mark Rose explains in his study of the invention of modern copyright, issues of the writer's literary property in the sense of economic interest and his personal propriety in the moral sense developed together, "like the twin suns of a binary star locked in orbit."[40] According to Rose, despite a foreshadowing in the Copyright Act of 1710, it was not until the arguments in the case of *Millar v. Taylor* of 1769 that legal discourse recognized total authorial interest in a work. The writer's right to such property was based on the concept of his "personality" or genius embodied, uniquely, in literary labor, rendering the result, the text, a "work of original authorship."[41] With the widespread acceptance of this concept in practice during the latter third of the eighteenth century in Britain, and its codification in the letter of the law by the Copyright Act of 1814, writers became owners of their texts. They became agents endowed with the full responsibility and credit for the production of their "works".

The book represents the final stage of the emergence of "the author" as a cultural ideal or type of self-identity. As the critic of modern autobiography Philippe Lejeune explains, the author is a value arising from a unique combination of practices, among which publication is paramount. According to Lejeune,

> The author of a text is most often the one who wrote it, but the fact of writing is not sufficient to be declared an author. One is not an author in the absolute. It is a relative and conventional thing: one becomes an author only when one takes, or finds oneself attributed, the responsibility of the emission of the message (emission that *implies* its production) in a given circuit of communication. . . . the notion of author refers as much to the idea of *initiative* as much as to *production*.[42]

The mass publication made possible by print, along with the level of responsibility and credit implied in the concept of the author's copyright, together brought into being this sense of initiative in the figure of the author of a book text. The printed book, legally protected as intellectual property, displays the writer at the summit of his narrative capacities. In addition to the personalized voice in narration and the unity of its plot, therefore, the physical form of the autobiographical text completes the sum of its authoritative effects. An autobiographical book is not only the most substantial, it is also the most potent form of authorial self-identification.

Although every detail of a book – its dimensions, paper, size and style of type, layout, decoration, price, edition size, etc. – connotes an aspect of the initiative taken by its producer, and symbolizes his identity as an author, the chief emblem of authority is the title-page. Title-pages are textual devices serving to promote the author as a formal ideal, establishing an indissoluble connection between an object, a text, and a creator. In an autobiographical book, the title-page represents what Lejeune calls the "autobiographical signature," establishing a contract between the producer and consumer of the book that all of the credit for the work, from the individuality and authenticity of the narrational voice to its unity, substantiality, and initiative, accrues to the person designated there as "author." In a way, perhaps, the actual content of the modern autobiographical narrative matters less in itself than what it contributes as the physical backing for the title-page, which most succinctly and directly communicates the fundamental message of the text: the narrative authority of the autobiographer. This unequal relation between the title-page and the rest of the discourse is more plausible if we recall the autonomous function of title-pages as advertisements in the seventeenth and eighteenth centuries. Then title-pages functioned much as dust jackets do today. They did not merely distinguish the contents of one book from another (most of which were of course sold unbound), they also graphically epitomized the work for prospective purchasers and other readers. The title-page was literally an advertisement for the text; it was displayed on its own in booksellers' shops, and sometimes was posted up or cried out in the streets.[43] Eighteenth-century newspaper advertisements for books typically excerpted the contents of the title-page.[44] The title-page was a performance of the work in miniature. Moreover, writers understood the connection between the title-pages of their books and their personal reputations; the playwright–poet John Gay, for instance, in his "Trivia, or the Art of Walking the Streets of London," first published in 1716, concluded by bringing the poem and its reader round to a view of its own title-page: "High-rais'd on *Fleetstreet* Posts, consign'd to Fame, / This Work shall shine, and Walkers bless my Name."[45] Thus the public's recognition of an autobiographer's self-identity would depend, in the most basic sense, upon the immediate impression made by his work's title-page.

Few people alive in Lackington's day witnessed as many title-page performances as he did, and few were likely to have possessed a better developed concept of print values than he. It is not unreasonable for us to assume therefore that, along with the novel, the spectacle of authority constituted by the title-pages of books tacitly informed his autobiographical performance. Several features of the title-page of the *Memoirs* attest to Lackington's sense of its importance. Besides the prominence and authority it gave to his name, his address, the intentional structure of the first forty-five years of his life, and his active voice, the work featured as its frontispiece an engraved reproduction of an oil portrait of Lackington. The book-

seller was evidently proud of this object, his picture, which along
with the other accoutrements of status – his country house, clothes,
carriage, and so forth – announced that he had "made it" in society.
In a postscript to the very last letter of the *Memoirs*, he acknowledged
"the approbation it [i.e. the portrait] has been honoured with by all
who have seen it, as a striking likeness" (1791, pp. 341–2). As such,
it added a finishing gloss to the text by providing a visual complement
to the verbal image of its subject. Of course the inclusion of a portrait
of the author in a printed work was hardly unusual by the eighteenth
century – graphic representations of authors can be found even in
medieval manuscripts, and became increasingly common and personalized in books as time passed and reproductive technology developed
– but "heads" as detailed and expressive as the portrait of Lackington
were limited to the most expensive and important of books, such as
a celebrated author's posthumously collected works, in folio. Such
images as these – think of the engraved portrait of Shakespeare
appearing as the frontispiece to the First Folio edition of 1623, or the
image of Dryden in the first volume of Tonson's two-volume folio
edition of Dryden's *Works*, published a year after the author's death
in 1701 – identify and individualize the voice constituted in the
literary corpus by connecting it with a specific face, giving readers a
sense of the writer's material presence, and contributing yet another
dimension to his aura of authority. For a living writer such as
Lackington, with no previously published books and no other
legitimate cause to make his face and stature worthy of public
recognition, let alone approbation, to have included so fine an image
of himself in an otherwise run-of-the-mill octavo volume, priced at
5s., in boards – a "popular" book in its material as well as its verbal
form – was highly unusual.[46]

But for that matter so was the *Memoirs* itself. By the end of the
eighteenth century, it was not unusual for men and women of any
class to maintain a personal diary, and even for many of them to
write their diaries up in narrative form, as brief autobiographies. Yet
it was unusual for the products of this practice to find their way into
print. If personal diaries or narratives were printed, it was still usually
done for a specific purpose unrelated to the writer himself. Extracts
of religious diaries were sometimes published to promote piety;
indeed, that was the point of Wesley's serially published *Journal*.
Occasionally, the recollections or notes of a public figure, such as one
involved in national religion or politics, like Richard Baxter or the
Earl of Clarendon, or a notorious criminal, like John Sheppard,
warranted publication. A printed biography of a public figure might

adduce examples of its subject's original prose, drawn from letters or commonplace books, to illustrate a point. Personal appearances in print such as these were, with few exceptions, arranged posthumously, by editors and publishers, and not by the subjects themselves. Memoirs might be written and left for posterity, but printed "autobiography" was unheard of – there was no term invented to describe such a practice. The very few autobiographical works which their authors boldly printed – John Bunyan's *Grace Abounding*, John Wesley's *Journal*, George Whitfield's *Journal*, John Dunton's *Life and Errors*, Colley Cibber's *Apology*, Charlotte Charke's *Narrative*, George Anne Bellamy's *Apology*, and a handful of other less known works – typically served an impersonal purpose. Though some were epistolary, perhaps in imitation of *Pamela*, none were emplotted as stories in which their authors acted as heroes. Thus, while it is possible for us to see how each of the separate strands of Lackington's work may be unoriginal in its own right, we must also keep in mind the momentous and unprecedented originality of his having combined them in the form of a single work.

No other aspect of the *Memoirs* expressed Lackington's precocious use of print for self-promotion better than its imprint, which in the first edition reads as follows: "Printed for and sold by the AUTHOR, No. 46 and 47, Chiswell-Street; W. Bulgin, Bristol; and all other Booksellers." Lackington was the work's single copyright owner, and the sole initiator of its publication. The *Memoirs* was printed "for" him: Lackington was the person whose capital and reputation were at stake in its book form. He also acted as his own distributor; though he depended on other retailers for assistance, they had no shares in the copyright, and bore no fiscal and legal responsibility for it.[47] Lackington owned his *Life*, and all the credit, symbolic and economic, ensuing from the thirteen editions which appeared in his lifetime accrued entirely to him.

At least this is what his title-page declared to the public, and what the reception of the work, which I shall consider briefly later in my epilogue, sanctioned. However, the ultimate value of any book depends upon collective effort – the collaboration of papermakers, printers and binders, as well as purchasers and other potential readers – despite the fact that only one person may be designated as its author. Indeed, as the historian Roger Chartier explains, and as the succeeding chapters of this book will demonstrate, the author is always dependent on and constrained by aspects of textuality and contextuality beyond his control:

He is dependent in that he is not the unique master of the meaning of
his text, and his intentions, which provided the impulse to produce the
text, are not necessarily imposed on those who turn his text into a book
... or on those who appropriate it by reading it. He is constrained in
that he undergoes the multiple determinations that organize the social
space of literary production and that, in a more general sense, determine
the categories and the experiences that are the very matrices of
writing.[48]

This condition of dependency and constraint is of course also true of
the self-identity manifested by the text. Self-identities are always the
effects of interpersonal negotiation, and thus are products of collaboration; yet this is a fact which, like the collective responsibility for a
book, individuals in modernity persistently, obsessively overlook.
The legacy of anti-modernist thought inspired by Nietzsche has
argued, compellingly, that just as every text is an articulation of the
relations between texts, every author – indeed, every self – is the
articulation of an identity structured within and around the discourses available to it at any moment in time.

So from the perspective of ontology and epistemology, in order for
Lackington to have been more accurate, rather than "everything I
read I made my own," he ought to have written "everything I read
made my 'I.'" His autobiographical performance, a weaving together
of everything from Biggs's handbill to *Tristram Shandy*, obviously
demonstrates the latter rather than the former judgment. But for
Lackington to have understood his self-identity as a product of
discursive relations was a historical impossibility, for he was a pre-
modern rather than a post-modern person. His claim to be a
sovereign subject was a natural product of the discourse of his age,
which the cultural historian and philosopher Michel Foucault has
characterized as that of "anthropological sleep." Like the self-identity
constituted in Lackington's *Memoirs*, the modern individualist self is
hypnotized by the illusion of individual personal authority, a will to
autonomous self-creation sustained by the practice of modern autobiographical narrative. As Lejeune explains, "We are never really the
cause of our life, but we can have the illusion of becoming its author
by writing it, providing that we forget that we are no more the cause
of the writing than of our life."[49] Lackington's *Memoirs* is the first
eruption of this modern pathological forgetfulness, a symptom of the
assumption by the popular personality of individualist self-identity.
Let us now turn back two centuries before its publication, to consider
how such a pathology developed in personal discourse.

Part II
Early Ancestors: The Sacred

The knowledge of letters is certainly one of the greatest blessings that ever God bestowed on mortals; their uses are innumerable; they ease our memories, by committing to writing what would otherwise have been burdensome to retain, or else have been totally forgot. By this means our predecessors have transmitted to us their various exploits and transactions, and we hand them down, together with our own, to future generations. Thus also we have accounts of what is done in the remotest parts of the world; and they again the same from us. Thus excellent men by their writings, in all faculties and sciences, enjoy a sort of immortality upon earth, by having their memories hon-oured by succeeding generations who never saw their faces in the flesh.

But the greatest blessing of all that has by this means been transmitted to us, is in the revelation of God's will to us in the Holy Scriptures; wherein is contained all that we need to know, or to do, in this life, in order to be for ever happy in the next. For had not the apostles committed their doctrine to writing, how short and uncertain an account should we have of it; then there would have been large room for introducing oral traditions at pleasure.

And we, who live in these latter ages, have still greater reason of thankfulness to Almighty God for the great improvement of the use of these letters, by the wonderful and almost miraculous invention of the art of printing; which is now come to so great perfection, and has already done so much good in the world. . . .

Several good men have been careful to publish to the world an account of the lives of such men who have been eminently serviceable in their day and station, and whose lives have been exemplarily pious; and I doubt not but much good has been done by this means, and that many others have been thereby provoked to follow 'em in love and good works.

"A Family History Begun by James Fretwell" (1739)

3
Christian "Experience"; or, The Discourse of Life and Death

Experience is a Copy written by the Spirit of God upon the hearts of beleevers. It is one of *Faiths* handmaids, and attendants, and *Hopes* usher.

Spirituall Experiences, Of Sundry Beleevers (1653)

It's a great work to learn to die, safely and comfortably; even the work of all our lives.

The Lives of Sundry Eminent Persons in this Later Age (1683)

In 1591, 200 years prior to the first publication of James Lackington's novel *Memoirs*, another pivotal text in the history of English individualism and autobiographical practice appeared. On 15 June in that year, Philip Stubbes saw published in London his narrative account of the life and death of his 20-year-old wife, Katherine Stubbes, who had been buried seven months and a day before, on 14 December, at Burton-upon-Trent in Staffordshire. Stubbes's work was a twenty-page quarto pamphlet printed in black-letter entitled, *A Christal Glasse for Christian Women.*[1] Both the text and its subject were, for contemporaries then as for us now, exceptional entities. *A Christal Glasse* ranks among the earliest English representations of the life of an ordinary person – neither prince nor canonical saint nor martyr – to appear in the form of an autonomous narrative text. In it the subject speaks at extraordinary length of her experience directly, in first-person singular discourse, which makes her one of the first ordinary people to have been (albeit posthumously, and at her husband's initiative) identified by a voice individualized through an extended narrative performance. Though not an autobiography,

Stubbes's *Christal Glasse* establishes the structure and intention of autobiographical discourse in the seventeenth century; though subject to the authority of both patriarchy and religion – she is adduced as "a mirror of woman-hood [and] . . . a perfect pattern of true Christianity" (sig. A2) – Stubbes the biographical subject establishes the characteristic form of expression of the individualist self.

Young Mistress Stubbes, née Emmes, the daughter of William Emmes, late citizen of London and a cordwainer by trade, married Philip Stubbes at the early age of 15, shortly after the death of her father. Though engaged in trade, William Emmes had been a man of some substance, if only in the eyes of a contemporary Londoner: *A Christal Glasse* describes him as one who "had borne divers Offices of worship in his Company, amongst whom he lived in great account, credit, and estimation all his dayes" (sig. A2). Stubbes, a restless, Cambridge-educated hothead and penner of pious ballads who had at the time of his marriage recently gained some notoriety by rebuking the world, and England in particular, for its backsliding with his tract *The Anatomy of Abuses*, was an odd choice for a husband for Katherine. However, she was the youngest child and only daughter among her siblings, and probably for financial reasons had to be married hastily, upon the division of whatever estate her father left his family. Stubbes likely praised God for his good fortune. His clamorous piety, at least, must have given his in-laws some assurance, despite his otherwise uneven character. For her part, Katherine proved a satisfactory wife to a well-traveled husband over fifteen years her elder. *A Christal Glasse* praises her submission both to scripture and to Stubbes. The narrator tells us, "She obeyed the Commandment of the Apostle who biddeth women to be silent, and to learn of their husbands at home" (sig. A2ᵛ). Indeed, "For true love and loyalty to her husband and his friends," she was, "the rarest Paragon in the world" (sig. A3). In the space of about four years she bore two children, both male. It was after the conception of the first child, however, that she became sensible of her impending premature death. According to the narrative, which throughout identifies "Mistris Stubs" as "this godly young Gentlewoman,"[2] she began telling both her husband and her neighbors, "not once or twice, but many times," that should she conceive another child, she would bear it, but that by doing so would die. In retrospect, this premonition was interpreted as a sign revealed to Mistress Stubbes by God, because remarkably, we learn, "according to her Prophesie, so it came to passe" (sig. A3ᵛ).

As the narrative represents it, the drama of Katherine Stubbes's death was the central event of her life. The details of her parentage, marriage, and godly and wifely demeanor – the only really personal topics introduced in the text – serve merely as a prelude to her death; they take all of three pages to relate. The reader is quickly and deliberately ushered to the scene of her sick-bed, where the main action begins. A sudden recovery followed the birth of the second child; but abruptly, after a fortnight of increasing strength, Katherine was struck "with an exceeding hot and burning Quotidian Ague," in which she languished for six straight weeks (sig. A3ᵛ). Throughout her illness, she expressed her desire to die, intermittently murmuring, "O my sweet Jesus, O my love Jesus, why not now sweet Jesus, why not now? O sweet Jesus pray for me, pray for me sweet Jesus" (sig. A4). We learn that "[t]hese, and infinite the like, were her daily speeches, and continuall meditations," despite the pleas of her husband and others that she pray to God for health (sig. A4). To such appeals, we are told, she answered,

> I beseech you pray not that I should live for I think it long to be with my God; Christ is to me life, and death is to me advantage: yea, the day of death is the birth day of everlasting life, and I cannot enter into life, but by death, therefore is death the door or entrance into everlasting life. I know, and am certainly perswaded by that great Judge, in the high Court or Parliament of Heaven, that I shall now depart out of this life: and therefore pray not for me, that I might live here, but pray to God, to give me strength and patience to persevere to the end, and to close up mine eyes in the justifying faith of the blood of my Christ. (sig. A4)

During this period also her countenance would sometimes brighten; she would smile and laugh without apparent cause. When asked to explain the source of her mirth, she replied, "O, if you saw such glorious and heavenly lights as I see, you would rejoice and laugh with me: for I see a bilion of the joyes of heaven, and of the glory that I shall go unto; and I see infinite millions of Angels attendant upon me, and watching over me, ready to carry my soul into the kingdom of heaven" (sig. A4ᵛ).

At what witnesses to her death would later come to see as the first moment of her last hour, Mistress Stubbes called one day for her newborn child, took it in her arms, kissed it, and handed it over to her husband, telling him that the infant "is no longer mine, he is the Lords and yours, I forsake him, you, and all the world, yea, and mine own selfe" (sig. A4ᵛ). Then her attention was drawn to her puppy, her loyal bed-companion, which she beat away, telling Stubbes, good Husband, you and I have offended God grievously, in receiving this Bitch many a time into our bed: we would have been loth to have received a Christian soule, purchased with the precious blood of Jesus Christ, into our bed, and to have nourished him in our bosoms, and to have fed him at our table, as we have done this filthy Cur many times: the Lord give me grace to repent it, and all other vanities. (sig. A4ᵛ)

Next, the narrator reports, "having thus godly disposed all things, shee fell into a Trance, or swound, for almost the space of a quarter of an houre, and so as every one thought shee had been dead" (sig. A4ᵛ). Then coming to consciousness, she turned to address the audience of "many, both worshipfull and others" assembled at her bedside, telling them that as "my houre-glasse is run out, and . . . my time of departure hence is at hand, I am persuaded by three causes to make a confession of my Faith before you all" (sig. B). She proceeded to state each of these causes: first, "that those (if there be any such here) that are not yet throughly resolved in the truth of God, may hear and learn what the spirit of God hath taught me, out of his blessed and alsaving Word"; second, "that none of you shall judge that I dyed not a perfect Christian, and a perfect member of the mysticall body of Jesus Christ"; and last, "that as you have been witnesses of part of my Life, so you might be witnesses of part of my Faith and Beleefe also." Then she introduced her confession as follows:

I would not have you to think that it is I that speaks unto you, But the Spirit of God that dwelleth in me and all the elect of God, unless they be reprobates. For S. *Paul* saith *Rom. 8. If any one have not the spirit of Christ dwelling in him, he is none of his.* This blessed Spirit hath knocked at the door of my heart, and my God hath given me grace to open the doore of my heart, and he dwelleth in me plentifully. And therefore I pray you lend your patience a little and imprint my words in your hearts: for they are not the words of flesh and blood, but the Spirit of God, by whom we are sealed to the day of our redemption. (sig. B)

There follows a break in the text, separating the ensuing monologue from the narration preceding it.

The monologue is entitled "A most heavenly confession of the Christian Faith made by the blessed Servant of God, Mistris *Katherine Stubs*, a little before she died." It occupies the space of over ten pages, more than double the amount devoted to her "life," and half of the entire text of *A Christal Glasse* (sigs B–C2). The "confession" addresses twenty-seven theological topics, each identified in the margin by a handy side-note, from the first, "What God is," through

"Christs comming to judgement, and our resurrection," "Her faith in predestination of God, and what it is," and "Sacraments, and what they are, whereof they do consist, & what they represent unto us," to the last, "We shall know one another in the life to come." The confession is constituted entirely of first-person discourse. We are meant to read it, as the title-page instructs us to do, as a transcript of her speech, "word for word as she spake it." Each transition is marked by the phrase, "I beleeve . . ." or a variant thereof, lending to the discourse a subtle and effective *accumulatio*. Taken as a whole, the "confession" represents Katherine Stubbes's personal creed, an individual distillation of the doctrine of the Elizabethan church. This testimony is followed by a transcript of her part of a disputation with Satan, who, it seems, appeared before her upon the conclusion of her address to her human audience. Her arguments rapidly vanquished the tempter (the transcript covers but two pages of text). This triumph became a denouement of sorts;[3] after putting Satan away, Mistress Stubbes sang a psalm, asked her husband not to mourn her and, smiling,

> lifting up her whole body, and stretching forth both her arms, as though she would imbrace some glorious and pleasant thing, said: I thank my God through Jesus Christ, he is come, he is come, my good Jaylor is come to let my soule out of prison. O sweet death, thou art welcome, the messenger of everlasting life . . . strike sweet death, strike my heart, I fear not that stroke: now it is . . . O most holy, blessed and glorious Trinitie, three persons and one true and everlasting God, into thy blessed hands I commit my soul and body. (sig. C3ᵛ)

At which words, the narrator informs us, in conclusion to the narrative, "her breath stayed, and so moving neither hand nor foot she slept sweetly in the Lord" (sig. C3ᵛ).

The Katherine Stubbes emerging from this performance fulfills the narrative's promotion of her as a "rare and wonderful example" (sig. A2) in many different ways, not the least of which is as an individualized voice. Besides the lessons of scripture (helpfully identified by the printed side-notes), her discourse imprints in the patient reader's heart a powerful testimony of personal capacity, however embedded it may be within the institutional discourse of Christianity and patriarchy. Though young, inexperienced in life, and obedient to the doctrine of female silence, Mistress Stubbes displays a remarkable verbal ability. Not only is she able to deliver a longwinded monologue after enduring six weeks of sleepless fever; in her health she was apparently also prone to engage papists and atheists in argument whenever occasion called, "and convince them; yea, and confound them" with her testimonies, as well as to "reprove . . . sharply" any filthy tongues in and about her home (sig. A2ᵛ, sig. A3). Yet no one found her either loquacious or, worse, a scold; indeed, "She was never known to fall out with any of her neighbours, nor with the least child that lived: much less to scould or brawl, as many will now adaies for every trifle, or rather for no cause at all" (sig. A2ᵛ). By her confessional style and manner of disputation with Satan she appears to have been as well schooled in the art of rhetoric as most ministers and probably many lawyers in her day, though the narrative makes no mention of her ever receiving any formal education. Moreover, although at the start of her confession she claimed to speak only "as the Spirit of God shall illuminate my heart" (sig. B), she displays a studied knowledge of both the old and new testaments, citing specific passages of the latter text in her monologue twelve times. Her neighbors found her "alwaies poring upon a Book, and reading" (sig. A3), and we learn as well that "her whole delight was to be conversant in the Scriptures, and to meditate upon them day and night. Insomuch as you could seldome or never have come into her house, and have found her without a Bible, or some other good book in her hand" (sig. A2ᵛ). Finally, for a layperson, let alone a woman, she shows a potentially dangerous grasp of theology, which she acquired from liberal conversation with Stubbes, for "when she was not reading, she would spend her time in conferring, talking, and reasoning with her husband of the word of God, and of Religion" (sig. A2ᵛ). Though unable ultimately to write her own narrative, and therefore to authorize an individual self-identity, Katherine Stubbes displays at least the potential to do so, providing the example of a person able to read, and reason, and speak for herself. This was something wonderful indeed.

Paradoxically, however, every word of *A Christal Glasse* – whether attributable to Mistress Stubbes or to the narrator of her tale – serves to negate both its human subject's individuality and her personal capacity. She was able and eloquent only because her faith told her that she was one of God's instruments. Recall how she began her confession: "I would not have you to think that it is I that speak unto you, But the Spirit of God that dwelleth in me and all the elect of God, unless they be reprobates . . . [my words] are not the words of flesh and blood, but the Spirit of God, by whom we are sealed to the day of our redemption." Thus, in spite of Katherine Stubbes's awesome textual presence, the true subject of *A Christal Glasse* is not self-authorization, but the annihilation of self. Human mortality is its major theme, as the narrator explains in its opening sentence:

Calling to remembrance . . . the finall end of mans Creation, which is to glorifie God, and to edifie one another in the way of Godliness, I thought it my duty as well in respect of the one, as in regard to the other, to publish this rare and wonderful example, of the vertuous Life, and Christian Death of Mistris *Katherine Stubs*: who whilest she lived was a mirror of woman-hood: and now being dead, is a perfect pattern of true Christianity. (sig. A2)

The work's minor theme, as we have seen earlier, is the necessity of female subjection to male authority. In either case, the text suggests, death becomes her. This is the implicit message of Katherine Stubbes's life, which she aptly described as a "prison." She was imprisoned by the culture of the patriarchal family: "she would very seldome or never, and not then neither, except her husband were in company, go abroad with any, either to Banquet or Feast, Gossip or make merry as they term it" (sig. A2ᵛ); as well as by the nature of Christianity: "my body is nothing else but a stinking prison to my soule" (sig. A4). And it was the explicit message of her death, which the text represents as a liberation: "O send thy messenger death to fetch me . . . send thy Jaylor to deliver my soule out of prison" (sig. A4). Death was her desire, for which she relinquished all: seeing "a bilion of the joyes of heaven and of the glory that I shall go unto," "she was willing to forsake her selfe, her husband, her child, and all the world besides" (sig. A4ᵛ). From a modern, individualist, perspective, Katherine Stubbes embodies a rather perverse concept of personal freedom – she was at liberty only in the most extreme posture of self-denial.

Yet this was the message most early modern Christians, both male and female – the intended audience of *A Christal Glasse* – were prepared to receive. The fact that a woman was the subject of Stubbes's work was arbitrary. Being, to the contemporary eye, the weaker of the two human vessels, the female was therefore the more pliant, and thus the more susceptible to temptation; but by the same token she was also the more capable of perfection. In either case, her value as an exemplary subject was that she was more prone to extremes, and therefore offered a more vivid pattern for readers to follow. However, self-denial *per se* was not enjoined exclusively on Christian women. Even Philip Stubbes, the originator of the written narrative and an eye-witness of most of the events it relates, took pains to deny himself a voice in the text. He appears in his work not as its author but rather as a character, "her husband," and ascribes the actual narration to a disembodied voice, the imaginary "I" of the narrator. As Stubbes well knew, death became *every* body. The crucial matter was to learn to die well, by living in self-denial.

A Christal Glasse was therefore intended partly as an extension of a literary tradition which had, by the late sixteenth century, firmly planted itself in several generations of the popular imagination. Iconic representations of "Moriens," the dying man, confronted by a variety of temptations, originated in the fifteenth century. In England in the early sixteenth century a number of vernacular works on the practical "crafte" or "art" of dying appeared, forming a body of literature which culminated, from a literary formalist standpoint, with Jeremy Taylor's *Holy Dying* in 1651.[4] Taylor explained the commonplace Christian understanding that "*He that would die holily and happily, must in this world love tears, humility, solitude, and repentance.*"[5] One must prepare for a holy and happy death by diligent and frequent self-examination, which in Christian practice constituted an act of self-denial: "we are here to follow S. *Pauls* advice; *Judge your selves and you shall not be judged of the Lord.* The way to prevent Gods anger is to be very angry with our selves, and by examining our actions and condemning the Criminal, by being Assessors in Gods Tribunal, at least we shall obtain the favour of the Court" (vol. II, p. 55). To show the wisdom of this course, Taylor cited Ecclesiastes 19:1: "*He that despiseth little things, shall perish by little and little*" (vol. II, p. 57). Similar advice was available over a century before, in the devotional treatise attributed to Thomas à Kempis, *De Imitatione Christi*, fully translated into English and printed in London around 1531 as *The Folowynge of Cryste*. This work instructed that "the most high and profitable learning is this, that a man have a soothfast knowledge and a full despising of himself. Also not to presume of himself, and always to judge and to think well of others, is a sign and token of great wisdom, and of great perfection and singular grace."[6] Such was the self-knowledge Katherine Stubbes exemplified for her contemporary audience. She herself explained that "Christ biddeth me, *Love not the world, nor any thing in the world,* affirming that if I love the world, *The love of the Father is not in me*" (sig. A3^{v}). The experience of mortification, the personal foundation of the faith she confessed, made her certain of her election, and able to die in joyful anticipation of everlasting life with God. The abnegation of her individual personality continued even after her death, with the representation of her experience in a book bearing her name. Philip Stubbes saw in his wife's life and death an experimental proof which might edify other Christian souls. He represented her death as incontrovertible evidence of the justness of her faith, and as a mirror by which others might know God, and themselves. In *A Christal Glasse*, "Katherine Stubbes" signified a universal pattern for which Christ was the prototype. She was not an individual person; her "life" was a conduct book; her "experience" structured by side-notes (fifty-four in all) for the information of others. Readers studied her life not to know Mistress Stubbes, but to use her pattern to mortify themselves.

Yet however familiar the function of *A Christal Glasse* may have been to its audience, its design was something new. Apart from the figure of Christ, historical subjects, and especially speaking subjects, were unknown to the *ars moriendi* tradition in England. The peculiar genius of Stubbes's work was its emphasis on personal praxis, by its use of biographical material and the personal voice as a vehicle for abstract doctrine. Stubbes may have taken his cue from the epistles of Paul, the scriptural authority most frequently cited by his wife in her discourses. Like Paul's, Katherine Stubbes's voice made her piety palpable for the ordinary reader. This was a trick even the stylistic brilliance of Jeremy Taylor could not achieve. At the conclusion of his chapter in *Holy Dying*, on the "general preparation towards a holy and blessed death," Taylor conceded that "the victory which holy souls receive by the mercies of Jesus Christ, and the conduct of Angels is a joy that we must not understand till we feel it . . . let us enquire after it no further, because it is secret" (vol. II, p. 67). But by preserving the private meditations and visions of a real-life dying person, Stubbes offered his readers a foretaste of that secret knowledge. Even though, so long as they lived, Christians could never be certain of their end, the confidence of Katherine Stubbes's relation from her own death-bed, so proximate to the gates of heaven and in view of its "glorious light," might inspire expectations of certainty in her readers. The voice of real experience, more familiar and accessible than theological abstraction, offered more convincing hope than the metaphor-laden prose of a doctor of divinity.[7] The enormous popularity of Stubbes's work attests to the effectiveness of its innovation: at least thirty-four separate editions of *A Christal Glasse* had appeared in print by 1700, twenty-eight of them before 1650. The book was clearly a best-seller among the gentry and wealthy merchants of London: the Elizabethan popular publishing tycoon Richard Jones first owned its copyright; after Jones's retirement from trade in 1602 it was acquired by John Wright, a founding member of the "ballad partners" group specializing in the backlisting of cheap popular classics. In 1635, "Katherin Stubs" – as the book was commonly known – was described in a comedy by William Cartwright as a staple in the selection of miscellaneous religious tracts hawked beside playhouse doors:

I shall live to see thee
Stand in a Play-house door with thy long box,
Thy half-crown Library, and cry small Books.
Buy a good godly Sermon Gentlemen –
A judgement shewn upon a Knot of Drunkards –
A pill to purge out Popery – The life
And death of *Katherine Stubs*.[8]

Moreover, purchasers used "Katherin Stubs" well – of the editions known to exist today, all but four survive by virtue of unique copies. The perishability of the text is a mark of its indispensability to its readers, who literally read it to death.

Though new to the *ars moriendi* tradition in the late sixteenth century, the narration of personal experience and use of first-person discourse occupied a fairly well-established position in some other contemporary literary traditions, especially those pertaining to civility and Christian morality. While neither directly advocated self-denial, each of these traditions also sought, in part, to uphold institutional orders larger than individual persons. And, like the art of dying well, each also contained the seeds of practices tending to place the individual person before the larger order, in spite of the practitioner's best intentions. Works teaching the art of politics and good government emphasized the honor and privilege of noble blood. John Lydgate's *The Fall of Princes*, composed in verse c. 1431–9, and printed in four different English editions by 1558, described the tragic experience of historical personages. Lydgate followed the narrative strategy of Boccaccio, from whom *The Fall of Princes* was adapted, by having deceased characters appear before him in a vision or dream and narrate their lives in the first-person singular.[9] These narrations were obviously fictional, but the personal voice of ghosts served as an effective exhortatory device. The same strategy was employed by the authors of the compilation of princely tragedies known as *A Myrroure for Magistrates*, a kind of continuation of Lydgate's work, which appeared in 1559. This text, as its title indicates, also helped to popularize the notion of personal history as a mirror. In his dedication of the work, William Baldwin explained that "here as in a loking glas, you shall see (if any vice be in you) howe the like hath bene punished in others heretofore, whereby admonished, I trust it will be a good occasion to move you to the soner amendment."[10] The metaphor of the glass originates in the medieval concept of the speculum, functioning as both a mediating instrument and a reflector. The text as mirror enables the reader to see himself by seeing through the experience of others.[11] Following

the example of Lydgate and the *Myrroure for Magistrates*, the value
of history as a tool for personal information, especially in the conduct
of politics, was often cited as justification for its publication in the
sixteenth and seventeenth centuries, as it was by Henry Wright, in
his work *The First Part of the Disquisition of Truth, Concerning
Political Affaires* (1616), in which he claims, "History is auaileable
to instruct any priuate man (of what degree soeuer) how to frame his
life, and carry himselfe with commendation in the eye of the world,
when, as in a glasse, he shall see how to beautifie & compose it,
according to the pattern of other men's vertues."[12] Though still
within the bounds of the community of nobility, Wright's reader
finds himself contemplating the "priuate" person, the embryo of the
autonomous individual, in public.

Personal history and first-person discourse were used to teach
Protestant piety as well as civic virtue. Texts in this tradition
emphasized the godly "community of saints."[13] While *A Christal
Glasse* owes itself partly to the tradition of medieval hagiography –
for example in its use of the quasi-miraculous "prophesie" of
Katherine Stubbes's death as a portent of her election, linking her
with such saintly predecessors as Margery Kempe – the more
proximate and influential mode of Christian biography was that of
Protestant martyrology, represented by John Foxe's *Acts and Monuments*, known popularly as *The Book of Martyrs*, first published in
England in 1563. In fact, Philip Stubbes had collaborated with Foxe
in this work, by contributing verses to the revised and augmented
fourth edition of *Acts and Monuments*, published in 1583.[14]
Although a book of truly monumental proportions – in the edition of
1583, two folio volumes containing 2,154 pages of text – the work
was enormously popular, and many abridged editions appeared after
Foxe's death in 1587, the first in 1589. If not actual eye- and ear-
witnesses of the experience of the Marian martyrs in the 1550s,
Stubbes's potential audience was likely to have been familiar with
Foxe's representation of it, as was Stubbes himself. While Katherine
Stubbes was not herself a martyr, either in her life or in its narrative
representation, *A Christal Glasse* bears evidence of the absorption of
Foxe's histories, in its manner of placing her within the community
of the elect. In Stubbes's work we can observe, as in Foxe's, the
importance ascribed to contemporary personal experience, and the
need to preserve the best instances of it by embalming them in print.
In his preface, Foxe tells the reader that "I thought it not to be
neglected, that the precious monuments of so many matters, and men
most meete to be recorded and registyred in bookes, should lye

buried."[15] Likewise, the title-page of *A Christal Glasse* states that the discourse of its subject is "worthy to be printed in letters of Gold, and to be engrauen in the Table of euerie Christian heart." As a result of this similarity of purpose, there are parallels in form between the two works, the chief of which is the use of first-person discourse.

In addition to reflecting the modern understanding of the martyr as sufferer, Foxe's relations of the experience of his subjects also retain the primitive Christian conception of the martyr as a witness of God. They do this by incorporating the discourse of the sufferers themselves. The full title of *Acts and Monuments* advertises that they were "Gathered and collected according to the true copies and wrytings certificatorie as wel of the parties them selves that suffered, as also out of the Bishops Registers, which wer the doers thereof." This provenance defined the method of the book. Foxe was a compiler; he spun the thread of his narratives from contemporary accounts of the martyrs' examination and execution, derived either from witnesses present or from "papers" left by the participants themselves.[16] An example of the latter source material, a "true copy" of the examination speech of John Rogers, written in Rogers's hand, was found in a corner of his prison cell after his death by his wife and son. Foxe obtained a transcription of this text, and built his account of Rogers's martyrdom around these "Admonitions, Sayings, Prophesyings," as he identified Rogers's paper, creating what the literary historian John R. Knott describes as a "social drama" of heroic resistance, exemplifying "the fundamental conflict of authority and individual conscience that runs through the *Acts and Monuments*."[17] The individual conscience appears in Foxe's dramas because they represent real protagonists and actual dialogue, instead of allegorical figures and imaginary speech. Indeed, Foxe crammed authentic discourse into his narrations whenever possible – even indirectly, as in the case of Rowland Taylor, burned at the stake shortly after Rogers and who, Foxe tells us, though he left no paper of his own, at his parting from his son gave him a Latin book, "containing the notable sayings of the old martyrs" gathered from Eusebius. This book was probably *Apothegmata . . . collecta ex Eusebii Historia Ecclesiastica*, printed in London in 1552.[18] If the martyr generated no quotable text of his own, the words of others could serve him instead. But such words had meaning only in the mouths or from the hands of persons noted for their piety, industry, sobriety, austerity, charity and, in general, self-sacrifice. By featuring authentic discourse in this context, Foxe's *Acts and Monuments* attempted not so much to dramatize the individual conscience as to expand the dimensions of the godly community, by creating a new mine of Christian *sententiae*, a body of "godly sayings" possessing the authority of scriptural rather than individual truth. Undoubtedly Katherine Stubbes had such sayings in mind when she counseled her audience to "lend your patience and imprint my words in your hearts: for they are not the words of flesh and blood, but the Spirit of God, by whom we are sealed to the day of our redemption." By imprinting his wife's words on paper as well as in his heart, Philip Stubbes, like Foxe, and St Paul before him, was promoting the word of God.

The praxis of *A Christal Glasse* thus marks the intersection of the *ars moriendi* tradition with elements of the traditions of books of civility and Christian biography. The significance of this meeting of traditions in a single pivotal text in 1591 is the inauguration of a practice which would become increasingly regular in the course of the seventeenth century: that of preserving the private expressions of ordinary persons, and representing them, for the edification of posterity, in the context of individual, autonomous biographies, both to demonstrate the biographical subject's Christian conduct and to bind together the godly community. Philip Stubbes's hasty transcription and publication of his wife's words began a new technology for promoting piety; both the content and the form of her printed *Life and Death* were imitated in a widening stream of biographical narrations thereafter.

In these publications, autograph "papers" such as those featured by Foxe acquired increasing importance. Like *A Christal Glasse*, another early example of this hybrid form, *A Brief Discovrse of the Christian Life and Death of Mistris Katherin Brettergh*, first printed in 1602, contained discourse compiled, according to its writer, "out of the fresh memories of those that were present, and eye-witnesses as wel as my selfe."[19] But subsequent lives were narrated, in part, by the first-person discourse preserved in the devotional writings of the deceased subjects themselves. For example, *A Faithfull Remonstrance of the Holy Life and Happy Death, of John Bruen* (1641), whose title-page identifies the subject as "brother to that Mirrour of Piety; Mistris Katherin Brettergh," illustrates Bruen's "carefull observation of the ways & works, mercies and judgments of the Lord" with verbatim transcriptions (printed in inverted commas) of several personal anecdotes from a written text, "which [Bruen] calleth a declaration of some of the works of the Lord, to the praise of his glorious Name, power, and mercy: adding and annexing that exhortation out of *Job, remember that thou magnifie his works, which men behold, Every man may see it, man may behold it a far off.*"[20]

The "Narrative" of Mrs Elizabeth Wilkinson's *Godly Life and Death*, written by Edmund Staunton and appended to the printed version of the sermon he preached at her funeral in 1654, incorporates four full pages of "a Narrative coppyed exactly out of her own hand writing, of God's gracious dealings with her soul;" this account briefly described her spiritual awakening in her teens.[21] Staunton's own "care and diligence in self-examination" was praised by Richard Mayo, who in his *Life and Death of Edmund Staunton* published passages from Staunton's *Journal or Diary of God's Mercies*.[22] In at least one case, the practice of self-examination conducted by means of writing daily or weekly personal "experiences" in a notebook was so extensive that it supplied the basis of the subject's posthumous *Life*. The preface to the *Account of the Life and Death of Mr. Philip Henry*, written by his son Matthew, explains that

> [m]uch of our Materials for this Structure we have out of his own Papers, (especially his Diary) for by them his Picture may be drawn nearest to Life, and from thence we may take the truest Idea of him, and of the Spirit he was of. These Notes being intended for his own private Use in the Review, and never Communicated to any Person whatsoever; and appearing here (as they ought to do) in their own native Dress, the candid Reader will excuse it, if sometimes the Expressions should seem abrupt, they are genuin, unforced, and unstudied Breathings of a gracious Soul.[23]

Perhaps no seventeenth-century soul took more breaths of this sort than Mary Rich, the Countess of Warwick. The surviving parts of the "diary" she kept, a record of her spiritual experiences and meditations during the years 1666–72, fill thousands of MS pages.[24] Thus did Anthony Walker's claim in the funeral sermon he preached for her that "indeed *prayer was her very element*, in which she *lived*, and *actually* died; and 'twas as the vital breath of her Soul, and the wing that wafted it immediately to Heaven," strike the reader aware of the extent of her writings as no exaggeration.[25] Walker took as the text of his sermon Proverbs 31: 31: "Give her of the fruit of her hands; let her own works praise her in the gates," and accordingly devoted a significant part of his discourse of the Countess's *Life* to outlining her habits of writing, for example:

> [she] recorded dayly the *frame of her own heart* towards God, his *signal providences* to her self, and sometimes towards others, *his gracious manifestations to her Soul, returns of prayer, temptations resisted, or prevailing,* or whatever might be useful for *caution* or

encouragement, afford her matter of *thankfulness* or *humiliation*. And by this means she had arrived at such experience, that she could conclude, at least make strong conjectures of the events of things she spread before the Lord in prayer, by the frame of her own heart.

Moreover, "*meditation*," we are told, "was her *Master-piece*"; in this "she *exceeded* her self."[26] Appropriately appended to her *Life*, under a separate title-page, are two printed works "By the Right Honourable *Mary*, late Countess Dowager of *Warwick*" herself: one entitled *Occasional Meditations upon Sundry Subjects*, and the other, *Pious Reflections Upon Several Scriptures*. These, along with the excerpts from the "diary" quoted by Walker in the sermon serve to identify Mary Rich as a writing as well as a speaking subject.[27] For her, both speaking and writing were essential to the practice of living and dying well.

In the comparatively short space of the eighty-seven years separating Mary Rich from her predecessor Katherine Stubbes, the medium of expression of the discourse of Protestant piety had shifted from speech to writing. Toward the end of the seventeenth century in England, those ordinary people who died happy did so in part because they wrote well, or at least extensively; their personal writings served to make their lives "worthy to be imprinted" in books, as well as in the table of Christian hearts.[28] Indeed, the book, the public epistle, became the conventional metaphor for the Christian heart. Thus George Newton described the heart of his biographical subject, Joseph Alleine, as "an Epistle, written not with Ink, but with the Spirit of the Living God." This verbal heart was metonymically connected to the identity of the person. Matthew Henry wrote of his father that "he was himself, in his whole Conversation, *an Epistle of Christ*."[29] By the close of the seventeenth century, the practice of composing such epistles of self-denial had evolved to the point where the resulting product verged upon, but ultimately fell short of, modern self-representation in narrative autobiography. An example of such a product appeared in London, in 1714, as *The Life of the Reverend Mr. Geo. Trosse Late Minister of the Gospel in the City of Exon Who Died January 11th 1712/13 in the Eighty Second Year of his Age. Written by Himself, and Publish'd According to His Order*. Not only were Mr Trosse's expressions preserved in the context of his biography, the biography itself was his original expression, and Trosse ensured the posthumous publication of his text on his own, before he died. Indeed he seems to have been the author of himself.

But as in the case of Katherine Stubbes, such blatant self-promotion constitutes a paradox for us: though the Christian subject wrote his own personal epistle, Christ remained its author, in the sense of being the original after which all Christian identities were copied. Christian subjects were, like Philip Henry, "epistles of Christ," not original, autonomous personalities. Therefore, a concept of individual genius had no place in this mode of self-identification: such epistles expressed the dispositions of the *heart*, rather than the cogitations of the *head*. The practice of Protestant piety by ordinary people at this point in time still concerned passion, not reason. Thus, however modern the texts of subjects like Trosse and his cohorts appear to us, we should not take them as expressions of modern self-identity. In addition to Trosse himself, other biographers also narrated his life, one of whom explained the significance of Trosse's performance in terms both Trosse and his contemporaries would have best understood: "For a man to draw up a Narrative of many Quires of Paper, of his Sins and God's Judgments, for the use of near Relations, while he was yet alive: And, when he was above Sixty Years of Age . . . to abridge it, and order it to be Printed after his Death, discovers the Zeal for the Glory of God, such Love to Souls, such deep Humility and Self-Denial, as are scarce to be parallel'd."[30] Trosse's text and others like it remained exceptional, and were designed primarily to "discover zeal for God" rather than unique self-identities. Let us look more closely at how this tradition of preserving pious experience in first-person discourse developed in the seventeenth century.

4

Writing on the Heart
Preserving Experience in
First-Person Discourse

Not long before he fell sick, he said to one that lay with
him, that he slept very little in the nights; adding, when I
lye waking in my Bed, I sometimes run through the course
of my whole life; and if a pen-man were ready by me, I
could relate many observable passages of Gods Providence
about me: his friend said, Sir, you may do well to write
them down as they come into your thoughts: he made no
answer to that.

The Holy Life and Happy Death of Mr. John Angier (1684)

Do you not know who hath said to you so often, *Remem-*
ber me? How often have you heard that sweet Word since
you came hither? What? Do you think it is enough to
remember Him for an Hour? No, but let it be a Living,
and Lasting remembrance. Do not you write that Name of
his in the Dust, that hath written your Names upon his
Heart. Your High Priest hath your Names upon his Heart,
and therewith is entered into the Holy Place, and keeps
them there for a Memorial before the Lord continually. O
that his remembrance might be ever written upon your
Hearts, as with a Pen of Diamond, upon Tables of Marble,
that might never be worn out!

The Life and Death of Mr. Joseph Alleine (1672)

In the early modern period England witnessed the growth of the
habit of keeping separate notebooks relating to personal experience.
These texts represent the primitive form of a practice which would,
by the nineteenth century, produce the narrativized autobiography
and the concept of the individualist self. Though it may seem so to

us, this development was not inevitable. Writing, personal experience, and self-identity have no intrinsic affiliation; their merging and maturation together depended upon a relationship being created, codified, and acculturated. The process of the invention and rationalization of what we inelegantly call "self-writing" began in the late sixteenth century and accelerated during the seventeenth century.

Though ship's logs, business ledgers, corporate chronicles, and family estate and household account books had been utilized since medieval times at least, the use of private notebooks by individual persons to record matter pertaining to their own experience was something new in 1600. The advent of the interleaved pocket almanac book certainly contributed to this novelty. The first English printed almanac intended for use as a diary or memorandum book seems to have appeared in 1565; it contained a blank page facing the calendar for each month. A year later was published *A Blancke and Perpetuall Almanack*, designed for the user to note financial matters and, it said, "things that passeth from time to time (worthy of memory to be registered)." An edition of 1571 described itself as "a book of memory, necessary for all such, as have occasion daily to note sundry affairs."[1] Such diaries became common in the seventeenth century, and a number containing MS notes have survived.[2] However, the types of memoranda these tiny books allowed – the average dimensions of a pocket-sized bound "blank" almanac were about two inches by four – were hardly the means by which an individualized narrative identity could be realized. More pertinent to the development we are tracing are the more discursive personal notebooks, sometimes composed with the aid of memoranda contained in pocket almanacs, kept mostly by persons of intense Protestant piety. It is a commonplace of European cultural history that these so-called private spiritual confessionals were largely responsible for the emergence of a so-called autonomous, interiorized self-identity in the early modern period. Yet little has been done in the way of empirical research to document the circumstances directly contributing to this new mode of self-configuration.

In his classic account of the rise of Puritanism in England, William Haller wrote that "The usual practice of the saint was to begin his new life by setting down on paper an account of his spiritual rebirth, which account also he frequently continued in the form of a daily written record of his subsequent spiritual struggles."[3] This is a sweeping generalization crying out for qualification, but we have taken it as given for quite some time. Yet we now know that at least two persons of exceptional piety, the Mistresses Stubbes and Brettergh, failed to produce writings of their Christian experiences for their biographers to draw upon. It is likely that many others whose faith was no less intense also neglected to write anything about themselves. In fact, such documentation was not a necessary passport into heaven. A seventeenth-century sermon assured its illiterate hearers that "Though you cannot read a letter in the book, yet if you can, by true assurance, read your name in the *Book of Life*, your scholarship will serve. . . . If you cannot write a word, yet see you transcribe a fair copy of a godly, righteous, and sober life, and you have done well."[4] Historical research into literacy suggests that throughout the early modern period the habit of writing may have been the exception, rather than the norm, of "Puritan" piety. Unfortunately, we have only written records to draw upon for knowledge, which tell us little about the "usual" practice of pious illiterates. Still, through written texts we can interpret the nature of the practice of recording personal experience, at least for those saints and others who could and did write.

According to the literary scholar Brian Vickers, "the Renaissance was – to an extent which never ceases to surprise one – a notebook culture."[5] This statement makes sense only if we recall that but a tiny proportion of the total population actually participated in such culture. To use a notebook, a person had to be capable of taking and reading manual notes. The distribution of literacy within the British population in the early modern period is nearly impossible to know accurately. As the historian Margaret Spufford has convincingly argued, probably more people could read than could write, because many children were removed from school after the teaching of reading, but before they had completed lessons in writing, which commenced only after pupils had obtained basic reading skills.[6] However, most studies of literacy in the early modern period are based upon evidence of the ability to write. The historian David Cressy's analysis, for example, uses signatures to depositions taken in ecclesiastical courts in the south-east of England. Though they probably underestimate the number of readers in the population, Cressy's conclusions are meaningful to us because our notebook culture was composed exclusively of writers. Cressy determines that writing skills were limited to 30 per cent of the total male population and only 10 per cent of the female population by 1640, reaching 45 per cent and 25 per cent respectively by the accession of George I.[7] Thus we can see that, even as late as the end the seventeenth century, the number of potential participants in the notebook culture comprised a minority of the total population.

In the lifetimes of Katherine Stubbes and Katherin Brettergh, however, writers were probably even scarcer than they were in the Stuart period. Outside the monasteries, writing skills were indispensable only to persons engaged in trade. With the dissolution of the monasteries in the mid-sixteenth century the general demand for writers increased, but the ability to write was not absolutely required of entrants to the grammar schools until about 1570, the same time at which Roger Ascham, in his *Scholemaster*, first proposed the method of written rather than oral exercises in the teaching of Latin.[8] A consensus about the utility and necessity of writing skills for those obtaining a classical education – typically young men intending to pursue careers in the church or the professions, such as law – seems therefore not to have been reached by educators until about the time of Mistress Stubbes's birth. It is not surprising that she left no writings despite her extensive study of scripture: she probably was not taught to write, as in her youth there was undoubtedly a dearth of qualified writing tutors available to parents wishing to expose their children, male or female, to this new technology. The wealthier young gentlemen stood at the head of the line for writing instruction; their sisters were probably fit in as opportunities arose. The first English self-education manual to include lessons on learning how to write appeared in 1596. Books on domestic duties in pious households did not begin to hint at the necessity of writing instruction until about 1620.[9] Reading remained the dominant and only really necessary skill to the practice of piety recommended by such manuals until the mid-seventeenth century.

Moreover, even when instruction was available, the apparatus of writing itself was for many prohibitively expensive. To write required, in addition to time to practice it, the purchase of pens, ink (or the ingredients to concoct it), and paper. Before the advent of printing in the late fifteenth century, most texts were written on parchment, which did not readily lend itself to recreational composition.[10] Though paper was in use alongside parchment from the fourteenth century, it did not gain ascendancy as a vehicle for writing until Tudor times. Even then, most of the paper used in England had to be imported from the Continent, which added to its cost. Until about the second decade of the seventeenth century, a quire (24 sheets) of small folio-size white writing-paper cost retail purchasers between 4*d.* and 5*d.* – about as much as a laborer's daily wage.[11] A blank notebook of several quires bound and covered either in vellum (recycled) or calf was not cheap; even as late as 1647, a diarist noted paying 11*d.* for "inkle and a dyurnall."[12] The cost was enough to preclude a habit of writing for purely personal purposes. After paper manufacture in Britain began in earnest toward the end of the seventeenth century its price became less prohibitive. But before then ordinary people probably found little cause to consume paper in any quantity, and even those who could write likely used what they could afford sparingly. Last, we should also consider the prohibitions on writing imposed by the need for space in which to do so, especially for writers of personal notebooks. Such work would have to take place at home, as the manipulation of pen and ink made difficult all but the rudest shorthand note-taking away from a proper writing-desk, and the one public location in which extensive composition might be feasible, the alehouse, would not normally allow sufficient privacy for writing of a personal nature. The coffee-houses of the late seventeenth century were hospitable to readers, but less so to writers. Even at home, privacy was scarce. In most houses, solitude was obtainable only late at night or in the early morning, when the rest of the household was asleep. Few but the very wealthy had access to private studies, or "closets," as they were called; but these do not seem to have been commonly fitted for writing before the mid-sixteenth century, and not purpose-built for it until the seventeenth.[13] In short, before the mid-seventeenth century at the very earliest, a person wanting to pursue "the usual practice of the saint" by writing a personal record of any kind, let alone a daily one, had to be both unusually wealthy and determined.

But even more than this, a person possessing the means to render his spiritual experience in writing had also to have a motive for doing so. Reasons to write about oneself in any manner are hard to come by before the mid-seventeenth century. The earliest mention of a personal spiritual diary in a printed book appeared in 1641, in *The Holy Life and Happy Death of John Bruen* which, in a side-note, identified a paper of Bruen's entitled "declaration of some of the works of the Lord," as "A book of Rememb." However, neither the extracts quoted from it nor the surrounding narration offered an explanation of why Bruen produced this book, or what part it played in his spiritual practice.[14] The first manual of piety to advocate diary-keeping explicitly, Isaac Ambrose's *Media: The Middle Things, in Reference to the First and Last Things*, was printed in London in 1652. This work, treating "the Means, Duties, Ordinances, Both Secret, Private, and Publike, for continuance and increase of a Godly life," recommended the use of a diary especially as an aid to the exercise of "Self-Tryal," or "a Discussion of a man's life, that his thoughts, Words and Deeds may be seen, and censured according to the Rule of God's Law," "besides many other uses" unnamed. In the diary of self-trial, Ambrose explained, the Christian does the following:

> 1. Hereby he observes something of God to his soul, and of his soul to God.   2. Upon occasion he pours out his soul to God in prayer accordingly, and either is humbled or thankful.   3. He considers how it is with him in respect of time past, and if he have profited in grace, to find out the means whereby he hath profited, that he may make more constant use of such means; or wherein he hath decayed, to observe by what temptation he was overcome, that his former errors may make him more wary for the future.

Ambrose also supplied extracts from his own personal diary, to suggest appropriate types of entries for the reader.[15] Though *Media*'s title-page claimed that Ambrose compiled his treatise "for the most part, out of the most eminently Pious, and learned writings of our Native Practical Divines," the addition of diary-keeping to the Christian exercise regime appears to have been Ambrose's own innovation. No prior text in the canon of printed handbooks of Christian duty, either in English or in any other language, made explicit mention of making accounts or keeping diurnal records of personal experience in writing.[16]

In the sixteenth and early seventeenth centuries, treatises on the forms of Christian devotion and directions to Christian practice published in English were typically translations of Jesuit works from the Continent. These texts recommended routines of daily prayer and meditation as a means to ensure personal salvation.[17] For example, the *Institutio Spiritualis* of 1551 explained that

> If the spiritual beginner is careful to exercise his soul daily in the manner laid down, and thus to unite himself to God; if, through internal conversations and loving desires, he strives without ceasing to join himself to God; if he takes care to persevere constantly in self-denial and mortification and never gives up his holy purpose, either on account of his frequent falls or because he becomes discouraged by the innumerable distractions of his mind, he will certainly arrive at perfection and mystical union, if not in this life at least in death.[18]

In adapting such practices for their own purposes, English Protestants advocated regular performance of meditation and prayer as a sign of the practitioner's election.[19] In one of the first treatises on meditation originally written in English, the Church of England bishop Joseph Hall explained that its practice was "the pastime of saints, the ladder of heaven and . . . the best improvement of Christianity. Learne it who can, and neglect it who list; hee shall neuer find ioy, neither in God nor in himselfe, which doeth not both knowe and practice it."[20] But for both Catholics and Protestants, meditation was an exercise of the imagination, rather than of the hand. It began in oral prayer and then turned steeply inward, toward the mental image of God. In Hall's words, it was "a bending of the mind vpon some spirituall obiect, through diuers formes of discourse, vntill our thoughts come to an issue."[21] Richard Rogers, in another early Protestant guidebook, called meditation a "practice of musing;" it was the Christian's "secret talking with God, and with [his] own heart."[22] Self-examination played a supporting role in such musing. According to Hall, "the soule must . . . bee purged, ere it can profitably meditate"; hence self-examination was promoted as a mandatory preparation for prayer and meditation.[23] And, like meditation, it was also to be performed as a purely mental exercise.

Although the technology of script is absent from English devotional guides of the Tudor and early Stuart period, almost from their inception such works employed the script-related metaphors of print and engraving to illustrate aspects of Christian practice. The anonymous *A Dyurnall for deuoute soules to ordre them selfe thereafter*, printed by Robert Wyer in London sometime before 1533, for example, instructed the reader at night to "imprynte . . . in your mynde with purpose to confesse them to your ghostly father" both the benefits of the Lord and his own negligence in word, deed, and thought occurring in the course of the day. Making reference to "our frayle and oblyuyous memory," it recommended that "by often rehersynge," Christians could cause such instructions to "be depely wryten and grauen in oure stony hertes."[24] But the use of paper evidently was not an option, either for recording such instructions or for carrying them out: "heart" was a metonym for soul, whose repository was the unaided memory. This relation of heart–soul–memory made sense, since "writing on the heart" was more feasible for most would-be practitioners of piety than writing in notebooks. However, a puzzle still remains for us. Haller's "usual practice" cannot be found inscribed in the letter of Christian duty before the mid-seventeenth century, yet spiritual diaries survive from the late sixteenth century. Ambrose actually merely reflected rather than inaugurated the notebook tradition. How then did the practice originate? Let us search the diaries themselves for clues.

One of the earliest spiritual diaries to have survived from the sixteenth century belonged to Richard Rogers, the "Puritan" lecturer and acting curate of the parish of Wethersfield, Essex, and the author of *Seven Treatises*, probably the first book of Christian direction by an English Protestant to be printed in England, in 1603. Though his more than 600-page treatise never once mentions the utility of notebooks, Rogers kept a personal record on paper at least for a portion of his lifetime. The text we have, written in his hand, consists of an unbound paper book measuring approximately six by eight inches, now in the possession of Dr Williams's Library in London, where it arrived as part of the manuscript papers of the seventeenth-century Presbyterian divine Richard Baxter.[25] Within this mass of documents Rogers's book was scattered. In 1858 the antiquarian R. H. Black reconstructed the text in the course of his efforts to catalogue the library's manuscript collection. Following the original numbering of leaves apparently in Rogers's own hand, Black was able to rearrange in consecutive order pages numbered 13–46 and 51–98. Thus, in addition to the twenty-fourth and twenty-fifth folios, the first six have been lost, as well as an unknown number of others from the end, because the text breaks off abruptly at the bottom of the verso of the forty-first folio. We therefore cannot know with certainty where and how the text began and concluded. It may be possible that the work commenced and was continued in other notebooks which have not survived. What we have today consists of entries beginning 28 February 1587 and ending 25 July 1590, when Rogers was in his late thirties (he died in 1618, at age 67). Thus his work is the product of a practice conducted during the prime of his life.

But what practice does it represent? M. M. Knapper, the modern editor who published a version of the text in 1933 found it remarkably devoid of anything other than "ethical" content. Among its omissions, he noted that the diary mentions little of Rogers's family beyond births, baptisms, and deaths; it takes no notice of the physical environment in which Rogers lived; it says nothing of Rogers's activities in the classis of which he was a member; and it contains very few comments on contemporary politics. On these grounds the work was judged to be "faulty, both in being so preponderantly ethical, without regard to the intellectual and aesthetic sides of man's nature, and in prescribing a conduct involving a mental concentration continued beyond the limits of human endurance."[26] This criticism is grounded in modern expectations of what a personal diary should be: a reasonable yet full representation of "man's nature." However, if we appreciate the text as it was, rather than demand it to be something it was not, an entirely different concept of the spiritual notebook emerges.

Rogers's work is fundamentally a diary: it consists of discrete, dated entries which reveal a pattern of writing at regular intervals. At first Rogers made entries bi-weekly or monthly, then, starting in late 1587 and continuing to the text's end, he made them almost weekly, though there were occasional periods of omission. One entry suggests that the writing was done in the evening.[27] All the entries record, as the first one states clearly, "things worth the remembr[ance]" occurring in the time following the previous record (fo. 1). These worthy "things" are quite particular: they typically concern Rogers's sense of his spiritual state, and his practice of religious worship, especially the triad of private prayer, meditation, and study. Indeed, the constancy of his performance of these godly duties appears consistently in the text as the yardstick of Rogers's faith. Not surprisingly, given the view of human nature to which all Christians then subscribed, the major theme of Rogers's book is corruption; its minor theme is the impossibility of a mortal's ever attaining Christian perfection. Therefore inconstancy, or neglect of duties, is paramount. The text repeatedly registers the basic finding that, as Rogers noted, "I beare not my selfe in such a course as that I perceive constancy [of grace] in all my lif, but in many partic[ulars] unsetlednes . . ." (fol. 3ᵛ).[28] Recording his inconstancy caused Rogers no end of grief, but grief he seems to have valued as a necessary condition for relief. He wrote that "when I doe my duties without feare of mine owne corruption and without watchfulnes I must confesse that thei are to my selfe unsavory, and without comfort" (fo. 4).

While it provides some explanation for both the work's apparent futility and the ethical quality which Knappen regretted, this statement also suggests the purpose served by the notebook: keeping it was an aid to meditation and prayer. Writing in the notebook was a preliminary exercise enabling Rogers to assume the posture of personal humiliation and supplication required in the performance of Christian duties to obtain the benefits of grace. After a particularly torturous recollection of the "buffetings of mine hart" in which, he wrote, "god sheweth me . . . that Sathan is not wanting" (fol. 4ᵛ), Rogers appended a brief written reflection on the writing itself, explaining its effect: "This I wrot this eveninge. And good chaunge by sensible feelinge of mine unworthines there was in remembering and settinge downe theise thinges, over there was before, for before I had gone about this I was utterly unsetled both in study and minde and nothing could be gone about roundly" (fo. 5). In the margin, at a later date, he epitomized the process thus: "This writing of my estat

was a kind of repenting." On a different occasion he called the
writing "this constant settling mine hart uppon good thinges"
(fo. 35). The notebook exercise functioned for Rogers as an instrument for self-examination. It was a personal speculum through which
he saw the condition of his own heart. It exhibited plainly his need
for the grace of God, and thereby helped to focus his attention in
professing his faith and asking for mercy. Had Katherine Stubbes
kept such a book, she would have turned to it during the moment at
which instead she concentrated her attention upon her dog. As
Rogers's notebook did for him, Mistress Stubbes's puppy served to
remind its owner of her sinful and corrupt nature, and so became the
catalyst for her repentance and her meditative soliloquy. Some
mnemonic device, be it a dog or a notebook, seems to have been
indispensable to practitioners of meditation.

For Rogers who, unlike Katherine Stubbes, enjoyed the personal
luxury of writing skills, the written record ensured a degree of
efficiency unattainable by bare memory. Rogers continued the passage on writing cited above by explaining that "this profit I have oft
reaped of the useinge of it that sometime I am drawn to not the time
past in writeinge, haveinge propounded it with my selfe, whereas
otherwise I feare I should not have entred into no consideracions at
all about such matters as did necessarily geve me cause to weigh them
deeply. To be sure I should soone forget them" (fos 4^v–5; the larger
entry of which this and the passages cited above are part, for 20 June
1587, is entirely omitted in the printed text). If Rogers followed the
conventional regime of daily prayer and meditation he himself
endorsed, the product of a weekly act of writing could, on the six
other days of practice, assist him in the performance of a purely
mental method of self-examination. In his *Seven Treatises* Rogers
propounded the importance of each Christian's "entring into [his]
owne estate and heart . . . to draw matter from [his] owne experience
to meditate on."[29] Personal experience and matters of divinity,
commonly expounded in sermons, were the two great mines of ore
for Protestant meditation, recommended to the laity and ministers
alike.[30] Occasionally in his diary Rogers identified single entries as
"meditations," implying that he found in them subject-matter for
private duties. He also sometimes mentioned reading over the notebook in the morning. This exercise probably occupied part of the
"hour in reading, [and] med[itation]" Rogers noted that he performed alone each morning, "to prepare me for priv[ate] prayer."[31]
The extensive amount of writing in the margins and between the
lines of many entries, most of it done sometime after the entry was

first made, suggests the part played by the notebook in this prepara-
tory practice. Its scribblings indicate the frequency and intensity with
which the book was reread and to a certain extent reworked as a tool
for meditation. From the nature of the material added, it is apparent
that Rogers was neither polishing the style nor correcting matters of
fact; instead, he was marking and arranging his text for the purpose
of extracting matter for meditation. Among the many types of
marginalia scattered throughout the text, the simple "note" appears
at least once on every page; "Read this oft" and "Reade this oft and
profit by gods mercy" are also pervasive, along with longer notes
designed as apothegms, such as the aforementioned "This writing
was a kind of repenting" and "[I]n this complaining more grace may
be seen to have been then in much reioicing although not evel" (fo.
6). Rather than a diary in the modern sense, Rogers's notebook was
a book of commonplaces taken from personal experience. It served
him as a sourcebook for the invention of personal meditations and
prayers.

If we wish to read it as a representation of self-identity, we must
appreciate how the notebook's function informed both the text and
the "experience" of its user. This process of self-information Rogers
himself understood, and resolved to promote deliberately with the
help of his notebook: "I have firmly purposed to mak my whole life
a meditation of a better life, and godlines in every part even mine
occupacion and trade, that I may from point to point and from
steppe to steppe with more watchfulness walk with the lorde"
(fo. 10). Rather than to discover his peculiar human nature, Rogers
wrote to leave his nature – which was universal, and depraved, after
all – behind. In this scheme the diary was the medium, but not the
message: a means to the end, not the object of the exercise. Moreover, though private, and intended for what was conventionally
called "secret duty," it was not a sacred or special text. Its status
was equal to the variety of other miscellaneous notebooks Rogers
probably kept beside it on the shelf, or to the individual contents
of the mass of unidentified manuscripts comprising the Baxter
papers, of which it eventually became a part. Its model or prototype
can be found in the reading notebook Rogers was no doubt instructed to keep as a student, both in grammar school and at the
university.

Although humanist educators never explicitly urged personal jour-
nal- or diary-keeping *per se*, commonplacing, the practice of extra-
polating and recording on paper pithy matter for personal use out of
the various texts one read, was central to the method of study they

advocated. In his *Introductio ad Sapientiam*, which was printed in twelve editions between 1539 and 1623 (eleven in English translation), Juan Luis Vivès (tutor to the Princess Mary) instructed students to

> Make a book of blank leaves of a proper size. Divide it into certain topics, so to say, into nests. In one, jot down the names of subjects of daily converse: the mind, body, our occupations, games, clothes, divisions of time, dwellings, foods; in another, idioms or *formulae docendi*; in another, *sententiae*; in another, proverbs; in another, difficult passages from authors; in another, matters which seem worthy of note to thy teacher or thyself.[32]

Such a book could then be used to assist the practice of dialectics. The considerable number of commonplace books surviving from the sixteenth and seventeenth centuries shows that tutors at the universities echoed these instructions throughout the early modern period.[33] In the mid-seventeenth century, for instance, the Cambridge tutor Richard Holdsworth advised his students to

> Get some handsome paper books of a portable size in octavo, and rule them so with ink or with black lead that there may be space left on the side for a margin and at the top for a title. Into them collect all the remarkable things which you meet with in your historians, orators and poets. . . . These collections you shall render so ready and familiar to you by frequent reading them over on evenings, or times set apart for that purpose, that they will offer themselves to your memory on any occasion.[34]

Though this method of reading was originally advocated for the study of pagan texts, it proved equally applicable to religious matter, both written and spoken.

For Protestant Christians, the school notebook proved a useful aid to worship. The seventeenth-century gentleman Simonds D'Ewes claimed that his habit of noting down sermons, "[b]y which means I had attained before my going to Cambridge a great insight into the very body of divinity," was held up by his schoolmaster as an example to his fellow students – one presumably of both Christian scholarship and piety. Moreover, the writing made him, D'Ewes wrote, "a rational hearer" in church.[35] The most diligent and pious students followed this habit of rational audition well beyond their schooldays. For the better part of his life, John Bruen displayed "conscionable diligence in hearing and observing, writing and recording, from the mouth of the Ministers, whatsoever they taught and preached unto edification." He also kept a separate commonplace book, for "collections of promises, precepts, comforts, mercies, judgements, marks of God's children, brands of wicked men, and many other good things, as he found them in the way" of his reading. Along with the personal diary or "Book of Rememb[rance]" mentioned earlier, these notebooks "he made the matter, or ground of his meditation, and the means to inlarge himself in this exercise."[36] With similar intent, from the age of 11 or 12 to his death, Philip Henry made it his "constant practice" to take notes in church and transcribe them fair over afterward, at home. According to his biographer, Henry "recommended this Practice to others, as a means to engage their Attention in Hearing, and to prevent Drowsiness, and to help their Memories after Hearing, when they come either to meditate upon what they had heard themselves, or to communicate it to others." Henry also used an interleaved Bible for study, "in which he wrote short Notes upon the Texts of Scriptures as they occur'd." This notetaking practice he cultivated in his children, whom he taught "in their own reading of the Scriptures, to gather out such Passages as they took most notice of, and thought most considerable, and write them down. . . . He also directed them to insert in a Paper Book, which each of them had for the Purpose, remarkable *Sayings* and *Stories*, which they met with in reading such other good Books as he put into their Hands."[37]

Though they could not attend the universities, women in strongly pious Protestant families were also encouraged to use writing in the performance of worship, if the family fortune could afford the teaching of the requisite skills. Printed funeral sermons and the brief character sketches appended to them praised their female subjects for zeal in note-taking. The sermon for Lady Anne Walker described her as "a constant Writer of Sermons [who] wrote them in her Heart as well as in her Book." It was said that Lady Elizabeth Brooke "wrote the substance of them and digested many of them into Questions and Answers, or under Heads of common Places, and then they became to her matter for repeated Meditation."[38] Elizabeth Wilkinson was "very carefull to remember, and took much pains in writing Sermons, and collecting speciall notes out of practicall Divines." She also "kept a Diary of Gods dealings with her soule, and of those various dispensations she met withall [and] she was much busied in prayer, meditation, and self-examination."[39] Katherine Clarke, according to her grandson Samuel, the Protestant life-writer, was "frequent, and constant in Secret Prayer, and Meditation." She read scripture and other "good books" daily, "[a]nd in reading of them she used to transcribe such passages as most warmed her heart." In her cabinet after her death were found, among other papers, two "little books." The first, in which she "had collected sundry Texts of Scripture, which might minister grounds of great Comfort against Satans Temptations" "by frequent using was almost worn out." The second gave "the account of her self and of Gods gracious dealings with her."[40] We have already seen the Countess Warwick remembered for her artistry in meditation; the preacher described her as a *"Spiritual Bee,"* because, like a bee, "she would suck Honey from all occurrences, whole Volumes of which she hath left behind her." It may be that the many handwritten pages of hers that survive represent the contents of but a few cells of a vast honeycomb of devotional practice now lost to us.[41]

These examples show us how the records of personal experience generated by Protestant saints were originally embedded in a context quite different from that of modern self-representation. The usual practice of saints, at least in the early stages of English Protestantism, was to keep a personal notebook of miscellaneous experiences and other writings, some original but many gleaned from sermons and printed books, as a useful (though not essential) aid to the daily ritual of devotion. Thus, to segregate the purely self-reflexive parts of it in order to isolate an individual and self-authorizing "life" controlling the text, as modern scholarship has displayed a propensity to do, is to distort the original design and function of such works. The great gulf of meaning standing between the original texts and their modern misconstrual can be observed in the case of the "diary" of Samuel Ward, Master of Sidney Sussex College in Cambridge from 1610 to his death in 1643, printed along with Richard Rogers's diary in *Two Elizabethan Puritan Diaries.* In this edited version, Ward's text is a chronological series of notes on personal experience, the first dated 11 May 1595, and the last 2 March 1630. For the first few months, Ward made entries nearly daily, after which sporadic periods of month-long omission appear, until the diurnal quality is lost altogether after 1598. There are a handful of entries dated between then and 1621, followed by some others dated in the 1620s. In general the contents of these notes are comparable to those of Rogers in their exclusive focus on duties and sin, though Ward's entries are on the whole less expansive than Rogers's, especially those which Ward wrote daily. Like Rogers, Ward intended his notes for use in meditation; the phrase "Think of . . ." usually precedes entries which are more than a mere list of sins. However, Ward's text is actually quite different from that of Rogers in its physical form, a critical fact which the edited version fails to convey.

Whereas the printed text of Rogers's diary represents the extent of the extant notebook with passages taken from the first folio to the last, the printed version of Ward's "diary" comprises but a fraction of the extant book, which contains, in addition to the discourse printed as the diary, many blank pages and a variety of writings in Ward's hand. The five- by six-inch manuscript notebook begins with fifteen folios of sermon or lecture notes, the first one commencing "Chatt 7 March 1591/2."[42] At this time Ward was an undergraduate at Christ's College; "Chatt" designates Laurence Chaderton, Master of Emmanuel College, whose lectures Ward attended and transcribed in his book for personal reference. The notebook is also written from the back. The first five folios commencing there consist of Ward's notes on his own scripture reading (fos 91–5). Besides these the book contains the self-examination notes dated 1595–9, written while Ward was a postgraduate at Christ's and fellow of Emmanuel College (a post to which he was elected in 1598), which form the bulk of the printed version (fos 15^v–37^v); then a gap of several mostly blank leaves (on part of one – fo. 43 – is written a short prayer) before a list of "Gods benefits" (fos 46–46^v); some journal entries of uncertain date (fos 46^v–47); another blank leaf (fos 48–48^v); then a six-folio commentary on the Lord's Prayer which commences with the heading "Here is sett downe 6 petitions" (fos 49–55^v); some miscellaneous lists of sins, "mercies," "considerations," "motives," and instructions (fos 56–63), part of which (fos 61–3) appears as the end of the diary in the modern version; and, last, a large gap of blank leaves (fos 63^v–90^v) before the final section of reading notes.

In the light of these complete and heterogeneous contents, we can see that the diary actually kept by Ward was far from the deliberate, unified, focused and autonomous text presented to modern readers.[43] Ward's notebook was not devoted exclusively to self-representation or even to self-examination; instead, it was merely a component of a larger experiment in the practice of religious study and worship – a means to an end, but hardly an end in itself. Accordingly, it had no intrinsic structure or design. It remained open, permeable, amorphous. And if we look beyond this particular text, to consider the larger body of papers of which it was a part, its lack of integrity becomes even more apparent. The notebook containing the diary was but one of several such books kept by Ward, in which he wrote a variety of personal reading notes, lists, commonplaces, dialectics, meditations, prayers, historical memoranda, and letters.[44] Instead of just a diary, Ward produced a pile of papers representing his practice of piety, throughout which his self-identity is distributed and, it appears, disintegrated and therefore appropriately mortified.[45] Moreover, he was not alone in producing such a heterogeneous mass. Besides the books of sermon notes, commonplaces, self-examination, and meditation already mentioned, several other sets of diverse and extensive quasi-autobiographical personal religious papers survive from the early modern period.[46] In preparing such materials for later audiences, modern editors have tended to boil these complex soups down to a simple residue, the autonomous "diary" or "autobiography" text representing an individual "life." Such fare would have been unpalatable to early modern men and women without at least the broth of religious worship to dissolve the substance of individual personality and self-reflexivity in it. The point of such writings was to reduce the self-identity of the individual voice, rather than to help it to coagulate.

On the other hand, the precedent for the modern predilections clearly lies in the early modern period. By the mid-seventeenth century, the personal diary text had already achieved a special kind of aura in the contemporary imagination, arguably because of its latent self-reflexive quality rather than its exemplary self-mortification. The Manchester nonconforming minister Henry Newcome, for example, began keeping a personal diary in 1646, at age 19, while he was an undergraduate at St John's College, Cambridge. He did so, he later wrote, "chiefly . . . upon the occasion of hearing that Dr. Ward . . . had left a diary of his life in his study, from his being sixteen years of age. I thought it was a very brave thing to have such a thing left from so early a time of his life, and so set upon it."[47] If Newcome had in mind the diary text which survives today, contemporary legend had pretty quickly made a mountain out of a molehill. It is possible that Newcome meant another text now lost to us; but in either case, his focus on the "diary" as a representation of Ward's "life," and his description of the practice of keeping it as a "brave thing," mark a considerable shift in the meaning of personal note-keeping.[48] In the decade before Ambrose recommended the practice in print, godly parents privately instructed their children to keep diaries. At the same time, preachers promoted the use of them from the pulpit.[49] However, even earlier some of these supposedly private documents generated a public notoriety either through direct exposure or hearsay.[50] The printed funeral sermons and their character sketches also collaborated in making personal writings and their writers publicly appreciated. In his memorial of John Bruen, William

Hinde wrote that "I have seen and read what he hath collected and set downe . . . under his owne hand, which I approve of, and like so well." Hinde represented Bruen's sermon notebooks as a public spectacle: they were "so many volumes of Manuscripts . . . set up in a comely order in his owne Study, as is scarce credible to report, being yet there to be seene, as so many worthy monuments of his conscionable diligence and faithfulnesse in the Lords service."[51] Likewise, the publication, each under a separate title-page, of a selection of the Countess of Warwick's meditations and of her scripture notes, as an appendix to her funeral sermon – whose text, as mentioned above, was Proverbs 31: 31: "Give her of the fruit of her hands; let her own works praise her in the gates" – brought such "worthy monuments" into the direct sight and sensation of an admiring audience, whose approbation served to imbue the residue of a private practice with a life of its own, and its source with a public authority.

This transubstantiation, witting or unwitting, of writing on the heart into a physical corpus with a special integrity can be seen in the reader response of Ralph Thoresby, the Leeds antiquary who, in his diary for 1680, at age 22, wrote that he had read the recently printed sermon for the Countess of Warwick, and was "mightily taken with her pious Diary, religious life, heavenly meditations, &c." A few months later Thoresby noted that he spent the better part of two days indoors, "imitating the picture of the virtuous Lady Mary . . . writing and abbreviating the life of that incomparable lady."[52] From the standpoint of a practical divine like Richard Baxter, whose sermons Thoresby sometimes heard, the young man's time would have been better spent imitating the picture of Christ by the practice of prayer and meditation. Though Baxter concurred with the contemporary estimation of printed pious lives as an effective tool for Christian instruction (the legacy of Katherine Stubbes), he also expressed fears that some readers valued persons and products more than practice, a fault for which he blamed the texts rather than the readers: "Conscionable mens Histories are true; but if they be also wise, they tell us but some part of Truth, concealing that which would do harm, and which the depraved world cannot bear without abusing it."[53] To some observers in the latter half of the seventeenth century, the funeral sermon as a religious form had regressed to its secular roots in the funeral orations of antiquity, because it contained too much praise of the dead and too little instruction for the living about death, resurrection, and the judgment to come.[54] Furthermore, the personal "diaries" these sermons often praised and quoted from were similarly judged as being, if not too secular, at least too much of a distraction from the performance of more essential Christian duties.[55] In his notebook for 1671 the minister Philip Henry recorded his lament that, in general, "there is oftentimes nowadays a great deal of precious time lost among professors in discoursing of y^{cir} escapes & adventures, not to give God glory, but to set up self – also in telling how they met & such a one preacht & twas a good sermon, but no profiting by it."[56] Without anyone's deliberate advocacy, it seems, toward the end of the seventeenth century the balance was beginning to tip toward an entirely different conception of personal religious papers. Some ministers articulated what others grasped unconsciously, that the spiritual notebook was losing its status as instrument, and acquiring a new status as an object created by a subject; that is, as an autonomous text deliberately wrought by an individual intending it to represent some aspect of his personality.

The symptoms of this change can be found almost from the beginning, in the treatment of diaries and related personal papers by their keepers themselves. Neither Ward nor Rogers valued his private notebooks above any of his public works – at least there exists no evidence in any of their surviving personal papers to suggest that they did. This is not the case with other notebook-keepers of the early modern period, however. Henry Newcome, for instance, during a period of forced retirement from his public ministry from about 1663 or 1664 to 1666, worked intermittently on Sundays and in spare evening hours "to contract and methodize" material from the almanacs and pious notebooks he had been keeping since his undergraduate days into an "entire narrative" of his life. Citing the precedent of François Du Jon, the sixteenth-century Dutch divine, who "left his own life writ by himself," and Bishop Hall, who likewise "left some choice memorials of his own life," Newcome explained that he designed his account "especially for the use of my children after me, that they may remember the God of their father, to the end that they might have their hope in God, and not forget the works of God, but keep his commandments."[57] He was 39 years old when he brought the narrative up to the present, in 1666.[58] During the time thereafter, almost to the day of his death in 1695, he continued his project of transcribing notes from the smaller books into the larger "methodized" one.[59] He also made efforts to ensure the preservation of these and related papers. In a memorandum written two months before his decease, Newcome instructed that his personal manuscripts be divided between his two sons: "my collections upon my readings all my time, comprised in six quartos and four octavos, with the index, a book by itself, and also an old Bible, (in which some scripture references are)" went to Peter; those "which are of modern passages and various concernments, with my almanacks, diaries, and all other private papers" went to his namesake, Henry. They were to share the books of sermon notes equally.[60]

Newcome treated his private notebooks as if they were an extension of his public person. The printed funeral sermon for him largely underwrote this attitude. Its preface noted that "There was in him a large stock of *Solid Learning and Knowledge, always* ready for use; for *Ostentation, never.*" The sermon itself characterized him as "a Person of good natural parts, one that has enough of a Genius to master what he applied himself to, and to make up the Figure of a great Man: These natural Abilities were cultivated by extraordinary Industry, which began very early, and continued all his Life; witness the many Volumes which he left behind him written with his own hand."[61] But Newcome would have been disappointed, I think, to find that neither of his sons, nor any of his surviving colleagues, nor even – a last resort – a member of his congregation, had compiled an account of his "Christian life and death" to be printed with the sermon, from the narrative he had so diligently prepared. He likely had such a view of its use in mind when he wrote it: at the time Newcome began to contract and methodize his diaries into a single account, he had before him not only the necessary leisure and the precedent of Du Jon and Hall, but also the contemporary example of his colleague and close friend John Machin, who died in 1664, leaving among his papers a notebook containing what Newcome described as "some *Memorials* . . . of himself and family for the use of his sonne," begun in 1655 and continued to the last year of his life. Machin wrote in his "Memorials" that "The occasion of making and writing this Book, was a thought I had, what was become of all my Fore-fathers, and what price I should set upon one of their Manuscripts concerning the State of our Family, Nation or Church of God in it 500 years since. Whereupon I resolved this work for my Sons sake, and Posterities imitation."[62] Whatever posthumous value Machin imagined his book might claim, Newcome treated the work and its writer as if they were dear. He explained in the account of his own life how from Machin's text he "gathered what I could, and put it into a method, as a Narrative of the Life of our precious brother Machin."[63] It took Newcome roughly five months to complete this work, which as printed consists almost entirely of quotation of Machin's original manuscript. During the time that he was busy compiling Machin's "narrative," perhaps for inspiration, Newcome read David Lloyd's biographical compilation, *The States-men and Favourites of England* – an odd choice for a man of religion, given its secular subject-matter, but a revealing one. Newcome noted in his diary that, reading Lloyd, "I thought it was much to think what brave men we have had, how vast and gallant their spirits have been, have attempted high and brave things; and why should we not do as much so? Sure the business of souls is noble and gallant, and the bravery of the course of holiness transcends. I would by these examples enoble my soul."[64] This reflection contains the seed of Newcome's retrospective description of Ward's diary as a "brave thing," and the implied valuation of the diarist as a rare kind of hero. Ward, Machin, and Newcome himself were, in Newcome's view, ennobled by virtue of their exemplary piety, and particularly by their habit of preserving their actions in writing.[65]

To be sure, there is a defensive quality to Newcome's self-ascribed heroism. After all, the leisure which enabled him to compose his personal memoir was the consequence of his refusal to meet the king's demand for religious and political conformity. In the eyes of many, such refusal was treasonous; it warranted severe punishment. Even before the Restoration government began a systematic effort to eject clergymen failing to conform to its religious and political dictates, Henry and Machin observed together how "[m]en were now seeking to turn out ministers." As the first real proofs of the government's intention surfaced, Henry noted in his diary his "great fear": "If I do fall into reproach for not providing for my family (for this is now my constant fear, lest I die and shall leave nothing for my wife and children;) and so men will say, This was his strictness, and this his Puritanism! see what it gets them! what it leaves to wife and children!"[66] Though Newcome's fear proved in the event unwarranted (he never suffered imprisonment, or loss of his estate, as many did), it provided an effective motive to prepare a record of self-justification, lest history be written only by the victors. From his perspective, Newcome's sense of his personal worth was no mere fancy.

Nor was it his alone. Many other ejected ministers also drew up memorials from the raw material of their diaries, intended to represent their nonconformity as both conscionable and consistent with their personal sense of piety and honor. About the same time that Newcome began his large abstract, Robert Blair, the deposed minister of St Andrews, began a long personal memoir from his many "short notes," a project he justified as follows: "I think myself obliged to leave some notes concerning the chief passages that have occurred to me in my pilgrimage, that my wife and children, at least, might have these to be a memorial of the way that I kept in the world, and that they may be the better furnished to answer the calumnies and reproaches that have been, and possibly may be cast upon me."[67] Blair was 70 when he began his work; his revision had progressed to the year 1636 before he fell ill and died, in 1666. A much younger nonconformist, Oliver Heywood, the minister of Coley, Yorkshire, began a relation of his life, covering his infancy to about age 40, in 1661. He continued to enlarge the text in a manner similar to Newcome's, rendering it a diary, with regular entries to within five days of his death, in 1702.[68] In a single day in January, 1664, John Shaw, the ejected vicar of Rotherham, Yorkshire (and a distant relative of Heywood by marriage), wrote a "hasty" memoir in the form of a letter addressed to Benjamin Shaw, "the son of my old age" (Shaw was 57; he died eight years later). Shaw began by explaining to the boy that "I think it not amiss to leave behind me for your use a few words that may give you some knowledge of me, and of the lineage whereof you are descended . . . and also some directions for the better ordering of your life and affairs thro' your pilgrimage here below."[69] To us this letter makes explicit the implicit intention of such personal memorials: to teach and to incite, as well as to vindicate, conscientious religious nonconformity.

In these texts we finally recognize examples of the "usual practice of saints" described by Haller: that is, the production of a seamless narrative account of one's spiritual growth, continued in the form of a serial record of trials and tribulations in and for the faith. In making this discovery we must note, in addition to the number of qualifications already registered in the course of our enquiry thus far, two further particulars. First, that instead of being written at the start of a "new birth," such accounts were typically made toward the end or at the middle of the saint's life, long after his spiritual awakening. Furthermore, despite their retrospective perspective, the texts fail to conform to the classic "conversion narrative" pattern – of the conviction of sin, the conversion through grace, and conse-quential harmony with Christ – typically ascribed to them.[70] The presence of this plot, or, for that matter, of any other story-like structure, working to integrate and totalize these discourses, is a fiction projected onto them by the modern critical imagination.[71] This is not to say that the pattern of conversion itself was not real. Seventeenth-century evangelical Protestant divines frequently wrote of "conversion," or "convincement" in their practical works, and their congregations no doubt talked of it extensively. However, this pattern, modeled as it was on the life, death, and resurrection of Christ, was an ideal form which mere mortals could only strive for in their own experience, and hope to achieve in death. The concept of predestination and the depraved state of mortals dictated that peace and rest of conscience could only come at the end of life, when all would be revealed. John Bunyan, the darling of modern scholars promoting the concept of early modern "spiritual autobiography," himself acknowledged the impossibility of narrativity at the very beginning of his own personal history, *Grace Abounding to the Chief of Sinners*, where he explained, "*My dear Children*, [t]he Milk and Honey is beyond this Wilderness."[72] Only God, the true author of history and of the fate of each Christian soul, could impose a narrative pattern on each human life by writing its end. Uncertainty and doubt were the lot of the poor Christian sufferer here on earth. In his limited capacity, the best a human writer could do was to string together a list of evidences of God's grace, to express his sincere desire for salvation. The structure of such memorials is paratactic, rather than narrative. Their chronological quality is arbitrary, a consequence of the fact that their contents were transcribed from diaries. Moreover, their endpoints are equally arbitrary; they appear abruptly, at the moment the writer found himself too weak to support the pen any longer.

The second and more significant deviation from received wisdom about these works worth noting here concerns their motivation, of which we have already seen some hint in the quotations taken from the texts themselves. They were not the pure products of a "private self." Despite their largely personal and spiritual focus, public pressures informed the memorials as much as, and perhaps even more than, private desire did. At the very least, we must say that the texts were products of interaction between private and public relations. The saint who transcribed his diary into a record "at large" was more conscious of writing to defend himself from the hostile accusations (both real and imagined) of neighbors and others than he was of an urge to represent the spontaneous expression of piety in his soul. The works do not constitute a retreat into the interior recesses of the mind, but instead an advance from those recesses into the realm of publicity, and (modest) self-promotion.

As such they emulate the secular tradition of personal historiography identified in the previous chapter by such works as *The Fall of Princes* and *A Myrroure for Magistrates*. These were superseded in the Elizabethan and early Stuart period by more ambitious but equally instructive texts such as, for instance, Camden's *Annals*, Lord

Herbert of Cherbury's *Life and Reign of Henry VIII*, Sir Robert Cotton's *Short View of the Long Reign of Henry III*, and Francis Bacon's *Henry VII*, among others, and a legion of cheap knock-offs and compilations, done in the same vein as Lloyd's *States-men and Favourites of England*.[73] By the mid-seventeenth century, this tradition had sired a small but influential subgenre of customized first-person advice books prepared by aristocratic fathers for their sons, to remind heirs of a family's noble history and instruct them in the practice of virtue. Though originally intended for personal use by specific family members, some advice books were preserved and handed down to succeeding generations, while others – especially those of controversial figures like Sir Walter Ralegh – gained public notoriety and circulated widely in manuscript or even printed editions.[74] Because the concept of honor imagined by the aristocracy largely depended upon wealth, power, and public service, the precepts such texts contained were practical, and defensive in nature; they focused on getting, spending, and political relations in the world and especially at court. Naturally the writers drew upon their own experience both to formulate and to illustrate their advice, which transformed maxims into memoirs. Indeed many works of this sort were indistinguishable from family genealogies and chronicles of *res gestae*, especially those emphasizing native honor, which reflected not only the English advice tradition but also the Continental traditions of *ricordi* and *libri della famiglia*.[75] The Scottish courtier Sir James Melville, for example, in the late 1590s, at age 64 or so, composed a memoir which incorporated personal experience, family history, and national politics. The work was addressed to his son, to whom Melville explained that

> Sone, sen thou hes schauen thy self sa willing to satisfie my expectation of the, in folowing and observyng many of my formar preceptis during the yong yeares, I grant now unto the thy requestis the mair glaidly, quhilk is to put in wret for thy better memorie sindrie thingis that thou had hard me rehers betymes, baith concernyng maneris, with some meit preceptis for thy barnely age; and also how to temper the rage of furious youth be the reule of godlynes and raisoun; . . . And now entering in my rype age, to let the with what tred of lyf I had during my perigrination throw the maist part of Europe.[76]

Thanks to the efforts of a grandson, Melville's manuscript found its way into the hands of an editor who printed it during the seventeenth century. In the editor's view, which reflected the early modern consensus, honorable public service deserved both public remembrance and imitation.[77] Given the nonconforming minister's familiarity with aristocratic culture, made at university, during tenure as a domestic chaplain or a tutor in a godly household, or by participation in local and national politics, it is natural that he would assimilate its memorial tradition as part of his own experience.

The emphasis on *res gestae*, on public acts, in aristocratic personal memorials also explains why comparatively few pious women transcribed their personal notes into large accounts. Haller in fact never considered why his "usual practitioners" should nearly always be male; but the negligible number of female transcribers is puzzling in the light of the evidence for a significant number of female notebook-keepers. In fact, women were constrained from writing up their notebooks into a memorial not merely because they were instructed to be silent in public – we have seen how exceptions could be made, as, for instance, in the case of Katherine Stubbes – but also because they were confined to the domestic sphere, where "service" has consistently not counted as such. Women's domestic actions passed largely unappreciated in public; hence most women found little cause either to seek reward or to defend themselves there by producing memorials of their experience. Still, within the family, women were expected to perform duties essential to its survival, by managing the household economy and seeing to the education, both secular and religious, of the children. Also, a woman could act in a more prominent public role by filling a breach caused by the sudden incapacity of male family members.

This extra-domestic female position is reflected in the mere handful of personal memoirs prepared by women possessed of an extreme sense of religious piety and family duty, of which the "three Books of my owne Meditations and Transactions of my Life" composed by Alice Thornton are typical. Thornton transcribed her spiritual meditations into a "Book of Remembrances" shortly after her husband's death in 1668. She later amplified the contents of this single book into three large notebooks, which upon her death in 1709 she willed to her daughter, along with "the best coppy of my fathers Book of Advice to his son George Wandesford." The pairing of her own books of "perticuler remembrances of [God's] favours, both spirituall and temporall" with the book of her father's advice suggests the motive informing Thornton's text.[78] Thornton's father, Sir Christopher Wandesford, served as Lord Deputy of Ireland, and the family suffered greatly both as a consequence of the Irish rebellion and of its royalist stance during the Civil War. Despite this trouble, Thornton worshipped her father, who died on the brink of the family's downfall. Both she and her mother treasured the memory preserved in his book of advice, which her mother without apparent irony called "the richest jewell she had, to be continued in the family." Thornton herself "esteemed [the book] a great mercy to me in perticuler, whose councell was most percing to my heart." She regretted that "noe good freind's pen could have leasure, in those sad times, to write us an account to the world of his eminent, holy, wise, prudent, and pieous life and conversation; whose virtues were soe eminent that he lives fresh in the memoryes of all that knew him; [which] if it had been writ out 'twould contineue his memory for ever."[79] Her own books of meditative remembrances were intended to serve this purpose, as well as to explain the "inevitable ruin" suffered by the Wandesford family and its fortune during his children's generation. The extent of detail recalled in each meditation transformed Thornton's compilation into a personal memorial. Despite her sincere profession of faith in God, "Who both sees my distresse, and I hope will pity my condicion," there is a tone of self-vindication underlying Thornton's religious exercises as they appear in transcription – a tone reminiscent of the memorials by the nonconformist ministers. Consider the following passage from her "Act of submission in my poverty":

> But since I am now reduced to the degree of losse in those riches which God had given me, I humbly beg His grace, and patience to be supported under the hand of God, which he did see fitt to bring me to, under great burdens, and debts, and losses, which I no waies was contributary to, either by my pride, extravagancy, voluptuousness, excesse, or waistfulnesse of what the Lord had given me, nor by any way of imprudence in the managery of what was under my caire or part to perform in my power. I hope that God and my owne conscience will not condemn me for any of these things, since what I did doe in poynt of housekeeping, diett, apparrell, or entertainments, was ever designed and practised to keepe within bounds of moderation, decency, and necessity, nor ever I affected to conforme myselfe to the modes or quirkes of new fashions and affected novelties, either in meate, drinke, apparrell, of the gaieties of the world – not even in the prime of my youth, when, as Job siaeth, *The candle of the Lord shined uppon me.*[80]

This is a far cry from the humble acknowledgment and acceptance of the burden of the depraved state of all humans so evident in the diaries of Rogers and Ward. Yet, despite its spiritual arrogance, Thornton's book is an unironic memoir of a dutiful daughter. The sense of personal responsibility demonstrated in the text exemplifies the limited experience of women in Thornton's society: her public-minded self-defense is limited to aspects of personal consumption and domestic economy, reflecting a sense of woman as ornament and, in a less passive mode, household manager. Though in one sense it seems to transgress the bounds of convention pushing onward toward modernity, it ultimately falls back to a traditional early modern stance.[81]

To conclude this chapter, we should now acknowledge that the usual practice of saints was, in the first place, not usual at all. It depended upon the acquisition of writing skills, and the possession of sufficient leisure time and a situation in which it was possible to write. Moreover, it developed in two distinct phases. The first phase was that of commonplacing from experience, of compiling lists of personal matter pertinent to religious meditation. In the second phase, which began with the Restoration, the lists began to be enlarged, and treated as historical source materials. Some notebooks were written over into personal memorials intended to be preserved for the family, to vindicate writers vilified for their piety. It is these later books that Haller likely had in mind when he described the usual practice. Finally, in this practice we can observe the stirrings of a personal voice and an individual self-identity structured in written narrative discourse. This concept of personality is still latent, and altogether pious. But a tendency to place the person before the piety had begun to emerge, and would be made more palpable by the advent of print.

5

A Press of Witnesses
The Impact of Print

O labour to *hold forth the Word of Life*, that such as have labour'd among you, may *rejoyce in the day of Christ*, that *they have not run in vain, nor labour'd in vain*. Let it appear you are the *Epistles of Christ, ministered by them, to be known and read of all Men*; So what there appear'd of Christ in them, will, as in another Edition, be seen in you.

> *The Glorious Reward of Faithful Ministers Declared and Improved* (1696)

I am as A white Paper Booke without any line or sentence but as it is Reuailed & written by ye Sperit ye Reuailer of secrets. . . .

> Letter from Richard Farnworth to George Fox (1653)

In September of 1683, an 18-year-old Essex-born apprentice named Elias Pledger began to keep a notebook of his spiritual experience since the day of his birth, which he maintained as a diary until he obtained his freedom at age 24, and continued sporadically thereafter – largely annually – until his late fifties.[1] At first glance, there is nothing unusual about Pledger's text: it is a four-and-a-half by seven-inch blank paper book containing 185 folios (though originally there were more, as several have been removed) bound in vellum over boards. It is written from both ends, and several leaves in the middle are unused. Its contents include the miscellany of spiritual observations typical of such books: in addition to the diary, focused largely on performance of religious duties and the "frame" of Pledger's heart, there are observations on self-denial, considerations on the existence of God, and a meditation on his father's death. The notebook appears, in short, to have been produced in the same occasional and spontaneous manner as others of its kind – for instance the late sixteenth-century manuscript diaries of Richard Rogers and Samuel Ward.

Yet, despite its apparent spontaneity, there is a formality to Pledger's text, particularly in the diary portion (which occupies the bulk of the written text – fos 2–85), that sets it apart from its predecessors. The formality is manifest in several ways. For one thing, there is the matter of the missing pages. Early in the book a large section of several leaves probably treating the period roughly from June 1688 to May 1689 has been cut out and replaced by a single sheet of writing in Pledger's hand glued to the edge of one of the cut pages, containing a memorandum of his being made free, which occurred in November 1689 (fo. 10). Evidently Pledger was displeased with either his discourse or that portion of his experience it represented, and so reworked it. But why should blemishes (if such they were) in a private spiritual diary require tampering of this nature? After all, Pledger must have understood that his God was omniscient, and that Christian consciences were not so easily repaired as paper books. Furthermore, the purpose of such diaries was to expose personal defects, not to hide them. Yet one is struck as well by the almost total absence of particular sins from this text, which rather too frequently finds its writer in a "good frame." Another oddity is the transcription into the text of letters Pledger apparently sent to ministers and other religious friends, optimistically discoursing upon the status of either his or their faith. Though a tradesman, Pledger appears to have fancied himself a minister of sorts, if we judge by the evidence of these epistles. Indeed, having read as far as the first fifty folios or so of Pledger's diary, the reader cannot help but notice how much the text resembles the printed lives of pious ministers, not only in its content but also in its form. After the letters – which are not unusual *per se*, but whose incorporation within the body of a spiritual diary is – one almost expects to come upon a section of "passages from my diary" within the diary, as if the notebook was not really a diary at all, but instead Pledger's own biographical account of his "life and death," with extracts from his personal papers carefully inserted to illustrate aspects of his saintliness.

In fact, I believe that such a text is precisely what Pledger set about creating, albeit unconsciously, in the hubris of youth, when he began writing his notebook. During the period that he made entries frequently enough to recall such details, Pledger noted his reading of several different pious lives from the seventeenth century, each of which did, in his words, "much affect me" (fos 11ᵛ, 37 – this was the only reading-matter he noted). Indeed, one life caused him to begin keeping the book in the first place: "In Sept 83 I read John Drapers life which did much affect me & made me set about writing this account of gods various providences to me, & my cariage to him" (fo. 8). This influence might explain the differences between his diary and others, like Ward's and Rogers's, which were conceived and executed in a context largely devoid of the exemplary books that so affected Pledger. It also accounts for the confusion of pronouns in the opening sentences of Pledger's diary, which begins: "Elias Pledger was born in that fatal year of 1665 in ye month of July in ye parish of little Baddow in ye County of Essex. ~~He~~ I was born of godly parents; my father being a minister of the presbiterian perswasion, I had the happy advantage of a Religious Education" (fo. 2). This trivial mistake suggests the extent to which both the culture of piety and the representation of self-identity had changed in England during the century separating Pledger from Rogers and Ward. When he took pen in hand, Pledger found himself faced with a choice inconceivable to his predecessors, that is: am I subject or object unto myself? Whether he appreciated it or not – and I would lay odds that he did not; that he crossed that "he" out in an instant, not dwelling on it for a second – in making that mistake Pledger encountered the possibility of one person being simultaneously both subject and object, both an "I" and a "he." A person so self-aware is capable of organizing his experience as if he were a character in a story; he is a person whose personality is apparent to himself. In the event Elias Pledger proved that he was not such a person, but his very character-conscious notebook suggests that autobiographical practice in early modern England had evolved to the point where a person like that could emerge. The text almost represents an individual and self-determined rather than a collective and prescribed self-identity.

This chapter will consider the rise of a critical influence upon writers of Pledger's day and age: the printed biographical text. As Pledger's practice shows, the movement in individual consciousness from biographical to autobiographical self-identification was sudden. The production and preservation of biographical discourse in print was a key factor in the acculturation of modern autobiographical practice and the making of individualist self-identity. But, as in the case of diary-writing, the advent of the printed biography, especially the biography of ordinary people, was hardly inevitable. The second half of the seventeenth century marks a crucial stage in the proliferation of biographical discourse in print. What kinds of biography were appropriate to this new mode of representation? Who was responsible for producing the texts? Who consumed them? Why? The answers to these questions will help us better to understand the values informing the practice of proto-autobiographers like Elias Pledger and his contemporaries.

The acculturation of a character-conscious self-identity depends ultimately upon the availability to many readers of a variety of personal narratives. By consuming such narratives, readers acquire a perspective of personality inaccessible from within the web of direct contact with other people and even with themselves. The act of reading is a disembedding mechanism. It temporarily disengages the reader's consciousness from the immediacy of real time and space. Reading biographical narrative allows a person to enter into an autonomous expression of the subjectivity of another person while retaining his own sense of self. By participating in the process of constructing the biographical subject as he reconstructs the text word by word and episode by episode, the reader experiences personality as a creation of discourse. Thus a reader of biography encounters the potential contingency of his own self-identity. The apprehension becomes a form of practical knowledge retained and utilized unconsciously in everyday experience.

Some early modern writers display traces of this reading knowledge in their personal notebooks. Pledger, for instance, wrote how he "was much affected wth reading some observations in Mr Wadsworth Life concerning ye dealing of god wth his Soul wch did suit my case in many pticulars. I find I am most enlarged . . ." (fo. 11^v). On reading the *Confessions* of St Augustine at age 23, Robert Blair observed "how [Augustine] in his old age laid to heart his childish faults . . . [and] I was thereby set to work to ponder the paths of my youth."[2] In the previous chapter I showed how Henry Newcome was affected by his reading of John Machin's personal memorial and Lloyd's *States-men and Favourites of England*; Newcome also explicitly stated,

> When I read the lives of some of the German divines, that notice was taken of their inclinations in their youth, and the delight that one had when he was a child to sit aloft above his companions, and to seem to read to them, was taken for a presage of his being a Doctor of the chair, &c., I cannot but remember that my fancy ran much after preaching, it being my ordinary play and office to act the minister amongst my playfellows.[3]

Moreover, this process was not confined to religious subjects. The diary of Edmund Bohun, for example, the sometime licenser of the press and chief justice of South Carolina, contains a number of self-reflections derived from his reading of Roman history.[4] And of course the medieval concept of the personal history as a mirror reflecting the reader's own experience takes for granted this almost involuntary self-reflexive response to biographical discourse. In the contemporary view, the rhetoric of personal history functioned to incite readers to act heroically to preserve the social and political status quo.[5] No one at the time could comprehend the revolutionary side of this design. By reading biography, people like Pledger not only learned to behave, they also discovered the singularity of their self-identity, a dimension of personal experience previously unknown to them. They could not have done so without the advent of print.

Print was responsible for the dissemination of a variety of biographical materials to a diversity of readers. This is not to say that manuscript texts failed to do this; some circulated, and quite far in terms of distance, but rarely widely in terms of readership. In contrast, the process of mechanical reproduction increased the number and to some extent also the variety of biographical texts in circulation, helping them to reach a larger and more diverse audience than a manuscript could ever hope to find. Print also changed the way its audience consumed a text. Because they were cheaper and somewhat more portable than the average manuscript, printed books were much more likely to become personal possessions, and therefore to be read privately. Though reading aloud in groups would not necessarily preclude the self-reflexive responses of readers noted above, profound introspection was more possible in silent reading done alone. In this way, print opened individual horizons.

At the same time, however, print had a peculiar way of closing them down, or finely focusing them, by imposing its form and its contents on the reader's imagination in a manner unprecedented by the artifacts of oral or manuscript culture. Much more than talk or handwriting, print reified discourse and its referents. The printed book, with its title-page, its dedication, its binding, its commodity value in the market – in short, its material and immaterial substance – connoted objectivity. Even a poorly printed text represented discourse as totalized, a "finished" object. By comparison, the average manuscript appeared less finished, more permeable and open to addenda (rather than errata, which are tacked on to printed texts). Print constituted a fixed and unchangeable order. And though a printed book might be burnt as a symbolic gesture, it would never endure the humiliating fate shared by many manuscript texts after the dissolution of the monasteries, whose meticulously handwritten parchment and vellum leaves became common wrappers, paper book bindings, scouring pads, and stuffing for scarecrows.[6] There was something sacrilegious about the destruction of a printed book. A book exuded the aura of definitiveness and authority which readers seem to have immediately respected. To a large degree, this aura extended to the discourse books contained. A printed biographical text gave its subject a definitive shape, substance, authority, and value.

The early portions of Pledger's notebook manifest the tendency of readers to internalize and emulate the definitive qualities of printed lives in their own experience. Even if we allow that the diary was begun as part of a sincere attempt to perform an essential Christian duty, it remains apparent that it was considerably informed by the books of Christian lives Pledger read, rather than solely by the spontaneous motions of his heart. Pledger's valuation of the printed biographies caused him to regard some aspects of his own experience as more significant than others. Where the doctrine of grace offered Christians a universal and therefore highly flexible allegory with which to frame their experience, the printed biography was very particular in its detail. It showed Pledger exactly what actions, feelings, and expressions became a Christian character, as well as the particular order of relation they should follow in the ideal experience. It made him even more literal-minded than he perhaps already was, and excessively conscious of textual self-presentation. These effects are evident in the editorial attention he bestowed on his diary notebook: the impersonal style (which persists even after the change of pronouns), the unusual transcription of supporting documents, and chiefly the excision of large chunks of text, and the replacement of some of these with alternative versions. In Pledger's experience, the diary had ceased to serve as a means to an end and had become an end in itself. It was a kind of mirror of its writer, rather than a means of displaying Christ in him. As such, it acquired a new representational meaning. It was the draft of a self-identifying text whose destiny was to appear in public as a printed book.

Of course Pledger's text fell short of this ultimate intention, perhaps because the unconscious knowledge originally motivating its writer was superseded by different, more pressing priorities later in his life. But other writers were not so deterred. In the late seventeenth and early eighteenth centuries, several persons ordered their private papers and left directions to posterity to see to their posthumous printing.[7] And many others less perfect in their emulation of the printed biography at least began their personal memorials by citing as justification for writing the variety of biographical texts which had appeared in print during the course of the seventeenth century.[8] Some of these writers might have at least considered the possibility of posthumous printing, without actually expecting or demanding it. In any case, the tendency to justify the existence of a personal notebook by making some reference to print suggests the degree to which diarists had internalized the values of the printed biographies available to them. After the mid-eighteenth century, few writers could claim innocence of biographical self-identity, such as it was constituted in printed books.

Little evidence survives to tell us anything about the production of printed popular biographies in early modern England beyond the texts themselves. With but a handful of exceptions, they always appeared after the deaths of their subjects. The roots of this tradition lie in the printed epitaphs, elegies, and other verses designed as memorials of deceased nobility and gentry. Such texts belong mostly to the first half of the seventeenth century, when they contributed to the latter half of a century-long rage among the gentry for ostentatious funeral ceremonies and monuments.[9] The point of elaborate gentry funerals was to represent symbolically the worthiness of the family of the deceased in an awesome public display of the dead subject's honor and virtue. The great figured tomb was designed to sustain this worshipful image, and the copious epitaph inscribed upon it literally underwrote the projected image as a caption does a photograph.[10] A separately printed book served as an optional complement to the tomb-text, extending its message verbally, into the homes and hopefully the memories of friends unable to experience (or re-experience) the total spectacle on site. The book also usually offered evidence to support the epitaph in the form of additional verses containing testimonies of articulate friends and others to the worth of the deceased. In this way the funeral book was quasi-biographical. However, specific references to an individual life were limited to a brief record of *res gestae* or descriptions of honorific qualities whose ultimate source lay in the family's noble blood rather than the peculiar qualities of the person to which they were ascribed.[11]

About the responsibility for producing these texts we can only speculate. The dead themselves were rarely involved, though later it was not unusual for a person to write his own epitaph. The verses were generally compiled by near kin, such as spouse, sibling, or child. In the case of city merchants, a "brother" of his company might see to the work instead.[12] Sometimes, depending upon ability and wit, the compiler included a specimen of his own writing. The expense of printing the text was likely borne by the survivors as part of the cost of the funeral itself. Copies of the finished book, which might be elaborately bound in velvet or calf with detailing in gilt, were probably given away by the family to mourners like other tokens of remembrance, such as rings, hatbands, or gloves. Less expensive copies (which could of course be custom-bound as the purchaser desired) might be sold by local stationers to interested friends, with the understanding that the family would pay for the remaindered sheets (which it would then control, and perhaps distribute gratis). In considering the means of distribution we are also left to conjecture; an apparently unique work printed in 1692 by the bookseller John Dunton, entitled *The Mourning-Ring, In Memory of Your Departed Friend*, suggests some possibilities. The purpose of this book, which contained a hodge-podge anthology of writings on the topic of death taken from a variety of sources, Dunton explained as follows:

> it were to be wished that this Mourning-Ring, which is so Entituled, that it might be given at Funerals instead of *Gloves, Bisquets and Wine*. And those that think it proper, may print in a Sheet of Paper, the most Material Passages, in the Life of their Dead Friend, and bind it up with those Mourning-Rings they give away at his Funeral; and for the more effectually perpetuating the Memory of the Party Deceased. There is room left in the Title of this Book, for inserting his Name and Place of Burial. And indeed, all serious practical Books are proper for this Design and[,] if Bound in Black, with a Cypher of Mortality, as in this Mourning-Ring, should be given at Funerals.[13]

Dunton cited as a precedent for his *prêt-à-donner* product the fact that "many have put in Practice this useful Design of giving Books at the Interment of Friends."[14] However, it is difficult to imagine anyone actually deigning to distribute one of Dunton's poorly made artifacts on any occasion. In the copy I examined, the space for a name and place was blank, and no biographical leaves had been added. Moreover, few examples of this "second" edition survive, and none do of the supposed first edition. Should families prefer a couture funeral text assembled from original material, as most seem to have done, the number of items produced in an edition was probably low, in the hundreds, which made the labor required to print them quite costly. Very few texts of this kind met with a demand sufficient to require more than a single edition.[15]

Of course the spectacle of gentry funerals and their accessories was designed for the sake of the living, rather than for the dead. This fact was driven home by a sermon, which became an increasingly common element of the funeral ceremony during the course of the seventeenth century, even after the vogue for other forms of pomp died out. Pious Protestants who could afford the gratuity frequently appointed a sermon in their wills or on their deathbeds. Some even desired a specific text and preacher. In general the rhetoric of funeral sermons, especially those by and for evangelical Protestants, was didactic. The discourse usually avoided pleading for the deceased's election (which in most cases was either taken as a given or ignored), and turned instead to propound the doctrine of grace to the living. The oration consisted of two parts: in the first, the preacher expounded the selected scripture text; in the second section, sometimes so short as to be a mere coda to the first, he characterized the life of the deceased as an example of how to live and die gracefully.

If the family or friends desired it, or if the preacher himself deemed his discourse worthy, the sermon might be printed, for the further edification and comfort of the living. Prefaces and dedications to such books often explained that they were prepared "at the request of some of [the deceased's] dear Friends."[16] The title-page of William Hinde's *Life* of John Bruen recommended the book "as a Path and President of Piety and Charity for the Inhabitants of the Famous County Palatine of Chester," where the Bruen family was long established and well known. On occasion another writer, usually a minister, might step in to revise the text, especially if the preacher did not know the deceased well enough to do the life convincingly.[17] More rarely, an auditor taking notes or some other second party might see to the sermon's printing, with the preacher's permission.[18] In the event of publication, the minister was listed on the title-page as author, and it is likely he rather than the family of the deceased handled publication arrangements with the bookseller. The fact that the sermons characterized the deceased as an example for all Christians expanded the potential audience for the printed version. If the preacher was widely known, a net profit might result from sales. A bookseller would not normally agree to publish a work without some guarantee of a return, or at minimum of no loss to himself for his efforts. The regular arrangement between the bookseller Thomas Parkhurst, who issued several pious lives in the second half of the seventeenth century, and the nonconforming minister Oliver Heywood, who wrote *The Life and Death of John Angier* among other works, entailed payment for the manuscript in bound copies of the book rather than cash. Parkhurst also expected Heywood to buy a significant portion – a hundred or more – of the edition at a discounted price for distribution among his colleagues, congregation, friends, and patrons.[19] This kind of arrangement was a little less like private publication in its modern sense than those for secular books of epitaphs and elegies, and we can assume that it was typical of those for other sermonized lives.[20] Sales of the remainder of the edition would be the responsibility of the publisher, who would distribute copies in London and in the local community of the deceased, especially if the minister was not settled there. Provincial demand could be quite high. This, along with the writer's obligatory purchase, could alone account for the sell-out of an entire edition. One of Parkhurst's apprentices noted his master's "very strange success" in selling off whole impressions of some works, "before the book has been almost heard of in London."[21] In a few cases demand was sufficient for subsequent impressions: Heywood's *Life of Angier* saw three editions in the space of eight years, though these were probably editions of 500 or thereabout, rather than the trade standard of 1,000–1,500 copies.

Also, in setting up the dead as examples of piety, the sermons took a page from the book of Katherine Stubbes. Increasingly during the seventeenth century, printed funeral sermons appropriated the key concept in the title of *A Christal Glasse*, identifying their contents as constituting an exemplary "Life and Death."[22] Non-sermon funeral books soon also appropriated this design.[23] By mid-century it was conventional for all printed memorials to contain a prose character sketch of the deceased, representing what one writer described as "an Historicall surveigh of [her] Religious life, so that though [she] bee now taken out of your sight and to bee seene among you no more, [she] may yet so remain in your minds, as to be a memento and motive unto you for imitation of that faire patterne [she] set before you, while [she] lived with you."[24] In this manner, the tradition took a big step toward becoming more formally biographical.[25] However, in each instance the overriding didactic intention caused writers to limn a character type rather than an individual personality. This biographical subject was consistent with the ideology of Christian community and self-denial. No matter whose experience went into a *Life*, a one-dimensional image of a generic saint came out in the text.

Moreover, the logic of these "historical surveys" was paratactical, rather than either chronological or analytical. The index, or "Table of the Principal things contained in these Lives," included in Samuel Clarke's large anthology of biographies, each of which was originally published individually as a funeral memorial, provides a good example of the tradition's logical priorities. "Principal things" were typically abstract qualities like "Faith, Fidelity, Friendship . . . Humility, Hypocrisie, Industry . . . Joy, Liberality, Love . . . Meekness . . . Modesty . . . Mortification," etc.[26] By contrast, specific people, places, events, actions, thoughts and opinions – the stuff of narrativized historiography – hardly figured at all. Tracking the order of discourse in the lives is rather like completing a connect-the-dots portrait; the text rambles from one topic to another, without concern for cause-and-effect relations or meaningful personal development. The biographical element was confined to a bare sense of chronology in the relation of birth, parentage, and education. Beyond that the typical pious life was more akin to the Theophrastian character than the modern biography. In spite of the considerable promotion of the deceased subject's name, his or her personality remained unknown. However, writing in the later decades of the seventeenth century began a shift toward more historical detail in *Life* and *Death* accounts.

The Civil War and Interregnum period precipitated events which touched the personal experience of most pious Christians profoundly. Their imprint can be seen and read in many of the lives published after 1660, when the restoration of Charles II to the throne heralded an effort to return the nation to its pre-revolutionary peace and stability. A number of liberties established and enjoyed by evangelical Protestants in the years following 1642, which Charles and his parliament interpreted as potentially seditious licenses, were removed in an attempt to reconstruct the episcopal Church of England along the lines of the 1559 Elizabethan Act of Uniformity and its Book of Common Prayer. The Act of Uniformity[27] approved by the king on 19 May 1662 to be enforced on 24 August of that year was far more rigorous than its predecessor. It required that the newly revised (and popishly inclined, in the radical view) Prayer Book alone be used in all places of worship and that every beneficed clergyman publicly declare his assent and consent to the book's contents. Any minister failing to do so was *ipso facto* deprived of his office. Further, it required incumbents to subscribe a declaration of non-resistance to the king, of intent to conform to the liturgy, and of the nullity of the Solemn League and Covenant of the Long Parliament of 1643 (which had established an alliance with the Scots and led to the ascendancy of Presbyterianism in England). Last, the Act recognized only episcopal orders as valid. Any incumbent not episcopally ordained before 24 August 1662 would lose his living. By the end of that year over 2,000 ministers, chiefly Presbyterian, stood ejected.[28] These dissenters from the Act and its principles of exclusion were publicly recognized as "non-conformists."

Charles's treatment of religious deviants did not end there. More than the comparatively moderate Presbyterian incumbents, Charles perceived radical sectarians such as Independents, Fifth Monarchists, Baptists, and Quakers in particular as fractious and seditious. This bunch had already separated itself from the established church long before Charles returned, on the grounds that, even under its accommodating Presbyterian discipline, it remained insufficiently reformed. For the sectarians, faith rather than national allegiance was the only qualification for church membership. They perceived the line dividing members from non-members as that which divided the converted from the unconverted. Worse, from Charles's point of view, the Quakers, the best-organized and most active element of the radical fringe, loudly proclaimed their obedience to no authority but Christ. Not only did they refuse to attend Sunday services and pay tithes, they ignored the power of the local magistrate and habitually neglected petty but symbolically resonant conventions of social decorum, such as the removal of hats and bowing before men of rank. In this way Quakers offended many others besides the king, and set a provocative example for would-be challengers of authority. To make these matters even more politically ominous, they and other separatists commonly met for worship in secret, at which time, popular rumor had it, they plotted to overthrow the government.

To disrupt these seedbeds of insurrection and to further manage Presbyterians and other ejected incumbents who might also align themselves and their congregations in opposition to the state, magistrates were directed to enforce existing Tudor and Stuart statutes against conventicles, vagrants, popish recusants, and refusers of oaths, and the king approved a series of new Acts known collectively as the Clarendon Code. The first of these, passed in 1664, was the Conventicle Act,[29] which forbade all religious meetings of five or more people not conducted according to the liturgy of the established church. A first offense incurred a £5 fine or three months' imprisonment; a second, a £10 fine or six months in gaol; a third, £100 or transportation. The Five Mile Act,[30] enacted in 1665, was directed against those in holy orders who had "taken upon them to preach in unlawful assemblies, conventicles, or meetings under colour or pretence of exercise of religion . . . [and] settled themselves in divers corporations . . . thereby taking an opportunity to distill the poisonous principles of schism and rebellion into the hearts of his Majesty's subjects." Such persons were forbidden to come within five miles of any city, corporation, or parliamentary borough or any place they had ministered without having first taken an oath similar to that required by the Act of Uniformity. A violation incurred a £40 fine, which was divided three ways between the Crown, the poor of the parish in which the offense occurred, and the informer whose disclosures secured a conviction. The second Conventicle Act,[31] passed in 1670 following the lapse of the first Act in 1669, gave an even more prominent place to informers, and opened the way to a summary and arbitrary exercise of authority. It empowered not two (as before) but any single justice of the peace, on the evidence of a confession, two witnesses, or simply "by notorious evidence and circumstance of fact," to convict a suspect of conventicle attendance. The justice's personal opinion on matters put before him sufficed as a conviction, and he was empowered to secure it by breaking and entering any house or place where a conventicle was suspected, and to seize and sell personal goods to raise cash for payment of penalties. Though this new Act reduced the fines imposed on offenders, it created an additional class of fines intended to encourage its enforcement: £5 on persons failing to inform and £100 on justices neglecting to prosecute. It was commonly known as "the Informing act."[32]

Given such official encouragement, unscrupulous informers flourished. The Act was often invoked selectively as a lever in personal vendettas having little to do with national security. In fact, the whole of the Clarendon Code was not nearly as systematically enforced as it could have been. Still, many did suffer severe oppression because of it, and all who stood in violation lived under constant threat of sudden apprehension and prosecution.[33] Whether indicted or not, nonconformists of every stripe, from the most innocuous Presbyterian to the most infuriating Quaker, were viewed in the eyes of the law and of a majority of the conforming population as social pariahs, at least until the Glorious Revolution of 1688 and the subsequent promotion of political consensus and religious toleration. In the meantime the Clarendon Code served to arouse mutual suspicion and create an atmosphere of paranoia in which rumor and gossip quickly escalated to accusations and lies.

The consequences of these conditions for the production of pious biography were twofold. First, the printed book achieved preeminence as a tool of the evangelical ministry. This occurred in part because books were getting cheaper to make and the number of people able to read them greater, but it was chiefly due to the more immediate fact that the new laws prevented direct contact between ministers and their flocks. To be sure, the law could be broken, but violators sometimes landed in gaol, which precluded direct relations with a congregation almost absolutely. Under such circumstances the utility of writing in general and books in particular became apparent. While copies of letters containing news and specific messages addressed to a small audience circulated in manuscript, printed books were used to publicize general information widely. According to Richard Baxter, the most renowned and most published Presbyterian of his day,

> The Writings of Divines are nothing else but a preaching the Gospel to the eye, as the *voice* preacheth it to the ear. Vocal preaching hath the preheminence in moving the affections, and being diversified according to the state of the Congregations which attend it: This way the Milk cometh warmest from the breast. But Books have the advantage in many other respects: you may read an able Preacher when you have but a mean one to hear. Every *Congregation* cannot hear the most judicious or powerful Preachers; but every *single person* may read the Books of the most powerful and judicious; *Preachers* may be silenced or banished, when *Books* may be at hand. . . . If Sermons be forgotten, they are gone. But a Book we may read over and over till we remember it: and if we forget it, may again peruse it at our pleasure, or at our leisure. . . .
>
> Books are (if well chosen) domestick, present, constant, judicious, pertinent, yea, and powerful sermons . . . especially when Vocal preaching faileth, and Preachers . . . are persecuted and forbid to preach.

Moreover, Baxter reasoned, fallaciously, "Knowledge hath abundantly encreased since Printing was invented: Therefore Books have been a means to it."[34] On these grounds, nonconformists enlisted the book in their efforts to comfort and rally their co-denominationalists and to vindicate themselves and their cause in the eyes of the general public.

The printed *Life* of the nonconformist came to occupy an important place in both the local and the national publicity campaigns. On the local level, nonconformists better appreciated its value as a vehicle for the instruction and edification of their congregations, especially among people of little experience and sophistication. As Baxter explained, "In the Lives of Holy Men we see Gods Image, and the Beauties of Holiness, not only in Precept, but in Reality and Practice; not *Pictured*, but in the *Substance*. . . . And *Holiness* in visible Realities, is apt to affect the World more deeply, than in Portraiture and Precept only."[35] Therefore, he continued, "this kind of History . . . is fitted to Insinuate the Reverence and Love of Piety into *Young unexperienced Persons*: For before they can Read much of *Theological* Treatises with understanding or delight, Nature enclineth them to a pleasure in History, and so their Food is sugared to their Appetites, and *Profit* is entertained by *Delight*."[36]

But this was just an explicit statement of what Philip Stubbes had confirmed in the popular response to *A Christal Glasse*, and what printed funeral sermons had been taking for granted ever since. More novel was Baxter's concept of the *pious* life as a vehicle for revisionist historiography, which made it useful at the national level. Noting how "[i]t is the Custom of the Devil to write infamous Lies of the best men when they are dead, which would be believed if those that knew them while they lived, did not say that which should refute the lies," Baxter movingly explained in the preface he contributed to Samuel Clarke's *Lives of Sundry Eminent Persons of this Later Age* that

> We live in a time of mental War, when it is the Devils great and daily business to belie the best of men, and make the ignorant believe that they are a Generation of walking Plagues, movers of Sedition, teaching men to Worship God contrary to the Law, enemies to *Caesar*, Preaching up another King, one Jesus, and turning the World upside down, not keeping the Tradition of the Fathers; the Cry is loud, *Away with such Fellows from the Earth; It is not fit that they should live.* Most odious Lies are published of them with so great confidence, as that Strangers may think they are bound to believe them. . . . And so much of God, of Christ, of the Holy Ghost, of the Gospel and of Religion, and of the Church and Souls of men, doth lie upon the true representation of the Faithful, and the vindication of Gods Image upon them, and confuting Satans lies, as that it is no small part of the Duty of all Christs Servants to endeavour it.[37]

Furthermore, to the end that the Presbyterian cause might be articulated by a chorus of voices describing this "true representation of the faithful," Baxter called for more writers of pious biographies. Citing the examples of the Continental ecclesiastics Thuanus,[38] Scultetus,[39] and Junius,[40] whose relations of their own "life and times" were known to most serious university-educated men in England, Baxter put autobiographical texts first in the canon of the historiography of the Protestant church: "It were to be wished that more did as . . . [they who] give us a Breviate of the most considerable Passages of their own lives: Because no man knoweth usually those intimate Transactions of God upon mens Souls, which are the Life of such History." But unfortunately, Baxter observed, few are moved to write their own lives, for fear of appearing vain. Given this modesty, he argued that someone from among the holy person's "intimate Friends" should become his biographer in the breach.[41] Baxter's call for more autobiographers and biographers was echoed in an editorial note accompanying Samuel Clarke's self-penned narrative of his life, included in Clarke's posthumously printed *Lives of Sundry Eminent Persons* at the request of its publisher Thomas Simmons. Explaining that Clarke's work was "a bare relation of matters of Fact, which cannot be so fully done by any other as by a man's self," it expressed a desire "that others, whom God has made eminently instrumental for the service of his Church, would write after his Copy, and follow his Example herein."[42] Such public petitions were apparently also made privately by godly ministers to their congregations. Philip Henry taught parents how to instruct their children to compose personal histories, by beginning a memorial book of each child's experience, to be passed along to the child for continuation when he was able to keep it himself.[43]

Though few nonconformists actually stepped forward to write their own lives as Clarke did, several were motivated to create small archives of personal historical materials out of which others might fashion a biography worthy of print. The fairly widespread production of such source materials was the second significant consequence of the Clarendon Code for pious biography. Under the imminent threat of persecution, anxious nonconformists learned to make a habit of documenting "matters of fact" (a common phrase apparently related to the law) pertaining to their actions and movements lest they be accused of being someplace they had not actually been or doing something they had not actually done. To this end, many ejected ministers maintained diaries of their personal movements and general historical occurrences, in addition to those relating to the motions of their hearts (or they included personal historical memoranda along with spiritual notes). Though any kind of notebook could (and did) serve this purpose, interleaved (or "blank") pocket almanacs were ideal, and were used, for example, by the ejected minister Philip Henry, who recorded events in copies of Goldsmith's almanac from 1657 to 1696, and William Allen, who was ejected from the mayoralty of Plymouth in 1662, and whose annotated copy of Rider's *British Merlin* for 1671 has survived.[44]

But note-writers had to take care to protect their books, for an almanac could provide evidence to convict as well as to defend a minister. The *Life* of Philip Henry describes how during a journey to London in 1665 Henry's friend, the ejected minister Richard Steele of Flintshire, was stopped and searched by authority of a warrant issued against both Steele and Henry, from JPs acting "under Colour of the Report of a Plot." Finding nothing to incriminate Steele, his would-be apprehenders seized instead "his *Almanack*, in which he kept his Diary for that Year; and it not being written very legibly, they made what malicious Readings and Comments they pleas'd upon it, to his great Wrong and Reproach."[45] Their report, "a dreadful story," according to Henry Newcome, who recorded the incident in his diary, caused "a great noise in y country," according to Philip Henry, who likewise noted the incident in his. Henry added to his record a memorandum that "I shall take warning & bee more Cautious, for malice may take that with the left hand which is written with the right." The modern editor of Henry's diary surmised that the manuscript's many erasures were made by Henry himself, out of fear of possibly sharing in Steele's misfortune.[46] To maintain secrecy, some wrote in a personal cipher; others wrote in Greek or Latin, to prevent the unlearned from browsing.

This habit of necessity followed chiefly by ministers and other persons liable to attack was also recommended to the less vulnerable laity for somewhat different reasons, in the practical manual written by the Essex minister John Beadle, published in 1656 as *The Journal or Diary of a Thankful Christian*.[47] The book contained an elaboration of a sermon Beadle had preached as early as 1644 in his parish at Leighs, home to the aforementioned "spiritual bee," the Countess of Warwick, who described *The Journal or Diary* as one of her favorite books.[48] Advertised as "Some Meditations upon Numb. 33.2" (treating God's command that Moses keep a record of the trials of the ancient Israelites under the diaspora), Beadle's sermon became the first and only manual of practical piety devoted solely to the maintenance of a spiritual diary. The book offered instructions more minute than those previously available in Isaac Ambrose's wide-ranging *Media*, first published in 1652. Moreover, Beadle's advice differed from Ambrose's by advocating that, besides private sins, a personal diary should contain records of "Nationall, and more publick" events as well. Though Beadle acknowledged the traditional need for diurnal self-examination "to encrease in us that self-abasement & abhorrency of spirit that is most acceptable in the sight of God," he stressed that notebooks had also to serve a new need: that of the true Church for materials to function as "a Stone of witnesse."[49] Diary documentation of historical events was required, claimed Beadle, "[i]n times of commotion, when the bands of love are broken into several parties and factions, as they have been lately among us." By the public records contained in private journals, iniquity – the "Nationall Epidemicall sin of the time" – would be readily revealed both to contemporaries and to posterity. To this end, Beadle instructed diarists to take note of such public occurrences as the demeanor of kings, princes, magistrates, and governors, especially what religion they embraced or opposed; also "the various and changeable condition of the Times in the Countrey where we live;" and "the severall and most remarkable judgments that God hath in our time inflicted upon notorious offenders, whether persons in high places, or such as moved in a lower orb."[50]

The need for public witnesses also affected the range of materials to be accounted as noteworthy "private concerns." The list of these grew to include matter more worldly than spiritual. According to Beadle, "All the instruments, all the men and means that God hath in providence at any time used for our good, must not be forgotten." Thus the thankful Christian ought to take note of his parents and their efforts for his sake, his schoolmasters, other "bountiful Benefactors" in his education and career (essential for any type of success in this age of patronage), as well as his own calling, and the duties committed to and performed by him in it.[51] The general thrust of Beadle's concern is indicated by his title's suggestion that the writer conceive of his diary as a "journal." A journal connoted a text more historical or news-oriented than the Christian notebook had hitherto been. In becoming a journalist, the pious Christian added a dimension to his experience as a saint. Not only was he Christ-like in self-denial, he acted like an Old Testament prophet as well, bearing witness to posterity of latter-day iniquity.

As a direct result of these consequences of the political and religious upheaval from 1640 to 1689, when the Act of Toleration ending persecution was passed,[52] the printed pious biography in England became more generally historical in both form and content: its detail became more personal, specific, and concrete, and its structure more subservient to the order of chronology and the narratologic of cause and effect. Above all it adhered to the new secular concepts of plausibility and truth. In contrast to what one text characterized as the "ridiculous" practice of "Romanists," whose hagiography contained "some *Sainted* that were scarce *men*, and their *legends* bundles of lyes the very stain and infamy of Christianity," Protestant biography in the latter half of the seventeenth century adopted the rhetoric of proof and verification in order to secure credibility.[53] We can observe the valorization of historical truth in the increasing tendency of title-pages after 1660 to identify the pious *Life*'s contents as a "narrative," an "account", a "relation", or a "history," instead of as a "mirror" or "pattern." Though exemplarity remained a significant feature of the post-Restoration memorial book, it had to share the bill equally with the function of witnessing. Only the memorials of pious women, whose actions were largely domestic and therefore removed from history as it was then understood, remained predominantly exemplary. But even in representing the generic and nondenominational female pattern of piety, preserving truth became paramount. In his memorial of his wife, the Anglican minister Anthony Walker explained that "I have not writ her Life as the *Roman Historians* did the Lives of their Great Men and *Heroes*, made Speeches for them, and put Words into their Mouths, rather fit to be spoken by Men of their *Figure* and *Character*, than really spoken by them. But all that's *Comma'd* in the Margin is transcribed, *verbatim*, from her Writings, which I have shew'd to many *Witnesses*, and am ready to show to any Friend, who shall desire it."[54] Increasingly, biographers adduced authentic first-person discourse as the vehicle of truth.

Because their presence eliminated the need for a potentially biased second party, the words of the biographical subject constituted the most ideal witness of his pious life, and of his iniquitous times. Hence biographers quoted such discourse verbatim, or at least cited it as a source of information as often as possible, as Henry Newcome did the nonconformist minister John Machin's words in his "faithful narrative" of Machin's life, discussed in the previous chapter. Over two-thirds of the printed text is set between inverted commas, reflecting Newcome's deliberate intention to allow Machin to speak for himself. Thus the pious biographer became more like a compiler and editor than an author, and the discourse of biography itself more autobiographical in form. Newcome's method was followed by nearly every writer able to draw upon a diary, notebook, or other personal paper in preparing a memorial. Hardly any pious *Life* printed after 1660 neglected to feature some original paper or fragment of authentic discourse, which leads one to wonder whether it was possible for a person to have achieved textual memorialization without first leaving some shard of reified speech behind him, written either on paper or on the hearts of intimate friends. In any event, the greater prominence given to the writings of the biographical subject set up a subtle tension between the particularity of the subject's presence as a historical entity and a textually embodied voice on the one hand, and the universal truth he was meant to articulate and champion on the other. Unintentionally, the nonconformist biography veered sharply toward the precipice of modernity by constituting the voice of an individual authoritative subject.

So far I have considered Presbyterian practice, which actually followed rather than led the biographical tradition in the second half of the seventeenth century. The more radical nonconformists and sectarians made up the true avant-garde of pious biographers. Their use of print as an evangelical tool started by spontaneous combustion in the heat of controversy during the 1640s, when many came forward with their own plans to carry the unfinished (in their collective view) project of reforming the Christian church to completion. Quakers, Baptists, Seekers, Ranters, Muggletonians, Fifth Monarchists, and others propounding a vision of a "true church" flourished during the Interregnum period, after the abolition of episcopacy, the collapse of regulation of the press, and in the absence of an effective national policy of church government.

Though doing so fails to represent adequately the variety of opinions within this heterogeneous group, for our purposes we can reduce the bone of contention between the radicals and the more conservative Protestants to the marrow of emphasis on individual conscience. Most radicals – Seekers, Ranters, and Quakers especially – emphasized a religion of divine inspiration, of personal and direct contact with Christ. Here began their problems with all forms of worldly power, including the comparatively tolerant Commonwealth and Protectorate regimes. By following their consciences in the pursuit of religious perfection, the radicals replaced obedience to civil and ecclesiastical institutions with their own prophetic authority. The warrant for such authority lay in each saint's ability to testify publicly to his experience of divine inspiration. Such testimony issued forth in the form of scripture-inspired personal bearing of witness to the "Truth" or "Light" of Christ within. Without public expression, the experience of personal inspiration was ineffectual, and the saint powerless. Radical saints gave the ability to speak (or not to speak, if doing so ran contrary to the wisdom of inner inspiration) in public new importance for the ordinary person. The control of discourse became for them a sign of self-identity; it signified election and solidified faith. It was the rock upon which the truly reformed Christian church would be built. For this reason an unprecedented amount of personal discourse treating prophetic "experience" found its way into print between 1640 and 1660.[55]

The testimony or profession of faith had of course always mattered to evangelical Protestants. But, as we have seen, it belonged properly to the practice of private meditation; the only occasion such discourse might decently issue forth in public was on a death-bed, as in the case of Katherine Stubbes, whose dying speeches served to secure her spiritual life in the face of worldly corruption. Her witnessing was a public performance designed to demonstrate the embodiment of scriptural truth in the person of piety – but this kind of Protestant transubstantiation was appropriate only to physical death. The sectarians, on the other hand, made it a condition of everyday life. The sectarian saint's sense of self depended upon total and absolute self-denial, upon the constant embodiment of the word of Christ in his or her own person. The reifying tendency of print made this embodiment all the more palpable.

The radical saints' testimonies of their spiritual callings resulted in some of the first appearances of personal discourse in print. Moreover, many testimonies were published during the saint's lifetime, suggesting a precocious modernity in sectarian identity. But in fact the speaker's control over his words remained minimal – to call the religious radicals "authors" of their printed books in the modern sense would be premature. It is best to regard these works as crude transcriptions of oral discourse into a written text, and to note how most lack the narrative sophistication displayed by discourses originally conceived in writing. We must also observe how the circumstances of composition constituted textual concessions to group rather than individual (or individualist) ideals. On the whole, the seemingly modern textual performances of the radical sectarians remained mired in their pre-modern context. However, the saints' use of the print medium deserves our attention, for it cleared a path for future innovators to follow, with different results. Let us first look briefly at a couple of radical texts conceived with no foresight of print, before considering those deliberately designed for it.

The quasi-autobiographical short relations of "experiences" collected and published by ministers of Independent or Congregational churches served to validate the true church by declaring publicly the witness of Christ in the whole body of the congregation, not merely in the person of its head, or mouth, the minister. In the radical lexicon, "experience" denoted the personal sense of the "*Call* to *Christ*" or "the *work* of *grace* upon [the] *heart*."[56] Despite their characterization by scholars as "spiritual autobiographies," the saints' relations of such experiences were hardly biographical. Instead of a total life, the testimonies described only the circumstances of the receipt of Christ's call, what was sometimes identified as individual "conversion" or "convincement." For example, the several "experiences" collected and printed for the minister John Rogers of members of his Dublin congregation each respond to the same three concerns, identified by side-notes in the printed text, as follows: (1) when and where the person was called; (2) how called; (3) the effects of the call. Each testimony therefore amounts to a very brief and formulaic account of a single event in the saint's life, offering little in the way of biographical character or novelistic plot. Usually the call came in a lecture by an evangelical minister expounding scripture, and was afterward confirmed for the saint in a dream. The only substantial variety among relations is that of particular names, dates, places, and scripture texts.

Such accounts as these were ad hoc compositions made to satisfy the demand of a voluntary church congregation for "evidences" or "testimonies" of sincere and firm faith from persons seeking admission. Experiences were to be spoken by the candidate before the assembled congregation, which might also designate a member to question him further in front of the group regarding matters of faith. In exceptional cases where a candidate for admission was unable to speak publicly, the congregation appointed a member to hear the account privately, and either to transcribe it in writing or to repeat it orally for the rest.[57] The emphasis on oral discourse not only tended to heighten the emotions of participants, it was also pragmatic, as probably only a minority of radical church members were able to read a written text, and even fewer able to compose one. Thus writing and printing were actually unusual; most testimonies faded into space after being spoken, which is why so few survive. Those experiences preserved in the printed anthologies were transcribed and usually abridged by the ministers expressly for use by Christians outside the congregation. Rogers claimed that his unique historical moment required the printing of experiences so that they might serve as signals for pilgrims who had lost the way: "Now *darkness surprises* us, and *adversity* comes upon us; and in a *time of darkness, when we see no light; yet we shall obey the Lord, and hear his voice* (having continual *experiences) to direct us.*"[58] Though the subject-matter was new to print, Rogers's rationale was hardly original; it was an appropriation of the traditional evangelical purpose of religious publication, adapted to the special circumstances of the 1650s.

The same can be said to describe the publication of the Newcastle Baptist saint Jane Turner's *Choice Experiences*. In general, because women were not barred from speaking in radical churches, their testimonies found their way into print alongside those of men. The female experiences contained in the congregational anthologies constitute some of the earliest instances of first-person discourse in English by women to appear in print during their own lifetimes. Jane Turner's book was unusual in that it was exclusively devoted to her words and her experience, thereby setting an original example of personal textual autonomy. The text was prepared at the insistence of Turner's husband and his colleagues, who believed that her testimony would provide "a glorious example for all Christians to follow, in a serious observing the passages of God's providence and Grace." Turner's "word from the Author to the Reader" suggests her own discomfort with this public appearance. Apologetically, she confessed her sense of "walk[ing] in an untrodden path, having never seen anything written before in this manner and method."[59] But it would have been more accurate for her to have said that she had never seen anything *printed* as such, because her text actually represented extracts from a private notebook written by Turner to pass time spent in her husband's absence. In the published version, selected diary entries were arranged to constitute what it called "a gradual narration of the Lords various dealings with her many years, both in, and after Conversion," answering the same three concerns identified in each of the experiences in Rogers's collection.[60] Thus all aspects of the text but the printing were conventional either in mainstream Protestant practice or the rituals of the sectarian congregations, and hardly in need of an apology.

As for the printing, Quakers at least would have found no problem in it. They were prepared not only to accept the printed discourse of a woman on her own, but even to find it worthy of rebuttal. Shortly after Turner's text was published, the Quaker Edward Burrough saw printed his tract entitled *Something in Answer to a Book Called Choice Experiences, Given forth by One J. Tvrner*. Burrough's reply was typical of early Quaker attitudes toward saintly discourse in both its taking the print for granted, and finding the words grounds for contention. Whereas the more conservative Protestant might have objected to a vain sally forth into print by any person, male or female, especially in order to speak chiefly of his or her particular spiritual affairs, Burrough found no fault with Turner's action. For him, public testifying was a godly imperative. It was the only way to discover the true Christ within. Unfortunately for Turner, Burrough's close reading of her testimony found it falling short of the mark of saintliness. Burrough wrote that she "declareth . . . of being brought out of *Babylon* into *Syon*, but all along through her *Booke*, her language is one and the same . . . I know her voyce, its the language of her City where she now dwells, which is in confusion *Babylon*."

He argued further that "Satan is now transformed in her into an Angel of light by which she is deceived; and whereas she *talkes* of her *choyce experiences*, death yet raignes in her, and is no whit subdued." This criticism displays the two most pronounced features of Quaker testimony: the prominence of the active voice of the saint, and a literal-minded application of scripture to personal experience. Though all radical discourse emulated these features to some degree, the early Quakers treated them as absolutes. A typical Quaker response to Christ's call resulted in the literal, total, and irreversible negation of the worldly or outward self, and its replacement by a new inward self, the person of Christ. Of Turner's case Burrough concluded that "the Image of God ... is a mystery hidden from the eye of *I. Turner* and from all vulterous eyes; and this mystery is within, in life and power consisting of the new man Christ Jesus, who is the Image of God made manifest within the saints, in whose Image man is *like* God, godly."[61]

The god-like identity of the converted Quaker and his words provided the warrant for the prodigious amount of print issued by "Friends," as Quakers called themselves. The Friends' print differed from that of other radical sectarians in that it did not occur as an afterthought. Print was a deliberate component of the Quaker ministry, helping to articulate the collective identity of the Friends almost from the beginning of the movement. The Friends did not comprise a disciplined, organized church but were instead a loose association of "brethren" (male and female) bound together by a common belief in "no lord or commander, no shepherd nor preserver, but the Lord Jesus Christ alone." Membership in this community of believers was determined by a person's willingness continually to observe the peculiar social imperatives following from the Friends' literal interpretation of scripture, such as the refusal of hat-honour, of tithes, of the Sabbath, and so forth, rather than by a discrete testimony of experience within the shelter of a church. For these and other infractions of civility and its laws individual Friends were routinely harassed in public, either by taunts, chiding, fines, or imprisonment. Through such personal trials each Friend verified his or her sainthood on a daily basis in the world at large. Friends were known to each other and to the world by their actions and their words; for them speech constituted a form of action. All Friends imagined themselves, Burrough explained, as being "chosen ... as vessels of [God's] glory, and instruments in his hand, to bear and publish his name in the world." To this end, he continued, many were "continually exercised in preaching the gospel, in answering books and manuscripts put forth against us, and in disputes and contentions with such as opposed the Truth."[62] This was literally true in the first three decades of the Friends' existence. From 1652, when two works by Friends were printed, to 1660, when 278 appeared in print, the average output of the society was 122 titles a year; in the 1660s the average was 117 titles, or approximately 13 per cent of the national total of publications listed in Wing's short-title catalogue. In the 1670s output slipped to sixty-five titles annually, though as a proportion of national production it remained significant at 7 per cent of the total.[63] These figures are impressive when we consider that, by 1715, Friends represented a mere 0.73 per cent of the total population of England and Wales.[64] And though a few Friends – Burrough, George Fox, and William Penn in particular – wrote many books each, a wide variety of Quaker writers actually saw their words printed. John Whiting's catalogue of Friends' books printed in or before the year 1708 contains the names of over 525 different writers.[65]

From the late 1650s, accounts of personal experience written deliberately for publication comprised a significant part of printed Quaker discourse. In the early days, itinerant ministers sent news or "journalls" of their travels in dictated letters to Friends at Swarthmore Hall in Lancashire, where they were transcribed into several copies and sent abroad to ministers in England and elsewhere.[66] In 1657, after they had firmly established themselves in London, the Friends hired a scrivener to oversee this internal correspondence.[67] But even earlier they had secured the London printer and bookseller Giles Calvert to publish books for them, thus enabling some texts to circulate among a wider audience of Friends, and the world besides.[68] We can observe the desire to reach a large public in such titles in Burrough's print bibliography as *A Generall Epistle, and greeting of the Father's Love to all The Saints* (1657) and *A Declaration to all the World of our Faith, and what we Believe. And this is written that all people upon Earth may Know by whom, and how we are saved* (1657).[69] Though the majority of Quaker books treated general doctrinal matters, some described personal conversion experiences not unlike those testified by members of independent congregations;[70] others related personal travels and sufferings at the hands of persecutors, with short, detailed accounts of historical events.[71] Though not autobiographical narratives in the modern sense, these texts represent the beginnings of such a mode of expression, containing narrations of personal experience written in first-person discourse.

Starting in the 1660s, with the decease of the original generation of itinerant or "public" Friends, a host of quasi-biographical *Life and Death*-type memorials of the departed were printed. They included whenever possible at least a fragment of an authentic "declaration" or "testimony" made by the deceased person himself, and so blended the abstract discourse of Quaker prophesying with the mundane detail of the more mainstream pious lives.[72] Sometimes the amount of authentic discourse available in writing resulted in the publication of a memorial volume of collected "works," which usually included a brief historical "journall of the life" of the writer composed by himself.[73] In cases where personal historical writings were extensive enough to allow it, a separate quasi-autobiographical "journall" volume might be printed instead.[74] A study of early Quaker books by type and year of publication shows a total of eighteen individual autobiographical and biographical publications in the 1650s, climbing to twenty-five in the 1660s, thirty-eight in the 1670s, ninety-two in the 1680s, and sixty-three in the 1690s. As a proportion of the total printed output of Friends, these works represented a mere 2 per cent in the 1650s, but reached 15 per cent in the 1680s and 13 per cent in the 1690s.[75] Though perhaps unimpressive to us, such numbers represent a tidal wave in contemporary terms, drowning the books of the lives of all other dissenters as well as those of the established church combined. Moreover, they were the result of a systematic, top-down effort to ensure that Quaker voices be heard even during the period of government censorship and suppression of illegal or "private" presses, from 1662 to 1689. Some attention to this effort is in order, as it offers the best perspective we are likely to gain of the collective forces responsible for individual printed pious biographies and autobiographies in the latter half of the seventeenth century.

In the 1650s Quaker publication was ad hoc. Still, an editorial procedure was in place for writers with manuscripts intended for print. In 1653 Thomas Aldam wrote to George Fox that "I doe Reioyce to heare that the wisdome of god doth soe Order that all Bookes may come to thy hand, to be vewed bee fore they bee printed, & such as are printed or to bee will bee sent diuers wayes in Order as they may bee passed abroad in seruice."[76] The cost of publishing before the mid-1650s was probably borne largely by the private donations of Margaret Fell (later the wife of George Fox), whose husband during a business trip to London early in 1653 contacted the bookseller Giles Calvert to see about printing two replies to Lancashire clergymen co-written by George Fox and James Nayler.[77]

Though not a Friend himself, Calvert had radical sympathies, and was one of but a few willing to risk harassment from Commonwealth authorities seeking to suppress Quaker activity (Calvert's shop at St Paul's was twice raided in attempts to seize Quaker books).[78] After the establishment of regular meetings throughout the north and in London between 1653 and 1660, at which collections for the relief of prisoners and support of the ministry were taken, all Friends subsidized the costs of publication.[79] At least 600 copies of each edition were sent to northern Friends for distribution by itinerants there at meetings and in public squares on market and lecture days; the rest were sold in London shops and cried out in the streets by Quaker women, or distributed gratis at Westminster or in the yard of St Paul's. Some were sent to ministers abroad, in Wales, Ireland, Holland, Germany, Italy, and Barbados.[80] This ad hoc publication system continued to be used, apparently with success, even after the government's attempt to censor dissent with the Licensing Act of 1662.[81]

In 1672, however, the process became more formalized. The first Yearly Meeting of county representatives appointed a committee of ten to oversee the distribution of Quaker books outside London, and "to see they be Carefully corrected and that none be printed but what are done by friends order."[82] A year later George Fox established another committee, the Second Day's Morning Meeting, to issue that order. The Morning Meeting relieved Fox by taking on the tasks of receiving and evaluating manuscripts by Friends intended for the press, as well as those of monitoring the publication of anti-Quaker propaganda, and ensuring the issue of an appropriate response.[83] In 1675 the Yearly Meeting called into being yet another body, the Meeting for Sufferings, to deal with relief of prisoners suffering under the Clarendon Code.[84] Part of its duties included organizing the collection, printing, and distribution of accounts of particular cases, as a means of applying pressure to magistrates. Perhaps in recognition of the fact that the Meeting for Sufferings' duties overlapped somewhat with those of the other two bodies, in 1679 the Yearly Meeting virtually dissolved the committee of ten and codified the Meeting for Sufferings' relation to the Morning Meeting. The Morning Meeting was left to act as an editorial board, and the Meeting for Sufferings was to oversee "the inspecting[,] ordering and regulating the press and printing of bookes."[85] The procedure thus established required that all manuscripts be sent to the Morning Meeting (except those of cases of suffering, which would come first to the Meeting for Sufferings, to be passed on to the Morning Meeting), which would usually appoint a committee of three members to read the text and determine its print-worthiness. If printing was recommended, the Morning Meeting passed the manuscript to the Meeting for Sufferings, which would make arrangements with a printer about the number of copies to be printed, the format of the text, the quality of paper, the type of binding to be used, the correcting of proofs, and the manner of distribution.[86]

These latter duties were instituted in order to control costs, which were covered both by the society's National Stock account (supplied largely by general collections in local Quarterly Meetings, as ordered by the Yearly Meeting) and by the Public Stock of individual Quarterly Meetings, which paid printers for copies of books sent to it for its own use and for distribution to individual Friends and the public.[87] In general, Quaker books were cheap tracts of one to thirty or so pages – rarely over a hundred – in length, retailing for a few pennies. In the 1670s and 1680s, however, anthologies of the writings of deceased Friends were printed, several of which required a hundred or more sheets, making the books expensive to produce. Moreover, it seems that printers often sent the Quarterly Meetings more books than they could dispose of and pay for. For this reason the Meeting for Sufferings stipulated a revised distribution procedure. Previously, according to a directive of the Yearly Meeting, printers were to send a fixed number of copies of each edition of all books printed to every Quarterly Meeting.[88] This procedure guaranteed a minimum return to the printer for taking the risk of making unlicensed books. But in 1680, partly because of abuses and partly because of a lapse of the Licensing Act in 1679, the Meeting for Sufferings removed the guarantee, stipulating instead that printers send out only those books requested in numbers specified in writing, and that "the way of exposing books to sale, bee for the future by sending them to Market Townes to such Friends and shopkeepers as will expose the same to sale in their shopps and houses."[89] This procedure seems to have stood even after renewed efforts by the government to regulate the press began in 1682.[90] At roughly the same time as it did away with the quota system, the Meeting for Sufferings clarified the matter of right of copy, which had previously been murky. It gave writers the power to dispose of their copies as each saw fit for the first, second, and third impressions of a book and allowed for a change of printer after each impression, if the writer desired it. It added that in cases "where the Author is deceased or absent, or gives no order, then ye Friends of ye 2^d days meeting to dispose thereof." We might regard this attempt to shift the burden of financial responsibility from the society to individual writers and booksellers as a small step in the direction of loosening the reins of institutional control on individual publications.[91] It would also edge the books closer to the open market for print (such as it was) where, through relatively free exchange between producers and consumers, their potential commodity value would be enhanced.

Yet, in their immediate context, the consequences of the Meeting for Sufferings' decisions hardly appear so liberating. Indeed, some contemporaries and most modern scholars have regarded the Friends' publishing practices throughout the seventeenth century as effectively transforming the potential variety of Quaker voices into an echo of the society's leadership, thereby undermining the credibility of individual prophets and possibly destroying the grounds of the personal authority of Quakers altogether. Originally, the Morning Meeting in particular came under severe attack from Francis Bugg, a former Friend, who complained that

> This Meeting doth much resemble his Majesty's Privy Council: For the King, by and with the Advice of his Privy Council, can do many things ... So can this Meeting; ... they can alter, and change any Message, stop any Prophesie, stifle any Revelation, silence the Voice uttered by the Spirit of the Lord, thro' their most eminent Prophets, in what respect they please, and make it speak louder and more shril, where they think there is most Service, or may be more conducive to their Designs; ... they are the Wheel within the Wheel, which move all the whole Work ... For all Books Printed and Reprinted, pass thro' the fiery Tryal of their Infallible Examination; they Govern, they Rule, they Steer the Vessel, but all INVISIBLY.[92]

Bugg's barrage of metaphors contained a kernel of truth, which recent scholars have done their best to document. Though they avoid his hyperbole in preference to the moderate terms of "regulation" and "control," modern scholars largely agree with Bugg, finding for instance that in the seventeenth century the Meeting for Sufferings and the Morning Meeting "tended to impose a unity, characterized by caution and extreme political sensitivity, which had been absent in the 1650s."[93] This unification of course affected the nature of supposedly authentic personal discourse, especially autobiographical writings. It has also been argued that the editorial agenda of the leadership caused the "toning down" of original voices as it "repressed" the "spiritual ardency and expressive vigor" present in earlier discourses.[94] On such grounds we have been further cautioned against reading Quaker journals as expressions of individual personalities, because "to some extent the similarities between the various journals owe more to their editors than to their writers."[95] Rather than an avant-garde, the Quakers appear in this light as the shock troops of a fundamentally reactionary literary movement tending toward a kind of medieval absolutism rather than modern individualism.

But though these criticisms are accurate in detail, their emphases distort our perception of seventeenth-century Quaker discourse, and the whole later seventeenth-century tradition of pious biography of which it was a part. They do so by implying that the regulation and control exercised by the two meetings suppressed a host of unique, autonomous personal voices, making them over into mere reverberations of an official ideology. This implication is false, for two reasons. First, Quaker discourse in the 1650s was no more original or personal in expression than it was a quarter-century later. All of the early writings were conceived for a single purpose, to demonstrate scriptural authority. To that end they all drew upon the same treasury of scriptural figures and tropes, and all display the same repetitive, incantatory style of narration. From the perspective of the performance of individual authority, there is little in the way of either content or style to distinguish, for instance, Thomas Green's first-person narrative, *A Declaration to the World, of my Travel and Journey out of Aegypt into Canaan* (1659), from, say, John Perrot's first-person narrative, *Immanuel the Salvation of Israel*, published a year earlier. Though originating from different writers, the two texts are largely identical in form and meaning. So instead of the *imposition* of unity onto heterogeneity, we ought rather to describe the advent of editorial controls as the *substitution* of one form of unity for another. Earlier, a more scriptural discourse prevailed; later, a different, more mundane one took hold. In both periods, the immediacy of a larger source of authority, either the word of God or the concerns of the society itself, precluded the manifestation of individual style and personality in Quaker personal writing.

Second, as we have seen, the discourse of other religious nonconformists after 1660 was no less impersonal than that of Quakers. While first-person narration went public, so to speak, in the context of religious controversy in England during the second half of the seventeenth century, it did so largely as a means of signifying God's truth. While it was less biblical in form, it remained biblical in content, providing an impersonal chronicle of historical fact. The mode of discourse attributed to the imperatives of the Morning Meeting is comparable to that of most other pious biographies in the last few decades of the seventeenth century, all of which were published in the interest of religious truth while also seeking to avoid further political controversy.[96] Though none would abandon the principles of their group, all sought to locate grounds for toleration and concord. The desires of individuals were inconceivable in this context. Either a person identified himself with some larger body, and expressed himself in its terms, or he did nothing to identify himself at all – for then there was no alternative to the tradition of pious biography.[97] Therefore, to regard the first-person discourse of seventeenth-century piety as a form of individual expression is to treat it anachronistically, as the finished product of a process of cultural secularization and the individualization of personal experience then only in its infancy, which would not mature until the advent of Romanticism in the early nineteenth century.

In fact, rather than stifle personal expression, the Quaker editorial system actually succeeded in bringing to print a variety of voices and lives the likes of which would not be seen again at least until the advent of the letters to the editor and the obituary columns in the provincial newspapers. Even by 1700, the only means of publication available to a writer unable himself to pay in advance for a complete edition of printed books was a speculating publisher, most of whom could not afford the risk of investing in the manuscript of an unknown writer dealing chiefly with personal experience.[98] The Friends' commitment to print offered their entire membership access to a unique and unprecedented means of subsidized publication, on the condition that writers seeking to use it submit to the editorial judgment of the Morning Meeting. It is impossible to know with precision how harsh this judgment was in practice, because no copies of original manuscripts showing the corrections or "marks" mentioned occasionally in the Morning Meeting's minute book survive. However, if the minutes represent accurately the number of manuscripts actually submitted to it for evaluation, we can at least be sure that comparatively few were either rejected outright or radically altered.[99] Among those manuscripts not immediately printed by the society, some were ordered to be "laid by" because their timing was inappropriate;[100] some were recommended for manuscript circulation, because of the sensitive or esoteric nature of their contents;[101] some were sent back to the author for resubmission because they were illegible or incoherent;[102] some were approved, but for publication at the author's expense.[103] In fact, most works appear to have been "ordered for the press" one way or another with little difficulty. The only writers encountering frequent or extensive problems were the society's chief controversialists, in particular Fox and Penn.

Meanwhile, the Friends' leaders actively encouraged rank-and-file members to compose their own biographical memorials. A minute from the Yearly Meeting of 1688 advised Friends to "put in mind again to draw up a Memmorial of the lords support, to be printed after Decease." This advice expanded upon an earlier instruction from the Yearly Meeting "that always care be taken to bring distinct Accounts of all such Friends as have dyed in Prison or Prisons for their Testimony to the Truth . . . with their Names[,] Ages[,] Dwelling Places[,] Education[,] Callings[,] Time of Convincement[,] And the places of their Travail & Service & Time of Sufferings & Death."[104] From the very beginning of the movement attempts were made to keep comprehensive records of individual cases of suffering, in order to plead to magistrates for relief, and to document the Friends' struggles for the cause of truth; some of these were printed when it was deemed expedient to do so.[105] After the establishment of the Meeting for Sufferings in 1675 expressly to administer matters of relief, the historiographical process became more systematic. Materials relating to individual cases were to be sought out, collected, and written up in brief abstracts by local correspondents working as part of a worldwide network of 110 writers organized and main-tained by the Meeting for Sufferings.[106] This network not only ensured that few Friends would suffer unnoticed, it also provided even the remotest of them with a direct, accessible link to the national membership and its leaders, including the Morning Meeting.[107] By this means Friends were taught the value of personal experience, both their own and that of others, as well as how to preserve it in writing, and how to put it into print.

That these lessons were well learned is obvious from the range of biographical and autobiographical texts individual Friends submitted to the Morning Meeting, and which appeared in print. When an important first-generation leader died, the Morning Meeting itself took the initiative and directed correspondents to enquire after and send to the meeting any and all available books and manuscript papers by or about the deceased, so that a memorial volume could be published. When the materials arrived, a committee of three was assigned to read them over and mark them for the press, one of whom typically contributed a testimony or short preface to the volume. The Morning Meeting did this for William Dewsbury, Alexander Parker, John Burnyeat, Steven Crisp, and, most famously, for George Fox; all but Parker were memorialized individually in a printed book (in Fox's case, uniquely, two folio books).[108] Others took it upon themselves to memorialize the lives of less renowned

Friends. Theophila Townsend's first printed work was her narration of the life of her acquaintance Jane Whitehead, which she submitted to the Morning Meeting's judgment and saw printed in 1676.[109] In 1675 Joan Whitrow contacted the Morning Meeting about publishing a memorial of her only daughter Susannah, who had just died at age 15. The meeting promptly appointed Rebecca Travers to speak or write to Whitrow about it. A manuscript was brought in and assigned to Travers and another Friend to correct, with the meeting's instruction that "what is chiefly to [Joan Whitrow's] owne praise be left out." The result was a collection of testimonies and authentic discourse written and compiled by Whitrow, and introduced by Travers; it was Whitrow's first printed work.[110] Whitrow's was but one of several memorial books written by parents in memory of their deceased children, which together constitute a tiny tradition of their own, sanctioned by the Morning Meeting, it seems, for the edification of Quaker children.[111]

Other books were intended for less specific purposes, and may have been paid for in part by local meetings or the families of the dead. John Beck sent up from Westmorland several testimonies made at the bedside of his recently deceased wife Sarah, which the Mourning Meeting "read & agreed to be printed." The result was John Beck's only printed work.[112] Richard Samble's wife and other Friends in Devonshire prepared his papers and wrote out testimonies to his memory, which were printed; Thomas Briggs's daughter sent up from Cheshire her father's journal of his life along with her own testimony to his memory, printed; John Haydock of Lancashire personally delivered to the Morning Meeting his younger brother Roger's "Journall and Testimonys concerning him in Manuscript . . . to be prused in ord^r to print," which was done under the editorial hand of John Field.[113] As their titles indicate, these books were quite conventional productions. If we put aside the matters of doctrine they contained, the printed memorials of Friends were almost identical in form to the pious *Life and Death* accounts of Presbyterian and other nonconformist ministers appearing at the same time. This should not surprise us, because the Quaker works were meant to serve the same purpose as those of their less radical religious counterparts.

What set Quakers apart from other nonconformists was their remarkable efforts to use print to the advantage of the society. Baptists, Presbyterians, and others imitated this practice, but failed to equal the Friends' intensity. Thanks largely to the Quaker initiative, all pious Protestants by the end of the seventeenth century shared the understanding, expressed anonymously in the preface to the Friend John Burnyeat's works, that

> The *End* of *Books* is the *End* of *Preaching, viz*. Informing the Inquirer, Stirring up the Careless, Stopping the Gainsayer, and Comforting and Building up those, whose faces are turned already *Sion-ward*; and that are attended with many *Exercises* in their *Journey* to *Everlasting Habitations*. And as the *End* is the same, so where the *Servants of Christ* cannot come, *Books* may; that are the *Testimony* of their *Care* and *Ministry* for others: They remain also with us, and are a *Memorial* of those that writ them, when they are Gathered to their Fathers: and by them the *Living* often Converse with the *Dead*; who yet *Die* not but *Live* in their Labours, in the *Children* they beget to god; in their *Writings* they leave behind them, as Pledges of *Love* and *Care* for the Flock.[114]

While it was obviously meant to describe the book as an evangelical instrument (a physical extension of the role of the writer himself as a "pen in God's hand"), this praise also portrays, in muted tones, a certain respect for the individual writer and his labor. It was perhaps the kind of awe a contemporary like Elias Pledger might have felt for the figures of the Presbyterian Richard Baxter, and the Quaker George Fox, the two prominent leaders of nonconformity in the Restoration period, when he encountered the massive folio volumes containing their individual lives.[115] Both Baxter and Fox had carefully prepared their personal papers for posthumous publication, for the vindication of their respective religious causes. But despite these intentions, each text would be read by future generations principally as an autobiography, as a monument to its writer's personal individuality and self-expression, rather than as an impersonal history.

By now two aspects of this practice should be clear. First, deliberate self-representation was not a conscious intention of those who ordered pious biographies for the press. Second, the modern meaning – we might call it a "strong misreading"[116] – of such works was manifest in them as soon as they reached the eyes of their intended audience, an unanticipated outcome which would be repeated increasingly by consumers of such texts in the eighteenth century, to the point where biographical discourse would beget an unholy offspring in the form of modern autobiographical discourse. Pledger's neglected notebook represents for us the first stirrings of a new kind of personal writing emerging out of strong misreading, which would in turn interact recursively with, and permanently change, the very models it set out to imitate. In the eighteenth century biography was secularized, as personal matters of an intimate though less spiritual nature came to replace the universal truths dictated by God. People learned to see themselves as objects of their own making, and biographical discourse served as a prominent site for the construction of such self-knowledge.

Part III
Immediate Precursors:
The Profane

A very considerable Share of veracity is commonly allowed
to [Mrs Phillips's] Memoirs of her own Times, and consequently we may look upon them as a very just representation of the present Age, and, considered in this Light, no
doubt they will do us extraordinary Honour with Posterity
... these admirable Adventures, will afford indubitable
Proofs that Pleasure was the reigning Taste; that Profusion
passed for Magnificence; that Show and Equipage gained
Admittance every where; that Money was the one thing
necessary, and that all Ways of coming at it were esteemed
lawful amongst those who lived in a continual State of
Dissipation. It will teach them, I mean Posterity, how they
came to be left so poor, and whence they derived those
comfortable Legacies of Debts and Taxes which we have
been so charitably disposed to leave. It will point out the
real Causes of those Misfortunes which would otherwise
wear a very mysterious Appearance, explain our Peaces
without Quiet, our Wars without Actions, and our
Expeditions without End. In short, it will shew what Sort
of Folks we were, and thereby serve as an admirable Key
to the History, Politicks, and Learning of the *British*
Nation during the eighteenth Century.

The Parallel; or Pilkington and Phillips Compared (1748)

6

True Confessions
John Dunton and the
Subject of Repentance

It goes hard with the *pride* of human nature, and the
principle of self-love, to take a Review of our past Lives,
and to make a Collection of Mistakes and *Errors*; though
it would certainly be the ready way to amendment, and I
am resolved to give the world a precedent of this nature.
St. Austin informs us, that he who repents is almost
innocent; and I may add, that Confession is the best
companion of sincere Repentance.

The Life and Errors of John Dunton (1705)

Let him whose Fate it is to write for Bread,
Keep this one Maxim always in his Head:
If in this Age he wou'd expect to please,
He must not cure, but nourish [our] Disease;

.   .   .   .   .   .

In Vain the sober thing inspir'd with Wit,
Writes Hymns and Histories from scared Writ;
But let him *Blasphemy* and *Bawdy* write,
The *Pious* and *Modest* both will buy't.

Reformation of Manners, a Satyr (1702)

In 1705 the notorious London bookseller John Dunton published his
own *Life and Errors*, to absolutely no public acclaim. In fact, the
reception of Dunton's book was so chilly that its sales, he publicly
regretted a year after its appearance, "han't bore the Charge of Paper
and Print."[1] What made the book's failure even more lamentable was
that Dunton had produced it as a means to earn himself a quick
profit. Heavily laden with debt (in 1704 Dunton did time in the Fleet,

and completed the *Life and Errors* while hiding from creditors), he desperately needed cash to sustain his trade as a bookseller. To his "mortification," as he explained, with characteristic irony, he therefore became his own hack, and reckoned himself "among the number of Scriblers, for my (present) Income wou'd not support me, did I not stoop so low, as to turn Author."[2] In fact, the *Life and Errors* was among the first of Dunton's projects to identify him on a title-page "in the reputation of the Author," rather than in that of the publisher. But the book failed to raise either the financial or literary credit of its writer in any timely manner. This double failure is remarkable, if we consider that Dunton had by 1705 over twenty years' experience in the book trade, having published at least 300 separate titles bearing his imprint.[3] We might reasonably expect a better assessment of contemporary taste from a person as deeply immersed in it as Dunton was.

What went wrong, and what does this addendum to the list of Dunton's personal errata contribute to our understanding of narrative self-representation in England at the start of the eighteenth century? To answer this question, this chapter will consider Dunton's practice as both a bookseller and an author in the context of late seventeenth- and early eighteenth-century popular print culture. Our venture is justified by the fact that, as we shall find, the activity of entrepreneurial publishers and writers like Dunton accelerated the drift of their culture toward secular institutions, of which the modern autobiography was one. Of course, a number of factors contributed to the broad cultural transformation which began in earnest after the Glorious Revolution of 1688. Here, however, I shall focus on two which seem to have operated in tandem, and so doing also paved the way for the tradition of secular autobiographical practice to follow. Almost hand in hand, innovations in journalistic publishing and in social control occurring around the turn of the century helped to establish in the popular imagination a new form of self-consciousness: the concept of an active, independent, and secular personality – the kind of character perceived as unique and, more importantly, individually responsible for what passed in public (sometimes in print) as his "life." In this light, despite its failure, Dunton's *Life and Errors* was an important text. Dunton's folly is the most substantial early example we have of what was in its day an increasingly common form of personal discourse. In what follows I attempt to account for this fact, and to consider its implications for the advent of modern, narrativized autobiography and the individualist self.

Recently both Dunton and his literary remains have been disinterred by scholars and repositioned within the nexus of discourses leading up to the novel. So resurrected, the *Life and Errors* is now acclaimed as possibly "the first full-scale autobiography in English that is *not* almost totally a spiritual autobiography."[4] The argument for this seminal role is reasonable, yet not lacking in paradoxes, which I want further to explore here. In the many works bearing his name, Dunton loudly proclaimed his predilection for novelty and invention. Whether as a publisher or as an author, he seems always to have endeavored to deliver the shock of the new. As he explained in the *Life and Errors*, "unless a Man can either *think or perform something out of the oldbeaten Road*, he'll find nothing but what his Forefathers have found before him" (pp. 247–8). With this willful precocity in mind, the unpopularity of the *Life and Errors* has been ascribed to the immaturity of its contemporary audience, rather than to any fault of the text or its writer. Dunton's book arrived, we are now told, "a generation ahead of the public taste, pointing onward toward a loosened expressiveness of self before readers were quite aware that that was what they wanted."[5] Apparently Dunton, who died unnoticed in 1732, his assets divided among creditors, suffered in life the fate of the visionary artist largely unappreciated by his contemporaries. Both he and his *Life and Errors*, in short, came out of nowhere, and for that reason rapidly returned thence.

But to accept this interpretation would be, I think, to take Dunton and his work on his own rather dubious terms. Indeed, reading through the variety of Dunton's imprints one gets the impression that a good deal of his discourse was produced with a wink and a nudge, as if it was part of some elaborate but half-baked swindle. This impression is especially strong in texts dating from the latter half of his career, beginning in the late 1690s. Thereafter, he seems to have had regularly to defend himself against the charge of maggotry. While it is true, as we shall see, that Dunton was an innovative publisher, it is also true that he was the P. T. Barnum of stationers in his day. He was expert at putting old wine or even plain vinegar into new bottles, and selling it to a gullible book-buying public apparently eager for the latest literary sensation. Despite the hyperbolic promises of his title-pages to deliver discourses never before seen at large, the texts they fronted were often compilations of extracts from Dunton's previous publications, or thinly disguised paraphrases of works already printed by someone else. The *Life and Errors* constitutes a fine example of Dunton's entrepreneurial chicanery. He closes his prefatory address "to the impartial readers" of it by arguing that "if

PURE NOVELTY will be any Recommendation of this Book, I may expect, that even the *Criticks* themselves will be kind to it, for . . . the History of my LIFE and Errors is . . . wholly gathered from my own Breast; neither is [it] stolen from any thing else, but my own Thoughts" (sig. A5ᵛ). But this puff resonates with irony, which all but the dullest of readers (likely the only truly impartial ones to be found) would have appreciated even before they left the bookshop.

For, despite his claim to be the "author" of his text, a cursory perusal of its contents reveals that Dunton should at best be called its compiler. Though it advertises itself as a "True History" of Dunton's "secret" life (containing a frank confession of his sins which he promised to relate "so far as my Diary serves me"), the whole digested into seven phases (in accord with the "seven ages" of man), each containing an original reflective commentary or, in Dunton's description, "an idea of a new life" showing how Dunton "would think, speak, and act, might he live over his Days again" (sig. A5ᵛ, title-page), the book actually forsakes this self-reflexive narrative project almost from the beginning. The seven stages are in the event but four, with the fourth stage left incomplete. To the end of the third stage, at page 95, which comprises less than a fifth of the book's entire contents, Dunton offers a conventional resumé of his *res gestae* up to the time of his marriage at age 23, narrated in first-person discourse, but largely in the impersonal style of the pious biographies of his day. The "secret history" of sins proves wanting, and the "idea of a new life" proves long on moralistic meditations on Christian topics like filial duty and education and short on the revision of errors. Worse, even in this early portion of his text Dunton seizes every opportunity to interrupt what he facetiously calls "the Thread of History" by inserting discourse by or about people other than himself: letters from his family and lovers, elegies, his father's dying counsel, extracts of sermons, and the like. Of course, as we have seen, there was a precedent for this method of textual compilation in the tradition of pious biography; but typically the interpolated segments of discourse were by and about the biographical subject, intended to demonstrate some quality of his piety. In contrast, Dunton adduces his extra-personal materials seemingly to avoid rather than to attempt representation of his life and errors.

This strategy of digression is fully realized at stage four, where the text finally abandons any pretense of interest in Dunton to become instead a miscellany comprising, among other heterogeneous odds and ends, the text of Dunton's marriage certificate; his wedding-song; a travelogue of his journey to North America; witty dialogues with the colonial ladies, and their characters; a review of some of his more successful publications (with large excerpts from some, running to several pages each); characters of authors, stationers, auctioneers, provincial booksellers, printers, stationers, binders, engravers, rolling-press-men, licensers, and customers; a list of customers whose characters he did not draw, but might possibly do in the future (thus extending the range of those who might purchase a book because their names are printed in it, a scheme which suggests the increasing attraction of print to contemporaries); a "comprehensive view of the life and death of Iris" (his first wife); a list of people he forgot to characterize; a reply to slanderers regarding his debts – all of which extend the text to page 412, where Dunton abruptly and incomprehensibly recalls his personal history, stating: "And so much for that OLD Life I repent of, and that NEW Idea I wou'd (seriously) practice, might *I live over my days again.*" But there remained a considerable amount of unused pages in the quire; so, Dunton carries on, explaining, "Having here some VACANT PAGES, *I shall add a* BRIEF *Character of some Eminent Persons . . .*" (p. 412). They are followed by a relatively short series of additional textual detritus, terminating, at last, with several lines of doggerel identified as "My Last Prayer." Above the "Finis" in the copy at the Huntington Library, a contemporary reader has added, in manuscript, "canst thou Be"; which no doubt expressed the exasperation of even Dunton's most impartial readers. In sum, the *Life and Errors* fails to offer a coherent principle of textual composition and structure which might enable a reader to identify Dunton as its "author."

Furthermore, while the text presents many of the miscellanea as new and original, most of them were neither. For instance, though its title-page advertises "the New Discoveries the Author has made in his Travels Abroad," the passages in the *Life and Errors* describing the places, customs, and persons of New England were lifted from contemporary travelogues and character-writings.[6] The characters of eminent persons used to fill out the last quire had appeared in 1702 as part of a serial project begun and immediately abandoned by Dunton entitled, *The History of Living Men.*[7] And those items which we cannot precisely identify as being already in print we may at least assume were not written by Dunton. Though he entered the trade in 1682 with a catalogue of apparently legitimate and original publications, Dunton very soon began to publish the products of anonymous hacks, whose work he sometimes attributed to respectable writers; he also sold slightly revised versions of his own previous imprints with title-pages implying, if not claiming outright, that the contents were entirely new; and more rarely, though apparently without scruple, material taken verbatim from other booksellers' copies.[8] By the time of the publication of the *Life and Errors*, no buyer familiar with the still quite parochial world of print in England could have imagined John Dunton capable of producing a completely original or novel book.

This is why Dunton candidly anticipated that some would call the *Life and Errors* "one of *Dunton's Maggots*" (sig. A5). In fact, the book is one big joke about Dunton's bad reputation, written specifically for skeptics, the "impartial readers" Dunton addresses in his preface, where he explains that "besides the *Satyr* here and there scattered in this LIFE, there are many things which want a KEY" (sig. A6ᵛ). This key, left wanting in print, is simple: the text is an exercise in irony. Irony explains the jest of the book's full title, which describes Dunton as the "Late Citizen of London," and the work as "Written by Himself in Solitude." Neither statement could have been further from the truth. The only problem was that apparently no one found Dunton's personal puzzle compelling or amusing, least of all those who knew him well (and to whom he probably owed money). For just about everybody, it seems, the *Life and Errors* proved to have been one maggot too many. Dunton's potential audience had seen his lines before, and had in all likelihood grown weary if not angry with the ironist.

Such is my alternative explanation for the failure of the *Life and Errors* to create a ripple in the contemporary pool of literary interest. It also hardly bears remarking that Dunton's text is far from being a "full-scale autobiography" in the modern sense. Not only does it lack a unifying narrative design, its compiler appears allergic to any form of sustained discursive attention to himself. As Dunton explains, in one of his book's few sober and self-reflexive passages, "where e'er I come, I love to be quest at, not known, and to see the World unseen" (p. 320). This quality at least the book adequately represents. Also, ironically, the sections of it which are recognizably autobiographical, in the sense of being a first-person account of Dunton, for the most part follow the conventions of the pious biographies of his day. Though not "spiritual autobiography" in the more radical sense of scriptural prophesying, Dunton's account of himself to the stage of his marriage would not have been too out of place had it appeared in a contemporary anthology of Presbyterian lives.

This is not surprising, given Dunton's extensive contact with the culture of post-Restoration English Presbyterianism. In his "introduction" to the *Life and Errors* Dunton admits that "the world, it is true, has given me that partial and precise name of *Presbyterian*," but he claims to renounce it "for ever" (sig. B2). That was in 1705. Dunton was born in 1659, the son of John Dunton, the minister of Graffham, Huntingtonshire. Dunton's father was the third in a succession of John Duntons who were ministers, and he intended his son to become the fourth. Accordingly, the boy was tutored at home in preparation for university. But he proved an unwilling scholar, and so what learning he had acquired was put to use instead in the book trade. In 1674 Dunton was apprenticed to Thomas Parkhurst who, we will recall from the previous chapter, was Oliver Heywood's publisher, and whom Dunton characterized as "the most eminent Presbyterian Bookseller in the three kingdoms" (p. 281). The seven years Dunton spent in Parkhurst's employ obviously influenced his expertise in trade. The early, legitimate Dunton imprints were mostly works of practical piety. At the peak of his business in the mid-1690s, Dunton joined Parkhurst and two other former Parkhurst apprentices in jointly publishing Sylvester's *Reliquiae Baxterianae*, for which Dunton took subscriptions in his shop.[9] And, upon arrival there, the subscriber would have been greeted by Dunton's wife, Elizabeth Annesley, a daughter of Samuel Annesley, one of the most eminent Presbyterian ministers in Restoration London. Her death in 1697 marked the start of the steep decline in Dunton's business. Though scholars attribute Dunton's difficulties in trade to his dislike of shop- and book-keeping (duties he left to Elizabeth), it may also have been the case that Elizabeth Annesley's presence in Dunton's shop accounted for most of his bread-and-butter custom with her co-denominationists, who abandoned the apostate publisher immediately upon her decease: Dunton issued no works of divinity of any sort after 1697.[10] The strange fact that Timothy Rogers's funeral sermon for her was published by John Harris rather than Dunton suggests the extent of Dunton's estrangement from Elizabeth Annesley's friends and family.[11] Whether or not this inference is correct, it would be understating the case to say that Dunton was familiar with post-Restoration pious biography.

Still, his life was hardly worthy of biographical memorial, as the tradition of pious biography had defined it: Dunton was neither a reverend minister nor even an exceptionally godly layperson. He had no legitimate warrant to promote the memory of his experience with a printed *Life*; what did he think he was doing with a book claiming that "the Burthen" of his discourse was "no less than the Business of the *Christian Life*" (sig. A3ᵛ)? If unsuspecting readers were lured by such bait, few could have taken its meaning literally after reading a few pages. It was obvious that Dunton had no serious evangelical agenda to pursue; his book did not attempt to represent its subject as a true "epistle of Christ." On the contrary, it advertised the "[t]okens of corrupt Nature and intemperate Passion" in Dunton much more than it promoted the dull (but sheet-filling) pirated homilies of his alleged "new life" (p. 8). Yet even his grand promise "to make the World my Confessor, and to publish every Error and Mistake that I can possibly recollect" proved to be false (p. 69). Not far into the *Life and Errors* it becomes evident that Dunton had no clear biographical intention, pious or scandalous. The alleged "life" was a clever package for what amounted to a heap of printed sheets in some way related to John Dunton, cheaply bound and offered for sale at 5*s*. a copy.

Despite this ungraceful or (depending upon one's perspective) downright profane performance, Dunton apparently expected to be regarded by his readers as a wit, if only for his "New and Surprizing" idea of identifying himself to the public in such a bizarre manner (sig. A5). Witty or not, the *Life and Errors* was indeed an unprecedented text. Although before it there had appeared a couple of parodies of the printed pious biography as political propaganda, no person prior to Dunton had attempted to make himself the subject of such a text, either in seriousness or in jest.[12] In retrospect, then, credit is due to Dunton for being one of the earliest in England to attempt to represent his experience in an extensive printed biographical narrative while yet alive. Moreover, in doing so he appears to have perceived the utility of the self-written biographical book as an individual performance able to command considerable public attention, and thereby to influence its estimation of the writer–subject's self-identity. Unfortunately for Dunton, though, he lacked either the genius or will to render his textual performance either memorable or credible.

Where did the inspiration to attempt such a performance come from? Not solely or, I want to argue, even chiefly from the tradition of Protestant biography, despite Dunton's participation in the publication of such works during the early part of his career. Though separately printed memorials of godly ministers would continue to appear throughout the eighteenth century, the golden age of pious biography ended in 1702, when the last of the most eminent nonconformist divines were dead and Edmund Calamy published his *Abridgement of Mr. Baxter's History of his Life and Times*, in which he included an "Account of . . . those Worthy Ministers who were Ejected after the Restauration . . . till the Year 1691." In 314 pages Calamy memorialized the lives of 2,435 persons, mostly Presbyterians, Independents, and Congregationalists, who suffered for the cause of nonconformity.[13] Eleven years later Calamy saw printed as a separate volume his revised version of this account, then totalling 2,523 names, entitled *An Account of the Ministers, Lecturers, Masters and Fellows of Colleges and Schoolmasters, who were Ejected or Silenced after the Restoration in 1660. By or before the Act of Uniformity. Design'd for the Preserving to Posterity, the Memory of their Names, Characters, Writings and Sufferings.*[14] Different versions of Calamy's work were printed throughout the eighteenth century; by the 1770s it was known simply as *The Nonconformist's Memorial.*[15]

Calamy intended his text to be a comprehensive record of individual suffering. To produce it, he explained,

> I took the pains to consult the printed Lives, and scatter'd Characters, and Funeral Sermons, of as many as I could meet with, Collecting thence what appear'd suitable to my purpose. I added an Account of some few, my own Acquaintance with whom, put me into a Capacity of giving their just Character. And had Memoirs concerning several others, (of whom no Account was ever Printed before) communicated by divers Friends in City and Country, who were best able to do them justice.[16]

Though its treatment of individuals was unbalanced – some persons had only the mention of their names, while others received extensive and detailed attention (the account of Philip Henry was the longest: ten pages in its original version) – Calamy's text became the definitive biographical statement of Restoration evangelical Protestantism. It superseded all of the individually printed biographies, copies of which had become scarce even by then. At almost the same time, perhaps in imitation of Calamy, the Quakers compiled their individual sufferings together in a massive, definitive printed memorial.[17] Thus both *Reliquiae Baxterianae* and George Fox's *Journal*, the two compendiums of nonconformity written by the leaders of Restoration religious dissent, were relieved of their broad historiographical duties, and effectively made obsolete (neither was reprinted until the twentieth century). Moreover, the conditions of heroic nonconformity had by 1700 largely been eradicated. The Act of Toleration of 1692 put a permanent end to religious persecution and took the wind out of personal evangelicalism (at least until its revival by George Whitfield and the Wesleys in the 1730s). With the passing of these virtual institutions of English Protestantism, early modern pious biography lost its *raison d'être*, and consequently suffered an immediate irreversible decline.

However, the appetite for printed narrations of personal experience among the broader population actually waxed rather than waned. Throughout the second half of the seventeenth century secular culture continued to expand and diversify, to the point where it threatened to subsume the domain of the sacred. Besides drama, among the most insidious artifacts of the rising secular culture were the newsletter and the serial journal – the half-sheet quarto tract and by the end of the century the half-sheet folio broadside (the modern-day tabloid) – carrying accounts of current events and other matters of ephemeral or occasional interest. Though the English "newsbook" or newspaper originated during the 1620s, its growth accelerated after 1688, in the more liberal political climate, and especially after 1695, when the Licensing Act was allowed permanently to lapse, enabling greater competition and experimentation in all forms of publishing.

The newsbook format stimulated and was itself encouraged by popular demand for contemporaneous information of all kinds. Occasional reports of natural catastrophes, represented as acts of providence (the sacred continued to supply a warrant for many secular interests), were common among the discursive products catering to this taste; but the chief part consisted of accounts of the actions and rationalizations of persons involved in public events. Political traitors and Jesuits, murderers, informers, and other perpetrators of intrigue in the paranoid atmosphere of late Stuart London predominated. Subjects like Titus Oates and the popish plotters, the killers of Sir Edmund Berry Godfrey, the false witness Thomas Dangerfield, and the gangs of people hanged at Tyburn received meticulous attention to the details of their experiences in a variety of "accounts," "narrations," "memoirs," "confessions," and "relations" vying for the urbane reader's attention and the contents of his purse.

In keeping with the historiographical standard established over a century before by Foxe's *Acts and Monuments* and revisited in the pious biographies of Restoration nonconformists, the most successful of these journalistic accounts featured authentic discourse, either the first-person narration of an eye-witness, confessor, or the speeches or writings of the protagonists themselves. The emphasis on detail and authenticity possibly peaked at the height of absurdity with the publication of Thomas Dangerfield's *Memoires* in 1685, while he lay in prison at Newgate under the charge of *scandalum magnatum* brought against him by the Duke of York, for writing a libelous *Particular Narrative of the late Popish Design to Charge those of the Presbyterian*

Party with a Pretended Conspiracy against his Majesties Person, and Government, printed in 1679. The *Particular Narrative* reproduced Dangerfield's "digest" of a written deposition he voluntarily gave to the Lord Mayor and magistrates of the City of London, alleging how he was solicited by friends of the duke to spread false information about a plot by dissenters against Charles II. News of Dangerfield's testimony had leaked out and, as he explained in his *Narrative*, "some others have undertaken . . . to Publish Relations of what I then Deposed; In which upon perusal of the same, I find some things omitted, others mistaken, or not so fully and particularly related as I could wish." He therefore resolved to see printed "a particular and exact Relation of the Designs that were formed against [the Presbyterians], from my own hand."[18] With the appetite of his audience already whetted for precise details of the plot, Dangerfield no doubt earned a hefty fee for the right to print his *Narrative*.[19] Other publishers sought to profit from this affair, and Dangerfield became notorious in London, with nearly twenty different pamphlets by or about him printed between 1680 and 1685.[20] In August of 1684 the Duke, having read and heard enough, ordered Dangerfield's arrest. He was found guilty, fined, and sentenced to be whipped, immediately after which he died accidentally of a blow to the eye from a bamboo cane brandished by a heckling spectator on the road back to Newgate from Tyburn.

The *Memoires*, published while Dangerfield awaited trial, consists of a verbatim transcript of his "Distinct Diaries of his Motions, Receits, and Expences," written, the title-page advertised, "by his own hand," while a fugitive from the law, from Tuesday, 2 December 1684 to Thursday, 19 March 1685, a few days before his arrest. Each daily entry contains three parts: his "Adventures," "Expenses' and "Receits" – the usual contents of a blank pocket almanac, in this case possibly brimming with secret information. But the only remarkable detail it revealed was a record of his robberies. A typical entry runs as follows:

Wednesday, Dec. 3d.

I Rode all day in the Vale of Ailsbury, untill 2 a Clock, and then bad weather forced me into the Oxford Arms, at Thame, where I lay all night, and wrote 3 Letters, one to my Dear, one to my Sister, and one to my Friend.

Of a Farmer in the Vale,	6s.	0
Of a Parson in the Vale,	6s.	0
Of a Woman in the Vale,	5s.	0
Of a Farmer in the Vale,	5s.	0
	22s.	0

Lost 5s.
Demands not paid 5s.
Spent at Thame,   10s. 6d.[21]

The *Memoires* took the concept of authentic detail to its extreme; it was a text perhaps for fans only, intended, as the preface explained, merely "to pick up, and to Furnish Fresh Matter toward the Just History of His Adventures."[22] But many readers had become fans and armchair historians, addicted to petty personal details and whatever else counted as genuine fact. Dangerfield's *Memoires* displays the tendency of newsbooks and related publications to promote in secular culture both an interest in the minutest knowledge of personal experience and, more importantly for us, the authority of texts – whether diaries or complete narrations – composed of genuine first-person discourse. The appetite for news propelled the development of autobiographical discourse in the secular domain.

To be sure, Dunton, the maven of (re)invention, catered to the public's growing hunger from the start of his publishing career. While apprenticed to Parkhurst, he distinguished himself as a partisan of the Whig cause, which put him in position to exploit the anxious atmosphere generated by party politics, of propagandistic innuendo circulated as "news."[23] His own publications, however, largely sacrificed political principle for the sake of personal profit. In 1683, after little more than a year of doing business on his own, Dunton was arrested for his alleged part in the publication of a work entitled *Truth Will Out, or, a Sermon Preached Upon the First Discovery of this New Plot, on the 20th June, 1683, by a London Minister*. Upon inquiry, the authorities found that the text was actually a verbatim transcription of Jeremiah Burroughes's *Irenicum*, published in 1646 – hardly "news" in 1683.[24] Shortly thereafter, in a blatant attempt to inject an old story with new life, he published a *Full and Impartial Account of the Notorious Life of this Present Pope of Rome Innocent the 11th*, written, the title-page explained, "to Revive the Remembrance of the Almost Forgotten Plot against his Sacred Majesty and the Protestant Religion."[25] He also exploited the rise of informers and informing by publishing a little compendium of the practice, called *The Informer's Doom*, which advertised itself as "a Full and Pleasant Account of the Arraignment, Tryal, and Condemnation of all those Grand and Bitter Enemies, that Disturb and Molest all Kingdoms and States, throughout the Christian World."[26] Dunton dabbled in exposés of popery, especially its Jacobite manifestations.

And one of his most successful publications was a *Life* of the perpetrator of the "bloody assizes" of 1685, Chief Justice George Jeffreys, published shortly after Jeffreys's death in prison in 1689.[27] Dunton managed to issue the substance of this work under six different title-pages all in the same year, resulting in the sale of over 6,000 copies.[28] A follow-up, a *Life* of Richard Talbot, Earl of Tyrconnel, the leader of the military forces in Ireland loyal to James II, was also popular, though it does not appear to have sold as well as the *Life* of Jeffreys.[29]

Both of these latter works and the *Life* of Innocent XI exhibit how, in the secular domain, the biographical text had become a popular medium for the transmission of historical fact. However, as in the case of sacred biography, little interest was attached to the biographical subject himself; he was merely an example or, like the metaphor used to describe pious persons, an "instrument" of the larger cause or corporation with which he was associated. While the lives issued by Dunton purported to represent their subjects from the cradle to the grave, the narration of fact in them actually focused largely upon the situation in which the subjects were involved. This impersonal concern is epitomized by the short titles of the lives of both Jeffreys and Talbot: *The Bloody Assizes*, for Jeffreys, and *The Popish Champion*, for Talbot. Jeffreys's *Life* featured "a true Account of his unheard of Cruelties, and Barbarous Proceedings, in his whole Western-Circuit," including as well the experience of the victims of his justice, "[w]ith their undaunted Courage at the Barr, their Behaviour in Prison, their Cruel Whippings afterwards, and the remarkable Circumstances that attended their Executions" (title-page). Talbot's *Life* advertised "a true Account of his Birth and Education, his Advancement and Honours," but also "his Treacherous Disarming of the Protestants, and Cruelties towards them." The latter topic occupied the bulk of the narrative, with "a relation of all the Skirmishes, Battels, Sieges, and Remarkable Transactions which have hapned under his *Government*; with the Particulars of the *late bloody Fight* in the North, the manner of the late King's Landing at *Kinsaile*, with what remarkable has hapned since," and "[a] brief Description of the Kingdom of *Ireland*" (title-page). With such huge loads of impersonal fact to bear, these texts contained little space for the emergence of a pure biographical concept.

But the impersonality of the occasional newsbooks was less pronounced in the biographical subjects appearing in serial journals, several of which catered to a popular interest in matter other than hard fact. In the serials of the late seventeenth century a forerunner of the personal profile or the "human interest" story emerged. Some journals specialized in narrations of personal experience which penetrated beyond the surface of mere fact, to disclose the peculiar emotional and psychological responses of real people to specific historical circumstances. In rare but significant instances not just the variety of experience, but also the variety of human character became perceptible – biographical subjects became personalities in their own right, rather than corporate instruments, patterns, or types. One of the first sustained publications contributing to this development was Dunton's *Athenian Mercury*, the first issue of which appeared on 17 March 1691, as the *Athenian Gazette, Resolving weekly all the most Nice and Curious Questions proposed by the Ingenious*. It was made of a folio half-sheet, and sold for 1*d*. The *Gazette* proved so popular that within a fortnight Dunton was publishing it semi-weekly. He continued to do so with but two periods of suspension, until 17 March 1697, when competition from imitators and his own personal and financial difficulties forced him to quit.[30]

What made the *Athenian Mercury* (early on Dunton changed its name for copyright reasons) so popular is difficult to know for sure from our distance in time; however, we can speculate that the personal and familiar nature of its contents excited the interest of a variety of contemporary readers seeking something more than the unessential trivia and occasional satire which were the *Mercury*'s stock-in-trade. Dunton's innovative format engaged the participation of the public in the production of each issue, and tapped its narcissistic and voyeuristic potential. The "ingenious" proposers of the questions "resolved" by the *Mercury*'s anonymous writers were its readers, whom Dunton encouraged to submit their queries by penny-post letter to Smith's coffee-house (nearby Dunton's shop in the Poultry). In his first issue he offered specimens of the kind of concerns he proposed to print: "Whether 'tis Lawful for a Man to beat his Wife?" "How came the spots on the Moon?" "Where was the soul of Lazarus for the four days he lay in the Grave?"[31] The *Mercury* has been identified as a predecessor of the modern *Notes and Queries*,[32] but such a description fails to reflect the significance of the bulk of its contents, which are more akin to the modern "Dear Abby" newspaper column. While it regularly treated matters of science, magic, and religion, the *Mercury*'s most prominent topics of discussion concerned the more personal issues of love and matrimony. Questioners' letters appear to have been printed verbatim, or digested so as to retain the style and personality of the original. Though their names were withheld from print, correspondents often related their concerns in the first person, and digressed in detail upon their own private experience or that of persons with whom they were intimately acquainted, in a style which still rings true even when the authenticity of a letter might otherwise be suspect. It is likely that the spontaneity, originality, and intimacy of the questions and answers accounted for much of the *Mercury*'s appeal to contemporaries, in the same way that such discourse continues to appeal to the audience for similar texts today.

In effect, the *Athenian Mercury* printed a small yet unprecedented secular body of individual public confession.[33] Literary historians regard it as an important source of the tradition of representing personality in narrative which would eventually culminate in the novel. George Starr, for instance, has argued that the *Mercury*'s treatment of personal matters as secular "cases of conscience" partly initiated the concept of experience as a series of situations, events, actions, and episodes, and the concept of persons as characters with their own "individual identity."[34] To be sure, the lead taken by the *Athenian Mercury* was not limited only to the discourse of the novel. We may also assume that its representation of personality influenced the composition of biographical texts and subjects to the same degree that it did fictional ones. Indeed, I believe, we ought to regard it, rather than the tradition of pious biography, as the main motor driving the idea of Dunton's *Life and Errors*. Doing so will help us further to account for the apparent failure of this text to reach the stage of modern autobiographical narrative.

Though it was his most sustained effort, the *Athenian Mercury* was not Dunton's only experiment in non-news journalism, nor was it the only forum he constructed in which authentic and original first-person accounts of personal experience were prominently featured for mass consumption. Dunton created several other serial or part-publications supplying the burgeoning interest in individual humanity, though he abandoned most of them after one or a few issues.[35] Perhaps the most important of all of his serials for the history of autobiographical practice, because it foreshadowed the concept of the *Life and Errors* most directly, is *The Night-Walker*, which appeared in eight monthly parts from September 1696 to April 1697. Each part was made up of five quarto sheets (with 25–30 pages of text per issue) and sold for 6d. It is impossible to judge precisely the popularity of this work; however, according to Dunton, whose statements we must always regard with suspicion, *The Night-Walker* was "well receivd." Whatever this statement might mean, the fact that he remained interested in the project long enough to publish eight parts, quitting only after his hired writer "was quite out at the *Elbows*, for want of Matter," suggests that it was indeed a lucrative endeavor.[36] If the level of interest of today's public in salacious personal history is any measure, then we can assume that *The Night-Walker* commanded a large and dedicated readership in its day. The full series title describes the essence of its contents, while appealing to the baser desires of readers: *The Night-Walker: or, Evening Rambles In search after Lewd Women, With The Conferences Held with Them, &c. To be publish'd Monthly 'till a Discovery be made of all the chief Prostitutes in England, from the Pensionary Miss, down to the Common Strumpet.* Perhaps because of its subject-matter, literary scholarship has largely ignored this work; when scholarly ignorance has proved impossible to maintain, *The Night-Walker* has been the subject of condescending mention and no serious discussion.[37] But such neglect is regrettable, for *The Night-Walker* is a seminal text in the history of modern autobiographical discourse: it preserves some of the earliest and most accessible examples of personal history narrated by the subjects themselves, in which individual peculiarity is appreciated for its own sake, and the beginnings of a unified structure or plot are apparent in the written narration.

The first issue of *The Night-Walker* presented its readers with an unnamed first-person narrator–protagonist, identified only as "a Good Country-man, Citizen, and Christian."[38] Though this character remained a constant presence throughout the series (except for the last part, when Dunton apparently attempted to take over the writing himself, and invented a pair of handsome young out-of-habit clergy-men to replace him), he is not its main focus of interest. Rather, he is the lens or narrative filter through which the reader encounters the variety of malefactors constituting *The Night-Walker*'s true subject-matter. The good countryman, citizen, and Christian is a kind of vigilante. Out of the sweetness of his bourgeois heart, he takes upon himself the task of making nightly rounds of the seediest sections of London, with the intention of bringing vice to light, in order to see it wither and die. His operation is humane, however: rather than incite further malice by making it the center of a humiliating public spectacle, he fixes upon his prey in the open, then accompanies it back to its nest, there discreetly to reason it into a confession of its errors and a sincere expression of repentance. As he explains to the reader, "I chose this Method of Accosting the offenders in person, where-ever I could have an Opportunity, in such a manner as I thought most conducible to reclaim them from their Errors."[39] The other advantage of this procedure is for the reader: it maximizes the voyeuristic potential of the good countryman's activities, which constitute the principal, though unstated, reason for their publication. Like the true-crime television series *Cops*, now popular in the United States, in which an anonymous video cameraperson silently records every incident of a police officer's beat for home viewers seeking a safe but microscopic perspective on crime in all of its banal detail, each issue of *The Night-Walker* purports to offer a thorough, unedited record of a dusk-to-dawn expedition into the stews of London, from contact in the open street to penetration of the deepest recesses of the backstairs apartment. At the conclusion of the first issue, it whetted the reader's appetite for more, proposing,

> to SEARCH, not only for *Houses of avowed Profanity, but even unto the Closets and Bedchambers* of some who little think, that their Wickedness is so well known as 'tis — Nor shall we confine *our Search* only *within* Doors but shall now and then make a Visit to *St. James' Park, Lincolns-Inn, and Grays-Inn-Walks,* the Playhouses, Musick-Houses, Exchanges, *&c.* And shall also saddle our Horse once a Year, and take a turn to *Tunbridge, Epsom, the Bath,* &c. That, if it be possible, we may Shame the Gallants of *both Sexes* out of these wicked Practices.[40]

The use of the first-person plural in this passage suggests the degree of proximity, someplace just shy of perfect identification, the reader was meant to achieve with the ostensibly "good" citizen in his stimulating ramble. Yet the preface to the first issue of *The Night-Walker* flatly denied its voyeuristic appeal, claiming that "*The Design of the* Undertaking, *is not to minister Fuel to* Wanton Thoughts, *or to please the* prophane Pallats *of the* Beaus *and* Sparks *of the Town, but to display* Monthly *their Abominable Practices in lively Colors, together with their dismal Consequences, in order to frighten or shame them out of them if possible.*"[41]

This defense was actually not as hypocritical as it may seem. In publishing *The Night-Walker,* Dunton took advantage not only of the permanent lapse of the Licensing Act in 1695 and the death of his influential father-in-law in 1696 – the two principal sources of censorship of his endeavors – but also of the new enthusiasm for the suppression of private vice, which acquired terrible momentum shortly after the accession of William and Mary. Dunton seized on the initiative taken by the new monarchs, who with unprecedented energy indicated their desire for a national reformation of manners. In 1689 William wrote to the two archbishops and to the Bishop of

London expressing his concern to restore public order by regulating private conduct and requesting them to read to their congregations the statutes against blasphemy, swearing, perjury, drunkenness, and profaning the sabbath. William's letter also ordered each parish priest to see that his churchwardens presented all persons guilty of adultery and fornication, and to preach often against such sins. Every minister was commanded "to suppress impiety and vice, and to reform all disorders as far as in you lies."[42] Two years later, Mary wrote to the Middlesex justices urging that they set a good example and prosecute immorality. In addition to letters, William and Mary jointly issued a proclamation in 1688, to be read four times a year from the pulpit, in the courts of law, and in public places throughout the kingdom, which acknowledged the divine source of their own and the kingdom's preservation from popish tyranny and, warning that this blessing could be reversed by the population's manifest wickedness, ordered all officers of the law to execute the statutes against profanity and vice. On his own William, and later Anne, renewed these concerns in subsequent proclamations of 1698, 1699, 1702, 1703, and 1708.[43] A sort of war on vice had been declared.

The crown's concern was met with a groundswell of public support, from Anglicans and dissenters alike. Local grassroots "societies" dedicated to the suppression of vice sprang up in metropolitan areas throughout England and Wales during the 1690s. By 1701 there were nearly twenty such groups operating in London and its suburbs, along with at least twenty-three others in provincial towns throughout the kingdom.[44] Composed mainly of younger men employed in the skilled crafts, such as carpentry, coach-, wig-, or shoemaking, or in the trades, such as butchers, bakers, drapers, grocers, and tailors, these Societies for the Reformation of Manners (as they were officially known) met periodically to hear an invited lecturer inveigh against vice, and, so fortified, to pursue their self-appointed duties in society. Chief among them was taking information.[45] As the Anglican minister Samuel Wesley, Dunton's brother-in-law and sometime publishing partner, explained in a lecture sponsored by the London societies, "*Good Manners* are the *Bond and Cement* of all *Societies*, and *good Laws* the life of *good Manners* . . . and they can never be *executed*, unless *Information* be given against those who transgress them." He therefore recommended that the best way for conscientious citizens to assist the magistrates was by informing: "there is no other effectual way but by giving *Information* against *Ill-men* and *scandalous Livers*."[46] Wesley was merely repeating the instructions the Middlesex justices had been propounding to citizens since the receipt of Mary's letter in 1691.[47] In response the societies organized local campaigns to indict, prosecute, and convict targeted offenders. To facilitate this process they saw to the printing and distribution of blank warrants (which enabled persons to give information simply by inscribing a few details into a generic text), an annual "Black Roll" or report of successful prosecutions initiated by the societies (which helped to identify likely offenders as targets of surveillance), promotional pamphlets describing the history of the organization, its rules and procedures, and the statutes it sought to enforce (enabling anyone who could read to organize his own local society), and copies of sermons preached as part of its lecture series, on topics such as the duty to inform, and the wickedness of sin (to provide examples of good conduct).[48]

That Dunton exploited this popular movement almost from its inception should by now be no surprise. In 1694 he published an apparently legitimate tract for "the Society for Reformation" entitled *Proposals for a National Reformation of Manners, Humbly offered to the Consideration of our Magistrates & Clergy.*[49] With high-minded and high-toned piety, the anonymously written main text argued for "[t]he Necessity of a Present National reformation," on the grounds that

> All *men agree, that* Atheism *and* Profaneness *never got such an high* Ascendant *as at this day. A thick* gloominess *hath overspread our* Horizon, *and our* Light *looks like the* Evening of the World. . . . Impiety *abounds, even after our angry God hath* shaken the foundation of the Earth [a reference to the then recent earthquakes in Jamaica and Sicily]; *and that he hath herby, so loudly called the* Christian World, (*to this* Nation *and* City *also, in a more especial manner*) to awake *from deep* slumber, *and to* amend our *ways, by an* Universal Reformation, *of our* Lives *and* Manners. . . . (sig. A2)

The tract also declared a means or "instrument" of effecting this reform; specifically, that

> We who are Inhabitants of the Cities of *London* and *Westminster*, and Parishes adjacent, both in the Counties of *Middlesex* and *Surry* . . . agree, upon our own Costs and Charges to imploy and maintain a competent Number of such fitting Persons, as we shall choose, to assist the several Constables and other Officers . . . in putting in Execution those good laws aforesaid; *viz.* by observing and taking notice of all those, that for the time to come, shall impudently dare, in Rebellion against the Laws of God and Man, to Swear and Curse, to profane the Lord's day, or be Guilty of the loathsom Sin of Drunkenness; also by

searching out the lurking Holes of Bawds, Whores, and other filthy Miscreants in order to their Conviction and Punishment according to Law. (pp. 28–9)

This proposal was followed by a "true relation" of the detection of "several *Barbarous Villanies* and *Murders*" in which some members of the society assisted the London constables, intended both to demonstrate the moral problem and its solution and to *"have some Influence on all Good Men, to Excite their ardent Sighs and Prayers to GOD that he would New-animate our Pious* Magistrates, *and* Clergie *in a more especial manner, to improve their great Interest to Promote and Encourage such a* Society *(or* Societies*)*" (p. 30). The tract concluded with what appears to have been the first of the annual lists of names of persons successfully prosecuted for vice at the initiative of the society, the "Black Roll" for 1693 (p. 34). The next and very last page of the text contained an advertisement for books lately printed for Dunton, among which was "An earnest call to Family Reformation, Price 6d. or 50 of them for 10s. to those Gentlemen that bye them to Disperse." On the evidence of this publication, it appears that Dunton was not only well acquainted with the Societies for the Reformation of Manners and their activities, he even assisted them in carrying out their endeavors, at least indirectly. Thus, superficially, *The Night-Walker*'s claim to constitute a deterrent to vice was consonant with a rationale already in practice.

But the moral legitimacy of *The Night-Walker* is of less concern to us than how it represented contemporary perceptions of reality, especially of personality and self-identity. The assault conducted by the Societies for the Reformation of Manners and their allies directed attention to aspects of personal experience which had hitherto remained largely overlooked and essentially unremarked in public. What matters is not whether the practices being accounted as "vice" were actually on the rise (anyhow, such a fact cannot be proved in the absence of data for comparison), but rather that, by virtue of the attack on them, they attained a presence at the forefront (as opposed to the background) of discursive consciousness. Though many factors contributed to this shift in attention, among them especially those which scholars have recently identified as constituting an "urban renaissance" commencing around 1680 in both London and the provincial towns, much credit is also due to the moral campaign of the 1690s for causing private life to be talked and written about in England as never before. Within this new moral and social discourse, new epistemes of personal experience emerged to occupy the horizon of subjective consciousness, even though, in an objective sense, they had always been present in it. Indeed, what counted as vice in the closing decades of the seventeenth century represented almost a new variety of sin, quite unlike the sins of omission harped on by Tudor and early Stuart divines in England. The public preoccupation with both vice and the literature surrounding it was part and product of a novel conception of human personality.

Though not a complete departure from the so-called "Puritan" tradition in England, the spotlight on vice was largely a component of the new orientation of the Restoration church, which adopted a practical theology intended to be more rational and accessible to everyone, not merely Protestant "saints." The church put away the abstract concept of predestination propounded by Tudor and early Stuart divines and replaced it with a simple doctrine of universal redemption. Securing salvation or grace was made thereby an entirely personal and individual matter, dependent upon a faith expressed in very practical terms; not by Katherine Stubbes's Christ-like mortification but by a new life practiced here on earth, begun in sincere repentance and continued with dedicated self-discipline. Faith was proved by action rather than conviction, by the resolve of the head triumphing over the passions of the heart. Repentance, which had hitherto played but a minor role in English Protestant theology, became the linchpin of this faith. During the Restoration period, repentance was probably the most common theme of Anglican sermons on ordinary Sundays, where ministers expounded it as a process, beginning in "consideration" and self-examination, leading to a sincere breaking of the hard heart in "contrition," and from there to "resolution" for amendment of life. For salvation, successful completion of this process was, as the title of Jeremy Taylor's treatise on repentance put it, *Unum Necessarium*. Likewise, the author of the *Whole Duty of Man*, the most popular book of any kind in the Restoration era, stressed that "repentance is, in short, nothing but a turning from sin to God, the casting off of all our former evils, and instead thereof constantly practising all those Christian duties which God requires of us. And this is so necessary a duty, that without it we certainly perish. We have Christ's word for it (Luke xiii.5), *'Except ye repent, ye shall all likewise perish.'* "[50] But repentance was not to be left till the death-bed; neither was it adequately addressed by "conversion" (which was in the view of the Restoration church a matter of almost blind belief), nor by the Roman Catholic sacrament of penance (which made faith too easy). It was a personal imperative to be undertaken immediately upon one's realization that one was living in sin: in other words, as soon as one perceived the evil course of one's life.

Moreover, despite the absence of penance in its liturgy, the Restoration church strongly emphasized auricular confession as an essential aid to understanding the nature of one's sinfulness, and as an inducement to repentance. As Robert South explained in a sermon, "the disburdening of a troubled conscience ... to some knowing, discreet spiritual person for his advice and resolution ... [is] a sovereign expedient."[51] The resort to confession is consonant with a general emphasis on casuistry in post-Restoration theology, including that of dissenters still clinging to the concept of predestination. By contrast, however, confession and repentance in the doctrine of the Anglican church was not an occasional matter. It was understood to be a single, life-defining action. In confession the penitent soul identified the peculiar downward spiral or chain of causation in his personal history which led to his turning away from God in sin. This consideration would enable the penitent then to renounce his way-ward path, and commit himself to conquering the personal weaknesses and/or circumstances leading to his iniquity. If the confession and repentance were sincere and subsequent self-discipline strong, then salvation was assured. And even in cases where the opportunity for life amendment was absent, such as those of criminals sentenced to death, the confession and renunciation of sin were necessary for any hope of salvation. Hence the intense attention paid to the dying speeches of persons hanged at Tyburn and elsewhere in the kingdom during the latter part of the seventeenth century.

In any event, the significance of this doctrinal turn toward the confession and repentance of sin for the discourse of personal history is monumental: not only did it alter the content of experience by focusing it intensely on those practices which the penitent himself was best able to observe – that is, his own "secret" or individual vices (whereas previously he was trained to notice the signs of God's providence working in and around him) – it also added the element of narrativity to it. In a primitive manner, persons began to be perceived as the products of unique circumstances and actions over which they exercised some degree of control, and for which they could be held individually responsible. Narrations of personal experience in the confessional mode dimly reflected this new personal authority. Additionally, the emphasis on confession and repentance turned the first-person narration of experience into a performance which displayed the moral character of the speaking subject. Salvation depended upon one's being able first to represent one's life-course accurately and sincerely. The predominance of the confessional mode enhanced the dimension of individual conscience in narration. The self as author began to appear in written autobiographical discourse.

Dunton's *Night-Walker*, then, must be read as one of the early artifacts of this reorientation of personal consciousness, displaying the extent to which the secular domain had appropriated the Restoration church's ideas and attitudes. By late 1696, when the first issue of *The Night-Walker* appeared, the momentum of the movement for moral reform had abated considerably, largely because the societies had run aground on the sands of excessive use and abuse of the powers they had assumed. The vigilantes and their cause stood discredited, and subsequent efforts to revive the war on vice were doomed to remain forever on the margins of popular concern. But, despite this failure, the public consciousness of vice it had helped to stimulate, and the correlative interest in private life in general, as well as the confessional mode of representing it in discourse, continued with little inhibition; they even gained momentum. Undoubtedly *The Night-Walker* was conceived for and made successful by a secular readership. Though it made frequent mention of the Societies for Reformation and their cause, it did so to satirize rather than to promote the movement. The good countryman narrator appears not unlike de Sade's Justine, whose prudery leads her into the most ironic of situations, the representation of which is intended as a mockery of her naïvety. For instance, the third number, for November 1696, contained, among other things, lurid tales of child prostitution, the kidnap and rape of a young gentlewoman whose brother sold her to his friend, a clergyman's bigamy, a servant seduced by his master's wife, and an "Act of Uncleanness" (I infer it to be sodomy) between a harlot and two sparks in a public house. Some citizens, possibly members of the society, took it upon themselves publicly to burn this text, the most risqué of the series. Dunton responded by dedicating the next number, for December, to the Societies for Reformation, archly encouraging them to "take heart and redouble your Courage, you have the Laws of God on your side, and tho the Laws of the Land may be partly defective, and partly executed, yet when Vice is brought to the Test, it can never endure the Touchstone, but will hide its deformed countenance under the Cover of Virtue. . . ."[52] Readers likely to have been entertained by such fare were the coffeehouse wits, students, apprentices, and other urbane men-about-town, who turned to the pages of *The Night-Walker* for titillation, humor, and a glimpse of how their neighbors lived behind closed doors.

What they frequently found there, among a good deal of satirical
sermonizing, were several – between six and nine per issue – quasi-
autobiographical confessions of avowedly repentant sinners, printed
either as verbatim transcripts of discourse spoken directly in response
to an interrogation by the good countryman (who filled out the
account with his own additions) or as letters sent in by those moved
to confess by what they had read in or heard about *The Night-
Walker*. Of these discourses, the letters are the most autobiographical. At the end of the first issue, noting that some malefactors had
eluded him in the dark, the good countryman expressed his desire
"that they would send in an account to *The Night-Walker*, according
to Directions, how they came first to be led aside to such Lewd
Practices together with some Demonstration of their Repentance."[53]
The second issue began with a letter, freshly dated 27 October 1696,
commencing thus:

> *Sir,*
> I have perused your *Night Walker*, and cannot but applaud your
> design, therefore in order to the furthering of the same, I think fit to
> give you an account of my own former Wickedness, how I came to be
> engaged in those Courses, and by what means I was reformed, wishing
> that it may have some good effect towards the reclaiming of others
> who follow the like practice: But if it have not, this *poor effort* is one
> of the least things that I owe to the publick, whom I have so much
> injured by my former bad example.
>   I leave you at liberty to put my Matter in your own Words and
> Method, and shall begin my Story.[54]

The text, which occupies four printed pages, followed by a sequel
dated 1 November covering three more pages, appears to have been
transcribed verbatim. Of course its authenticity is suspect, along with
the authenticity of every alleged "Fact" in *The Night-Walker*; but
even so, the lengths taken to create the effect of its reality distinguish
it from previous modes of representing personality, such as allegory
and the ideal-type kind of character pattern. In either its epistolary
form or its confessional content (or in both), this letter and the others
like it in this and subsequent issues of *The Night-Walker* can be read
as predecessors of the quasi-autobiographical novels, such as *Pamela*,
and the quasi-autobiographical apologetic memoirs which began to
appear in England during the mid-eighteenth century.

   In a sense, *The Night-Walker* was not unlike today's *Penthouse
Forum*, with its plausible yet barely credible tales of sexual bravado,
except that whereas the logic of *Forum* is the description of a single

event, the first-person narrations printed in *The Night-Walker* nearly always discover a moral at the end of a chain of episodes, and therefore impose the logic of a rudimentary plot onto the penitent's experience. There was a crime, and then a history leading up to it, which the good countryman always demanded to know, in part because, as he explained, "sincere Repentance was always accompanied by a penitent Confession both to God, and to those whom we have offended."[55] Moreover, the history generated by confession enabled him to highlight a moral at each tale's end. For example, in the case of a 14-year-old girl being enticed away from the Sunday service by two old women who made her steal from her parents and then sold her to a couple who imprisoned and sexually assaulted her, the good countryman explained that "this sad instance may be a Warning to Parents to watch carefully over their Children, and especially to take heed that they keep good Company and observe the *Sabbath-day*, for many thousands have been ruined and brought to shameful Ends, by a failure in those two Points, as appears by the Confessions of most Criminals at the Place of Execution."[56] In fact, this tragic lesson proved in every case to be the only kind the good countryman was capable of dispensing, which made *The Night-Walker*'s little plot-lines rather repetitive, not to say unoriginal. What is important, however, rather than the originality of plot is the grafting of it onto a set of unique, purportedly real, and personal, circumstances, which resulted in the creation, in the case of each confession, of an original personality: an active, responsible, and sincere character confronting a unique and relatively complicated reality, over which he achieves some degree of individual mastery. Besides, readers of *The Night-Walker* were probably not much interested in its morals; if they had been, they would have purchased the text of a sermon instead.

What exactly they were seeking in Dunton's pages is impossible to know. What we do know is that, next to titillation and wit, the chief novelties offered by *The Night-Walker* were action, intimacy, and personality. Previous printed accounts of this sort, dating back to the Elizabethan and early Stuart period, typically treating some "Bloody Murther" rather than sex crimes, were comparatively static and impersonal. They focused on the relation of "Matter of Fact," and largely ignored the disposition and discourse of the perpetrators, which were controlled not by their personal and independent will, but rather by providence.[57] In contrast, *The Night-Walker* featured the criminal conscience as the key to understanding matters of fact. This new emphasis indicates a significant though not yet decisive shift in contemporary consciousness of self-identity. The individual discourses in *The Night-Walker* were neither novels nor modern autobiographies, but they were much closer to these genres than the discourse of pious biography. True, they had in common with all three discursive traditions the ability to elicit a self-reflexive reader response, and thereby to promote the mode of self-identity represented in them. Several letters printed in *The Night-Walker* began by explaining how the correspondent's own conscience was affected by the confessions appearing in previous issues, for instance as follows: "Sir, I have perused all your *Night-Walkers* that have hitherto been published, which brought my own faults to mind, and made my Wounds Bleed afresh, and therefore that other young men may take Example by my Misfortunes to avoid such a lewd Course of Life, I desire you would insert this following Account. . . ." Another candidly began: "*Sir*, Having perus'd yours for *October*, I was in no small surprize to find my self discovered thereby. . . ."[58] But what is distinctly modern about the selves discovered by readers of *The Night-Walker* is their uniqueness and autonomy – a feature of their individual responsibility – in contrast to the universality of previous subjects, whose self-identities were governed by providence. Dunton's short-lived series is perhaps the best early expression of a new first-person voice in written narrative, capable of assuming responsibility for the making of its own individual experience.

Indeed, this is what the *Life and Errors* purported yet failed to be. Though it bears some of the markings of the tradition of pious biography, the basic focus of interest it advertised itself as representing derived rather from the more recent and therefore more "novel" (in Dunton's sense) tradition of public printed confessions of repentant sinners, including, but certainly not limited to, those in *The Night-Walker*. That it was intended to be an extended confessional performance is frankly stated in the opening address "To the Impartial Readers" of the *Life and Errors* where, after arguing the case for the authenticity of his narration, Dunton turned to propound the reason for its publication. As he explained,

> perhaps some may own this Book for a *True History*, that may yet question my Discretion, for Publishing a *Secret History of my own Errors*: To this I answer, He that is asham'd to confess the *Ills* he hath been conscious of, shews too plainly he is *A great many Leagues from Repentance*, and is more in Love with his Sin, than his Amendment; but if *there is Joy in Heaven over one Sinner that repents*: I can't but think my Lamenting my OLD Errors (and resolving on a NEW Life) will set me beyond the VENOM of Ill Tongues (sure I am) no Good Man will

dislike anything that endeavours to promote *A Reformation of Man-ners*, but will love my Design more than my Performance, and approve my Future intended Innocence more than he will condemn the ERRORS of my past Life. *But however 'tis taken, (I am sure) 'tis honestly meant*; for I confess my *Errors*, on purpose to shame my self out of Love with 'em, and do add to 'em, my *Idea of a New Life*, as a Testimony against my self, if ever I fall into the like again.

But seeing I have been too Remiss in the *Former Part of my Life*, for those FEW MOMENTS I have yet left, I'll Endeavour (by the Grace of God) daily to act *Faith* and *Repentance*, and direct all the FUTURE STEPS of my Life towards Heaven; and if after all my Striving, I may bring up the REAR IN BLISS, it will abundantly recompence all the TEARS I have, or can shed for my Sins: And I heartily wish, that all my Readers may Repent of their OLD, and enter with me on a NEW Life. (sig. A6)

Of course, all of this is tongue-in-cheek, because Dunton well knew what those few impartial readers yet unacquainted with the book-seller were about to find out: that Dunton was no more capable of either sincere or sustained confession than he was of publishing an original work. But what matters more than his literary impotence is his appropriation of an apparently common cultural knowledge of confessional practice, which Dunton exploited in order to lure any readers, in his own ironically contemptuous phrase, "so vile, as to nibble at this CONFESSION" (p. 508, misprinted as "244"). In this novel undertaking, Dunton carried early modern autobiographical discourse one major step closer to modernity, by exploring without fully realizing the potential of a printed narrative performance to display an authorial self-identity. The *Life and Errors* was the seminal work of what in the first half of the eighteenth century hardened into a firm tradition of extended first-person confessional narratives printed as books, some of them fictional and some non-fictional. In fact the most successful of the early examples of this kind of text were realistic fabrications, such as the confessions of penitents like "Moll Flanders," "Colonel Jacque," and "Robinson Crusoe." In these works, and those of their less well-known real-life counterparts, the authorial self-identity typical of the individualist regime achieved a form which readers could intuit, and to some degree identify themselves with. Let us next consider some aspects of this practice more thoroughly.

7

The Trump of Fame
Self-Identified Heroes
and Heroines

Perhaps, when I wrote these things down, I did not forsee
that the Writings of our own Stories would be so much the
Fashion in *England*, or so agreeable to others to read, as I
find Custom, and the Humour of the Times has caus'd it
to be.

The History and Remarkable Life of the Truly Honourable . . .

Col. Jack (1723)

Scandal is the only thing that gives Life to Conversation,
and Libel is that single Sort of Writing that is not at present
out of Fashion. . . . Time was, that people looked out for
Books that might mend them, but such our Times are, that
the best Use a Man can make of his Pen is, to shew that
Amendment is an idle thing, and Repentance the only
Crime a man in this Polite Age ought to repent. . . . [Mrs
Phillips] has been infinitely more conspicuous in the polite
World, whose Actions have now employed the Trump of
Fame almost thirty Years, and who by recording them with
her own Pen, will, in all Probability, transmit them as
Monuments of her Triumphs to latest Posterity.

The Parallel; or Pilkington and Phillips Compared (1748)

In the eighteenth century, biographical subjects succeeded where
Dunton failed in his *Life and Errors*: they made themselves action
heroes, both as protagonists in narratives of their lives and as the
persons solely responsible for the configuration and transmission of
the narratives, and thereby earned popular acclaim. Not quite
"autobiographers" in the modern sense, these new biographical

subjects nevertheless emerged in striking contrast to the brave but passive and self-effacing patterns of Christian piety which had dominated the tradition in the seventeenth century.

The genre of biography – we may now legitimately call it that, for this was the period in which "biography" was regularly appreciated as such – was during the first half of the eighteenth century dominated by criminals, courtesans, castaways, comedians, "captains," quacks, and other peculiar characters, accounts of whose personal activities momentarily satisfied the seemingly insatiable popular appetite for novel (that is, deviant) experience. Once exposed to it, even readers of relatively refined taste grew to crave the personal individuality and autonomy embodied in a *Life* of unusual activity. At the same time, because of the volume of public demand for them, written biographical narratives of deviants became valuable commodities in the developing market for books. Early on, only nimble publishers and their hack writers were able to exploit the public's interest. However, by mid-century several biographical subjects had written and successfully published their own texts, bringing the nascent tradition of autobiographical narration to the threshold of its modern form. Through such practice, both the author-subjects and their readers discovered the importance, and eventually the necessity, of exercising discursive control over matters of personal fact. Not only did such control constitute a degree of material and existential personal freedom, it also enabled a subject to negotiate and ultimately to validate his self-identity in an increasingly anonymous and socially fragmented modernizing culture. In short, early eighteenth-century biographical practice emerged as the staging-ground for the individualist self.

Literary–critical discussions of early pseudo-autobiographical novels, such as those by Defoe, make reference, with insufficient clarity, to the mutual development of autobiography and individualism in the first half of the eighteenth century.[1] We may achieve a more precise view of this process if we look past the first-person prose fiction narrative to one of the principal forms of discourse it attempted to represent: the confessions and last dying speeches of condemned criminals and the biographies and autobiographies contrived from them. Though critics have acknowledged the function of criminal confession as a primer of popular taste for what was to come in the novel, we have largely neglected the significance of such confession as a tradition of autobiographical practice in its own right, and therefore have overlooked its contribution to the acculturation of individualist self-identity.[2] Yet this tradition's presence and popularity paved the way for the various apologies and other so-called "scandalous" memoirs which began to appear in the 1740s, which represent the closest precursors of modern autobiographies produced in eighteenth-century England. The discourses of the criminal penitents, the apologists and others writing in this new tradition informed public perceptions of personality differently than the discourses of their antecedents. Whereas the pious biographies represented their subjects as static patterns of self-mortification, the criminal lives strongly implied the personal individuality, agency, and authority of their subjects, many of whom embodied a powerful, charismatic ethos in spite of their physical annihilation by the state. Moreover, the narratives projected this outlaw self-identity far beyond the narrow confines of the criminal's presence in real time and space. Both the modern autobiography and its referent, the individualist self, are unthinkable without the development of the tradition of confessional literature in the criminal lives and the scandalous memoirs. Focusing principally on the criminals, this chapter will discuss the emergence of a tradition of secular confession in the first half of the eighteenth century, and the changes in self-identity accompanying it.

The office of the "ordinary" or minister of London's Newgate Prison and the authentic accounts of the last dying speeches of executed criminals published at his initiative have attracted the interest of historians, largely students of crime and public order in the eighteenth century, who have analyzed the printed texts and aspects of their production and consumption as evidence of the relations, both social and cultural, between the lower orders and those above them.[3] In the pursuit of their interests, these studies have outlined the practice of early modern criminal confession; yet much of it still remains obscure to us. For example, we have been told that, in the eighteenth century, "[a]s soon as a condemned prisoner learned the day of his execution, he immediately turned his final hours to writing his autobiography which would be sold at Tyburn."[4] Although, as Hogarth's engraved image of the hanging of Tom Idle in the well-known series "Industry and Idleness" suggests, last dying speeches were hawked at executions, the practice of making and distributing a confession was actually more complicated than we have been led to imagine, as it was the result of a tradition informed by a variety of competing concerns – few of them expressing the desires of the prisoner himself, at least at first. It is also very likely that the vast majority of condemned prisoners throughout the period were incapable of writing their names, let alone their autobiographies. And of course if a prisoner did actually compose his own first-person narrative of his life, he would not have identified it as an "autobiography," because the form was not yet available to him. Thus, further exploration is warranted.

Almost from the beginning of the institution of Tyburn (the place of execution of capital sentences), a criminal facing imminent death might profess at least his guilt or innocence in an auricular confession addressed to the magistrates and public assembled to witness his execution.[5] However, it is uncertain whether the practice of scaffold testimony was mandatory. By the mid-fifteenth century, if not earlier, the carrying-out of capital sentences incorporated a ritual process of preparation of the condemned, to ready him for his death, which included the taking of a confession by a designated auditor. For example, Gregory's chronicle of London for 1467 mentions the execution of a brace of thieves who had stolen from the sacristies of London churches as follows:

> And the same daye that they shulde dy they were confessyd. And thes iiij docters were hyr confessourys, Mayster Thomas Eberalle, Maystyr Hewe Damylett, Maystyr William Ive, and Maystyr Wylliam Wryxhan. Thenn Mayster Thomas Eberalle wente to masse, and that lokyer aftyr hys confessyon might see the blessed sacrament welle i-nowe, and thenne rejoysyd and was gladde, and made an opyn confessyon by fore the iiij sayde docters of devynyte. And I trust that hyr soulys ben savyd.[6]

These confessions were probably made privately, within the confines of prison, rather than publicly at Tyburn. Whether the condemned were either required by the magistrates or themselves volunteered to repeat their statements later at the place of execution is not clear, but the practice of scaffold testimony continued. By 1500, thanks partly to the advent of paper – that practical, portable writing substance – confessions were being taken beforehand in writing, and read out by the condemned as he stood on the scaffold.[7] It is likely that anyone who could not write had his words recorded by a scribe or a priest with the necessary skills, and that if he could not read his "paper" would be read for him at Tyburn by a designated official, upon the conclusion of which the penitent might testify to its veracity.[8] An Elizabethan engraving depicting the scene of an execution shows a prisoner with the noose about his neck standing with his hands clasped in prayer and his eyes directed heavenward; beside him in the cart is another person, possibly a minister, holding a handwritten paper which he appears to be reading to the prisoner and the assembled crowd: perhaps the text is the prisoner's confession.[9]

Probably extempore confession continued to remain an option, as did giving no confession at all.

The practice of making rehearsed statements in public seems to have become increasingly common during the sixteenth century. It has been suggested, on the basis of the formal consistency of several surviving texts of such discourses, that many confessions were actually written by the magistrates or their representatives for the broken and condemned prisoner merely to assent to, even in the case of fully literate and knowing persons sentenced for treason, such as Thomas More.[10] Whether or not this inference is correct, the authorities did approve and even ordered the posthumous publication of either the examination at trial or the private confession (or both) of certain prisoners, by means of printed tracts. From the monarch's point of view, the impact of justice could thus be projected beyond the courtroom and the place of execution into distant memory. Of course printed texts could serve the memory of the malefactor's cause equally well. John Foxe, for instance, drew upon printed accounts of heresy trials and executions, some of the first of such texts, in compiling his *Book of Martyrs*. Yet, despite their double-edged quality, by the reign of Elizabeth, official accounts of murders and acts of treason, and the trials and executions of the perpetrators, were frequently committed to the press, sometimes in competition with ballads and other unauthorized versions of the same events.[11] The authorized tracts typically contained an anonymously composed, succinct third-person description of the crime, trial and execution, with a paraphrase of whatever words the condemned uttered, said to have been "penned by" or "taken from the mouth of" him. In these accounts, as in the accounts of the deaths of saints like Katherine Stubbes, value was placed on authentic discourse, either spoken or written; also similarly, the voice of the prisoner was established to affirm the larger order, rather than his individual interests.

During the Elizabethan period a figure acting in the role later designated as that of "the ordinary" first appeared in descriptions of the scene at execution time. He is identified as "the minister," who exhorts the condemned man "to be penitent for his sinnes."[12] The emergence of the minister urging repentance at this time is puzzling, given the permanent turn taken by the Elizabethan church toward a more Calvinistic liturgy, without the popish sacrament of penance. However, the practice of making a confession after condemnation was by then an institution, and priests had undoubtedly assisted the condemned to prepare for death much earlier than this, despite their absence from contemporary accounts. We can assume that the role played by the Elizabethan clergyman was viewed as customary; at any rate, it could be interpreted as a necessary duty under the offices for the Visitation of the Sick.

The first person named as a regular visitor and minister to the souls of Newgate prisoners was Henry Goodcole, who in 1618 wrote a pamphlet entitled *A True Declaration of the Happy Conversion, Contrition, and Christian Preparation of Francis Robinson, Gentleman.* Possibly the earliest work of its kind still extant, this text indicates the official understanding of the relations between the Newgate minister and his hapless flock of gaolbirds, as well as the substance and style of criminal confessions, in the seventeenth and early eighteenth centuries. Its title-page describes Goodcole as "a Preacher of the Word of God" (although he was not beneficed by the church until 1637, as curate of St James's Clerkenwell), and as a "daily Visiter" to the prison. Goodcole's epistle to the "Christian reader" of the *True Declaration* explains that he wrote it *"for the publique good of my Countrey, to admonish them to take heede by other mens hurts and harms."*[13] The substance of the text is a compilation of discourses uttered by the condemned prisoner Robinson, Goodcole explained, "as he himselfe related to me" (sig. B). They are identified as follows: "the prayers wherein he was exercised day and night"; "certaine deuout inward comforts by him continually uttered and used" (each begins with the phrase, 'god grant me . . .'); "a prayer he said at the time of his death"; "portions of scriptures whereon he continually meditated, after these prayers were ended"; and "[h]is owne relation of the beginning and proceeding in his foule fact, spoken the same morning a little before he went to his execution." The last of these is the longest, and constitutes the confession proper. It is nearly a complete, though compressed, autobiography leading up to the commission of the crime. Goodcole's introduction to it reveals his own sense of administering care to the terminally ill soul, while at the same time certifying its authenticity as a record of fact: "So soone as ever I came unto him, he did like a poore, sicke, and wounded patient, desirous of cure, tell his whole griefe, not mincingly or sparingly, but faithfully and truly, that I might better apply and endeavor to comfort him, the beginning of his evils he tolde me, and how hee grew worse and worse by degrees, the manner he related, and as neere as I can from his own mouth spoken, delivered here the same" (sig. Bᵛ). But Goodcole was really ministering to the living, as appears in the moral he transmitted from Robinson to the reading public, to finish the relation:

And thus he concluded: Let all take heede, and beware of couetousnes, content themselves with what they have, labour honestly with their hands to their owne living: for the honest and industrious Labourer, God will ever blesse, but they that doe trust in lying vanities, to get wealth by deceitfull meanes and wiles, let them know, said hee, that though God for a while forbeare them, yet his Justice requires to render vengeance to them, as justly on me now he hath done. (sig. C3ᵛ)

Goodcole's text renders Robinson's words throughout in a third-person paraphrase as in the passage above, though Goodcole was careful to explain that "these were the wordes proceeding out of [Robinson's] owne mouth" (sig. B2ᵛ). This indulgence in Robinson's discourse was justified, according to Goodcole, because "[d]ying mens wordes are ever remarkable, & their deeds memorable for succeeding posterities, by them to be instructed, what vertues or vices they followed and embraced, and by them to learne to imitate that which was good, and to eschew evill" (sig. A4). Under Goodcole's treatment, Robinson represented the evil and more secular inverse side of the Katherine Stubbes coin.

To be sure, Robinson's subjection to Goodcole's ministration – to his discursive purges and moral balms – appears suspiciously ideal. Today's reader, if not an earlier one, is likely to wonder how much of what Goodcole reported as verbatim speech was actually uttered by the prisoner himself. Though impossible to resolve, this concern merits attention because it highlights the almost total control enjoyed by the minister of the Newgate congregation over the prisoners' confessions. In a sense, the minister was the author of their discourses, as he was the person responsible for initiating their production and transmission. We can see this in a different pamphlet by Goodcole, this one the case of a woman convicted of witchcraft in 1621. Here Goodcole made clear that the chief duty of his office was to elicit a confession from the condemned prisoner as a necessary preparation for death, "which is alone pertinent to my function . . . and to declare vnto you her Confession *verbatim*, out of her owne mouth delivered to me."[14] As much as it was his function to act as physician to sick souls, it was also Goodcole's duty both to obtain and to publish the prisoner's discourse as a public service. Indeed, in his prefatory "apologie to the Christian readers" of the same text, Goodcole explained that he had not wanted to reproduce the confession, but that he was forced to prepare it for the press because, he wrote, "I could scarce at any time be at quiet, for many who would take no nay, but still desired of me written Copies of this insuing Declaration." He added another reason: "to defend the truth of the cause, which in some measure, hath receiued a wound already, by most base and false Ballets, which were sung at the time of our returning from the Witches execution."[15] Hence the official version was published, as the title-page stated, "by Authority." Everyone looked to Goodcole for the authoritative version of the confession, despite its having been made orally in the chapel at Newgate in the full hearing of visitors, and a written copy of it read out before the public assembled at the place of execution.

The concentration of authority for the confessions in the person of the minister made his position a potentially lucrative one, especially in cases of crimes of some renown, because monies from the sale of the confessions to booksellers for publication were allowed him as a perquisite of the job of obtaining and preparing them. This potential for profit increased as the print market developed and expanded in the course of the seventeenth century. But after Goodcole's death in 1641 it seems that no one immediately replaced him in his post at Newgate. Reports of crimes and criminal confessions continued to be issued ad hoc, but from a number of different, usually anonymous, hands, none claiming the authority asserted by Goodcole. This situation continued even after the Restoration, until 1684, when the London Court of Aldermen decreed that the sheriffs, who organized the executions, should act as licensers for what they called "[t]he Speeches of the Malefactors."[16] This year marked the start of a serial publication entitled *The True Account of the Behaviour, and Confession of the Criminals . . . Executed at Tyburn*, later known as *The Ordinary of Newgate, His Account of the Behaviour, Confession, and Dying Words of the Malefactors who were Executed at Tyburn* (referred to below as the *Account*). In its original format the *Account* was a folio broadsheet printed on both sides and written by Samuel Smith, the ordinary of Newgate since 1675 (by appointment of the Lord Mayor, whose personal chaplain may in previous years have had the duty of acting as minister to Newgate prison), and published by a succession of seventeenth-century London trade publishers, who simultaneously published a companion serial, of similar format but anonymously written, begun in 1683 and licensed by the aldermen, entitled *The Proceedings on the Kings Commission of the Peace, Oyer and Terminer, and Gaol-delivery at Newgate, held for the City and County of Middlesex, at Justice Hall, in the Old Bailey* (referred to below as the *Proceedings*).[17] Together these serials represented the voice of authority in the spectacle of late seventeenth- and eighteenth-century English crime and punishment. Though Smith's name had appeared on a handful of criminal texts issued shortly before 1684 (and a printed sermon, dedicated to Sir Robert Viner, the Lord Mayor of London, in appreciation of his appointing Smith to the post of Newgate ordinary), the *Account* marked his entrance into the field of journalism proper.[18] The *Account* was published on average about eight times a year, on the morning immediately after each execution day. Mercury-women and other peddlers of ephemeral and chapbook literature cried it out in the streets, and sold it for a 1*d*. (3*d*. by 1725; 6*d*. in 1730). This practice was followed by Smith's successors after his death and replacement in 1697 until about 1760, when the *Account* finally caved in to competition from the daily newspapers.[19]

Smith's serial offered basically the same explanation for its existence as Goodcole's texts. In a slight twist, perhaps in order to puff his own success as a healer, Smith adduced the malefactors' own desire (rather than an official one) to see their confessions published:

> Now whereas several Malefactors condemned to Dye, do in the Prison of *Newgate*, desire the Ordinary to Publish their Conferences with him, thereby giving an account of their Penitency; and to warn others by their Example of suffering Justice, to avoid the same Crimes. The Ordinary thereupon thinks it a necessary Service to give a faithful Account of the said Condemned Malefactors Behaviour; hopeing thereby it will be a means to reclaim Vice in Youth.[20]

Smith also mentioned the old scourge of "false" reports.[21] Despite the licensing of the speeches, competing unofficial accounts of crime and confession continued to be issued without direct suppression by the authorities, which only raised the level of public interest in the perpetrator and his execution. Large crowds had attended Tyburn events in the past; an eye-witness to the hanging of two men convicted of robbing a booth in Bartholomew Fair in 1538 estimated a crowd of 20,000 was in attendance.[22] This number seems greatly exaggerated, at a time when the total population of London and its suburbs was at most about 120,000. Still, by the end of the seventeenth century, crowds of several thousand regularly turned out to see the malefactors they had read or heard reports of turned off. This trend continued throughout the nineteenth century, until public hangings were abolished in 1868. A record crowd of 80,000 attended an execution in Moorfields in 1767.[23]

The heightened awareness and particular expectations of spectators at executions created a new angle for the ordinary to exploit in his serial. According to Smith, the public now expected the performance of an auricular confession at Tyburn as part of the spectacle of execution. But he noted sympathetically that often the condemned "are somewhat Averse to it there, by reason of the Noise of the People, [and] besides the Consternation which is upon them, being ready to be Executed, makes them say little."[24] In the carnival atmosphere which prevailed during the procession to Tyburn and at the turning off itself hecklers, both verbal and physical, frequently harassed and intimidated the condemned – recall how poor Thomas Dangerfield, who was sentenced only to be publicly whipped, actually died after being struck by a spectator during the procession back to Newgate following the execution of his sentence. Though few were subject to abuse this extreme, others suffered severe humiliation in the presence of the crowd. The celebration and support of the malefactor as hero which some historians adduce to argue for a turning upside-down of a state-run display of power in public executions may have been the exception rather than the rule. In any event, even when a confession was made, not everyone in attendance could hear it. Smith's publication therefore guaranteed provision of the details should the malefactors' Tyburn performances fail to satisfy popular expectations.

Scholars still have much work to do before a satisfactory explanation of the early modern emphasis on public confession at executions can emerge. Both the Foucauldian thesis that it was a component of a theatrical display of state power, in which the criminal acted as a compelling spokesperson for the law, and its antithesis, that it was part of a charivari, an elaborate skimmington ritual conducted to critique the power structure, have been put forward to explain the execution procedure as a whole.[25] A third alternative, attempting to mediate between the other two extremes by emphasizing the *frisson* of horror or disapproval in some of the early printed literature of crime and punishment, has also been advanced.[26] While each of these interpretations offers valid and illuminating views, they all aim high, and overlook fundamental contemporary concerns about the nature and function of personal confession. In the previous chapter I noted the emphasis placed by the Restoration church upon repentance, which obviously underwrote the role of the Newgate minister as healer of individual souls, and may have been responsible for the official revival and institutionalization of the office of ordinary after 1675. But the process of individual salvation need not have involved the public so intimately as it did in the case of the condemned malefactors; according to the Church's prescription, confession to one auditor alone sufficed. There

172   *Immediate Precursors: The Profane*

was, however, an additional dimension to the theory and practice of penitence linking the individual malefactor to the local community and the nation, and obligating a public confession from him. According to the divine Christopher Love, a public confession is required of an individual person, "[i]n case of publique scandal given to the Church, whereof thou art a member, by falling into some notorious and known sin, when thy sin becomes scandalous and known to all that live about thee." This was typically the case with persons whose crime warranted the extreme sentence of death – word got around, especially with the publication of the *Proceedings*. Furthermore, Love added, public confession

> is equitable, because the Communicants of a Congregation, of a Church, are offended by thy scandal, and whilst thy sin is notorious they are scrupled: therefore there must be a publick repentance. And besides, publick scandal may bring Gods wrath on the Congregation, if the offender doth not confesse his sin. . . . Therefore for the good of Congregation and Church, whereof thou art a member; if thy sin becomes notorious and known, thou art bound to confesse it; not that every private sin must be confest to the Church, but in case of publick scandal, thou art then to compensate the congregation by manifesting thy confession.[27]

Though Love speaks of the "public" as comprising only a church, the term applied also to the nation (which was still considered the same body as the Church, despite advancing secularization); indeed, this relation between individual sin and the moral and physical fate of the nation lay behind William and Mary's call for a national reformation of manners in the late 1680s and thereafter. The public turned out to witness executions in part because it understood this relation, as the following printed description of the procession to Tyburn of two men convicted as accessories to the murder of Sir Edmund Berry Godfrey during the anxious period of the Exclusion Crisis makes clear:

> By the vast Multitudes that crowded to see them pass, and the general sense of the people, it was apparent how zealous the English Nation in general, and particularly the whole City is, in their respects to His Majesty, and how concern'd to bring all those to just punishment, that shall make any attempts against His Sacred Person, or endeavour to destroy the Protestant Religion, and introduce abominable Popery.[28]

The popular appreciation of the nation's connection to individual conscience and demeanor was, besides the baser lust for titillation, a major motivation for the public's zeal to see criminals confess, and explained the ordinary's concern to get his *Account* out and into print. By the late seventeenth century actual Tyburn performances involving criminals, magistrates, the ordinary, and spectators were enacted as extreme continuations of a relatively new and still expanding public discourse about individual conscience.

The *Account* consistently offered the same contents: the text of the ordinary's sermon preached in the chapel at Newgate on the Sunday before the scheduled day of execution; a brief biography of each condemned prisoner (decanted from his confession, if one was made; if not, the ordinary stated what he knew, usually name, age, and occupation) with a statement of his "disposition" (whether or not the convict admitted his culpability, expressed remorse, etc.); concluding with a description of his behavior at Tyburn (whether the prisoner showed signs of a penitent death). The biographical section, which reported the substance of the ordinary's attempt to get the prisoners to give some "account of their evil Lifes,"[29] is the most relevant for us, because it offers archetypal examples of the eighteenth-century criminal *Life*. Though the individual lives printed in the *Account* were filtered through the ordinary's moral sieve, so that only a chain of escalating evil actions was retained as their essence, and were presented not for their own sake but for the purpose of controlling public order, each did nevertheless constitute an original, individual autobiography in miniature. Consider the following two discourses from the *Account*, which are typical examples of their kind:

IV. *George Segar*, Condemned for Burglary, aged 26 Years, Born at *Portsmouth*. After his Father and Mother died, his Sister took care of him for a while, and she not being able to support her self, left him to the Parish to keep him, the Overseers of which placed him out to Spin Pack-thread, he left that Employment and took bad Courses; he was addicted to Gaming, Lying, and Stealing, to Swearing and Drunkenness: He wept and said, that it grieved him that he had Sinned against Christ who suffered Death on the Cross for Penitents, and hopes when he dies he shall come into a better World, tho' he was perswaded to commit this Crime, and that all his Sins now lye heavy on his Soul.

VI. *William Pierce*, Condemned for Treason as a Coiner of false Money: He said that his father intended him for the Study of Divinity, but he rather fancied to get skill in Physick, this he Practiced fourteen years, and that he thought he was bound in Conscience to give Physick to the Poor without paying for it; he confest that while he was a Youth he was often Drunk, but hath ten Years past been very sober; he Confest that his general faults were numerous, of which God in his

Mercy had made him sensible; he said, that he hopes he is prepared for Death, and that tho' he cannot weep as some do, yet that his Heart is truely contrite for all his Sins: My greatest trouble said he, is for the Diseases of my Soul; my sins are a Leprosy which make me unfit to appear in Gods sight, but with an humble Obedience and a contrite Heart I Prostrate my Self before his Foot-stool, for the Pardon of all my Sins, and with a steadfast Faith believe that Christ is able to save to the uttermost such who come to God by him. Oh that my saviours Blood may be a Balsame to heal all the Diseases of my Soul! I hope he was Penitent.[30]

These discourses, like the majority of the autobiographical confessions printed in the *Account*, were originally composed orally by the prisoner and transcribed and edited for subsequent publication by the ordinary or perhaps a paid assistant. In each case, the basic outline of the tragic plot is bare; all that is wanting to make it a complete narrative is more detail – fuller characterization and amplification of particular incidents.

In other instances, likely those of convicts able to write (though we cannot be sure who actually did the writing in any particular case, with only a printed text to go by), the *Account* reproduced verbatim the discourse of a written confession. For example, at Tyburn on 25 September 1696 Thomas Barlow, convicted of coining false money, "offered a Paper, and desired it might be printed," which the ordinary included in his *Account* for that day, as follows:

As I am noe going to depart this World, and launch out into Eternity; I hope God will give me that Grace not to dye with a lye in my Mouth, being willing to give some accompt of my former Life: I was born in the Year 1666, my Father had a small Estate, the which he lived above, but died in my Infancy; my Mother survived him two Years, at which time my Estate being then entangled, I being about Nine years of age, went to serve a Person of Quality, in the nature of a Page, in which station I remained Seven or Eight Years: after which I aboad five Years with one of her Sons, till I came to the Stature of a man, at which time I sailed up the *Straights*, in order to learn the art of Navigation, upon great promises of preferment, but the Commander did not prove so kind as I expected, which caused me to be extravagant in those Parts, and as soon as we returned into *England*, I left him, without taking any leave or acquainting any Friends therewith; getting most of my things on Shoar by stealth; during which time I got into Company with a young Woman, that helped me to make away with what I had, and after brought me into ill Company, to follow this course of Life I now dye for: I do not deny but that I have done many ill things, but not lately; neither do I deny this I dye for I protest as I am a dying Man, the Oath that *Anderson* Swore against me was wholly false & untrue, for I never had any discourse relating thereto as I hope to receive Mercy at the Hands of the great God of Heaven, any farther then when he charged me; I desire him to get a *Habeus Corpus*, to move me to *London*. Many People may be apt to cast Reflections on my Wife, and think she hath brought me to this untimely Death, but I do declare to the contrary: for would I have taken her Advice I never had known any of these Misfortunes, for it was wholly against her consent I engaged my self in any such way, the thoughts of which are very horrible to me at this time having a greater detestation against Sin, then ever I had a love for it; which I hope God will confirm in my Heart, and grant me salvation through the merits of my beloved Saviour, Jesus Christ.[31]

The appearance of this text in the *Account* was unusual. Most confessions given in writing by prisoners (or at least those identified as such by the ordinary) were printed separately as individual texts of their own, usually at the initiative of the ordinary but sometimes by friends into whose hands the prisoner delivered his paper, either beforehand in prison or at the place of execution.[32] However accomplished, separate printing was the normal procedure for publishing original and authentic written papers, which were usually too long to fit into the single-sheet format of the *Account*. The imprints on these works, most of them single-folio broadsheets or pamphlets of no more than six pages, indicate that they were handled by trade publishers (often the same ones responsible for the *Account*), who dispersed them in large editions (1,000–2,000 copies each) with rapid sales. Though small, this body of penny-printed texts constitutes the immediate forerunner of the modern autobiographical tradition.

One of the earliest of the separately printed written confessions to survive is the twenty-five-page quarto pamphlet version of the "last speech upon the ladder" of Nathaniel Butler, an apprentice cloth-drawer convicted of murder and executed in London in 1657. Butler's printed discourse, whose title-page described it "[a]n Exact Relation of his Life, from his Cradle to his Death. . . . Written with his owne Hand," was much longer and more detailed than that of Barlow, quoted above.[33] According to the preface to Butler's text, Butler was urged by a "friend" to write his story to counter the information published in a "lying scandalous pamphlet unjustly called his life & death" by an "unworthy" unnamed scribe "whose aim was at no better end than self-interest, taking all opportunities to inrich [himself] by so grosly and basely abusing others."[34] Butler's experience at the place of execution demonstrates why most confessions delivered from the scaffold fell short of complete life histories. An eye-witness to the event wrote that having ascended the ladder, Butler began his last speech unto the People; and but for the Presse and Noise of the Multitude he might have been heard afar off; for he stretched his voice exceedingly to be heard, insomuch that spending himself in reading of his Papers, he was seen to sweat very much, which occasioned his often wiping of his face, and encreased delay, so that he was desired to abbreviate himself in what he had to say, which accordingly he did; and delivered his papers into the hand of *Mr. Yearwood* [the Lord Mayor's chaplain, ministering at the execution] or some other of his acquaintance.[35]

Though they insisted upon having a confession spoken to them, the witnesses to executions demanded also that performers keep their discourses to a minimum. Anything extending beyond the length of time needed to read a paragraph or two was interpreted as a tactic of delay.[36] Perhaps that is why Richard Foulkes, the minister of Stanton Lacy in Shropshire, who was executed at Tyburn in 1679 after being convicted of infanticide, reassured the crowd assembled to watch him turned off that "he intended not, nor did he hope they expected any long speech there, but that he had otherways taken care that his confession should be printed and published at large, better than he could there express it in a few words."[37] Of course the weather may have been a factor as well: Butler was executed in August; Foulkes in January. On occasion the shoe was on the other foot, so to speak, and the crowd made the condemned person impatient. Margaret Clark, a domestic servant convicted of setting her master's house afire, for which she was sentenced to die, expressed her exasperation with the crowd, members of which kept interrupting her prayers with questions about her crime, to which she responded: "I have given an account in Writing, which I hope will satisfie the World; for I take God to witness, that all that I have written in that Paper is true: O Lord thou knowest I would not lie, I am coming to thee." The sheriffs immediately demanded to see this paper, which was written by another hand and signed by Clark, and then in the possession of the ordinary; afterward, it was printed, as the text's title-page attested, "for general satisfaction."[38] Situations such as these illustrate the willingness of malefactors to satisfy the public's demand for a succinct scaffold speech on the one hand, and its large appetite for detailed information on the other.

A cursory review of extant texts indicates that the practice of issuing separately printed copies of authentic confessional papers to supplement the discourses spoken at Tyburn increased steadily during the course of the late seventeenth and early eighteenth centuries.[39] A number of factors probably contributed to this trend, such as the improved level of writing skills among prisoners; the energy of the ordinary, at whose discretion official versions of written papers were ordered to be printed; the energy of publishers wanting to issue pirated or unofficial papers; and of course the willingness of the public to consume such texts. At the turn of the century all of these factors seem to have been on the rise simultaneously, especially the latter three. John Allen, who succeeded Smith as ordinary, was actually dismissed from his post by the London Court of Aldermen for extorting money from prisoners and for excessive license in taking and printing their confessions, some of which he apparently invented. Among other things, Allen was charged with "frequent prevarications in the printing and publishing the pretended confessions of the respective criminals that are executed at Tyburn, contrary to the duty of his place and function."[40] Allen's successor, Paul Lorrain, the most renowned of the ordinaries, was subject to similar charges, though he was never dismissed from his post.[41] A satirical look at Newgate published in 1717 singled Lorrain out for "Sincerity and Plain-dealing" in his capacity as ordinary. The work further complained that "the Characters of those Persons employed to induce [the prisoners to confession] are as low, as their Salaries, and under the Pretence of Benefiting others by the Terrors of Offenders Punishment, and the Odiousness of their Example, they only consult their own Interest, by committing those Confessions to the Press, for the Lucre that is obtain'd for so doing."[42] Shortly after Lorrain's death in 1719, *Mists Weekly Journal* reported that he left an estate worth £5,000, on a gross annual salary of only £180. Later it was claimed that the ordinary received £25 per issue of his *Account* from its publishers, a quite considerable sum.[43] These various allegations suggest the large financial incentive motivating the ordinary to produce confessions.

If he failed to move swiftly, the competition might soak up his profits. In the production and consumption of criminal biography during the eighteenth century, moral imperatives were shunted to the passenger seat in the publishers' drive for pecuniary advantage. Since the days of Smith, the *Account* had contained frequent warnings about competing versions purporting to be authentic.[44] By 1700 the press's piracy of criminal lives had become epidemic. Grub-street hacks regularly haunted Newgate in search of a printable story. Even Thomas Gent, a printer's apprentice, spent his off hours hanging about the Old Bailey with a notebook, on the lookout for material to write up; in 1723 he hit the jackpot with a book based on the execution for treason of Christopher Layer, "on whose few dying words," Gent explained, "I formed observations in nature of a large speech." Gent's text "had a run of sale for about three days successively, which obliged me to keep in my own apartments, the unruly hawkers being ready to pull my press in pieces for the goods."[45] Big sums of money were offered in exchange for access to a potential story, or for the ready copy itself. An observer at Newgate in the 1730s complained that he saw "a slender gentleman address himself to one of the criminals in a low tone to this effect, that he would tip him as handsome a coffin as a man need desire to set his a[r]se in, if he would come down but half a dozen pages of confession." In 1740 a Newgate turnkey admitted accepting bribes from writers seeking access to a renowned prisoner.[46] In 1751 it was reported that the minister attending the prisoners at the New Gaol in Southwark was auctioning the confessions he took from them to the highest bidder.[47] In 1733 the *Gentleman's Magazine* noted that the Reverend Piddington sold the confession made to him by the convicted murderess Sarah Malcolm for £20.[48] A bookseller would not have paid such a sum without some assurance of profit from sales of the printed text. Though we cannot know exactly how much was made from the retail of criminal confessions, we can infer from the stir caused by hawkers in the streets that the figures were high. A witness in the second half of the eighteenth century observed that "the sale of the speeches ... must have been very great, for the number of those who hawked them about was enormous; no one can form a conception either of their number or of the dischordant chant, and noise they made. Their number was indeed so great that in going along the streets, there was no cessation, no interval when the ear was relieved from the sounds of their voices." Another claimed that the *Account* "experienced a ten times greater sale than either the *Spectator*, the *Guardian* or the *Rambler*."[49] Some separately printed biographical texts and confessions appeared in many editions over a short period of time: *A Warning to Youth: The Life and Death of Thomas Savage* reached twenty-two editions in the early eighteenth century; *The Discoveries of John Poulter* reached seventeen editions between 1753 and 1779; and Defoe's *Narrative of all the Robberies, Escapes, &c. of John Sheppard* ran to eight editions (at 6d. a copy) in only two months in 1724.[50] If the seventeenth century was the period of the scaffold's manipulation for moral purposes, the eighteenth century witnessed its commodification for purposes of personal profit.

An unintended but equally conspicuous emolument deriving from the commodification of the scaffold was the celebrity accorded to the criminal himself, who otherwise failed to benefit from the reproduction of his discourse by others. The buzz in September and October 1724 about the thief and escape-artist John Sheppard, for instance, was described in a contemporary printed biography of him as being so intense

> that it was thought all the common People would have gone Mad about him; there being not a *Porter* to be had for Love nor Money, nor getting into an Ale-house, for *Butchers, Shoemakers,* and *Barbers,* all engag'd in Controversies, and Wagers, about *Sheppard. Newgate* Night and Day surrounded with the Curious from St. *Giles's* and *Rag-Fair,* and *Tyburn Road* daily lin'd with Women and Children; and the *Gallows* as carefully watch'd by Night, lest he should be hang'd *Incog.* . . . In short, it was a week of the greatest Noise and Idleness among Mechanicks that has been known in *London,* and *Parker* and *Pettis,* two *Lyricks,* subsisted many Days very comfortably upon *Ballads* and *Letters* about *Sheppard.*[51]

None of this popularity passed unnoticed by its subject, Sheppard, who had his portrait drawn for publication while in his cell, and cooperated in the production of yet another written narrative of his adventures, which he ceremoniously delivered into the hands of its publisher at the place of execution.[52] From at least the third decade of the eighteenth century forward, no malefactor facing execution could remain ignorant of the colossal attention his imminent death and printed *Life* would command. The impact of the spectacle of the execution of Sheppard and others in the eighteenth century, with all of its attendant festivities, is well known to us. A Scottish clergyman observing a mid-century hanging noted that

> [a]mong the immense multitude of spectators, some at windows, some upon carts, thousands standing and jostling one another in the surrounding fields – my conviction is that, in a moral view, a great number were made worse, instead of better, by the awful spectacle. Of the ragamuffin class a large proportion were gratified by the sight; and within my hearing many expressed their admiration of the fortitude, as they termed the hardness and stupidity, of one of the sufferers. "Well done, little coiner!" "What a brave fellow he is!"[53]

Magistrates found the popular cult of the criminal scandalous, and publicly complained, as Justice Henry Fielding did in 1751, that

> No hero sees death as the alternative which may attend his undertaking with less terror, nor meets it in the field with more imaginary glory. . . . The day appointed by law for the thief's shame, is the day of glory in

his own opinion. His procession to Tyburn, and his last moments there, all are triumphant; attended with the compassion of the meek and tender-hearted, and with the applause, admiration, and envy, of all the bold and hardened. His behaviour in his present condition, not the crimes, how atrocious, soever, which brought him to it, is the subject of contemplation. And if he hath sense enough to temper his boldness with any degree of decency, his death is spoken of by many with honour, by most with pity, and by all with approbation.[54]

Moreover, not just the interest of "the common People," but that of elites also secured the criminal's celebrity, especially through the production and consumption of printed texts. Though he deplored criminal charisma, Fielding deigned to compose a biography (albeit parodic) of the notorious thief-taker-turned-thief Jonathan Wild; though he complained of the "ridiculous rage" of buying criminal biographies, Horace Walpole himself purchased and kept several such texts in his home library, along with a portrait of the murderess Sarah Malcolm; and James Boswell confessed to having read criminal biographies in his youth, which he said gave him "a sort of horrid eagerness" to attend hangings.[55] Few persons, it seems, could resist the pathos encoded in the criminal *Life*, which exercised what Samuel Johnson identified as the biographical capacity to "enchain the heart by irresistible interest."[56] Why?

In the eighteenth century, the confessional criminal biography represented the apotheosis of the penitent: it functioned as a vehicle for creating and promoting a charismatic deviant, *individualist*, self-identity. It underwrote the image of the criminal as the subject of popular concern and even sympathy, transforming him into a kind of tragic hero, whose exploits culminated in his final moments before the crowd at Tyburn, when he demonstrated publicly his acceptance of personal responsibility for his actions. As I showed in the previous chapter, this grasping of responsibility by the malefactor was made possible by the anti-antinomian stance adopted by the Restoration church, which redefined the question of salvation as a matter determined by the conscience rather than the heart, and thereby placed personal authority within the reach of individual rational capacities. Before this shift, as Goodcole's pamphlets suggest, confession and repentance were formal gestures dictated as necessary by providence, which governed the whole chain of causation in individual experience from the cradle to the grave. The fate of the Tudor and early Stuart malefactor was inevitable; like marionettes, good and bad men alike merely responded to the manipulations of the divine hand. By contrast, the post-Restoration confessional literature demonstrated the importance of personal discipline in the making and unmaking of human careers. Rather than providence, personal choice dictated individual fate. We can witness this in the discovery made by Defoe's fictional malefactor Colonel Jack, at the end of his confession of his life of crime and adventure, that "in collecting the various Changes, and Turns of my Affairs, I saw clearer than ever I had done before, how an invisible overruling Power, a Hand influenced from above, Governs all our Actions of every Kind, limits all our Designs, and orders the Events of every Thing relating to us."[57] Although Jack's trope is archaic, referring not to his own agency but to a providential force, some godlike "first Mover, and Maker of all things," as he called it, the sense of his realization, coming at the end of a long confession in which his personal decisions are paramount, refers instead to a new source of human agency: his own ability to determine the course of his life. Though in literal terms Jack appears passively to accept the design imposed on his experience by providence, in figurative terms he is demonstrating his self-mastery; for he discovers the chain of causation by reason rather than divine revelation, through his own independent act of narrative "collection," as he put it. Jack understood his personal responsibility, but he lacked the words to describe it, so he utilized the old terminology. In the case of actual criminals standing in the cart at Tyburn, the penitent confession displayed a similar accountability, which everyone present understood unconsciously, without need for its explicit articulation. The catharsis occurring during the speeches at Tyburn was experienced chiefly by the witnesses who, after the malefactor settled the burden of blame for his evil squarely on his own shoulders, could express their thanks and relief for his demonstration of personal responsibility by celebrating his memory after seeing him turned off.

The moral encoded in the criminal biography, then, was self-control: it legitimated the malefactor's pathetic end, and made him "great" in spite of fate. In time, the lesson of personal authority in the printed lives of malefactors would become more pronounced – though never absolutely explicit – as the secularization of English culture continued and the rituals founded in Protestant practice were transformed by advancing deism. Religious terminology in confessional biography was eventually replaced by the emerging vocabularies of class, gender, and the law; in this context the significance of individual agency and power came to the fore. Early signs of this shift can be found in the collections of individual criminal lives which began to appear from 1710 and multiplied in the decades immediately after.[58] Most of these works seem to have been based originally on the ordinary's *Account*, the *Proceedings* and/or related texts, and therefore represent a synthesis of "authentic" biographical and autobiographical discourse.[59]

Consider, for example, the monumental folio book put together by one "Captain Charles Johnson" and published serially in 1734 as *A General History of All the Lives and Adventures of the Most Famous Highwaymen, Murderers, Street-Robbers, &c. To which is added, A Genuine Account of the Voyages and Plunders of the Most Notorious Pyrates.*[60] The book is a collection of nearly 200 discrete biographies of individual British outlaws, arranged in rough chronological order. Here the traditional, passive Christian "Life and Death" title motif has given way to the active secular one of "Life and Adventures," which becomes increasingly common, with some variation ("Life and Actions," "Life and Enterprises," "Life and Robberies," "Life and Intrigues," and so forth) during the eighteenth century, signifying the triumph of agency over self-mortification in narratives of personal experience. Further, the discourse of Johnson's introduction illustrates the extent to which a *Life* in his *General History* was informed by a secular order maintained by personal interest and self-control. It recommends the book to the reader on the grounds that

> Lives of particular persons have been commonly esteemed the most Useful Pieces of History; they display Human Nature more familiarly than General Histories, and the Impressions they leave are stronger. General History seems not so much the Concern of a private Man, who has nothing to govern but his own Passions; nor can he receive any extraordinary Advantage to himself from the greatest Acquaintance with it, unless he is Philosopher enough to apply the Convulsions of the Revolutions of State to his own Appetites and Inclinations. (sig. B^v)

In this argument we encounter the novel concepts of "particular persons"; an inherent "Human Nature;" the "private" domain as the "government" of one's "own Passions" and the related abstractions such as personal "Advantage," "Appetites and Inclinations." Moreover, the introduction identifies its subjects as "our Celebrated Heroes" (sig. B^v) – despite the fact that nearly every *Life* included ends in execution.

Recent scholars, especially historians attempting to use the criminal lives as source materials, have expressed concern about the veracity of such texts as these, especially in the light of contemporary allegations that the ordinary or some other writer fabricated individual confessions. Yet attempts to verify details have been largely positive, in the few cases where facts can be checked.[61] For us, however, matters of literal truth in the criminal lives are less important than the more fundamental issue of figuration, of how the "facts" are represented. In the collections especially the subjects are so excessively romanticized that their actions, we imagine, can hardly be true. But even so, should the details prove false, the mere fact of their glamorization is remarkable, for it is evidence of a shift in the status of the autobiographical subject and his self-identity. In Johnson's *General History*, for example, pathetic low-life subjects are represented as, to take just a few instances, a "thorough Master in the thieving Art" (p. 9); a "very bold Man" (p. 24); a "witty Rogue" (p. 70); a "great seducer" (p. 78); an "arch Villain" (p. 97); and a "dexterous Man," committing "Actions the most daring and artful that were ever known" (pp. 11, 14) – in short, they are treated as individual subjects of style, potency, and control rather than (as might also be said of all, not just one of them) objects "of base Extraction ... void of Education, good Manners, or any other Qualification that was amiable" (p. 9).

The potent self-identity manifest in the speeches and actions of the criminals themselves was the motor of desire driving popular interest in memoirs of malefactors such as these. Who could resist Captain Phillip Stafford, described as "a sort of Gentleman-Farmer" with an income of £50 a year, who was hanged for stealing from his neighbors, when told that "The Part of a gallant no Man performed better, nor imitated that of a Lover more naturally then *Stafford*: He had besides all that was graceful and engaging in his Behaviour, as well as his Person" (p. 78)? Moreover, even as a child he excelled: "Never a Lad in all the Parishes round, but would shudder at the Name of *Phillip Stafford*, and if he was not always the best Scholar, he was indisputably the Head Boy in every School he went to" (p. 77). Stafford could also sing, versify, and seduce women of every rank – all of which caused his *Life* to be heroic despite its awful end. Its final scene is worth quoting almost in its entirety to illustrate the extent of Stafford's heroic personal authority:

> While *Stafford* was in Prison, before his condemnation, he lived in a very grand manner: he had a Wicket made before the Jail Porch to hide his Fetters, where he used to sit frequently with one of the Keepers, and converse with Gentlemen of the best Fashion in the whole Town. . . .
> The Captain had a new light-coloured Suit of Cloaths made to go to the Gallows in (for he did not expect to be hanged) in which he appeared as tho' he had been going to a Wedding. He had a Nose-Gay in his Bosom, and his Countenance was without the least Appearance

of Concern all the Way. As he past by a Tavern, he ordered the Cart to stop, and called for a Pint of Wine, which he drank all off, and told the Vinter he would pay him when he came back. At the Gallows he stood up, and looked round him very wishfully some Minutes, still desiring more Time. At last when the Sheriff bid him prepare, and he saw no Remedy, his Colour was observed to change, and he trembled very much, but said nothing. Just at the Instant that the Cart was ordered to be drawn away, he delieverd a Paper to the Sheriff, and then was turned off in a great Deal of Confusion. The Contents of the Paper were as follows:

It is not merely in Compliance with the common Custom of Malefactors, that I write any Thing to leave behind me in the World; if there had not seemed a more than ordinary Necessity for this Declaration from me, upon the Account of my having been so universally talk'd of, I should have been contented to have suffered in Silence, what the Justice of the Law has required.

I confess not only the Fact for which I die, but also almost all those that are laid to my Charge, by common Fame, besides innumerable others of the same Nature, yet I hope that what I am about to offer, will Plead a little in my Favour, and in some Measure abate the Horror which many sober People are apt to conceive at the bare Recital of my Crimes.

I was brought up in Principles of Honour and Virtue by my Parents, and I continued to Act agreeably to those Principles for many Years, as several worthy Gentlemen now Living can testify. I can moreover call upon a greater Witness than any Mortal to attest, that I have always thought in my Soul nothing so mean and Unworthy of human Nature as Fraud, of what kind soever it might be. It was only the Iniquity of the Times, in which it had been my Unhappiness to have lived, that occasioned my abandoning in Practice what my Judgment always approved of; Notwithstanding the Pains I have taken to work myself into a Belief that Virtue is nothing but a vain Chimaera.

The Cruelty with which all the loyal Party was Prosecuted during the late Civil War, gave me a very despicable Opinion of those who executed it. This Opinion was afterwards strengthened when I beheld the same People dividing among themselves, and using an equal Severity towards each other, as any one Party got uppermost. I soon found that their Religion was but a Pretence, and their Appearance of Sanctity, nothing more than Hypocrisy; That Interest was the only Point they pursued, and their hyperbolical Cant concerning another World a mere engine to draw to themselves larger Possessions in this, which they had the Confidence to affirm they had learned intirely to despise. These things made me determine, when my Estate was quartered, and my Principles prevented my getting an honourable Subsistence, to take openly from some of those Hypocrites what they unjustly, though more craftily, had taken from better People.

What lies most heavily on my Conscience, is, my having ever condescended to deal with these Men in their own Way, by imposing upon them under a Shew of Piety: May God forgive me in this Particular! . . .

I shall not trouble the World with any more of these Things, which only relate to my Maker, and my own Conscience. Give me Leave to say, that as I have not been a common Offender, I would hope my Remains will be treated with a little more Decency, than the Bodies of the unhappy Wretches who suffer at this Place, commonly are.

As I die justly, I have no Occasion to say any Thing concerning the Instruments of my Death, who only execute what the Law demands. If there are any other Persons, who are conscious that they have given me just Cause of Offence, let them know that I forgive them from my Heart; and that I die in Peace with all the World, to which I can very calmly bid *Farewell*. (p. 85)

Stafford's parting confession completes his own and the spectators' perception of him as a self-made man. He shunned traditional corporate identity to operate in his own autonomous field of authority (note that he is not even a "yeoman," but a "sort of Gentleman-Farmer," defying even the most liberal category of traditional respectable identification). The personal ethic, native ability, and individual charisma embodied in Stafford epitomize the personae fleshed out in the narratives of the less articulate and less well-born malefactors in Johnson's *General History*, as also those of comparable works seeking to present their dead subjects as heroes. Such texts as these represent the malefactors as morally and physically powerful individuals, in control of themselves and therefore of their worlds. Consider as a final example Johnson's representation of Thomas Dun, a man "of very mean Extraction" but one who also "chang'd himself into as many Shapes as *Proteus*, being a Man who understood the World so well, that there was nothing he could not humour, nor any Part of Villainy that came amiss to him. To Day he was a Merchant, to Morrow a Soldier, the next Day a Gentleman, and the Day following a beggar: In short, he was every day what he pleased himself" (p. 24). The romanticized criminal was a free agent, socially mobile, and almost omnipotent. The image of total personal authority, he was the prototypical individualist self.

For less sophisticated readers, Johnson's text projected this message visually, with a series of twenty-six copperplate engravings each representing a single hero whose *Life* the *General History* contained. Such images, individual copies of which could be purchased separately, were the commoner versions of the finely engraved portrait "heads" of princes and other worshipful persons collected, like baseball trading-cards today, in the seventeenth century by exceptionally literate gentlemen such as Elias Ashmole, John Evelyn, Samuel

Pepys, and Ralph Thoresby.[62] Occasionally in their day engraved portrait heads were deliberately bound with a printed discourse as the book's frontispiece. This was rare in the case of most writers, whose stature remained in all respects well beneath that of worthy royalty and great statesmen. However, if a writer was a person of renown, or someone whose words had earned him an undisputed place in history – for example, Erasmus – then a publisher might include an iconic representation of him as part of the text, usually a magnum opus. *Reliquiae Baxterianae* contained as its frontispiece a fine engraved head of Richard Baxter; Samuel Clarke's *Lives of Sundry Eminent Persons*, which included his own *Life*, had a head of Clarke.[63] If the portrait were finely done, which was possible after the copperplate engraving surpassed the woodcut as the better method for reproducing images on paper in the late sixteenth century, it could add a powerful visual dimension to the personality projected by the written text. The unique physical features and expressions of Baxter and Clarke enhanced the reader's appreciation of each man's individuality as a biographical subject, paradoxically in contrast to the message intended by his words. But not too much: these representations were still very formalized and generic, despite their detail. Their content was dominated by the posture, countenance, and garb of the subjects, which suggested very strongly the character of the stereotypical "grave divine."

The portraits of the criminals, on the other hand, represented their subjects in such a way as to project not only their unique physical features but also their unique personal actions and style. Whereas the divines are disembodied heads (and sometimes chests and shoulders) set against the generic backdrop of a chapel interior, the criminals and pirates are full-bodied figures standing in specific, usually outdoor, locations, depicted in the process of enacting an episode from their lives. For example, the pirate Bartholomew Roberts stands on a coastal promontory, in fancy dress; his left hand is on his hip and his right holds a drawn sword; his feet are apart, in a stance of readiness for action; in the water behind him is his frigate with guns ablaze, their fire directed at a burning clifftop fortress; men from the ship are landing ashore with their swords drawn; the local inhabitants stand before them with arms raised in surrender (opposite p. 228). Captain Henry Morgan is similarly posed, his image's caption tells us, "before Panama which he took from the Spaniards" (opposite p. 278). John Sheppard, the notorious escape-artist, is depicted in the Stone Room at Newgate prison; his feet and hands are in chains, the feet secured with a padlock the size of his torso; he is well dressed, and seated, gazing reflectively out the heavily barred window: our hero is planning his next escape. The giant irons serve to emphasize the magnitude of his unstoppable personal power (opposite p. 461). As visual complements to the written texts, the criminal portraits helped to encode the message of individuality and potency.

Relatively cheap reproductions such as those intended for Johnson's *General History* no doubt adorned the walls of adolescent sleeping compartments in their day as posters of rock stars and sports heroes do today. At least one of Johnson's biographical subjects mentioned exchanging "pictures," possibly of malefactors, with a schoolmate as a youth (p. 70). It is likely that some portraits were also used for domestic decoration by adults of relatively unsophisticated taste – the more urbane, like Horace Walpole, would have had the portrait done in oils, as was the image of Sarah Malcolm in his library.[64] The others could have the engraving of her execution, included in Johnson's book. Though scarce today, Johnson's images were in their day cheap and plentiful, as were individual copies of the printed lives they accompanied. Today's reader finds Johnson's text an imposing folio, expensively bound as befits an artifact treasured by modern rare book collectors, but in contemporary hands it was treated as readers today treat magazines. The book was originally published in weekly parts made up of two sheets each, containing the texts of two or three lives. Each part retailed separately for 2*d*.; one could also subscribe to the whole series, and accept monthly home delivery by itinerant chapmen of eight sheets for 8*d*.[65] Once the complete series had been issued, readers could bring their collected parts to a binder to make a single book, or purchase a complete set from the publisher ready bound. Acquisition in the latter manner would have been prohibitively expensive for most of Johnson's readers. The typical consumer probably bought a few parts at random, rather than whole sets. This explains why complete books are now so scarce.

Serial publication of works like Johnson's *General History* helped to extend the renown of individual criminals, and thereby to promote the individualist self-identity they demonstrated.[66] This publishing scheme was still relatively new when Johnson's bookseller, James Janeway, attempted it. Its advantage to the common reader with but a few pennies to spend was that it made big books (or parts of them, at least) available and affordable. A bookseller could likewise benefit from selling more copies of a work to more people this way, with less of his own capital invested up front. Part-publication also mitigated the need for a precise calculation in advance of the length of the book and number of copies in an edition. Janeway could add (or eliminate) parts, or quickly have printed additional copies of any one part, in immediate response to demand. Most important of all for us, however, the advent of part-publication and its sister method, publication by subscription (by which means books were partially paid for in advance by purchasers judging the work by virtue of a prospectus) made the *self-publication* of a written *Life* a possibility for the truly motivated and intrepid person of small means, with little capital and no reputation in the market for print. Though they were never significant as a proportion of the total output of printed books at any time, the decade-by-decade totals of works printed for the author instead of a professional bookseller seem to have followed the general vogue for publication in parts and by subscription. A survey of the records of one eighteenth-century printing firm shows that no printing for authors was done before 1710. The practice became much more frequent from just before 1720 up to about 1755, with a peak in the 1730s. The general pattern is of rapid rise and gradual decline to about 1770.[67] During this half-century the window of opportunity for the emergence of the totalized autobiographical text – the work for which the author is completely responsible because he has shouldered the whole burden of its material as well as its literary production, and reaped the benefits personally – stood open. Indeed, the best evidence of the cultural reception of the individualist message encoded in the texts of criminal lives is the advent of the small but important number of imitative texts produced by persons acting, so to speak, as their own ordinaries – composing and publishing their own confessions, by their individual "allowance" or authority, without the support of patrons. I shall discuss a few of these self-published and self-sustaining works to conclude this chapter, for they represent the beginnings of a legitimate, fully secular mode of individualist self-identity in English autobiographical practice.

In his novel *Joseph Andrews*, published in 1742, Henry Fielding made a public gibe at the former actor–theater manager–Poet Laureate Colley Cibber (who in 1740 became also the first Briton to write and publish his own secular *Life*), by having its narrator mention sarcastically that Cibber's *Apology for the Life of Colley Cibber, Comedian*, "was written by the great person himself, who lived the life he hath recorded, and is by many thought to have lived such a life only in order to write it." This was not in fact the case for Cibber, whose *Apology*, written during retirement when he was in his late sixties, was an afterthought to his career; but it may be said with some accuracy that those immediately succeeding him as writers and publishers of their own life had to write it in order to live it. For this reason the apologetic, so-called "scandalous" memoirs issued by Cibber's daughter the actress Charlotte Charke in 1755, the poet-printseller Laetitia Pilkington in 1749–54, and the courtesan Teresia Constantia Phillips in 1748–9 claim attention. Though all three ladies were well born and bred, their status as public personalities remained marginal as a consequence of their gender. As women, Phillips, Pilkington, and Charke were the appropriate heirs of the criminal confessional tradition, whose practitioners came largely from the lower orders of society. Yet, by deliberate manipulation of autobiographical discourse, each women created and maintained an original and autonomous place for herself in the public domain as a kind of woman warrior, or female outlaw, liberated from the prison of the family, the domestic economy, patronage, religion, and ultimate subordination to traditional corporate authority, public and private. In their works we find individualist self-identity displayed in its most pronounced form before the appearance of Lackington's *Memoirs*.

Each of the three women produced a text relating a unique and eventful personal history which culminates, literally and figuratively, in her public presence as an authoritative personality. In *An Apology for the Conduct of Mrs. Teresia Constantia Phillips*, Phillips first appears as an unusually "frail Sinner," who has been brought low in the world by an excess of feminine "nature," which she has learned, too late, to conquer with reason:

> In her, indeed, it seems as tho' Nature had been profuse, on purpose that she might be the more conspicuous in her Unhappiness; for it is certain, whatever Preference she might have boasted in respect of Beauty, or other good Qualities, has been abundantly over-ballanced by her Sufferings: In Misfortunes, it must be confess'd, her superiority still remains, by her being, of all Women, the most unhappy in a Point which hardly any of them live to be convinced of; for Maturity of Reason has brought with it Reflection; and that Reflection, the stinging Remembrance of a Youth so ill managed, that no Time, or different Conduct, can retrieve.[68]

According to her *Apology*, Phillips's history properly commenced in 1722 at age 13, when she fled the "cruel usage" (vol. I, p. 23) of her gentleman father and stepmother at home. A comely young lady alone in the world, she was easy prey to predatory men. At age 15, Phillips attracted the attention of the future Lord Chesterfield. He seduced her with promises of protection, only to retract his interest and support after consummating his desire for her flesh. Thus broken, with nowhere to turn for assistance, Phillips committed one moral error after another in an escalating chain of sin and folly leading into marriage with a false savior, an unpredictably brutal Dutch merchant, Henry Muilman. Phillips's brief marriage to him was a protracted brawl terminating in divorce, in 1736. Muilman refused to pay alimony and Phillips plunged deeply into debt; in 1745 she served time in the Fleet. Ostensibly her *Apology* was an attempt to win public sympathy and support in order to shame Muilman into paying up, so that Phillips could free herself from creditors. She first tried to trade blackmail for silence, but when her attempts at extortion failed she resorted to the court of public opinion by publishing her tale. Yet there was more at stake in Phillips's work than the freedom money could buy. In fact, the real story told in the *Apology* is that related in its profuse digressions from the basic history of error, exploitation, and deception, of Phillips's own attempt to use narrative discourse to gain control of her self-identity. She judges that "scarce any story was brought to Light attended with such strange Circumstances as mine, I may also venture to say, never was Oppression equal to that attempted to be put upon me" (vol. I, sig. *). Phillips's *Apology* identifies her success as an author with her self-mastery and autonomy as a public and private personality.

When Phillips first attempted to bring her story to light, no bookseller would publish and no printer would print it, on account of the risk involved. Despite the precedents of Dunton's *Night-Walker* and the criminal lives, in Phillips's day a lengthy, authentic, and original account of domestic infidelity and abuse centered upon the experience of a single person was still unusual. Moreover, in her discourse Phillips named names. She accused living, powerful men of gross misconduct which, if the accusations were false, constituted libel for which the responsible parties were subject to fine and which, if they were true, might provoke attempts to suppress the work. (In the event, Phillips alleged harassment from both Muilman and Chesterfield.) Eventually Phillips found a printer willing to print her *Apology* for her in parts, to minimize his own risk. With a shrewd eye for her potential market, she hurried him to get the early numbers out before the landed gentry left town for the summer (vol. I, pp. ix–x). The first part of the *Apology* was entered in the Stationer's Register by Phillips as its "sole proprietor" on 11 April 1748, and advertised in *The General Advertiser* two days later as follows:

This Day is publish'd, Price I s.
NUMBER I.
And will be continued every Ten days 'till the whole is complete,
MRS. PHILLIPS'S Apology. This Wo[r]k will be regularly enter'd at
Stationers Hall, and whoever presumes to pyrate it will be prosecuted
with utmost Severity of the Law.
To be had only at her House in Craig's-Court, Charing Cross;
where Booksellers and Pamphlet-shops may be supplied, with the
usual Allowance.[69]

Each number of the *Apology* comprised six to eight half-sheets each, about sixty-four printed pages. There were seventeen parts in all, which when combined made a book of three volumes. Not only did Phillips take the unusual step of selling nearly every copy of all the parts herself, she also signed her name in ink at the bottom of the first page of each one, to authenticate it. The unusual method of publication, the unusual advertisement, and the unusual signature together strongly implied that Phillips's "conduct" (and so her "life") was her own property, over which she exercised single and total authority. In this manner Phillips demonstrated the extreme of autobiographical responsibility, figuratively and literally. After her first number sold out, professional booksellers showed interest, and several assisted Phillips in turn by acting as authorized wholesale distributors of subsequent numbers. Throughout, however, Phillips continued her practice of signing every copy sold. A second edition of the complete *Apology* was issued in 1748, a third in 1750, and a fourth in 1761. The *Apology* also generated a small body of paraliterature, which benefited Phillips as well as its hack writers and their booksellers.[70] As a publishing venture, Phillips's *Apology* was, in a word, a coup.

The work achieved its literary objectives as well, despite Phillips's professed uncertainty of her ability to carry off a narrative "Performance," as she called it. To compensate, she hired an unnamed hack to act as her ghostwriter. Thus the *Apology* consists mainly of third-person discourse. However, Phillips intrudes at length in the first person singular in the *Apology*'s several prefaces, which she apparently wrote herself to introduce individual numbers. These intrusions, coupled with her autograph on the first page of every copy of the parts of the first edition, convinced readers that the story was composed, if not narrated directly, by its subject. Besides reparation, Phillips wanted public attention, sympathy, and pardon for herself, as the *Apology* made obvious in the following pathetic appeal:

> Is it then wonderful, if deserted by him [i.e. Muilman] and *under Circumstances that of Necessity made the Nature of their Separation public*, a young Creature of Mrs. *Muilman's* extraordinary Beauty, and other Accomplishments, should draw the Attention and Admiration of Mankind upon her? Left to herself, without any Protection, or Friends to counsel or advise her, and in the Midst of these destructive Allurements, tho' she stray'd from that Path the Discreet and amiable Part of her Sex make the most shining Figure in, if the *Just*, the *Generous*, and the *Good* will but for a Moment turn their Thoughts inward, how will they lament! how pity her! for there they will see human Nature in its primitive Dress; and every Man and Woman of the least Discernment knows, when left to themselves, how little we are capable of, let the natural Bent of our Inclinations be what they will. (vol. I, p. 253)

She appropriated the discourse of the criminal penitents to redeem herself. Acting as her own ordinary, Phillips performed the public service of offering her story as a lesson in moral conduct by candidly indicting herself: so that, as the *Apology* explained, "Her Sufferings may, at least, serve as a Beacon, or Sea-mark, to warn from a fatal Ship-wreck those fair Adventurers, who may hereafter launch into the World, while Youth is their only Pilot, to steer so weak and perishable a Vessel as Beauty" (vol. III, p. 313). Boldly, at the same time, she also indicted the cultural double standard which held women accountable for crimes condoned when committed by men: "no Reformation is sufficient to expiate the Offences of the Fair, who seem the only Part of GOD's *Creatures* that are prohibited the Benefit of Repentance; and are so compleatly under the Curse of the Law, that she, who *offendeth in one Point*, is immediately denounced *guil[t]y of all*" (vol. III, p. 313). This latter judgment became the pivot upon which the moral argument of her account actually turned. Such was not Phillips's original intention. As the *Apology* explained, "[w]hen her Justification was attempted, our first setting out was not to vindicate the blameable Part of her Conduct: Quite otherwise; her Design was to humble herself in the most submissive Manner to the offended World" (vol. II, p. 242). But, in the course of her act of self-mortification, Phillips realized the more powerful strategy of self-vindication: by exposing the crimes of her antagonists, she could break the moral and material fetters she found herself in. Adopting the posture of the public penitent, Phillips discovered her own voice, and in its reverberations the grounds of personal authority.

By writing, Phillips became an action heroine. As she issued her numbers over the space of several months, her story evolved into an attempt to, as she put it, "talk upon paper" (vol. III, p. 312) and reinvent her identity through the weekly dialogue she had established with the reading (and gossiping) public. By the thirteenth number, her new self was literally manifest: "our Apologist . . . is formed with a Disposition very opposite to . . . *Female Supineness.* Her Misfortunes have shewn her the Necessity of becoming superior to them, and every new Oppression she meets with, adds fresh Vigor to her Fortitude" (vol. III, p. 34). The *Apology* justified this active stance by asking rhetorically, "Must she endure her shatter'd Character to be more broken by her Silence, while the more *blameable Person* revels in Ease and Affluence, unmov'd, deaf, and regardless of those Miseries, the narrow Supports of Life, which her *forgotten Bounty* to *those very Persons* have reduc'd her to?" (vol. I, p. 316). Moreover, Phillips's own mordant remarks on the process of publication, uttered in her prefaces, reveal how she came to grasp her performance as a means of establishing a personal moral authority normally denied to women by the code of female muteness. For instance, in an early preface Phillips explained that "I am at last reduced to this unpleasing Method of justifying myself to the World, as well as relieving my Fortune, at the same Time: I must beg Leave to assure you, tho' the last may be a material Consideration, the first is my principal and favourite View" (vol. I, sig. a). Elsewhere, taunting Muilman publicly, she wrote that, "I scorn any sordid View that can possibly be proposed to tempt me from the darling Consolation of giving you, once in my Life, a *Coup de Justice.* I thank Heaven that permits me to *speak* Daggers, tho' the Laws restrain me from the Use of them" (vol. I, p. 48). The "coup de justice" she envisioned was predicated on a new individual right, created by Phillips herself, who had learned to act as her own arbiter: "To infringe upon the Laws of private Society, to shew the corrupted Insides of fair and favourable Appearances, will admit of no Excuse, unless it will be allow'd *the Injur'd have a Right to complain*; and in some Measure, to ease their own Hearts, by laying the Ungrateful under equal Compunctions" (vol. I, p. 315). The *Apology* makes a strong case for this new kind of personal authority in its representation of the apologist. Phillips's story is that of the autodidact become autocrat become heroine. The wheel had almost come full circle, from Katherine Stubbes, who was praised for obeying the scriptural injunction that women "be silent, and . . . learn of their husbands at home," to Teresia Constantia Phillips, for whom both silence and husbands – indeed, the whole system of traditional patriarchal relations – were anathema.

The reading public sanctioned Phillips's self-defined heroism with its response to her *Apology.* The book sold well – demand was sufficient for three editions in two years, of a multi-volume work – and its author was generally commended for her literary efforts. The initial response was so positive, in fact, that in her preface to the fourth number Phillips could confidently write that "I have . . . already reaped considerable Benefit: And I have the Satisfaction to experience the Impartiality and Indulgence of the Publick, in acquitting, or condemning, only as Truth and Justice dictate: Nor can I help flattering myself they will be of Opinion, that I have, in some Measure, merited their favour" (vol. I, p. xvii). Her confidence was apparently warranted by experience. A disgruntled contemporary observer ruefully remarked that Phillips and her *Apology* commanded the "Taste of the Town."[71] Another wrote in 1749 that she "has, with so much Applause, for this last eighteen Months engrossed the almost general Conversation of the Public." Moreover, she "is at this Day countenanced by almost all the Ladies in *London*, from the highest Rank to the lowest." "Nor," he added, "throughout the Multitudes who I have heard speak of her since the Appearance of the Apology, did I ever hear one who accused her of a base, unjust, or dishonourable Action."[72] Children begged their parents for a copy of the mezzotint portrait (also signed in ink with her autograph) that Phillips issued with her sixth number, as a frontispiece to be bound up in the first volume; Phillips heard that her numbers were read aloud at the Smyrna coffee-house in Pall Mall, "to the Gentlemen then present . . . with general Approbation"; and an MP was overheard defending her book during a dinner discussion.[73] Phillips's autobiographical performance had vindicated her character, it seems; more importantly, it established her personal autonomy. In a Crusoesque touch, she retired to Jamaica, where she died in 1765.[74]

Though less aggressive and explicit about their intentions than Phillips, Pilkington and Charke enjoyed similar literary successes. In her *Memoirs*, Pilkington described herself as "an Heteroclite, or irregular Verb, which can never be declined, or conjugated" – an apt metaphor for the kind of autonomy she achieved, though she did not live to enjoy it for long.[75] In Dublin in 1737, at age 25, she was divorced from her husband, who accused her of adultery. She alleged that after the death of her father and the discovery that there was to be no fortune for his heirs, her husband wanted to be rid of her, and so entrapped her in a false intrigue to make him appear a cuckold. The incident became a public scandal and Pilkington, with her young son, fled to London. There she met Colley Cibber, the Poet Laureate, who befriended her by helping her to sell a few poems, which she had been writing since childhood, and to set herself up as a printseller. She thus became "the first of my Family . . . [to take] my Place behind a Counter" (vol. II, p. 241). She also hired herself out as a hack writer. Pilkington represented herself as a born author, "incorrigibly devoted to Versifying" (vol. I, p. 139). However, by her own account her poems earned great honors but small profits. If her native character was to become manifest, she would have to find a mode of discourse equal to her talents; she hit upon autobiography. According to Pilkington, the inspiration to write and sell her *Memoirs* came from Cibber. Hearing her relate her personal history to him over breakfast one morning, Cibber cried "Z——ds! write it out, just as you relate it, and, I'll engage it will sell" (vol. II, p. 88). It did, in three volumes, each one issued as Pilkington completed it, in response to public demand. In keeping with the tradition of personal confession first established by the criminals and then being appropriated and reinvented by Phillips, Pilkington conceived her discourse as "a lively Picture of all my *Faults*, my *Follies*, and the *Misfortunes*, which have been consequential to them. . . . I propose myself, not as an Example, but a Warning to them [i.e. "the *Female* Part of my Readers"], that by my *Fall*, they may stand the more secure" (vol. I, pp. 1–2). The audience for such fare was ready and waiting.

But Pilkington saw her *Memoirs* as more than just a bestseller. She had obviously been encouraged by the success of Phillips (whom she acknowledged as an influence – vol. II, pp. 349–54; vol. III, p. 129) to use her book as an instrument of self-justification and personal profit.[76] Pilkington deployed her text as an instrument to extort money from her husband and, it seems, any man who had ever crossed her. She demanded a guinea minimum subscription in exchange for her silence. As she explained toward the end of her first volume, "If any married Man, who has ever attacked me, does not subscribe to my *Memoirs*, I will without the least Ceremony, insert their Names, be their Rank ever so high, or their Profession ever so lowly" (vol. I, p. 245; cf. vol. I, p. 280). Before this threat was made, she noted, "[p]ersons were at first a little timorous, lest I should print a List of Subscribers, and by that means they might unwittingly give Offence; but when I declared no Names should be inserted, I had a numerous Contribution, from all the Nobility, Clergy, and Gentry" (vol. III, p. 212). By the time she began her third volume, however, she could say that "[m]any indeed are glad to become purchasers of it. Persons whom I know nothing of, come and beg I may not put them into the Third Volume; and they will subscribe" (vol. II, p. 2). The Dublin subscription edition was quickly succeeded by two London editions, which were distributed through normal retail sales;

they would help generate subscribers for subsequent volumes. More-over, like Phillips's work, Pilkington's also occasioned a considerable body of paraliterature, which also served to increase her fame.[77]

As a consequence of this popularity, Pilkington was not only guaranteed a small but apparently sufficient income, she also found herself able to set herself up as a kind of literary deity. At the start of her third volume Pilkington could claim with broad assent that her own "bold Undertaking . . . met with such unhop'd success, that I am quite encouraged to proceed; more especially as my Word is pass'd to the Publick; and my Word I have ever held sacred" (vol. III, p. 1). She died in 1750, before finishing the third part, which her son would issue posthumously, four years later. But toward the end of her second volume (which, because of the advanced state of her illness, she conceived as her last), Pilkington offered a final word on her experience:

> I have been a Lady of Adventure, and almost every Day of my Life produces some new one: I am sure, I ought to thank my loving Husband for the Opportunity he has afforded me of seeing the World from the Palace to the Prison; for had he but permitted me to what Nature certainly intended for me, a harmless household Dove, in all human Probability I should have remained contented with my humble Situation, and, instead of using a Pen, been employed with a Needle, to work for the little ones we might, by this time, have had.
>
> Now, after all my strange Vicissitudes of good and evil Fortune, I sincerely declare, that were I to have my Wish, tho' I should not now in the Decline of Life be able to struggle through Misfortunes, as in it's first sprightly Career; yet as by the Bounty, Compassion, and Kindness of all my noble, and honoured Benefactors, I have the unspeakable Happiness of being set above the low Distresses of Life. (vol. II, pp. 252–3)

Though considerably less bold in her literary undertaking than Phillips, Laetitia Pilkington nevertheless discovered in her auto-biographical endeavors the same sort of heroic self-identity whose grounds lay in the personal authority achieved by the *Memoirs* as a form of public action.

Charlotte Charke's *Narrative of the Life of Charlotte Charke* did the same with her self-identity. In the account of what she called her "UNACCOUNTABLE LIFE," Charke identified herself as "a NONPAREIL OF THE AGE" and an "Oddity . . . to be shewn among the Wonders of Ages past, and those to come," and so established the literary basis of her personal autonomy.[78] The youngest of Cibber's eleven children, she could never get along with her father, who in spite of his generosity to others like Pilkington, left her only £5 from his massive estate when he died in 1757. Raised to be an actress, Charke disliked the drudgery of housewifery; she married and divorced twice (with a daughter by her first union), then led her own troupe of itinerant stage-players, which earned her a bare living. By her account, Charke took "extravagant Delight" at seeing her name posted about town "in Capitals" on the playbills announcing her performances (pp. 56–7). Perhaps the desire to see her name permanently represented in printed letters, and the ready cash she knew could be had from the sale of her copy, led Charke to trade the stage for the pen as her chief means of support. Before returning to London she had begun but not finished a biographical novel entitled *The History of Henry Dumont*, which she intended to issue in weekly parts (pp. 263–4). As a preface to this work, she prepared "a trifling Sketch" of her life; however, friends "strongly urged" her to expand and publish it on its own, which she promptly did, in eight weekly parts beginning in March 1755.

Though far less vindictive than either Phillips's or Pilkington's works, Charke's *Narrative* was neither completely ingenuous nor lacking in titillation. Like her predecessors, she appropriated the criminal pose and even attempted blackmail. Her first number represented her as a "REPENTANT CHILD" wishing to "clear my Reputation to the World" (p. 15). In her sixth number she included a transcript of a letter she had sent to her father a week after the first number appeared, begging for his attention and support, but which Cibber returned without reply (pp. 118–20). Charke presumably then set about ordering for the press the next seven parts, seeing that no help was to be extorted by the threat of embarrassment to Cibber. The *Narrative* as a whole renders Charke more a laughing stock than either a temptress or an avenger, but readers were apparently as pleased to be amused by Charke as they were to be titillated, scandalized, and reprimanded by Phillips and Pilkington. Like those of the two others, Charke's book sold well partly because it was easy to obtain. Each part of the *Narrative* retailed for 3*d.*; subscribers to the whole series received gratis with the final number "a curious copperplate of Mrs. Charlotte Charke" and "a general title."[79] When the series ended the *Narrative* was immediately reissued as a duodecimo book, selling at half a crown. It went to two editions in 1755, and presumably served as an appetizer for Charke's next two works, each a biographical novel, *The History of Henry Dumont, Esq.; and Miss Charlotte Evelyn* (1755), and *The Mercer, or Fatal Extrava-*

gance: Being a True Narrative of the Life of Mr. Wm Dennis (1756), and other works which appeared before her death in 1760. These productions did not make Charke rich – in fact, the printer Samuel Whyte's account of his visit to her abode near Islington in 1755 describes it as "a wretched thatched hovel," and emphasizes the pitiful circumstances of Charke's apparent poverty[80] – but they did enable her to live autonomously, free from the charity of a patron.

The *Narrative* marked the start of Charke's career as an author literally, not just figuratively. Nevertheless for her as for her predecessors, Charke's autobiographical performance defined her personal individuality and autonomy first and foremost. It was the *Narrative* and the public's reception of it which Charke understood as the basis of her individual success. She closed her *Life* by offering her "sincerest Thanks" to her readers, to whom she owned herself "highly honoured," adding that "[a]s the World is sensible I have no VIEW OF FORTUNE, but what I must, by HEAVEN'S ASSISTANCE, strike out of myself, I hope I shall find a Continuance of the Favour I at present am blessed with, and shall think it my Duty most carefully to preserve; not only in Regard to my own Interest, but from a grateful respect to those who kindly confer it" (pp. 269–70). This gratitude sounds sincere, and most explicitly indicates what all three women came to appreciate through their autobiographical practice, that personal individuality, autonomy, and authority depended upon establishing and controlling a discursive self-identity through contact with the anonymous public.

Current scholarship has redirected serious attention to the proto-autobiographical efforts of these female authors, who have in the past been the victims of critical condescension and neglect. One recent study adduces the work of Charke, Pilkington, and Phillips to show how eighteenth-century women writers both reproduced and revised received ideas about female character in their private experience. On the one hand, each woman represented herself as a victim of male superiority which, in this view, implies female consent to domination by males. But on the other hand, we are told, the women contradicted male authority "by redefining the fall and the status of women, by exploiting a public forum to insist on the power of the printed word, and by resisting the textual production of a consistent and unified female identity that rests safely within middling common sense."[81] While this assessment of the importance of Pilkington, Charke, and Phillips works within the narrow field of meaning defined by female resistance to male authority, I believe we can appreciate their cultural impact even better if we demarcate their field of signification more broadly, by reading their work in the light of the transformation of autobiographical practice in general, and its impact upon the acculturation of the individualist self. For in this larger perspective it is less apparent that these women were resisting the production of unified identity and middling common sense than it is that they were actually contributing to the making of such discursive constructs, by reinventing biographical practice. In this manner, for better or worse, Charke, Pilkington, and Phillips acted as revolutionaries rather than reactionaries. Their proto-feminism unintentionally advanced a bourgeois paradigm.

The "autobiographical" tradition in the eighteenth century, such as it was, was in transition from constituting a largely religious discourse to a secular one, in which the historical particularity and self-identity of the person as an individual took priority over universal ideologies and corporate identities. During this transition period, no clear style or voice of authority had been established, either in terms of gender or of class. But the manipulation of criminal confession was pushing on toward a kind of personal authenticity which tended to be subjective, masculine, and non-aristocratic. The pattern or form of this new autobiography was also pushing toward the closure and unity of plot, especially in the case of texts designed as or modeled upon printed books, which required that a discourse be "finished" in a way that a manuscript text need not. However, even by the end of the eighteenth century the emplotted or unified autobiographical narrative was in actual practice the exception, not the norm. Rather than resist this new trend, the female authors actually participated in its further development, by offering popular and convincing examples of the autonomous, self-assertive, and authoritative form of auto-biographical self-identity which had been established by the criminal biography. They achieved this by appropriating and extending the confessional format as the framework for representing their own, non-religious, identity, and by publishing the results themselves, for personal profit. The endeavor earned each woman personal fame built precisely on the terms established by the particular and unique verbal contents of her book; as a corollary, each reaped a material profit which enabled her to act independently and autonomously in public space as an individual subject – a feat few men, let alone women, could manage at the time. The paradigm of personal responsibility displayed in the autobiographical practice of Charke and her female compeers was essentially masculine (indeed, each woman rejected traditional femininity completely by the action of putting her *authentic* speech into *print*) and middle-class, in that it represented the ideal of an upwardly mobile, self-made subject.

Finally, though each woman's narrative fails at the formal level to achieve the unity of closure found in emplotted stories, this omission seems less a consequence of her conscious rejection of a dominant, even repressive, form than the result of her inability to perceive such a form in any dimension of her experience. Although the criminal confessions contained the outlines of a tightly organized tragedy, thanks to the ordinary's habit of representing each case as a moral parable, none of the imitators appropriating their discourse appreciated or developed their parabolic structure in her own *Life*. The "thread of history" in each case was spun of one damn thing after another, in the manner of a historical chronicle. A conventional secular *Life* of action and adventure was therefore more open-ended, more comic, than tragic in form. Such a tragicomic format was appropriate, given that this was a period of perspectival transition from a divinely ordained universe to one made by human subjects.

There is also a practical explanation for the absence of plot. In the first place, the works were serials. If we take the prefaces and digressions within separate parts at their word, the narratives were composed incrementally, and therefore dialogically, in response to the public's reception of previously issued parts. This piecemeal method of assembling each text mitigated against the tightly woven structure of an overarching authorial intention. No end was figured from the beginning, as in the case of novels. Such projects as these could only end arbitrarily, as the waning of public interest, the intervention of legal authorities, the disinclination or actual death of the author (as in Pilkington's case), or some other accident of chance dictated. More importantly, however, apart from the criminal confessions, whose plots were hardly compelling, the cultural repertoire which Charke, Pilkington, and Phillips drew upon in composing their works – the she-tragedies on the contemporary stage and the popular "little histories" of women writers such as Delarivier Manley, Eliza Heywood, and Mary Davis – directed little attention to plot. In the theater the action, even in tragedy, depended largely upon constantly changing scene and hyperbolic, almost parodic, speech, rather than the meticulous unfolding of a complicated storyline. The effect of such texts was rather like that of television: motion, or flow, held the play together, rather than plot. In the romances of Manley and her cohorts, the story was the same: the reader participated in a dramatic spectacle of passion and emotion. The more cerebral process of following an intricate plot did not enter into the popular literary imagination until after the deliberate intentional structures of largely male novelists had been absorbed by a generation of readers.

In spite of this, a conclusion or denouement of sorts does surface in each woman's autobiography in the form of the discovery of personal authority. I argued above how Phillips and Pilkington made their own self-authorship the focus or aim of their discourses, through repeated reference to the writing and reception of their book texts. Though Charke appears less insistent on this point, she also managed to communicate the relationship between the production of an auto-biographical book and an authorial self-identity; about midway through her narrative, apropos of almost nothing, she interrupts her tale momentarily to explain to the reader how she came to accept her unfortunate experience because, she says, she realized that "I was then what I made myself" (p. 147). Perhaps that was the moment in her life when she decided unconsciously to quit the road and take up storytelling. If it was, she did not represent it as a turning-point in her *Life*. On the other hand, the message of personal responsibility and narrative self-control permeates her discourse, and lingers in the reader's memory as the residue of his encounter with the textual performance of Charlotte Charke.

Epilogue:
"The Author . . . Our Hero"

No youth did I in education waste;
Happily I'd an intuitive *Taste*:

.   .   .   .

Nature's my guide; all pedantry I scorn;
Pains I abhor, I was an Author born.

Lackington's epigraph, edition of 1792

The Hero as *Man of Letters* . . . is altogether a product of these new ages; and so long as the wondrous art of *Writing*, or of Ready-writing which we call *Printing*, subsists, he may be expected to continue, as one of the main forms of Heroism for all future ages. He is, in various respects, a very singular phenomenon.

Thomas Carlyle, On Heroes, Hero-Worship, & the Heroic in
History (1841)

The link between the autobiographical practice of the scandalous memoirists and that of our first individualist James Lackington is represented by the contents of a mixed bag of maverick writers who self-published their "memoirs" after 1755. These authors and their books represent the penultimate stage of the pre-modern autobiographical tradition. The books and the narratives were deliberately designed to establish the individual authority of their independent subjects–writers–producers–distributors. The only quality distinguishing such works from Lackington's *Memoirs* is the absence of story in the form of the narrative. If we credit the authors, their texts were produced to serve apologetic intentions; but in effect they seem to have been conceived chiefly for financial profit. For instance, Laetitia Pilkington's son John, who himself undertook the publication of the final, posthumous volume of her *Memoirs*, continued in his mother's wake by publishing his own *Life*, entitled *The Real*

Story of John Carteret Pilkington. It appeared in London in 1760. Like his mother's, Pilkington's book was sold to subscribers. He also imitated Teresia Constantia Phillips by autographing the title-page of each copy. Curiously though, *The Real Story* contained as its frontispiece a mezzotint of his mother, instead of an image of Pilkington himself. Upon reading the text one appreciates the appropriateness of this gesture; Pilkington was not really interested in telling his own story, he was instead attempting to cash in on his mother's reputation.

The other self-publishers leading up to Lackington included, for example, the Irish adventurer Captain Peter Drake, who in Dublin in 1755, at age 84, published his confessional *Memoirs* in a small edition of around 300 copies, of which nearly all were subscribed to in advance by friends and local acquaintances. However, Drake's family was scandalized by his account of his conduct and, fearing the book might besmirch their reputations as well as his, they rushed to the printer's shop and purchased and destroyed nearly all the copies of the *Memoirs*' first and only impression. Around the same time Simon Mason, a Birmingham quack at a low point in his career, published his *Narrative of the Life and Distresses of Simon Mason, Apothecary*. The point of this endeavor, Mason explained, was ostensibly "that I may convince the World that if my Knowledge in my Profession is deficient, my Industry and Application have not been wanting; and that I have done all that I could possibly do, in my Circumstances, to maintain myself and Family, in that small Sphere of Life I am plac'd in, with the greatest Assiduity; and if I have not some Qualifications requisite to make a Man prosperous in this World, yet I have endeavor'd to be as useful as it was in my Power."[1] He also intended his *Narrative* to get subscribers to his forthcoming treatise, *Practical Observations in Physick*, a prospectus for which was bound in at the conclusion of his narrative. The Scottish doctor James Houstoun published his own "memoirs" of his life and travels in a single volume in 1753, which he entitled his *Works*. Though it was obvious that Houstoun wanted money more than a literary reputation in exchange for his book, he nevertheless took time to offer a less mercenary rationale for his writing, which articulated the new perspective on biography and biographical subjects being embraced within the culture at large:

> Of all History I have always had the greatest Pleasure, satisfaction, and Edification from *Memoirs of Lives*, especially when wrote by the Persons themselves, from *Caesar's* Commentaries to *Colley Cibber's*

Life; for it is impossible, even for the best Limner, to draw a just Picture
to the Likeness, unless the Original is the Object of his Senses. It is true,
all Actions in human Life, especially the glorious Transactions of the
Great, are the Object of our Senses, but none know the original Source
and secret Springs of those Actions and Transactions but the Actor
himself.[2]

Houstoun's focus on "the actor himself" as the privileged knower of
"the original source and secret springs" of his own experience reflects
the increasingly widespread assumption that persons functioned
individually, as their own authors. The notion of persons as instruments of divine providence was withering away.

At the same time that Houstoun and his cohorts were pursuing
their financial interests, biographical discourse itself achieved unprecedented prominence in Britain, as the record of individual contribu-
tions to national achievement. In 1745 William Oldys commenced
the serial publication of his encyclopedic, six-volume folio book,
Biographia Britannica which, as its introduction explained, would
represent the "compleat *Body* of *British Biography*, and contain a
much larger, and more methodical Collection of *Personal History*,
than hitherto has ever appeared."[3] In Oldys's work, the deviant,
individualist values of less dignified collections such as Captain
Johnson's *General History of the Lives and Adventures of the Most
Famous Highwaymen* were embodied in legitimate, mainstream
subjects represented both for their own sake, in a "British Temple of
Honour" (as Oldys dubbed his book), and for the information of
like-minded readers. As the preface predicted, "this Body of Lives
being once in the hands of the Publick . . . every man of genius, every
person endowed with a generous and liberal spirit, will become more
steady and more assiduous, as well as more eager in pursuit of
knowledge and virtue, when he is sensible that his labours will not
be buried in oblivion, but that whatever he gloriously atchieves will
be faithfully recorded."[4] The representation of such lives suggests
that Britain was on its way to seeing itself as a nation of individual
"men of genius."

Furthermore, as the self-publishers were at work and Oldys's
volumes were trickling into being, Samuel Johnson was busy elevating
the general value and understanding of individual biography with
essays on it in the *Rambler* (No. 60, 13 October 1750) and *Idler*
(No. 84, 24 November 1759). He baldly stated that "no species of
writing seems more worthy of cultivation than biography, since none
can be more delightful or more useful, none can more certainly
enchain the heart by irresistible interest, or more widely diffuse

instruction to every diversity of condition" (*Rambler*). In this claim Johnson of course echoed earlier proponents of life-writing such as Richard Baxter; however the kind of discourse Johnson recommended was altogether different from the Christian/aristocratic tradition Baxter had in mind. Unlike Baxter, who believed life-writing should represent a universal pattern of virtue, Johnson rather shared his contemporary Houstoun's opinion that biography be particular, and delve beneath the surface of *res gestae* to reveal the original source and secret springs of authentic being in the making. Johnson wrote:

> biography has often been allotted to writers who seem very little acquainted with the nature of their task, or very negligent about the performance. They rarely afford any other account than might be collected from public papers, but imagine themselves writing a life when they exhibit a chronological series of actions or preferments; and so little regard the manners or behaviour of their heroes that more knowledge may be gained of a man's real character by a short conversation with one of his servants, than from a formal and studied narrative, begun with his pedigree and ended with his funeral. (*Rambler*)

Also like Houstoun, Johnson believed that the kind of discourse best suited to the task of discovering "real character" was that produced by the biographical subject himself: "Those relations are therefore commonly of most value in which the writer tells his own story" (*Idler*). To some extent this sentiment explains Johnson's tendency to read books in the light of their writers' biographies, as if they were instantiations of an authorial self-identity. This habit was promoted by such projects as his own *Lives of the Poets* and Boswell's epochal *Life of Johnson*, which together started a revolution in literary criticism, turning it away from mere description of the text toward analysis of its discourse as the key to the writer's character. A kind of ideal or construct, the self-identity of the author, was being forged in the critical alliance of his "Life and Works." As a result, it became normal to treat books as instantiations of individual personalities. As James Lackington put it, "books are our most constant and most faithful companions and friends" (1794, p. 454). Lackington's comment bears witness to the fact that the reciprocal pattern of recursive interaction between books and self-identities was being solidly established even among the least privileged of readers.

Lackington's *Memoirs* was both part and product of these cultural developments, moved along by the advent of the novel. The *Memoirs* represents its subject as both "ingenious author" and "hero" in an unconscious confluence of identities, explicit only in its table of contents, where Lackington appears in both guises, introduced first as "the author," the writing subject, and then mutating into "our hero," the acting one. In his story, writing and acting were unified by a single discursive structure. The text was a heroic performance, in which Lackington publicly demonstrated his own self-mastery, by representing the making of his peculiar genius. From our standpoint, the work was original in two senses. First, it was the earliest auto-biography to represent the life of its subject in novelistic terms, as an unfolding *story* of personal development. Second, as such, it was the first manifestation of a kind of self-identity which would become predominant in Britain and throughout the Continent in the nine-teenth century: that of the person as his own author, cultivating and nurturing the development of his unique "character," or self-identity, and who is therefore perceived in his social relations as being individually responsible for his life.

Of course, the authority of modern autobiographical discourse and individualist self-identity was not acculturated overnight. Comprehending narrativity is, as Robert Scholes has explained, "a matter of learned or acquired behavior, like the acquisition of a particular language."[5] We may abandon Scholes's simile and say that the advent of autobiography *was* the popular enactment of a new language of self-representation. One practitioner alone, even in the context of Johnson's and others' promotion of biography and individ-ual genius, could not in himself decisively turn the course of centuries of discursive practice; nor, indeed, did he attempt to do so. It is only in retrospect that Lackington's *Memoirs* appears so significant. As the contemporary response to the text shows, the ideological orien-tation evident in the *Memoirs* was but dimly appreciated in its day.

Still, the drift was hardly negligible, however slow. The small notice of the *Memoirs* in the *Gentleman's Magazine* for December 1791 called the book an "addition to modern biography," and noted the presence of those secret springs of real character Houstoun and Johnson demanded to know; it said the *Memoirs* would teach "religionists, how enthusiasm is supported, the lovers of the gentle craft how to earn a scanty livelihood, and the author's fellow-traders, and tradesmen of every description, how to acquire immense fortunes by SMALL PROFITS, *bound* by INDUSTRY, and *clasped* by OECONOMY. – "[6] Likewise, the *English Review* for July of the same year noted how "[a]s an author, Mr. Lackington is commendable in two points of view: he is entertaining, and he is useful ... the plain and undissembled manner in which he relates the means of his success, will instruct others, and act at once as a spur and guide to their industry." Further, it explained how his story inculcated "the best of lessons to a commercial nation; proving, by the convincing arguments of fact and example, that sobriety and industry, directed by good sense, will lead to opulence." The plot, it suggested, demonstrated how "minds of a peculiar stamp are superior to all situations, and burst resistless through barriers which are insurmountable to the herd of mankind."[7] None called Lackington an individualist or his book an autobiography, but the sense of these remarks is unmistakably close.

Even the negative criticism, such as Peter Pindar's printed satire of Lackington, *Ode to the Hero of Finsbury Square; Congratulatory on his Late Marriage, and Illustrative of his Genius as his own Biographer*, suggests that the novel message of the *Memoirs* had been received. The *Ode*, which appeared in 1795, the year of the publication of the "tenth" (probably the fifth) edition of the *Memoirs*, treated Lackington's virtual presence in his book as equal to his physical presence in his shop, newly removed to Finsbury Square, a stone's throw away from the former location in Chiswell Street. Pindar represented Lackington in terms which any reader of Romantic verse would easily understand:

> Oh! thou whose mind, unfetter'd, undisguised,
>   Soars like the lark into the empty air;
> Whose arch exploits by subtlety devised,
>   Have stamped renown on Finsbury's New Square,
> Great "hero" list! Whilst the sly muse repeats
>   Thy nuptial ode, thy prowess great *in sheets*.[8]

Pindar derived his caricature of Lackington from a perceptive reading of Lackington's "sheets" – his book, not his bed, though the conjunction is of course significant – as a total demonstration of its author's self-identity. This is explicit, for example, in Pindar's characterization of the work's frontispiece:

> Where is the Limner, that, with Skill transcendant,
>   On the proud Canvas fix'd the Image true;
> Plac'd the fine Form in Posture independent
>   And Bookseller and Author held to View?
> Ah, glorious Sight! What Feast for future Ages,
>   To view the Picture first – and then to read the Pages!!!
>   (p. 18)

Indeed, according to Pindar, "his sage Work o'er every Rival shines, / Tho' SMOLLETT droops – tho' GIBBON's Page declines" (p. 19). On the basis of this reading Pindar concluded mockingly, but nevertheless accurately, that Lackington was the "'EGO' Lord" (p. 23). The *Ode's* frontispiece Accompanying the *Ode* is a crude engraving depicting a rather unhandsome Lackington stepping into his coach with the aid of a stack of religious books as his step-stool (symbolizing his enlightened contempt for religion); a book entitled *My Own Memoirs* is under his arm; he is admired by a small crowd of Londoners (his popular audience); while his dog (who according to Lackington recognized his master in the original portrait) defecates on a copy of the new edition of his book, lying open in the street: the dog's target is its frontispiece. Without question, the message bound up in the pages of the *Memoirs* resonated in the contemporary imagination. The fact that Pindar's satire was directed as much *ad liberum* as *ad hominem* indicates that a significant part of the popular audience intuited the essential connection between Lackington's self-identity and his book. In this manner, the egotistical paradigm of individualist selfhood materialized on the printed autobiographical page.

Paradoxically, perhaps only Lackington himself remained insecure about the impact of his performance. He retired from bookselling in 1798, leaving his business in the hands of a third cousin, George Lackington, and removed himself from London to the country; first to Surrey, then to Somersetshire, and later to Devonshire, where he died in 1815 at age 70. Shortly after retiring he began to rethink his liberal views, and turned again to religion. He built several provincial meeting-houses for the Wesleyan Methodists, and endowed livings for a preacher in each one. These actions were complemented by the publication in 1804 of another autobiographical book, *The Confessions of J. Lackington*. The title was *not* a homage to Rousseau. The text is such a jumble of discourse that a hack, claiming that Lackington "really was doing no more than tacking together shreds and patches when he was preparing his volume," published a revised version of the *Confessions* in the same year.[9] Lackington intended the book to announce his spiritual rebirth, at which he renounced his former life as an "infidel," as he regarded himself to have been, and warned readers against the lessons of his *Memoirs*:

> In the latter end of the year 1791, when my Memoirs were first published, I had not witnessed, to its extent, the pernicious influence of infidel opinions upon all ranks in society. After I became better acquainted with the dreadful effects of infidelity in others, I was sorry

for what I had done, for I was then fully convinced, that the generality of mankind will always be much happier and better whilst under the influence of religious fanaticism, and even superstition, than when they have lost all regard to, or sense of, religion. Besides, I had known by myself and others, that for want of sufficient knowledge, many when they are reasoned out of fanaticism, are liable to go to the other extreme, by plunging into infidelity.[10]

Indeed, he confessed, "When I look into my memoirs, I shudder to see what I have done. I have wantonly treated of, and sported with the most solemn and precious truths of the gospel. O God, lay not this sin to my Charge!" (p. 185). Moreover, he placed the blame for his novel-reading squarely on the shoulders of his deceased wife, and singled out Amory's *Life of Buncle*, the novel by which means he said in the *Memoirs*, "my soul took its freedom up," as a "pernicious work" (p. 4). In effect, our modern author seems almost to have regressed to the status of a malefactor facing the gallows a century before, with an eleventh-hour, "hocus-pocus" conversion.

But if such was indeed his design, it lay within Lackington's prerogative as a modern author to enact such a deliberate role-reversal. For by renouncing his apostasy, he merely underlined rather than contradicted the encoded message of the *Memoirs*. He was the creator of his story, and therefore of his character. He thus retained the power to revise his account at any point in his life; after all, the *Memoirs* purported to represent only his first forty-five years. Further experience might change the particulars, while continuing to under-score the overarching action of original self-creation. The individual-ist self possesses the capacity to inhabit many particular selves, should the demand for a coherent narrative require such dynamic variety. In Lackington's case, all that was required to actualize the revised Lackington personality was a convincing discursive perform-ance. The *Confessions* were but another version of Lackington's self-identity – though a clearly nostalgic, rather than forward-looking representation, as the *Memoirs* had been. Perhaps the work's retro-grade character explains why it is so incoherent, and why few contemporaries found it worth their while. The *Confessions* lacked both a plot and an animated style, and so enjoyed no reputation with the public. The book entered literary oblivion after a single edition on each side of the Atlantic.

The *Memoirs*, in contrast, continued to entertain audiences even after Lackington's death. In 1830 it was reprinted as part of a series commenced in 1826 entitled *Autobiography; a Collection of the Most Instructive and Amusing Lives ever Published, Written by the Parties*

Themselves. According to its unnamed editor, the series was intended partly to distinguish the value of autobiography and autobiographical subjects each as entities in their own right: "There is such an essential distinction between self-composed and other Biography, that the principle literary object of our undertaking is at once apparent. It is ... to collect into one consecutive publication, genuine materials for a diversified study of the human character, by selecting the most curious and interesting Autobiographical Memoirs now extant."[11] This was the first time the word "autobiography" had been systematically applied to English biographical discourse. However, all thirty-four volumes issued in the series were reprints of works originally written (and a few actually published) earlier, mostly in the eighteenth century. As such, the series represented the culmination, as well as the canonization, of the vision encoded in lives written almost in anticipation of the Romantic era, among them those of Cibber, Hume, Lily, Voltaire, Drury, Whitfield, Ferguson, Charke, Mary Robinson, Gibbon, Cellini, and "our hero" James Lackington. We are told that his *Life*, "although a mere etching, has something special about it, which entitles it to a place amidst a collection of autobiographical portraits, in which originality and variety, rather than high finish and precision, form the leading objects of attraction" (1830, p. vi). Indeed.

Within a generation or two after Lackington – that is, in the imaginations of his young readers – modern autobiographical practice obtained hegemony within its discursive field, temporarily excluding though never completely annihilating other modes of self-representation. In Charlotte Brontë's novel *Jane Eyre* (1847), which arrived in its original format with the subtitle *An Autobiography* (a detail strangely suppressed in most editions produced today), modern autobiography even challenged authority in the field of the novel, a sign of its cultural ascendancy. Emplotted art and life were evidently intertwined. Likewise did the individualist self overtake the domain of self-identity, though it would be decades before such knowledge emerged from the space of practical consciousness and literary textuality to be explicitly articulated as a culture and an ideology, as it was, positively, by Burckhardt and others in the social sciences, and negatively by Nietzsche and his inheritors in the humanities. This paradigm shift, we may conclude, was not inevitable. It was the product of histories, and so will it continue to be, if it prevails.

Notes

Prologue: Advertisements for Myself

1 James Lackington, *Memoirs of the Forty-Five First Years of the Life of James Lackington*, 2nd edn (London, 1792), p. 260. Hereafter page references to this and other editions are cited by year of issue in the text. Lackington self-published several revised versions of the *Memoirs* in his lifetime. Those I refer to are: the first edition of 1791, with the slightly different title, *Memoirs of the First Forty-Five Years of the Life of James Lackington*; a second, "new edition," issued in 1792, considerably enlarged; a third version, a slightly enlarged version of the 1792 edition, also identified on its title-page as a "new edition," issued in 1794. I also refer to the edition of the *Memoirs* issued posthumously in 1830 by Whittaker, Treacher, and Arnot, which appears to be a reprint of Lackington's "new edition" of 1794.

2 George Whitehead, whom Wesley's executors originally proposed to write the authorized biography, figured that the book might earn profits of £2,000 in two years alone, according to Frank Cumbers, *The Book Room: The Story of the Methodist Publishing House and Epworth Press* (London: The Epworth Press, 1956), p. 78.

3 Quoted in ibid, p. 78.

4 Ibid.

5 *Rambler*, No. 60 (13 Oct. 1750).

6 Georges Gusdorf, "Conditions and Limits of Autobiography," trans. James Olney, in James Olney, ed., *Autobiography: Essays Theoretical and Critical* (Princeton: Princeton University Press, 1980), p. 31; hereafter page references are cited in the text.

7 For a lucid discussion of the arguments explicating autobiography's terminus, see Michael Sprinker, "Fictions of the Self: The End of Autobiography," in James Olney, ed., *Autobiography: Essays Theoretical and*

Critical (Princeton: Princeton University Press, 1980), pp. 321–42; also, Candace Lang, "Autobiography in the Aftermath of Romanticism," *diacritics* 12 (winter 1982), pp. 2–16.

Chapter 1   Narrative Subjects

1 Ian Watt, *The Rise of the Novel: Studies in Defoe, Richardson and Fielding* (Berkeley and Los Angeles: University of California Press, 1957), p. 60.

2 For two recent surveys, see Steven Lukes, *Individualism* (Oxford: Blackwell, 1973); Daniel Shanahan, *Toward a Genealogy of Individualism* (Amherst: University of Massachusetts Press, 1992).

3 For a discussion of the distinction between "person" and "individual" in the human and social sciences, see Michael Carrithers, Steven Collins and Steven Lukes, eds, *The Category of the Person* (Cambridge: Cambridge University Press, 1985).

4 Thomas C. Heller, Morton Sosna and David E. Wellerby, eds, *Reconstructing Individualism: Autonomy, Individuality, and the Self in Western Thought* (Stanford: Stanford University Press, 1986), p. 1.

5 Elizabeth Fox-Genovese, *Feminism Without Illusions: A Critique of Individualism* (Chapel Hill and London: University of North Carolina Press, 1991), p. 231.

6 Clifford Geertz, "'From the Native's Point of View': On the Nature of Anthropological Understanding," in Richard A. Shweder and Robert A. LeVine, eds, *Culture Theory: Essays on Mind, Self, and Emotion* (Cambridge: Cambridge University Press, 1984), p. 126.

7 Friedrich Nietzsche, *The Will to Power*, trans. Walter Kaufmann and R. J. Hollingdale, ed. Walter Kaufmann (New York: Vintage, 1967), pp. 267, 269.

8 Emile Benveniste, *Problems in General Linguistics*, trans. Mary Elizabeth Meek (Coral Gables: University of Miami Press, 1971), pp. 226, 227.

9 Kaja Silverman, *The Subject of Semiotics* (Oxford and New York: Oxford University Press, 1983), p. 52.

10 Jacob Burckhardt, *The Civilization of the Renaissance in Italy*, trans. S. G. C. Middlemore, 2 vols (New York: Harper & Row, 1958), vol. I, p. 43.

11 For a more recent assertion of this basic thesis see Walter Ullman, *The Individual and Society in the Middle Ages* (Baltimore: The Johns Hopkins University Press, 1966). Basing his account primarily on Roman and Christian law, Ullman extends the changed political climate back further than Burckhardt does, and expands its borders beyond Italy.

12 Alan Macfarlane, *The Culture of Capitalism* (Oxford and Cambridge, MA: Blackwell, 1987), p. 127.

13 Louis Dumont, *Essays on Individualism: Modern Ideology in Anthropological Perspective* (Chicago and London: University of Chicago Press, 1986), pp. 55, 65ff. Cf. Max Weber, *The Protestant Ethic and the Spirit of Capitalism*, trans. Talcott Parsons (New York: Charles Scribner's Sons, 1958).

14 Roger Chartier, ed., *Passions of the Renaissance*, vol. III of *A History of Private Life*, trans. Arthur Goldhammer (Cambridge, MA, and London: Belknap Press, 1989), p. 7.

15 Norbert Elias, *The Society of Individuals*, ed. Michael Schröter; trans. Edmund Jephcott (Oxford: Blackwell, 1991), esp pp. 121–51. See also his major work, *Über den Prozess der Zivilization*, translated as two volumes by Edmund Jephcott, *The History of Manners* (New York: Pantheon, 1976), and *Power & Civility* (New York: Pantheon, 1982).

16 Erving Goffman, *The Presentation of Self in Everyday Life* (Garden City, NY: Doubleday & Company, 1959).

17 Indeed, Goffman's repeated reference to "the individual" performer in *The Presentation of Self* reveals how much the study was a product of its time and place. But one need only substitute the generic human category "person" for "individual" in his book to open up the possibility of alternative performances.

18 In a social-theoretical study which has greatly informed my thinking, Anthony Giddens describes the modern self-identity as essentially a reflexively organized life-plan, at the core of which lies autobiography (Anthony Giddens, *Modernity and Self-Identity: Self and Society in the Late Modern Age* (Stanford: Stanford University Press, 1991), p. 76, passim.

19 For a discussion of one such possibility, within the culture of pre-Columbian Native Americans, and the form of "autobiography" appropriate to it, see Hertha Wong, *Sending My Heart Back Across the Years: Tradition and Innovation in Native American Autobiography* (New York and Oxford: Oxford University Press, 1992), esp. ch. 2.

20 For a discussion of the concept of "field" relevant to my study, see Pierre Bourdieu, *The Field of Cultural Production*, ed. and introd. by Randal Johnson (n.p.: Columbia University Press, 1993).

21 For Gusdorf, see n. 6 in the prologue. The terms "classic" and "modern" have been used, in turn, by Roy Pascal, *Design and Truth in Autobiography* (Cambridge: Harvard University Press, 1960), p. 36 and Wayne Shumaker, *English Autobiography: Its Emergence, Materials, and Form* (Berkeley and Los Angeles: University of California Press, 1954), p. 4.

22 For examples before 1600, see Georg Misch, *A History of Autobiography in Antiquity*, trans. E. W. Dickes, 2 vols (1907; repr. London: Routledge & Kegan Paul Ltd, 1950).

23 For a discussion of the term's etymology, see Robert Folkenflik, "Introduction: The Institution of Autobiography," in Robert Folkenflik, ed., *The Culture of Autobiography: Constructions of Self-Representation* (Stanford: Stanford University Press, 1993), pp. 1–5.

24 Lukes, *Individualism*, pp. 45–72.

25 Charles Taylor, "The Concept of a Person," in *Human Agency and Language: Philosophical Papers*, vol. I (Cambridge: Cambridge University Press, 1985), p. 97. In my account, Taylor's universal concept represents a historically specific entity: the person with an individualist self-identity. I doubt Taylor would endorse my historical qualification of his "person."

26 Ibid., p. 97.

27 Ibid., p. 104.

28 Charles Taylor, *Sources of the Self: The Making of the Modern Identity* (Cambridge: Harvard University Press, 1989), p. 47.

29 Alasdair MacIntyre, *After Virtue: A Study in Moral Theory*, 2nd edn (Notre Dame, IN: Notre Dame University Press, 1984), p. 205.

30 Ibid., p. 208.

31 Ibid., p. 212.
32 Ibid, pp. 213ff.
33 Ibid., p. 216. In my reading of MacIntyre, as in my reading of Taylor, I treat what he describes as a universal type – the narrative subject or narrative self – as a historically contingent mode of self-identity. I am not sure that MacIntyre would concur with my view.
34 Karl J. Weintraub, "Autobiography and Historical Consciousness," *Critical Inquiry* 1 (1975), p. 827.
35 Jean Starobinski, "The Style of Autobiography," trans. Seymour Chatman, in James Olney, ed., *Autobiography: Essays Theoretical and Critical* (Princeton: Princeton University Press, 1980), p. 75.
36 R. H. Tawney, *The Agrarian Problem in the Sixteenth Century* (London: Longmans, Green & Co., 1912); id., *Religion and Rise of Capitalism* (1926; repr. Harmondsworth: Pelican, 1938).
37 Christopher Hill, *Society and Puritanism in Pre-Revolutionary England* (London: Martin Secker & Warburg Ltd, 1964); C. B. Macpherson, *The Political Theory of Possessive Individualism: Hobbes to Locke* (Oxford: Oxford University Press, 1962).
38 Lawrence Stone, *The Family, Sex and Marriage in England 1500–1800* (New York: Harper & Row, 1977), p. 4.
39 Alan Macfarlane, *The Origins of English Individualism: The Family, Property and Social Transition* (Oxford: Blackwell, 1978), p. 163.

Chapter 2   A Novel Self-Identity

1 Watt, *Rise of the Novel*, pp. 62, 63ff.
2 John Feather, *A History of British Publishing* (London: Croom Helm, 1988), p. 124, credits Lackington as the first remainderer – the first to recognize that selling huge numbers of books at marginal profits could in the long term generate more income than selling fewer books at higher profits. See also Richard D. Landon, "Small Profits do Great Things: James Lackington and Eighteenth-Century Bookselling," *Studies in Eighteenth-Century Culture* 5 (1976), pp. 387–99.
3 Charles Knight, *Shadows of the Old Booksellers* (London: Bell and Daldy, 1865), pp. 282–3.
4 Watt, *Rise of the Novel*, pp. 75, 15.
5 [Daniel Defoe], *The Life and Strange Surprizing Adventures of Robinson Crusoe* (London, 1719), p. 75
6 Elizabeth W. Bruss, *Autobiographical Acts: The Changing Situation of a Literary Genre* (Baltimore and London: The Johns Hopkins University Press, 1976), pp. 6, 13.
7 Elizabeth W. Bruss, "Eye for I: Making and Unmaking Autobiography in Film," in James Olney, ed., *Autobiography: Essays Theoretical and Critical* (Princeton: Princeton University Press, 1980), p. 301. This essay presents a slightly revised statement of her concept of the autobiographical act.
8 For an account of the institutional transformations causing such disembedding of the person, see Anthony Giddens, *The Consequences of Modernity* (Stanford: Stanford University Press, 1990).
9 For a subtle discussion of the improvisation of discursive self-identity by

Aphra Behn in the context of the Restoration theater and the market for its printed discourse, see Catherine Gallagher, *Nobody's Story: The Vanishing Acts of Women Writers in the Marketplace, 1670–1820* (Berkeley and Los Angeles: University of California Press, 1994), ch. 1. Gallagher describes the result of Behn's practice as the constitution of "a split persona," of a private "true self" and a public "sold self;" in other words, of "a woman hidden behind her own representations" (*Nobody's Story*, pp. 17, 22). My study is concerned with the increasing cultural need for the creation of such "sold" or public selves not just by women writers but by nearly everyone acting in public, and also the concept of the integrity of such selves – to the point where the emphasis placed on articulating the public self is so great that it seems to subsume the true self, collapsing the split persona.

10 Though in her discourse Beauvoir displays a curiously excessive insistence on her individuality. One need only consider the number of times the "I" appears in the first paragraph of her *Memoirs* to find that her claim to what had long been a predominantly male mode of self-identification remained tenuous.

11 This point is made most persuasively by David Saunders and Ian Hunter, "Lessons from the 'Literatory': How to Historicise Authorship," *Critical Inquiry* 17 (1991), pp. 479–509.

12 [Defoe], *Robinson Crusoe*, p. 297.

13 Paul Ricœur, "Narrative Time," in W. J. T. Mitchell, ed., *On Narrative* (Chicago: University of Chicago Press, 1981), p. 167.

14 Robert Scholes, "Language, Narrative, Anti-Narrative," in W. J. T. Mitchell, ed., *On Narrative* (Chicago: University of Chicago Press, 1981), p. 206.

15 Paul Ricœur, *Time and Narrative*, trans. Kathleen McLaughlin and David Pellauer, 3 vols (Chicago and London: University of Chicago Press, 1984), vol. I, pp. 41, 66.

16 Paul Ricœur, "Life: A Story in Search of a Narrator," in Mario J. Valdés, ed., *A Ricœur Reader: Reflection and Imagination* (Toronto and Buffalo: University of Toronto Press, 1991), pp. 425–6; also *Time and Narrative*, I, pp. 33, 65–6.

17 For further discussion of the temporal aspect of narrativity see, in addition to the work of Ricœur cited above, Frank Kermode, *The Sense of an Ending: Studies in the Theory of Fiction* (New York: Oxford University Press, 1967); Peter Brooks, *Reading for the Plot: Design and Intention in Narrative* (New York: Vintage, 1985), esp. ch. 1; John Bender and David E. Wellbery, eds, *Chronotypes: The Construction of Time* (Stanford: Stanford University Press, 1991), esp. the chapter by Jack Goody.

18 Hayden White, "The Value of Narrativity in the Representation of Reality," in his *The Content of the Form: Narrative Discourse and Historical Representation* (Baltimore and London: The Johns Hopkins University Press, 1987), p. 21. Elsewhere in this essay White writes, "if every fully realized story . . . is a kind of allegory, points to a moral, or endows events, whether real or imaginary, with a significance that they do not possess as a mere sequence, then . . . every historical narrative has as its latent or manifest purpose the desire to moralize the events which it treats" (p. 14). For further discussion see Roland Barthes, "Introduction to the Structural Analysis of Narratives," in Roland Barthes, *Image–Music–Text*, ed. and

trans. Stephen Heath (New York: Noonday, 1977), pp. 79–124; Roland Barthes, "The Discourse of History," trans. Stephen Bann, in E. S. Shaffer, ed., *Comparative Criticism: A Yearbook*, vol. III (1981), pp. 3–20; and Louis O. Mink, "Narrative Form as a Cognitive Instrument," in Robert H. Canary and Henry Kozicki, eds, *The Writing of History: Literary Form and Historical Understanding* (Madison: University of Wisconsin Press, 1978), pp. 129–49.

19 Paul Ricœur, *Hermeneutics and the Human Sciences*, ed. and trans. John B. Thompson (Cambridge and Paris: Cambridge University Press and Editions de la Maison des Sciences de l'Homme, 1981), p. 138.

20 For a further elaboration of this concept, see, in addition to Ricœur's work and that of Saunders and Hunter mentioned earlier, Roland Barthes, "The Death of the Author," in Barthes, *Image–Music–Text*, pp. 142–8; Michel Foucault, "What is an Author?" trans. Josué V. Harari, in Josué V. Harari, ed., *Textual Strategies: Perspectives in Post-Structuralist Criticism* (Ithaca: Cornell University Press, 1979), pp. 141–60; Alexander J. Nehamas, "Writer, Work, Text, Author," in Anthony J. Cascardi, ed., *Literature and the Question of Philosophy* (Baltimore and London: The Johns Hopkins University Press, 1987), pp. 265–91.

21 For Whittington, see Caroline M. Barron, "Richard Whittington: The Man behind the Myth," in A. E. J. Hollander and William Kellaway, eds, *Studies in London History* (London: Hodder and Stoughton, 1969), pp. 195–248; for fictional characters see Laura Caroline Stevenson, *Praise and Paradox: Merchants and Craftsmen in Elizabethan Popular Literature* (Cambridge: Cambridge University Press, 1984).

22 Pepys, diary entry for 21 Sept. 1668, quoted by Barron, "Richard Whittington," p. 197 n. 2.

23 Wesley, of course, appreciated this fact. He wrote that "The work of grace would die out in one generation if the Methodists were not a reading people" (quoted in Cumbers, *Book Room*, p. 5).

24 He also likens himself to Dr Johnson's character Ned Drugget (1791, p. 250), whose progress Johnson epitomized in his *Idler*, No. 16 (20 July 1758). Lackington no doubt encountered Johnson's text in his youth.

25 In his *Prospecting: From Reader Response to Literary Anthropology* (Baltimore and London: The Johns Hopkins University Press, 1989), Iser writes: "The staged play of the text does not, then, unfold as a pageant that the reader merely watches, but is both an ongoing event and a happening for the reader, enabling and encouraging direct involvement in the proceedings and indeed in the staging" (p. 259). Hermeneutic theory in general asserts the participatory response of the reader as essential to the "reality" of written texts like novels. See, for example, Paul Ricœur, *Hermeneutics and the Human Sciences*, pp. 131–44. For further discussion of "staged play" in reader-response theory, see Susan R. Suleiman and Inge Crosman, eds, *The Reader in the Text: Essays on Audience and Interpretation* (Princeton: Princeton University Press, 1980); Jane P. Tompkins, ed., *Reader-Response Criticism: From Formalism to Post-Structuralism* (Baltimore and London: The Johns Hopkins University Press, 1980). For a historical account of readers and novels in the eighteenth century whose evidence supports the position advanced here, see Robert Darnton, "Readers Respond to Rousseau: The Fabrication of Romantic Sensibility," in his

The Great Cat Massacre and Other Episodes in French Cultural History (New York: Vintage Books, 1985), pp. 215–56.

26 This point is made most forcefully by Norman N. Holland, "Unity Identity Text Self," in Jane P. Tompkins, ed., *Reader-Response Criticism: From Formalism to Post-Structuralism* (Baltimore and London: The Johns Hopkins University Press, 1980), pp. 118–33. For a concurring view in psychological theory, see Stephen Crites, "Storytime: Recollecting the Past and Projecting the Future," in Theodore J. Sarbin, ed., *Narrative Psychology: The Storied Nature of Human Conduct* (New York: Praeger, 1986), pp. 152–73; and Kenneth J. Gergen and Mary M. Gergen, "Narratives of the Self," in K. Scheibe and T. Sarbin, eds, *Studies in Social Identity* (New York: Praeger, 1983), pp. 254–73.

27 The interrelationship between novel and autobiography in the eighteenth century is explored, largely from the vantage point of the novel, by Patricia Meyer Spacks, *Imagining a Self: Autobiography and Novel in Eighteenth-Century England* (Cambridge and London: Harvard University Press, 1976); see also her more recent book, *Desire and Truth: Functions of Plot in Eighteenth-Century English Novels* (Chicago and London: University of Chicago Press, 1990). Two critics of modern autobiography propound a conception of the genre as a positioning by readers: see Jonathan Loesberg, "Autobiography as Genre, Act of Consciousness, Text," *Prose Studies* 4 (1981), pp. 169–85; Janet Varner Gunn, *Autobiography: Toward a Poetics of Experience* (Philadelphia: University of Pennsylvania Press, 1982).

28 Tate Wilkinson, *Memoirs of His Own Life, By Tate Wilkinson, Patentee of the Theatres-Royal, York and Hull*, 4 vols (York, 1790), vol. I, p. xi.

29 [William Oldys, et at.] *Biographia Britannica; or the Lives of the most Eminent Persons who have flourished in Great Britain and Ireland, from the earliest Ages to the Present Times*, 7 vols (London, 1747–66), vol. I, p. viii. The politically controversial second edition of this work, begun in 1769, to which Lackington made his pitch for inclusion, was never finished. The death of its general editor terminated the project in 1795, at volume V, completed in 1793, ending at "Fastolff."

30 My discussion here and in the paragraphs following is informed principally by the work of Walter Ong, especially his article "Writing is a Technology that Restructures Thought," in Gerd Baumann, ed., *The Written Word: Literacy in Transition* (Oxford: Clarendon Press, 1986), pp. 23–50, and his book *Orality and Literacy: The Technologizing of the Word* (London and New York: Methuen, 1982).

31 Ong, "Writing is a Technology," p. 38.

32 Ong, *Orality and Literacy*, pp. 122, 132.

33 See D. F. McKenzie, "Typography and Meaning: The Case of William Congreve," in Giles Barber and Bernhard Fabian, eds, *Buch and Buchhandel in Europa im achtzehnten Jahrhundert* (Hamburg: Dr Ernst Hauswell & Co., 1981), pp. 81–125.

34 Ong, *Orality and Literacy*, pp. 133, 135, 143. It is therefore hardly coincidental that the first book printed in the English language was a romance, William Caxton's *Recuyell of the Historyes of Troye*, which he translated from the French and printed in the Netherlands in 1475.

35 Ong, *Orality and Literacy*, pp. 131–2. For a relevant application of this aspect of Ong's thought to a case study in eighteenth-century Britain see

Marlon B. Ross, "Authority and Authenticity: Scribbling Authors and the Genius of Print in Eighteenth-Century England," in Martha Woodmansee and Peter Jaszi, eds, *The Construction of Authorship: Textual Appropriation in Law and Literature* (Durham and London: Duke University Press, 1994), pp. 231–57.

36 However, Roger Chartier argues that the essential traits of the printed book which designate that author "were already typical of the manuscript book" in the fifteenth century; see Roger Chartier, *The Order of Books: Readers, Authors, and Libraries in Europe between the Fourteenth and Eighteenth Centuries*, trans. Lydia G. Cochrane (Stanford: Stanford University Press, 1994), pp. 51ff. Though Chartier may be correct, the mechanical reproduction of printed books institutionalized the designation of the author, by making his traits known to more people, especially to non-elites or non-professionals, such as James Lackington – a feat which manuscripts could never achieve. Also, my argument for the significance of mechanical reproduction runs counter to that of Walter Benjamin, who has famously claimed that mass reproduction diminishes a work's aura; for an important qualification of Benjamin's claim, which lends support to my argument here, see Gallagher, *Nobody's Story*, p. 64 n. 30.

37 Cf. "Verses occasioned by reading the life of Mr James Lackington. Addressed to the ingenious author by his unknown friend," *Memoirs*, 1792 edn, following the preface. The "ingenious author" is of course the respectable alternative to the hack, who is a kind of opportunistic upstart and rip-off artist, notorious since the late sixteenth century.

38 Recent discussions of the construction of the author in print include Lisa Jardine, *Erasmus, Man of Letters: The Construction of Charisma in Print* (Princeton: Princeton University Press, 1993); for the eighteenth century in particular, see Alvin Kernan, *Samuel Johnson & the Impact of Print* (Princeton: Princeton University Press, 1987); Julie Stone Peters, *Congreve, the Drama, and the Printed Word* (Stanford: Stanford University Press, 1990). See also Terry Belanger, "Publishers and Writers in Eighteenth-Century England," in Isabel Rivers, ed., *Books and their Readers in Eighteenth-Century England* (Leicester: Leicester University Press, 1982), pp. 5–25.

39 John Feather, "From Rights in Copies to Copyright: The Recognition of Authors' Rights in English Law and Practice in the Sixteenth and Seventeenth Centuries," in Martha Woodmansee and Peter Jaszi, eds, *The Construction of Authorship: Textual Appropriation in Law and Literature* (Durham and London: Duke University Press, 1994), p. 208. For an overview see Feather, *History of British Publishing*.

40 Mark Rose, *Authors and Owners: The Invention of Copyright* (Cambridge and London: Harvard University Press, 1993), pp. 82ff (the phrase quoted appears on p. 91).

41 Ibid., p. 114. See also Martha Woodmansee, "The Genius and the Copyright: Economic and Legal Conditions of the Emergence of the 'Author'," *Eighteenth-Century Studies* 17 (1984), pp. 405–8; and Gallagher, *Nobody's Story*, ch. 3, esp. pp. 158–62.

42 Philippe Lejeune, "The Autobiography of Those Who Do Not Write," in Philippe Lejeune, *On Autobiography*, trans. Katherine Leary, ed. Paul John Eakin (Minneapolis: University of Minnesota Press, 1989), pp. 192–3.

43 This fact of course explains the unusual length of so many titles, especially those for the eighteenth century; for a brief discussion see Philip Gaskell, *A New Introduction to Bibliography* (Oxford and New York: Oxford University Press, 1972), p. 183.

44 John Dawson Carl Buck, "The Motives of Puffing: John Newbery's Advertisements 1742–1767," *Studies in Bibliography* 30 (1977), p. 201.

45 John Gay, *Poetry and Prose*, ed. Vinton A. Dearing, 2 vols (Oxford: Oxford University Press, 1974), vol. I, p. 172.

46 Lackington published a cheap, 2s. edition of the *Memoirs* in 1695, with a different engraving of the same portrait.

47 The participation of other distributors in the sale of Lackington's book is a sign of its value as a commodity: any profits these others made would be a fraction of the retail price, depending on whether the distributor was a wholesaler or retailer or both.

48 Chartier, *Order of Books*, pp. 28–9.

49 Lejeune, "The Autobiography of Those Who Do Not Write," p. 192.

Chapter 3   Christian "Experience"

1 Philip Stubbes, *A Christal Glasse for Christian Women Containing, a most excellent Discourse, of the Godly life and Christian death of Mistresse Katherine Stubbes* (London, 1591). This title, which will be used in all subsequent references to this work, is from the edition of 1592; the unique copy of the 1591 edition lacks a title-page. Excepting the title, all quotations are from the 1591 edition; page references are cited in the text.

2 In the 1592 text, the writer is designated on the title-page as "P.S." (later editions have the full name, "Philip Stvbbes" or "Stvbbs"); the account is narrated by an omniscient narrator, appearing in the opening paragraph of the narrative as "I"; on the same page, "Philip Stubs" is designated as a character, "her [i.e. Katherine Stubbes's] husband."

3 According to Richard Wunderli and Gerald Broce, "The Final Moment before Death in Early Modern England," *Sixteenth-Century Journal* 20 (1989), p. 265, this rather popish encounter was retained in English Protestant theology as "a final test of election": after all was said and done about faith, the ability to confront Satan directly without despair was the ultimate litmus test.

4 Though a verbal masterpiece, *Holy Dying* was probably the least accessible of the works in this tradition. More accessible, and more popular, was Thomas Becon's *The sycke mannes salue*, which appeared in at least thirty editions between its first publication in *c.* 1560 and 1632. For a discussion of such works in Europe, see Mary Catherine O'Connor, *The Art of Dying Well: The Development of the* Ars Moriendi (New York: Columbia University Press, 1942); for England, see Nancy Lee Beaty, *The Craft of Dying: A Study in the Literary Tradition of the* Ars Moriendi *in England* (New Haven and London: Yale University Press, 1970).

5 Jeremy Taylor, *Holy Living and Holy Dying*, ed. P. G. Stanwood, 2 vols (Oxford: Clarendon Press, 1989), vol. II, p. 53. Hereafter page references are cited in the text.

6 Richard Whitford, *The Folowynge of Cryste*, ed. Edward J. Klein (New York and London: Harper & Brothers, 1941), p. 6.

7 Katherine Stubbes also offered a complete script for the dying person, made necessary by liturgical changes brought about by the Reformation in England. The role of the priest at the scene of the death-bed was diminished, and the dying person assumed the initiative in making a full confession of faith. For more on this see Ralph Houlbrooke, "Death, Church, and Family in England between the Late Fifteenth and the Early Eighteenth Centuries," in Ralph Houlbrooke, ed., *Death, Ritual and Bereavement* (London and New York: Routledge, 1989), p. 26.

8 William Cartwright, *The Ordinary, A Comedy* (written *c.* 1635), vol. III, p. v, quoted in Tessa Watt, *Cheap Print and Popular Piety, 1550–1640* (Cambridge: Cambridge University Press, 1991), p. 267. Watt provides the only discussion of *A Christal Glasse* I have been able to locate, on pp. 282–4 of *Cheap Print*.

9 John Lydgate, *The Fall of Princes*, ed. Henry Bergen, 4 vols (Washington: Carnegie Institution, 1923).

10 *A Myrroure for Magistrates*, ed. Lily B. Campbell (1938; repr. New York: Barnes and Noble, 1960), pp. 65–6.

11 In seventeenth-century English Christian literature, the glass was also a condition of human mortality, as in St Paul's words: "Now we see through a glass darkly ..." For further discussion of this meaning, see Frank Livingstone Huntley, *Bishop Joseph Hall and Protestant Meditation in Seventeenth-Century England* (Binghamton, NY: Center for Medieval and Early Renaissance Studies, 1981), p. 11.

12 Henry Wright, *The First Part of the Disquisition of Truth, Concerning Political Affaires* (London, 1616), pp. 71–2, quoted by Louis B. Wright, *Middle-Class Culture in Elizabethan England* (Chapel Hill: University of North Carolina Press, 1935), p. 301.

13 For studies of this aspect of the tradition see, for example, William Haller, *Foxe's Book of Martyrs and the Elect Nation* (London: Jonathan Cape, 1963); and, more recently, John R. Knott, *Discourses of Martyrdom in English Literature, 1563–1694* (Cambridge: Cambridge University Press, 1993).

14 *Dictionary of National Biography*, s.v. Stubbes, Philip.

15 John Foxe, *Acts and Monuments* (London, 1563), sig. AA2ᵛ.

16 Among the many contemporary sources available to Foxe was the archive published by Miles Coverdale: *Certain Most Godly, Fruitful, and Comfortable Letters of such true saints and holy Martyrs of God, as in the late bloody persecution here within this realm, gave their lives for the defence of Christ's holy gospel: written in the time of their affliction and cruel punishment* (London, 1564). This work contains just over 200 letters attributed to the Marian martyrs.

17 Knott, *Discourses*, p. 13. The quotation of Foxe is ibid., p. 21.

18 Ibid., pp. 33–4.

19 William Harrison's *Brief Discovrse* of Katherine Brettergh was originally annexed, with its own title-page, to two funeral sermons preached for her, one by Harrison and the other by William Leygh, in a book entitled *Deaths Advantage Little Regarded, and the Soules Solace Against Sorrow*, 2nd edn (London, 1602). The quote is from sig. M7 of this book. Beginning in

1612, the *Brief Discovrse* was published separately, as *The Christian Life and Death, of Mistris Katherin Brettergh.*

20 William, Hinde, *A Faithfull Remonstrance of the Holy Life and Happy Death, of John Bruen* (London, 1641), pp. 145, 147 (misprinted as "142").

21 Edmund Staunton, *A Sermon Preacht at Great Milton in the County of Oxford: Decemb: 9. 1654. . . .* (Oxford, 1659), p. 26. Mrs Wilkinson's "narrative," printed in italic, occupies pp. 26–34.

22 Richard Mayo, *The Life and Death of Edmund Staunton D.D.* (London, 1673), pp. 4–6, 33–5.

23 [Matthew Henry], *An Account of the Life and Death of Mr. Philip Henry*, 2nd edn (London, 1699), sig. A4ᵛ. The diary is cited in the following pages, 1, 6–7, 17, 23 (twice), 31 (twice), 42, 43, 46, 50, 62 (twice), 64, 65 (twice), 71, 75–6, 79, 95, 97, 102, 120, 123, 125, 130. Other autograph "papers" are cited as follows: "Reflections," 14; a "latin Narrative of his younger years," 15; his will, 54; an elegy he wrote, 88; a sermon, 81.

24 British Library, Add. MS 27351–5 and 27358.

25 Anthony Walker, *Eyphka, Eyphka, The Virtuous Woman Found. . . . With so Large Additions as May be Stiled the Life of that Noble Lady. To Which Are Annexed Some of Her Ladyships Pious and Useful Meditations* (London, 1678), p. 61.

26 Ibid., pp. 60, 61.

27 Diary quoted ibid., pp. 64–8, 74–7, 111–14.

28 In addition to the examples cited above, cf. Oliver Heywood, *A Narrative of the Holy Life, and Happy Death of . . . Mr. John Angier* (London, 1685); Richard Baxter, *A Breviate of the Life of Margaret . . . Baxter* (London, 1681); Timothy Rogers, *The Character of a Good Woman . . . In a Funeral Discourse . . . Occasioned by the Decease of Mrs. Elizabeth Dunton. . . . With an Account of Her Life and Death; And Part of the Diary Writ With Her Own Hand* (London, 1697); *The Life and Death of Mr. Vavasor Powell* (London, 1671); Theophilus Gale, *The Life and Death of Mr. John Rowe of Crediton in Devon* (London, 1673); *Some Remarkable Passages in the Holy Life and Death of the Late Reverend Mr. Edmund Trench; Most of them Drawn Out of His Own Diary* (London, 1693); Thomas Wadsworth, *Wadsworth's Remains. . . . With a Preface Containing Several Remarkables of His Holy Life and Death, From His Own Note-book, and Those That Knew Him Best* (London, 1680); Anthony Walker, *The Holy Life of Mrs. Elizabeth Walker* (London, 1690). See also the numerous references to "papers," "journals" and "diaries" in the anthology of early modern Christian biographies assembled by Samuel Clarke, *The Lives of Sundry Eminent Persons in this Later Age* (London, 1683).

29 George Newton, "An account of the Godly Life and Practice of Mr. Joseph Alleine," in [Theodosia Alleine et al.], *The Life and Death of Mr. Joseph Alleine* (London, 1672), p. 36; [Henry], *Life and Death of Philip Henry*, p. 151.

30 Issac Gilling, *The Life of the Reverend Mr. George Trosse, Late Minister of the Gospel in Exon.* (London, 1715), p. 86, quoted in *The Life of Mr. George Trosse Written by Himself and Published Posthumously According to his Order in 1714*, ed. A. W. Brink (Montreal and London: McGill–Queen's University Press, 1974), p. 43.

Chapter 4   Writing on the Heart

1 Bernard Capp, *English Almanacs 1500–1800: Astrology and the Popular Press* (Ithaca: Cornell University Press, 1979), p. 30.
2 For a list of examples, see ibid., p. 61.
3 William Haller, *The Rise of Puritanism*, Harper Torchbook edn (New York: Harper & Row, 1957), p. 94.
4 Quoted by David Cressy, "Levels of Illiteracy in England, 1530–1750," in Harvey J. Graff, ed., *Literacy and Social Development in the West: A Reader* (Cambridge: Cambridge University Press, 1981), p. 111.
5 Brian Vickers, *Francis Bacon and Renaissance Prose* (Cambridge: Cambridge University Press, 1968), pp. 76–7.
6 Margaret Spufford, "First Steps in Literacy: The Reading and Writing Experiences of the Humblest Seventeenth-Century Spiritual Autobiographers," *Social History* 4 (1979), pp. 407–35.
7 David Cressy, *Literacy and the Social Order: Reading and Writing in Tudor and Stuart England* (Cambridge: Cambridge University Press, 1980), tables 6.1–6.5. It should be noted that Cressy's evidence is drawn from a region exceptional in commercial activity and militant Protestantism, two factors linked by historians to high levels of literacy.
8 Foster Watson, *The English Grammar Schools to 1660: Their Curriculum and Practice* (Cambridge: Cambridge University Press, 1908), pp. 186–7.
9 John Morgan, *Godly Learning: Puritan Attitudes Towards Reason, Learning and Education, 1560–1640* (Cambridge: Cambridge University Press, 1986), pp. 165–6.
10 At least one London stationer sold blank membrane books, used for keeping the accounts of the royal wardrobe, in 1313. But this use of a parchment notebook was unusual. See G. S. Ivy, "The Bibliography of the Manuscript-Book," in Francis Wormald and C. E. Wright, eds, *The English Library Before 1700* (London: Athlone Press, 1958), p. 50.
11 D. C. Coleman, *The British Paper Industry 1495–1860: A Study in Industrial Growth* (Oxford: Clarendon Press, 1958), p. 11.
12 H. J. Morehouse, ed., "A Dyurnall, or Catalogue of All My Accions and Expences from the 1st of January, 1646[/7] – Adam Eyre," in Charles Jackson, ed., *Yorkshire Diaries and Autobiographies in the Seventeenth and Eighteenth Centuries*, vol. 1, Surtees Society Publications LXV (Durham, 1877), p. 36.
13 Mark Girouard, *Life in the English Country House: A Social and Architectural History* (Harmondsworth: Penguin, 1980), p. 166.
14 Hinde, *John Bruen*, p. 146, misprinted as "142."
15 Isaac Ambrose, *Media: The Middle Things, in Reference to the First and Last Things . . .*, 2nd edn (London, 1652), pp. 58, 72, 73–5.
16 Joseph Hall alludes to the practice in the proem to his *Occasional Meditations*, first published in 1620, where he begins, "I have heedlesly lost (I confesse) many good thoughts, these few my Paper hath preserued from vanishing; The example whereof may perhaps be more usefull then the matter" (Joseph Hall, *Occasional Meditations*, 3rd edn [London, 1633], sig. A7).
17 See Helen C. White, *The Tudor Books of Private Devotion* (Madison: University of Wisconsin Press, 1951).

18 Louis de Blios, *A Book of Spiritual Instruction: Institutio Spiritualis*, trans. Bernard A. Wilberforce (2nd edn, London: Art and Book Co., 1901), p. 95, quoted in Louis B. Martz, *The Poetry of Meditation: A Study in English Religious Literature of the Seventeenth Century*, revised edn (New Haven and London: Yale University Press, 1962), p. 19.

19 For an overview, see Helen C. White, *English Devotional Literature [Prose] 1600–1640*, University of Wisconsin Studies in Language and Literature, no. 29 (Madison, 1931).

20 Joseph Hall, *The Arte of Divine Meditation: Profitable for all Christians to knowe and practise* (London, 1606), p. 4.

21 Ibid., p. 7.

22 Richard Rogers, *Seven Treatises* . . . (London, 1603), pp. 239, 238.

23 Hall, *Arte of Divine Meditation*, p. 25; see also Martz, *Poetry of Meditation*, pp. 118ff.

24 *A Dyurnall for deuoute soules to ordre them selfe thereafter* ([London] n.d., sig. c.i^v, sig. a.ii).

25 Dr Williams's Library, Baxter MS 61.13.

26 M. M. Knappen, *Two Elizabethan Puritan Diaries by Richard Rogers and Samuel Ward* (Chicago: American Society of Church History, 1933), p. 35.

27 Baxter MS 61.13, fo. 40. Hereafter folio references are cited in the text.

28 Knappen's modern printed version displays this quality, but only a fraction as extensively as it appears in the original MS. Because Knappen wanted the text to represent variety, he edited out many of the entries which seemed repetitious, most of which were those concerning Rogers's obsession with his duties. So doing, Knappen obliterated the dominant theme and purpose of Rogers's practice.

29 Rogers, *Seven Treatises*, p. 245.

30 Cf. Hall, *Arte of Divine Meditation*, pp. 66–73. Protestant meditation differed from the Catholic form in its emphasis on the meditator's own experience, rather than the figure of Christ.

31 For example "meditation," fos 8^v, 12^v, 20; "reading," fos 2, 31^v, 23; "prayer," fos 35. Rogers distinguished "reading" from "study," which followed meditation and prayer.

32 Juan Luis Vivès, *Introductio ad Sapientiam*, quoted by R. R. Bolgar, *The Classical Heritage and its Beneficiaries* (Cambridge: Cambridge University Press, 1963), p. 273. For a discussion of Vivès and the notebook in Tudor education see Joan Simon, *Education and Society in Tudor England* (Cambridge: Cambridge University Press, 1966), pp. 109–10.

33 For a partial bibliography of extant commonplace books, see Margo Todd, *Christian Humanism and the Puritan Social Order* (Cambridge: Cambridge University Press, 1987), pp. 261–4. Todd discusses the practice of commonplacing by students on pp. 63–4, 82. See also Lisa Jardine and Anthony Grafton, "'Studied for Action': How Gabriel Harvey Read His Livy," *Past and Present* 129 (1990), pp. 30–78. Of course the rubrics and other notations contained both in the margins and in the body of the text, which flourished in many different types of books printed between 1500 and 1660 (including *A Mirroure for Magistrates*, *Acts and Monuments*, and *A Christal Glasse*), were designed to facilitate the taking of commonplaces. For a discussion of some of these, see G. K. Hunter, "The Marking of

Sententiae in Elizabethan Printed Plays, Poems and Romances," *The Library*, 5th ser., 6 (1951), pp. 171–8.

34 Quoted by Todd, *Christian Humanism*, p. 82.

35 James Orchard Halliwell, ed., *The Autobiography and Correspondence of Sir Simonds D'Ewes*, 2 vols (London: Richard Bently, 1845), I, 104, 95. For a discussion of the importance of sermon note-taking in early modern English Protestant education, see Morgan, *Godly Learning*, pp. 189, 198; for a discussion of its importance to gatherings of the pious out of church doors, see Patrick Collinson, "The English Conventicle," in W. J. Shiels and Diana Wood, eds, *Voluntary Religion*, Studies in Church History, vol. 23 (n.p.: Blackwell, 1986), esp. pp. 240–3.

36 Hinde, *John Bruen*, pp. 102, 142.

37 [Henry], *Life and Death of Philip Henry*, pp. 8, 19, 62.

38 Edmund Calamy, *The Happiness of those who sleep in Jesus* (London, 1662), p. 28; Nathaniel Parkhurst, *The faithful and Diligent Christian Described and Exemplified* (London, 1684), pp. 51–2, both quoted in J. T. Cliffe, *The Puritan Gentry: The Great Puritan Families of Early Stuart England* (London: Routledge & Kegan Paul, 1984), p. 26.

39 Staunton, *A Sermon Preacht*, pp. 23, 24.

40 Clarke, *Lives of Sundry Eminent Persons*, pt II, pp. 154, 157, 158.

41 Walker, *The Virtuous Woman Found*, p. 62. For a large selection prepared by her domestic chaplain see *Memoir of Lady Warwick: Also her Diary from A.D. 1666 to 1672* (London, 1847). Cf. Dorothy M. Meads, ed., *Diary of Lady Margaret Hoby 1599–1605* (London: Routledge & Sons, 1930).

42 Sidney Sussex College Library, Cambridge, MS 45, fo. 1. Hereafter folio references are cited in the text. The MS is covered by a modern leather binding. Other notebooks of Ward's at Sidney Sussex are bound in vellum (recycled medieval manuscripts) or calf, so it is likely that the book was originally similarly held together and protected.

43 We might compare it to the more secular diary of the gentleman-barrister John Manningham, kept during his terms at the Middle Temple, in the years 1602–3, which contains in a single notebook a mixture of commonplaces, anecdotes, observations and extensive sermon notes; or to the small autograph religious notebook kept in the latter half of the seventeenth century by Mrs Owen Stockton, which contains a miscellany of devotional writings made over the course of her lifetime. See John Bruce, ed., *Diary of John Manningham* ..., Camden Society Publications XCIX (London, 1868); Dr Williams's Library, MS 24.8.

44 The Ward papers at Sidney Sussex are meticulously listed and described by Margo Todd, "The Samuel Ward Papers at Sidney Sussex College, Cambridge," *Transactions of the Cambridge Bibliographical Society* 8 (1985), pp. 582–92.

45 This point is also made, with a somewhat different emphasis, by Margo Todd in her "Puritan Self-Fashioning: The Diary of Samuel Ward," *Journal of British Studies* 31 (1992), pp. 236–64. I endorse Todd's attempt to rescue the historical Ward and his text from what she calls the "unabashed condescension of modern scholarship," though I differ from her in seeking to reunite Ward's practice with the contemporary tradition of meditation. Todd instead considers the influence of individual teachers and books on

Ward's diary; among the books, she identifies the Bible and St Augustine's *Confessions* as being especially important. Her case for the latter text strikes me as rather tenuous. Though she cites numerous references to Augustine's works in works by Ward, Todd can only describe aspects of Ward's diary as being "reminiscent" of the *Confessions*. Superficial comparisons may be made, but the argument for influence requires more direct evidence if it is to be convincing. Despite our different emphases, however, the general thrusts of Todd's and my interpretation run, I think, together.

46 For a sense of the contents of a few of these, see Heywood, *Life and Death of John Angier*, esp. pp. 82–127; J. H. Turner, ed., *The Autobiography, Diaries, Anecdote and Event Books of the Rev. Oliver Heywood*, 4 vols (Brighouse, 1882–5), esp. vol. III, pp. 9–16; Linda Pollock, *With Faith and Physic: The Life of a Tudor Gentlewoman Lady Grace Mildmay 1552–1620* (London: Collins & Brown, 1993); *The Life and Death of Mr. Vavasor Powell*; Charles Jackson, ed., *The Autobiography of Alice Thornton*, Surtees Society Publications LXII (Durham, 1875); Paul S. Seaver, *Wallington's World: A Puritan Artisan in Seventeenth-Century London* (Stanford: Stanford University Press, 1985), esp. pp. 199–208.

47 Richard Parkinson, ed., *The Autobiography of Henry Newcome*, 2 vols, Chetham Society Publications XXVI and XXVII (London, 1852), vol. I, p. 14.

48 Newcome intended "brave" in contrast to his own "fear of my own tribunal" (vol. I, p. 15), but this still strikes me as a peculiar way to construe a Christian duty.

49 Upon leaving him at Cambridge in 1646, Oliver Heywood's father instructed him to "labour every day to get some sanctifyed thoughts, and spiritual meditations . . . and write them in a book and title it the meditations of my youth" and to "take short notes of every sermon, and write some faire over"; see Turner, *Autobiography . . . of Oliver Heywood*, vol. I, p. 160. Hugh Peter's sermon in London, 11 May 1643, noted by Nehemiah Wallington, in Seaver, *Wallington's World*, p. 11; see also ch. 5, n. 48.

50 In his diary, Richard Rogers mentioned "reading the writings of an other brother about his estate an houre and longuer" (fo. 27); the Scottish nonconforming minister Robert Blair wrote that he began a diary in 1622, at age 29, because he "heard of the practice of some diligent Christians, who daily took brief notes of the condition of their souls"; in Thomas M'Crie, ed., *The Life of Mr. Robert Blair* (Edinburgh: Wodrow Society, 1848), p. 31; Vavasor Powell complained that, at a moment of spiritual crisis early in his life, he went to take up his "little Diary" for help, "but having lent it to a Christian Friend that was far distant, could not" – which may be read as a warning to others doing the same with their books; see *The Life and Death of Mr. Vavasor Powell*, p. 12. Somewhat later, the Essex vicar and diarist Ralph Josselin wrote in 1657 that he "saw part of Mrs. Mabel Elliston's diurnal of her life, full of spiritual observation and sweetness"; see Alan Macfarlane, ed., *The Diary of Ralph Josselin, 1616–1683*, British Academy Records of Social and Economic History, new ser., III (London, 1976), p. 396.

51 Hinde, *John Bruen*, pp. 75, 102.

52 Joseph Hunter, ed., *The Diary of Ralph Thoresby*, 2 vols (London, 1830), vol. I, pp. 38, 46.

53 Baxter, *Life of Margaret Baxter*, sig. Aᵛ.

54 Clarke, *Lives of Sundry Eminent Persons*, part I, p. 129; Heywood, *Life and Death of John Angier*, p. 50.

55 Cf. Richard Baxter, who recommended that "To those Christians that have full leisure, this course is good; but, I urge it not upon all. Those that . . . cannot spare so much [time] . . . must . . . record only the extraordinary, observable, and more remarkable and memorable passages of their lives, lest they lose time from works of greater moment," in his *Practical Works* (London, 1838), vol. XVII, p. 601, quoted by Owen C. Watkins, *The Puritan Experience* (London: Routledge & Kegan Paul, 1972), p. 23.

56 Matthew Henry Lee, ed., *Diaries and Letters of Philip Henry of Broad Oak, Flintshire 1631–1696* (London: Kegan Paul, Trench & Co., 1882), p. 239.

57 Parkinson, *Autobiography of Henry Newcome*, vol. I, p. 2.

58 Ibid., vol. I, pp. 156–7.

59 One of the smaller notebooks has been published, in part; its contents were edited by Thomas Heywood, and printed as *The Diary of the Rev. Henry Newcome, from September 30, 1661, to September 29, 1663*, Chetham Society Publications XVIII (Manchester, 1849).

60 Parkinson, *Autobiography of Henry Newcome*, vol. II, pp. 285–6.

61 John Chorlton, *The Glorious Reward of Faithful Ministers Declared and Improved* (London, 1696), sig. A3ᵛ, p. 26.

62 [Henry Newcome], *A Faithful Narrative of the Life and Death of That Holy and Laborious Preacher Mr. John Machin* (London, 1671), pp. 3, 57.

63 Parkinson, *Autobiography of Henry Newcome*, vol. I, p. 147; cf. ibid., p. 143.

64 Ibid., p. 146.

65 Cf. the preface to Newcome's *Life and Death of John Machin* (not signed by Newcome), which claims: "'Tis to Record a great instruction to the World, to Write the Life of a good man, and he's a Public Benefactor to Religion that Rescues such a Treasure from the common Consumption of Time, and Stores it up for Posterity. 'Twere pitty, that what will be ever rewarded in Heaven, should be soon forgot upon Earth; or that the best Subject of Story should Silently Expire in Oblivion. We owe no small Additions both to Learning and Religion to such, who have transcribed the Lives of Excellent men, and thereby made them the Companions of Every Age" (sigs A4–A4ᵛ).

66 Parkinson, *Autobiography of Henry Newcome*, vol. I, pp. 125, 135–6.

67 M'Crie, *Life of Robert Blair*, p. 3.

68 Turner, *Autobiography of Oliver Heywood*, vol. I, pp. 133, 177; vol. IV, p. 305. See also the surviving fragment of a memorial by Thomas Jollie, the nonconformist minister of Altham, Lancashire, composed of materials transcribed from a diary: Henry Fishwick, ed., *The Note Book of the Rev. Thomas Jolly 1671–1693*, Chetham Society Publications, new ser., XXXIII (Manchester, 1895); and his "A short narrative of some of my sufferings these 20 years upon the account of nonconformity," Dr Williams's Library MS 12.78, fos 145–8, which covers the years 1660–79.

69 John Shaw, "The Life of Master John Shaw," in *Yorkshire Diaries and Autobiographies in the Seventeenth and Eighteenth Centuries*, vol. 1, ed. Charles Jackson, Surtees Society Publications LXV (Durham, 1877), pp. 121–2.

70 For example by Watkins, *Puritan Experience*, p. 37.
71 For a particularly inspired exercise in this mode of reading, see Patricia Caldwell, *The Puritan Conversion Narrative: The Beginnings of an American Expression* (Cambridge: Cambridge University Press, 1983).
72 John Bunyan, *Grace Abounding to the Chief of Sinners*, ed. Roger Sharrock (Oxford: Clarendon Press, 1962), p. 4.
73 For a discussion of this genre, see Louis B. Wright, *Middle-Class Culture in Elizabethan England*, esp. pp. 297–338.
74 For examples, see Louis B. Wright, ed., *Advice to a Son: The Precepts of Lord Burghley, Sir Walter Ralegh, and Francis Osborne* (Ithaca: Cornell University Press, 1962).
75 For a variety of examples from the late sixteenth to the early eighteenth centuries, see Sidney L. Lee, ed., *The Autobiography of Edward, Lord Herbert of Cherbury* (London: John C. Nimmo, 1886); John M. Gray, ed., *Memoirs of the Life of Sir John Clerk* (London, 1895); S. C. Lomas, ed., "The Memoirs of Sir George Courthorp 1616–85," *Camden Miscellany XI*, Camden Society Publications, 3rd ser., XIII (London, 1907), pp. 93–157; "Autobiographical Memoranda of Heneage Dering Dean of Ripon," in Charles Jackson, ed., *Yorkshire Diaries and Autobiographies in the Seventeenth and Eighteenth Centuries*, vol. 1, Surtees Society Publications LXV (Durham 1877), pp. 333–50; G. Davies, ed., *Memoirs of the Family of Guise of Elmore, Gloucestershire*, Camden Society Publications, third ser., XXVIII (London, 1917); James Fretwell, "A Family History Begun by James Fretwell," in Jackson, *Yorkshire Diaries and Autobiographies*, vol. 1, pp. 163–243; G. B. Harrison, ed., *Advice to His Son by Henry Percy Ninth Earl of Northumberland* (London: Ernest Benn Limited, 1930); Jonathan Priestley, "Some Memoirs Concerning the Family of the Priestleys, Written at the Request of a Friend, by Jonathan Priestley, Anno Domini 1696, Aetatis Suae 63," in Charles Jackson, ed., *Yorkshire Diaries and Autobiographies in the Seventeenth and Eighteenth Centuries*, vol. 2, Surtees Society Publications LXXVII (Durham, 1886), pp. 1–41.
76 James Melville, *Memoirs of his Own Life by Sir James Melville*, Bannatyne Club Publications XVII (London, 1827), p. 3.
77 George Scott, *The Memoires of Sir James Melvil of Hal-Hill* (London, 1683), preface.
78 Jackson, *Autobiography of Alice Thornton*, pp. 338, 335, 1.
79 Ibid., pp. 187–8.
80 Ibid., pp. 79, 269–70.
81 For a similarly intended work, see Lucy Hutchinson, *Memoirs of the Life of Colonel Hutchinson*, ed. James Sutherland (London: Oxford University Press, 1973), esp. pp. 278–89; for two less defensive memorials by pious aristocrats, see Pollock, *With Faith and Physic*, esp. pp. 24–5ff; T. C. Croker, ed., *Autobiography of Mary Countess Warwick* (London: Percy Society, 1848).

Chapter 5 A Press of Witnesses

1 Dr Williams's Library, London, MS 28.4. Folio references are cited in the text.

2 M'Crie, *Life of Robert Blair*, p. 6.

3 Parkinson, *Autobiography of Henry Newcome*, vol. I, p. 7. An eerie echo of this passage occurs in a biography printed six years after Newcome wrote these lines; see Theophilus Gale, *The Life and Death of Thomas Tregosse* (London, 1671), p. 4.

4 S. Wilton Rix, ed., *The Diary and Autobiography of Edmund Bohun* (Beccles: private printing, 1853), p. 35, *passim*.

5 For readings of early modern biographical discourse in this light see, Timothy Hampton, *Writing From History: The Rhetoric of Exemplarity in Renaissance Literature* (Ithaca and London: Cornell University Press, 1990); John D. Lyons, *Exemplum: the Rhetoric of Example in Early Modern France and Italy* (Princeton: Princeton University Press, 1989); Thomas M. Greene, *The Light of Troy: Imitation and Discovery in Renaissance Poetry* (New Haven: Yale University Press, 1982).

6 C. E. Wright, "The Dispersal of the Libraries in the Sixteenth Century," in Francis Wormald and C. E. Wright, eds, *The English Library before 1700* (London: Athlone Press, 1958), pp. 153, 165.

7 [Thomas Woodcock], *An Account of Some Remarkable Passages in the Life of a Private Gentleman [. . .] Left Under His Own Hand, To Be Communicated to the Publick after his Decease*, 2nd edn (London, 1711); Matthew Sylvester, ed., *Reliquiae Baxterianae* (London, 1696); [Thomas Ellwood et al., eds], *A Journal or Historical Account of . . . George Fox* (London, 1694); George Trosse, *The Life of the Reverend George Trosse*, ed. A. W. Brink (Montreal and London: McGill–Queens University Press, 1974).

8 For an exhaustive list of works most frequently cited by contemporaries, see the rambling prolegomena to the personal memorial prepared by Edmund Calamy, who died in 1731: John Towill Rutt, ed., *An Historical Account of My Own Life, with Some Reflections on the Times I Have Lived in. By Edmund Calamy*, 2 vols (London: Routledge, 1829), vol. I, pp. 1–51.

9 On aristocratic funerals see Lawrence Stone, *The Crisis of the Aristocracy 1558–1641* (Oxford: Clarendon Press, 1965), esp. pp. 572–81. On funerals in general, see Clare Gittings, *Death, Burial and the Individual in Early Modern England* (London, 1984).

10 Houlbrooke explains, in "Death, Church, and Family," p. 40, that Elizabeth's reign marked the completion of a general shift in the content of English epitaph texts from the late medieval invitation to pray for the deceased to the early modern emphasis on commemoration of the person.

11 See, for example, *Threnodia in Obitvm D. Edovardi Lewkenor Equitus, & D. Svsannae Coniugus Charibimae . . .* (London, 1606); and Anthony Stafford, *Honour and Vertue, Triumphing over the Grave. Exemplified in a Faire Devout Life, and Death, Adorned with the Surviving Perfections of Edward Lord Stafford, Lately Deceased; the Last Baron of that Illustrious Family: Which Honour in Him Ended with as Great Lustre as the Sunne Sets within a Serene Sky* (London, 1640).

12 See, for instance [Thomas Crashaw], *The Honovr of Vertve. Or The Monument Erected by the Sorrowful Husband, and the Epitaphes Annexed by Learned and Worthy Men, to the Immortal Memory of that Worthy Gentle-woman Mrs Elizabeth Crashaw* [London, 1620]. For a city merchant, see [Anthony Nixon], *Londons Dove: or A Memorial of the Life and Death of Maister Robert Dove, Citizen and Marchant-Taylor of London,*

and of his *Several Almsdeeds and Large Bountie to the Poore, in His Life Time* (London, 1612).

13 [John Dunton], *The Mourning-Ring, In Memory of Your Departed Friend, ... Recommended as Proper to Be Given at Funerals*, 2nd edn (London, 1692), sigs A2ᵛ–A3. Dunton's notion was taken up in the early eighteenth century by the divine Josiah Woodward, the chief advocate of the Societies for the Reformation of Manners. Woodward's own treatise on death, *Fair Warnings to a Careless World* (London, 1707), concludes with "A *Proposal* for the Giving away at *Funerals* some Practical Books of *Divinity*, instead of *Rings* and other the usual *Presents*, on such solemn *Occasions*, for the Promoting of *Religion* and *Virtue*" (pp. 225–36). This proposal echoes the *Mourning-Ring*'s preface almost verbatim, while adding some helpful clarifications, such as putting the family coat of arms on the cover of the gift books; that mourners leave tickets with their address at the funeral for the forwarding of gifts if they seem too heavy to carry with them; and a list of practical works suitable as gifts (p. 236). As for the biographical component, Woodward suggested this: "You may have the *Life* of the *Person* Deceased, Printed in one or more Sheets of *Paper*, or any Memorables thereof, to be bound up with the Book, *viz.* the Day of the Birth, Marriage, Death of the Person deceased, number of Children, their Names, how disposed of, or an Elegy or Copy of Verses on the deceased, or whatever else the surviving Relations desire" (p. 228). He also prepared sample memoranda for a wife, daughter and infant child.

14 [Dunton], *Mourning-Ring*, sig. A4.

15 Richard Baxter's *Life of Margaret ... Baxter* mentions that his wife directed in her will that a second edition of 500 copies be printed of the funeral sermon originally preached and printed by Baxter for her mother in 1661 (sig. A). Baxter carried out his wife's order, and the only surviving copies of the sermon are from this second edition, entitled *The Last Work of a Believer ... Prepared for Mary ... Hanmer ... [and] at the Desire of Her Daughter, before Her Death, Reprinted* (London, 1682).

16 As did that of John Duncon, *The Holy Life and Death of the Lady Letice, Vi-Countess Falkland*, 3rd edn (London, 1653), sig. A5.

17 As was the case in the *Life* of Jane Ratcliffe, of Chester, who suddenly died in London on a visit, and was buried there. John Ley, Ratcliffe's local minister, wrote her life when, he explained, "after a good time of waiting for it in vaine, I heard it was not to be expected at all" from the hand of the London minister who preached at the funeral. See John Ley, *A Patterne of Pietie* (London, 1640), p. 10.

18 This was the case stated in the advertisement to the printed text of Dr Whitehead's eulogy of John Wesley, *A discourse delivered at the New Chapel in the City-Road, on the ninth of March 1791, At the Funeral of the Rev. Mr. John Wesley*, 4th edn (London, 1791); but given the large number of sermon note-takers in the seventeenth century, it must have occurred then as well.

19 Harold Love, "Preacher and Publisher: Oliver Heywood and Thomas Parkhurst," *Studies in Bibliography* 31 (1978), p. 227, *passim*. Heywood may have accepted payment or donations in exchange for some of the copies he distributed. In describing his arrangements with the bookseller Nevill Simmons, Richard Baxter stated that he "took the fifteenth book

(for my Friends and self) and Eighteen pence more for every Rheam of the other fourteen" of each impression of most of his works. He also noted sometimes selling his fifteenth book for "about two thirds of the common price of the Bookseller (or little more) and oft less;" other times paying full price for hundreds more than his usual fifteenth, to distribute gratis Sylevester, *Reliquiae Baxterianae*, appendix VII, p. 118).

20 However, the imprint of Anthony Walker's *Holy Life of Mrs. Elizabeth Walker* indicates that it was printed by John Leake, "for the Author." Thus Walker paid for and handled all publication arrangements himself.

21 John Dunton, *The Life and Errors of John Dunton* (London, 1705), p. 289.

22 The full title of Ley's life of Mrs Ratcliffe epitomizes the tradition in 1640: *A Patterne of Pietie. Or the Religious Life and Death of that Grave and Gracious Matron, Mrs. Jane Ratcliffe Widow and Citizen of Chester. Of Whom the Discourse is Framed and Applied so as the Commemoration of the Dead May Best Serve to the Edification of the Living, Whether Men or Women, Whereof Part Was Preached, and the Whole Written.* Mid-century was a turning-point. Whereas Pollard and Redgrave's *Short Title Catalogue* lists no titles beginning with the phrase, "The life and death of . . .," Wing's lists fifty-six. Some memorials took even more than the title concept from "Katherine Stubs." Nixon's *London's Dove* (not a sermon), copied the long opening line of *A Christal Glasse* verbatim, altering only the name of the deceased (sig. A4). This constitutes further evidence of the influence of Stubbes's work, especially among the urban bourgeoisie.

23 For instance, Anthony Stafford's *Honour and Vertue, Triumphing Over the Grave*, whose title-page described the work as "A treatise so written, that it is as well applicative to all of Noble Extraction, as to him, and wherein are handled all the Requwisites of Honour, together with the greatest Morall, and Divine Vertues, and commended to the practice of the Noble Prudent Reader." Stafford had earlier penned a work entitled *The Femall Glory: or, The Life, and Death of Our Blessed Lady, the Holy Virgin Mary* (London, 1635), whose title-page described it as "A Treatise worthy the reading, and meditation for all modest women, who live under the government of Vertue, and are obedient to her lawes."

24 Ley, *A Patterne of Piety*, p. 4.

25 Hinde's *John Bruen*, written in 1626 but not printed until 1641, was even at the time of its eventual publication a breakthrough work, for its full chronological representation of its subject.

26 Clarke, *Lives of Sundry Eminent Persons*, sigs a*–a*^{v}. An alternative method of quickly tracking the paratactical quality would be to peruse the side-notes to each "Life."

27 14 Car. II, cap. 4.

28 Neil Keeble, *The Literary Culture of Nonconformity in Late Seventeenth-Century England* (Leicester: Leicester University Press, 1987), p. 32. I am indebted to this work, especially to ch. 1, for my account of the historical circumstances of nonconformity in this and the following two paragraphs.

29 16 Car. II, cap. 4.

30 17 Car. II, cap. 2.

31 22 Car. II, cap. 1.

32 Keeble, *Literary Culture*, p. 47.

33 For a history of persecution, see Gerald R. Cragg, *Puritanism in the Period*

of the Great Persecution 1660–1688 (Cambridge: Cambridge University Press, 1957), esp. ch. 2; for Quakers in particular, see Craig W. Horle, *The Quakers and the English Legal System 1660–1688* (Philadelphia: University of Pennsylvania Press, 1988), esp. ch. 3; for the general actions and attitudes of the gentry sympathetic to the cause of nonconformity, see J. T. Cliffe, *The Puritan Gentry Besieged, 1650–1700* (London and New York: Routledge, 1993).

34 Richard Baxter, *A Christian Directory* (London, 1673), pp. 60, 921.

35 *The Life and Death of Mr. Joseph Alleine*, pp. 2–3.

36 Ibid., p. 4.

37 Clarke, *Lives of Sundry Eminent Persons*, sigs a3ᵛ, a3.

38 Jacques Auguste de Thou (1543–1617); his *Historiarum sui temporis* ... *Libri CXXXVIII* (Geneva, 1620; Frankfurt, 1627) contained his own "De vita sua." De Thou's ecclesiastical history was well received and influential in England. The antiquarian and would-be historiographer Simonds D'Ewes cited de Thou as the model for the history of his life and times D'Ewes wrote up in 1636 from almanac diaries of "the sad and doleful events of Christendom" (written in cipher) kept annually since 1619. In his manuscript D'Ewes wrote of de Thou's work, which he purchased and read in 1633: "I have read over the greater part of his Latin story, penned in a most lofty and elegant style, and compiled with so much wisdom and judgment, as I was much delighted with the perusal of it; and often drawn into a just admiration of the author. A great benefit it is to the christian world. . . . And a blessed resolution it were, that Christian Princes would learn and practise his moderate and safe counsels, without oppressing the consciences and liberties of their loyal subjects" (Halliwell, *Autobiography and Correspondence of Simonds D'Ewes*, vol. I, pp. 136, 100). De Thou was also cited as an influence by the early eighteenth-century English ecclesiastical historiographers Gilbert Burnet and Edmund Calamy.

39 Abraham Scultetus, court preacher to Frederic, Elector of Palatine, *De Curriculo Vitae, Inprimis Vero de Actionibus Pragensibus Abrah. Sculteti* (Emden, 1625).

40 François Du Jon (1545–1602), *Opera Theologica* ... *Praefixa est* ... *Vita Auctoris ab Eodem Olim Conscripta* ... *et Narratio de Placido Ejusdem Obitu* (Geneva, 1607).

41 [Alleine, et al.] *The Life and Death of Mr. Joseph Alleine*, p. 5.

42 Clarke, *Lives of Sundry Eminent Persons*, p. 2.

43 Henry, *Life and Death of Mr. Philip Henry*, p. 9. No doubt this was part of the intention of personal memorials prepared for children by parents in their old age, mentioned in the previous chapter.

44 Lee, *Diaries and Letters of Philip Henry*, pp. vii–viii; R. N. Worth, "Notes from Two Plymouth Diaries," *The Antiquary* 13 (1886), pp. 242–4. Two other nonconformists, Henry Newcome and Sam Angier, also used almanac diaries; see Parkinson, *Autobiography of Henry Newcome*, vol. II, pp. 283, 286; Ernest Axon, ed., *Oliver Heywood's Life of John Angier* ... *also Samuel Angier's Diary*, Chetham Society Publications, new ser., XCVII (Manchester, 1937), p. 152.

45 [Henry], *Life and Death of Mr. Philip Henry*, p. 75.

46 Parkinson, *Autobiography of Henry Newcome*, vol. I, p. 154; Lee, *Diaries and Letters of Mr. Philip Henry*, pp. 173–4.

47 John Beadle, *The Journal or Diary of a Thankful Christian* (London, 1656). It was published by Thomas Parkhurst, who was to become the most prominent publisher of Presbyterian texts in England in the latter half of the seventeenth century, and the most regular publisher of Presbyterian biography of his day.

48 Beadle's sermon, delivered on 21 July 1644, caused Arthur Wilson, steward to the Earl of Warwick, Mary Rich's father-in-law, to begin a journal of his own life; see Arthur Wilson, "Observations of God's Providence, in the Tract of My Life," in F. Peck, ed., *Desiderata Curiosa*, 2 vols (London, 1732–5), vol. II, book XII, no. v, p. 25. On the Countess's favorite books, see Charlotte Fell Smith, *Mary Rich, Countess of Warwick (1625–1678): Her Family & Friends* (London: Longmans, Green & Co., 1901), p. 201.

49 Beadle, *Journal or Diary*, pp. 14, 179; the term "Stone of witnesse" was used by John Fuller in his preface to describe Beadle's book, sig. a7^v.

50 Ibid., pp. 25, 19, 22.

51 Ibid., pp. 58ff. A perfect example of this sort of diary, yet unprinted, is Owen Stockton's notebook of "Observations & experiences of gods wth my soul & other memorable passages of his providence recorded since Apr. 1st 1665," Dr Williams's Library, MS 24.7. It includes "A collection of memorable passages relating to my employment, both ministeral work and composing some treatises relating to ye glory of God & ye edification of his church since Au. 20 1677" (fos 90–2). Cf. the list drawn up by Thomas Jollie, presumably from his personal memorial, entitled "A short narrative of some passages of my sufferings these 20 years upon the account of nonconformity." Dr Williams's Library, MS 12.78, fos 145–8.

52 1 Will. & Mar., cap. 18.

53 Ferdinando Nicolls, *The Life and Death of Mr. Ignatius Jurdain* (London, 1654), sig. a^v.

54 Walker, *Holy Life of Mrs. Elizabeth Walker*, sig. A2^v.

55 For a recent and definitive overview of this literature, see Nigel Smith, *Perfection Proclaimed: Language and Literature in English Radical Religion 1640–60* (Oxford: Clarendon Press, 1989); for a study focusing on the meaning of discourse in public see Richard Bauman, *Let Your Words Be Few: Symbolism of Speaking and Silence among Seventeenth-Century Quakers* (Cambridge: Cambridge University Press, 1983).

56 John Rogers, *Ohel or Beth-shemesh.... An Idea of Church-Discipline, in the Theorick and Practick Parts* (London, 1653), pp. 363, 290. Book II, ch. 6 (pp. 392–439) of this manual teaching readers how to assemble and minister to their own radical church consists of testimonies taken from Rogers's Dublin congregation. Cf. also the bundle of experiences edited by Henry Walker, the minister of the congregation at Martins Vintry, London, cited by Rogers (p. 355) as an influence on his own collection: [Henry Walker] *Spirituall Experiences, Of Sundry Beleevers. Held forth by Them at Severall Solemne Meetings, and Conferences to that End*, 2nd edn (London, 1653); and Samuel Petto, *The Voice of the Spirit* (London, 1654), to which was appended a thirty-page tract containing the testimonies of two saints, entitled, "Roses from Sharon. Or Sweet Experiences Gathered up by some precious hearts, whilst they followed on to know the Lord. Published for publick Soul-Advantage."

57 Rogers, *Ohel*, pp. 290–3.

58 Ibid., p. 390.
59 J[ane] Turner, *Choice Experiences of the Kind Dealings of God before, in, and after Conversion; Laid Down in Six General Heads. Together with some Brief Observations upon the Same* (London, 1653), sigs B4–B4^v, B8.
60 Ibid., sig. B6.
61 Edward Burrough, *Something in Answer to a Book called Choice Experiences, Given forth by One J. Tvrner* ([London], 1654), pp. 3, 5.
62 Edward Burrough, "A Testimony Concerning the Beginning of the Work of the Lord, and the First Publication of Truth, In this City of London [1662]," in John Barclay, ed., *Letters, &c., of Early Friends* (London: Harvey and Darton, 1841), pp. 295, 296, 299.
63 Annual totals derived from David Runyon, "Types of Quaker Writings by Year – 1650–1699," in Hugh Barbour and Arthur O. Roberts, eds, *Early Quaker Writings 1650–1700* (Grand Rapids: William B. Eerdmans Publishing Co., 1973), pp. 567–76; percentages of national totals from David J. Hall, "'The Fiery Tryal of their Infallible Examination': Self-Control in the Regulation of Quaker Publishing in England from the 1670s to the mid 19th Century," in Robin Myers and Michael Harris, eds, *Censorship & the Control of Print in England and France 1600–1910* (Winchester: St Paul's Bibliographies, 1992), p. 59.
64 Michael R. Watts, *The Dissenters from the Reformation to the French Revolution* (Oxford: Clarendon Press, 1978), p. 270.
65 J[ohn] W[hiting], *A Catalogue of Friends Books; Written by many of the People, Called Quakers, from the Beginning or First Appearance of the said People* (London, 1708).
66 One such text, at the Friends' House Library, London, Swarthmore MS vol. III, 6, is an undated letter from James Naylor to Margaret Fell *c.* 1654, describing Naylor's preaching in the north of England at that time; it was later (*c.* 1675) identified by George Fox as "journall of j.n. 1654 abought," who wrote this on the back of the copy. Vols. I–IV of the Swarthmore MS collections consist almost entirely of copies of early letters of this sort, over 1,400 in all.
67 Norman Penney, "Our Recording Clerks," *Journal of the Friends Historical Society* (hereafter *JFHS*) 1 (1903–4), p. 16. By the time he died in 1681 the original clerk was earning a whopping £50 a year, which suggests the magnitude of his work.
68 Russell S. Mortimer, "The First Century of Quaker Printers," *JFHS* 40 (1948), p. 42.
69 For more titles of this sort see Joseph Smith, *A Descriptive Catalogue of Friends' Books*, 2 vols (London, 1867).
70 For instance Thomas Green, *A Declaration to the World, of My Travel and Journey out of Aegypt into Canaan Through the Wilderness, & Through the Red-Sea, from under Pharaoh, and Now Hath a Sure Habitation in the Lord, Where Rest and Peace is Known* (London, 1659).
71 Katharine Evans and Sarah Chevers, *This is a Short Relation of the Cruel Sufferings (For the Truths Sake) of Katharine Evans and Sarah Chevers in the Inquisition in the Isle of Malta* (London, 1662).
72 Edward Burrough, *A True Description of my Manner of Life, Of what I have been in My Profession of Religion unto this very Day: And What I am*

at Present, by the Grace of God (London, 1663); Francis Howgill et al., *A Testimony concerning the Life, Death, Trials, Travels and Labours Of Edward Burroughs* (London, 1662).

73 John Burnyeat, *The Truth Exalted in the Writings of . . . John Burnyeat, Collected Into this Ensuing Volume as a Memorial to his Faithful Labours in and for the Truth* (London, 1691), contains an "account of his convincement" and a "journal of his travels," pp. 1–72; Stephen Crisp, *A Memorable Account of the Christian Experiences, Gospel Labours, Travels, and Sufferings of . . . Stephen Crisp, in his Books and Writings herein Collected* (London, 1694), included, as its first item, "A Journal of the Life of Stephen Crisp, Giving an Account of his Convincement, Travels, Labours, and Sufferings, in, and for, Truth," pp. 1–60.

74 William Caton, *A Journal of the Life of . . . Will. Caton. Written by his own Hand* (London, 1689); [Ellwood], *Journal of George Fox*; Miles Halhead, *A Book of some of the Sufferings and Passages of Myles Halhead* (London, 1690).

75 Derived from Runyon, "Types of Quaker Writings," *passim*. I combined figures for texts Runyon classified as "autobiographical tract," "autobiographical journal," and "memoir or testimony to the memory of a deceased Friend." I left the "works" out of this calculation.

76 Swarthmore MS vol. III, 39.

77 Isabel Ross, *Margaret Fell: Mother of Quakerism*, 2nd edn (York: William Sessions Book Trust, 1984), p. 120; accounts of Thomas Willan and George Taylor to Margaret Fell between 1654 and 1657: Swarthmore MS vol. I, 207, 209, 213, 215, 221, 233, 234, 292, 312, 297. The two replies, the first Quaker books printed in London, were *Several Petitions Answered* (London, 1653), and *Saul's Errand to Damascus* (London, 1653).

78 For other printers see Mortimer, "First Century of Quaker Printers," pp. 43ff. On Calvert's troubles with the authorities, see John Hetet, "A Literary Underground in Restoration England: Printers and Dissenters in the Context of Constraints 1660–1689" (Ph.D. thesis, University of Cambridge, 1987), fo. 130.

79 Stephen C. Morland, ed., *The Somersetshire Quarterly Meeting of the Society of Friends 1668–1699*, Somerset Record Society Publications LXXV (n.p., 1978), p. 52.

80 Thomas P. O'Malley, "The Press and Quakerism 1653–1659," *JFHS* 54 (1979), pp. 172–4; Barclay, *Letters of Early Friends*, pp. 9, 84.

81 14 Car. II, cap. 33. For its effect on Quakers, see Arnold Lloyd, *Quaker Social History 1669–1738* (London: Longmans, Green & Co., 1950), pp. 147–50.

82 Friends' House Library, London, Yearly Meeting minutes (hereafter YM), vol. I, p. 3.

83 These full duties were not reflected in the minutes until 1674. Besides matters of publication, the Morning Meeting also looked after the public activities of London ministers. See Friends' House Library, London, Morning Meeting Minute Book (hereafter MM), vol. I, pp. 1, 4.

84 YM, vol. I, p. 25.

85 Ibid., p. 71.

86 Friends' House Library, London, Meeting for Sufferings minute book (hereafter MS), vol. I, pp. 101–3; vol. II, pp. 28–9.

87 Morland, *Somersetshire Quarterly Meeting*, pp. 20–1, 101, 133, 135, 168, 174, 209, 212, 230, 255–6, 258, 260.

88 The number sent varied according to the size of the meeting. The national total of copies ordered to be sent out was about 400 in 1672, when the first directive was issued. The Yearly Meeting revised the figures annually thereafter; in 1674 the national total peaked at about 600, and at that time another ninety were ordered for distribution overseas (YM, vol. I, pp. 3, 11, 12, 62).

89 MS, vol. I, p. 165. This order was renewed by the Yearly Meeting in 1682, YM, vol. I, p. 112.

90 *Epistles from the Yearly Meeting of Friends ... 1681–1817* (London, 1818), pp. 7, 19. Yet in the 1680s printers of Quaker books appealed to the Meeting for Sufferings for compensation for unsold stock, which request was honored as best as possible; see Morland, *Somersetshire Quarterly Meeting*, pp. 21, 230. In 1691, upon the recommendation of the Yearly Meeting, the Meeting for Sufferings instituted a simple revised quota system of sending two copies of every book printed and priced at under 6*d*. to every Quarterly Meeting, and one of each at 6*d*. or above. This enabled local reference libraries to be established in Quaker meeting-houses, and also served as a form of advertisement, making Friends aware of new titles in print (*Epistles from the Yearly Meeting*, p. 63; MS, vol. IX, p. 21).

91 MS, vol. II, pp. 5–6. But later the same year it recommended that only Friends print the Friends' books, which effectively limited the field to the two printers the Friends had been using in the previous decade: Andrew Sowle and Benjamin Clark (MS, vol. II, p. 28). One more was added in 1679: John Bringshurst, a former apprentice of Sowle.

92 Francis Bugg, *The Pilgrim's Progress from Quakerism to Christianity* (London, 1698), p. 73.

93 Thomas O'Malley, " 'Defying the Powers and Tempering the Spirit.' A Review of Quaker Control over their Publications 1672–1689," *Journal of Ecclesiastical History* 33 (1982), p. 85. See also Hall, "Self-Control in the Regulation of Quaker Publishing," and Luella M. Wright, *The Literary Life of the Early Friends 1650–1725* (New York: Cambridge University Press, 1932), pp. 97–109.

94 Jackson I. Cope, "Seventeenth-Century Quaker Style," in Stanley E. Fish, ed., *Seventeenth-Century Prose: Modern Essays in Criticism* (New York: Oxford University Press, 1971), pp. 227, 224.

95 Richard T. Vann, *The Social Development of English Quakerism 1655–1755* (Cambridge, MA: Harvard University Press, 1969), p. 216.

96 There is evidence to suggest that the Presbyterians and the Congregationalists may have had an informal system of pre-publication review similar to the procedure of the Morning Meeting. In a letter to the antiquarian Ralph Thoresby in the year 1695, Oliver Heywood mentions that "the London ministers expunged" some passages from his original draft of his *Life of John Angier* (1685). Heywood mentions this in the course of questioning "whether it be convenient to descend to the particulars of a diary" in an MS life of Mr Bowels, a nonconforming minister. Most of the renowned Presbyterian and Congregationalist ministers corresponded with each other, and shared Thomas Parkhurst as their bookseller, which would have made a system of review feasible. Harold Love, in "Preacher and Publisher,"

speculates that Parkhurst regularly circulated manuscripts to London clerics, who acted as "publisher's readers" (p. 234). Heywood's letter is printed in J. W. Vint, ed., *The Whole Works of the Rev. Oliver Heywood,* 5 vols (Idle, 1825–7), vol. I, pp. 434–5.

97 This was equally the case with political biography, best represented by Clarendon's *History of His Own Time,* an eyewitness account of the Civil War and its aftermath, finished in 1672 and first printed in 1704. In it Clarendon identifies himself throughout as "Mr. Hyde," a servant to the English monarch and, by extension, the English state.

98 Belanger, "Publishers and Writers in Eighteenth-Century England," p. 6.

99 Hall, "Self-Control in the Regulation of Quaker Publishing," pp. 65–6, surveyed the minutes for the years 1691–5 and found seventy-three "accepted," nineteen "not accepted." But his definition of "accepted" is "immediately put into print," at the expense of the society, leaving out the number of alternative publication options recommended and pursued. Hall's article offers an indispensable view of the Morning Meeting's communications with Quaker writers.

100 For instance MM, vol. I, pp. 5, 8; vol. II, p. 28.

101 Ibid., vol. I, pp. 3, 7.

102 Ibid., pp. 73, 98, 122.

103 Ibid., p. 11 (at the request of the author), 79; vol. II, 94, 213. This was common after 1682, when the meeting stipulated that writers held the rights in their copies.

104 YM, vol. I, pp. 202, 93; cf. *Epistles from the Yearly Meeting,* p. 2.

105 This was one of the tasks Ellis Hookes, the first recording clerk, was paid to perform; see Penney, "Our Recording Clerks," p. 15.

106 MS, vol. I, pp. 58–9; cf. YM, vol. I, pp. 8, 71, 92–3; *Epistles from the Yearly Meeting,* pp. 2, 5, 24. The original list of correspondents is printed in Barclay, *Letters of Early Friends,* pp. 346–50.

107 A fine example of this system in operation is traced by Evangeline and Charles Andrews in an appendix to their edition of the Quaker Jonathan Dickinson's journal of his shipwreck and journey from Jamaica to Philadelphia, which was printed by the Friends in 1699. See Evangeline and Charles Andrews, eds, *Jonathan Dickinson's Journal or, God's Protecting Providence* (New Haven: Yale University Press, 1945), pp. 204–33.

108 MM, vol. I, pp. 96, 98 (Dewsbury), p. 107 (Parker), pp. 130, 137–8 (Burnyeat); vol. II, pp. 8, 17, 18, 43, 61 (Crisp). References to the *Journal* and *Epistles* of George Fox are as follows: vol. I, pp. 163, 165, 166, 171; vol. II, pp. 17, 26, 28, 29, 31, 38, 44, 45, 52, 61, 62, 66, 68. The Fox case is documented by Norman Penney, "George Fox's Writings and the Morning Meeting," *Friends' Quarterly Examiner* 36 (1902), pp. 63–72.

109 MM, vol. I, p. 10; cf. T[heophila] T[ownsend], *A Testimony concerning the Life and Death of Jane Whitehead* (London, 1676).

110 MM, vol. I, pp. 17, 18; cf. [Joan Whitrow], *The Work of God in a Dying Maid, being a short Account of the Dealings of the Lord with one Susanna Whitrow* (London, 1677). Two editions were published in 1677, another one was printed in Dublin, 1696.

111 Other titles include: *The Living Words of a Dying Child, Being a True Relation of some part of his Words that came forth, and were spoken by Joseph Briggins on his Death-bed* ([London], 1675); [George Whitehead,

ed.], *A Seasonable Account of the Christian Testimony and Heavenly Expressions of Tudor Brain upon his Death Bed* (London, 1698); Sarah Featherstone and Thomas Browne, *Living Testimonies Concerning the Death of the Righteouss, or, The blessed End of Joseph Featherstone and Sarah his Daughter* ([London], 1689).

112 MM, vol. I, p. 30; cf. John Beck, *A Certain and True Relation of the Heavenly Enjoyments and Living Testimonies of God's Love ... Declared upon the Dying-Bed of Sarah, the Wife of John Beck* ([London], 1680).

113 MM, vol. I, p. 49, cf. Richard Samble, *A Handful after the Harvest-Man: or, a Loving Salutation to Sion's Mourners, being a Collection of several Epistles & Testimonies of ... Richard Samble* (London, 1684); MM, vol. I, p. 85; cf. Thomas Briggs, *An Account of some of the Travels and Sufferings of ... Thomas Briggs* ([London], 1685); MM, vol. II, pp. 173, 190, 303; cf. [John Field, ed.], *A Collection of the Christian Writings, Labours, Travels, and Sufferings of ... Roger Haydock. To which is added, an Account of his Death and Burial* (London, 1700).

114 Burnyeat, *The Truth Exalted in the Writings of ... John Burnyeat*, sig. A2ᵛ.

115 Sylvester, *Reliquiae*; [Ellwood et al.], *A Journal or Historical Account of ... George Fox.*

116 Thanks to Richard Dienst for suggesting this phrase to me.

Chapter 6 True Confessions

1 John Dunton, *Dunton's Whipping-Post: or, a Satyr Upon Every Body* (London, 1706), p. 2.

2 Dunton, *Life and Errors*, p. 320; hereafter, page references from the 1705 edition are cited in the text.

3 By Dunton's own estimate the number was 600 (*Life and Errors*, p. 217). However, according to the recent bibliography of extant works ascribed to Dunton, the figure is half as many; see Stephen Parks, *John Dunton and the English Book Trade: A Study of his Career with a Checklist of his Publications* (New York and London: Garland Publishing, 1976).

4 J. Paul Hunter, *Before Novels: The Cultural Contexts of Eighteenth-Century English Fiction* (New York and London: W. W. Norton, 1990), p. 333.

5 J. Paul Hunter, "The Insistent I," *Novel* 13 (1979), p. 21. In *Before Novels*, Hunter writes: "The *Life and Errors* is hardly a typical early-century work; it does not seem quite at home in its 1705 context, and its interests and strategies are, whatever else they may be, well ahead of their time" (p. 337). For a similar view of a different so-called "autobiography" by Dunton, see Robert Adams Day, "Richard Bentley and John Dunton: Brothers Under the Skin," in O. M. Brack, Jr, ed., *Studies in Eighteenth-Century Culture* 16 (Madison: University of Wisconsin Press, 1986), pp. 125–38.

6 C. A. Moore, "John Dunton: Pietist and Impostor," *Studies in Philology* 22 (1925), pp. 470–1.

7 Parks, *John Dunton*, pp. 152, 334–5. For other reprinted material in the *Life and Errors* see ibid., pp. 49–50; and Moore, "John Dunton," p. 480.

8 Moore, "John Dunton," *passim.*

9 Parks, *John Dunton*, pp. 311, 319. Other pious lives published by Dunton include: Henry Cuts, *The Life and Death of Mr. Francis Crow* (1693); *Some Remarkable Passages in the Life and Death of John Mason* (1694); Cotton Mather, *Early Piety, Exemplified in the Life and Death of Nathaniel Mather* (1689); id., *Life and Death of the Renown'd Mr. John Eliot* (1691; 2nd edn 1694); John Shower, *Sermon Preached Upon the Death of Mrs. Anne Barnardiston. . . . With a Brief Account of some Remarkable Passages of her Life and Death* (1682); Samuel Slater, *The Saints Readiness for their Lord's Coming: A Funeral Sermon Preached upon the Death of . . . Mr. John Oakes* (1689); Francis Spanheimius, *Funeral Oration to the Sacred Memory of the most Serene and Potent Mary II* (1695); these are listed in Parks, *John Dunton*, pp. 218, 236, 242, 257, 283, 299, 304, 308, 319.

10 Cf. Parks, *John Dunton*, pp. 326ff. The death of Samuel Annesley several months before his daughter also contributed to Dunton's decline; early on, Annesley persuaded some of his colleagues to sell their copies to Dunton; see ibid., p. 45, n. 27.

11 But the *Life and Errors* contains what appears to be Dunton's own "Comprehensive view of the life and death of Iris" (pp. 356–62), which is a textbook example (or parody, depending how one reads it) of such a life. In the year of his wife's death Dunton published a funeral elegy for his father-in-law, *The Character of the Late Dr. Samuel Annesley* (London, 1697), written by one of Annesley's parishioners, Daniel Defoe. Dunton also published Annesley's *Life and Funeral Sermon of the Reverend Mr. Thomas Brand* (London, 1692); cf. Parks, *John Dunton*, pp. 321, 270.

12 For two examples of printed parodies see *The Life and Death of Ralph Wallis the Cobler of Glocester: Together with some inquiring into the Mystery of Conventicleism* (London, 1670); *The Life & Death of Stephen Marshal, Minister of the Gospel at Finchingfield in Essex* (London, 1680).

13 Edmund Calamy, *An Abridgement of Mr. Baxter's History of his Life and Times* (London, 1702), pp. 183–497. Calamy's book was published by the same conger that published *Reliquiae Baxterianae* (Parkhurst, Jonathan Robinson, and John Lawrence), minus Dunton.

14 It was volume II of the second edition of Calamy's *Abridgement* (London, 1713). The work comprised 845 pages.

15 The first book published with this title appeared in 1775; it was reissued in 1777 and again in 1778; a second edition was published in 1802. The *Account* was severed from Baxter's *Life* in 1727, when it was printed in a two-volume edition of its own, entitled *A Continuation of the Account of Ministers . . . Ejected or Silenced . . . by or before the Act of Uniformity* (London, 1727).

16 Calamy, *Account* (1713), p. vii.

17 The first attempt was made by John Whiting, in the context of his own biography, in a book entitled *Persecution Expos'd, in some Memoirs relating to the Sufferings of John Whiting, and many others of the People called Quakers* (London, 1715). Whiting's effort was superseded by the more comprehensive work of Joseph Besse, *An Abstract of the Sufferings of the People Called Quakers for the Testimony of Good Conscience . . . Taken from Original Records, and other Authentic Accounts . . . to the*

Year 1666, 3 vols (London, 1733–8). This was later revised and completed in a two-volume folio edition by Besse, entitled *A Collection of the Sufferings of the People Called Quakers . . . from . . . 1650 to the Time . . . of the Act of Toleration* (London, 1753).

18 [Thomas Dangerfield], *Mr. Dangerfields Particular Narrative of the late Popish Design to Charge those of the Presbyterian Party with a Pretended Conspiracy against his Majesties Person, and Government* (London, 1679), sigs A, A^v.

19 Its printer, who presumably purchased the copy from Dangerfield, was fined £5,000 by the duke under the same charge brought against Dangerfield, which gives a sense of the stakes involved.

20 See the entries in Wing's *Short Title Catalogue*, and the bibliography in the *Dictionary of National Biography*, s.v. Dangerfield, Thomas.

21 Thomas Dangerfield, *Dangerfield's Memoires* (London, 1685), p. 1.

22 Ibid., unpaginated preface.

23 Parks, *John Dunton*, p. 13.

24 Title as entered in the Stationer's Register by Dunton, though actually published under the imprint of Thomas Manhood. See Parks, *John Dunton*, pp. 22–3, 223.

25 *The Devils Patriarck, or a Full and Impartial Account of the Notorious Life of this Present Pope of Rome Innocent the 11th* (London, 1683).

26 *The Informer's Doom* (London, 1683), title-page.

27 *The Bloody Assizes: or, a Compleat History of the Life of George Lord Jefferies, from his Birth to this present Time . . . Faithfully Collected by several West-Country Gentlemen, who were both eye and Ear-witnesses to all the Matter of Fact* (London, 1689).

28 Parks, *John Dunton*, p. 41; for other titles see ibid., pp. 234, 235, 236, 239, 242.

29 *The Popish Champion: or, a Compleat History of the Life and Military Actions of Richard Earl of Tyrconnel, Generalissimo of all the Irish Forces Now in Arms* (London, 1689). Dunton issued several other anti-Jacobite pamphlets, including *A Second Modest Enquiry into the Causes of the present Disasters in England . . . Being a farther Discovery of the Jacobite Plot* (London, 1690); the case of "the Pretender," James II's alleged son, interested Dunton, who facilitated three publications by the spy William Fuller in 1696, claiming to "discover" the mother of the Prince of Wales. Cf. Parks, *John Dunton*, pp. 63–4, 313, 314–15, 316.

30 For an overview see Gilbert D. McEwen, *The Oracle of the Coffee House: John Dunton's Athenian Mercury* (San Marino, CA: Huntington Library, 1972).

31 Quoted in Parks, *John Dunton*, p. 78.

32 Ibid., p. 76.

33 One innovative recent critic, investigating the *Athenian Mercury*'s discourse as an element of the construction of femininity in eighteenth-century England, has gone so far as to treat individual letters as "autobiographical narratives." See Kathryn Shevelow, *Women and Print Culture: The Construction of Femininity in the Early Periodical* (London and New York: Routledge, 1989), ch. 3.

34 George Starr, "From Casuistry to Fiction: the Importance of the *Athenian Mercury*," *Journal of the History of Ideas* 28 (1967), pp. 31–2, *passim*; see

also his *Defoe and Casuistry* (Princeton: Princeton University Press, 1971); Hunter, *Before Novels*, pp. 12–16.

35 For some of these see Parks, *John Dunton*, pp. 263, 330, 305, 307, 312.

36 Dunton, *Life and Errors*, p. 269.

37 As, for example, in the case of Roy M. Wiles, *Serial Publication in England Before 1750* (Cambridge: Cambridge University Press, 1957), p. 77.

38 *The Night-Walker*, Sept. 1696, p. 1.

39 Ibid., p. 2.

40 Ibid., p. 26.

41 Ibid., sig. B.

42 Quoted by Dudley W. R. Bahlman, *The Moral Revolution of 1688* (New Haven: Yale University Press, 1957), p. 16.

43 Ibid., pp. 26–7.

44 Ibid., pp. 37–9.

45 T. C. Curtis and W. A. Speck, "The Societies for the Reformation of Manners: A Case Study in the Theory and Practice of Moral Reform," *Literature and History* 3 (1976), pp. 47–8, 53.

46 Samuel Wesley, *A Sermon Concerning Reformation of Manners* (London, 1698), p. 35.

47 Bahlman, *Moral Revolution*, pp. 48ff.

48 Garnet V. Portus, *Caritas Anglicana or, An Historical Inquiry into those Religious and Philanthropical Societies that Flourished in England Between the Years 1678 and 1740* (London: A. R. Mowbray & Co., 1912), pp. 235–40, 251–4; Bahlman, *Moral Revolution*, pp. 54–66, Curtis and Speck, "Societies for Reformation of Manners," *passim*. Cf. [Josiah Woodward], *An Account of the Societies for Reformation of Manners, In London and Westminster, and other Parts of the Kingdom. With a Persuasive to Persons of all ranks, to be Zealous and Diligent in Promoting the Execution of the Laws against Prophaneness and Debauchery, for the Effecting a National Reformation* (London, 1699).

49 London, 1694; page references are cited in the text.

50 [Richard Allestree], *The Works of the Author of the Whole Duty of Man* (Oxford, 1684), vol. I, p. 48, quoted in John Spurr, *The Restoration Church of England, 1646–1689* (New Haven and London: Yale University Press, 1991), pp. 290–1. I am indebted to ch. 6 of Spurr's book, esp. pp. 281–96, for information in this paragraph.

51 Robert South, *Sermons*, 5 vols (Oxford, 1842), vol. III, pp. 364–5, quoted in Spurr, *Restoration Church*, p. 289.

52 *The Night-Walker*, Dec. 1696, sig. A2ᵛ.

53 *The Night-Walker*, Sept. 1696, pp. 24–5.

54 *The Night-Walker*, Oct. 1696, p. 2.

55 *The Night-Walker*, Sept. 1696, p. 17.

56 *The Night-Walker*, Nov. 1696, p. 7.

57 This point is made in a discussion of such texts by Peter Lake, "Deeds against Nature: Cheap Print, Protestantism and Murder in Early Seventeenth-Century England," in Kevin Sharpe and Peter Lake, eds, *Culture and Politics in Early Stuart England* (Stanford: Stanford University Press, 1993), p. 280 and *passim*.

58 *The Night-Walker*, Jan. 1697, p. 16; *The Night-Walker*, Nov. 1696, p. 18.

Chapter 7   The Trump of Fame

1 The best known remains Watt, *The Rise of the Novel*, discussed in ch. 2.

2 However, some studies offer provocative suggestions on the subject of criminal lives and personal individuality; see Lennard J. Davis, *Factual Fictions: The Origins of the English Novel* (New York: Columbia University Press, 1983), pp. 123–37; Michael McKeon, *The Origins of the English Novel 1600–1740* (Baltimore and London, The Johns Hopkins University Press, 1987), pp. 96–100; John Richetti, *Popular Fiction Before Richardson: Narrative Patterns 1700–1739* (Oxford: Clarendon Press, 1969), pp. 30–1, 52–3.

3 See, for instance, Lincoln B. Faller, "In Contrast to Defoe: The Rev. Paul Lorrain, Historian of Crime," *Huntington Library Quarterly* 39 (1976), pp. 59–78; id., *Turned to Account: The Form and Functions of Criminal Biography in Late Seventeenth- and Early Eighteenth-Century England* (Cambridge: Cambridge University Press, 1987); Michael Harris, "Trials and Criminal Biographies: A Case Study in Distribution," in Robin Myers and Michael Harris, eds, *Sale and Distribution of Books from 1700* (Oxford: Oxford Polytechnic Press, 1982), pp. 1–36; Peter Linebaugh, "The Ordinary of Newgate and his *Account*," in J. S. Cockburn, ed., *Crime in England 1550–1800* (Princeton: Princeton University Press, 1977), pp. 246–69; id., *The London Hanged: Crime and Civil Society in the Eighteenth Century* (Cambridge: Cambridge University Press, 1992); J. A. Sharpe, " 'Last Dying Speeches': Religion, Ideology and Public Execution in Seventeenth-Century England," *Past and Present* 107 (1985), pp. 144–67; W. J. Sheehan, "Finding Solace in Eighteenth-Century Newgate," in J. S. Cockburn, ed., *Crime in England 1550–1800* (Princeton: Princeton University Press, 1977), pp. 229–45.

4 Sheehan, "Eighteenth-Century Newgate," p. 238.

5 The first recorded instance of confession dates from 1239; Tyburn dates from 1108. See Alfred Marks, *Tyburn Tree: Its History and Annals* (London: Brown, Langham & Co., n.d.), p. 88.

6 Quoted ibid., p. 119.

7 Ibid., p. 121.

8 This was the case in the early seventeenth century with Elizabeth Sawyer, condemned to die for witchcraft, who made an auricular confession to a minister in the chapel at Newgate, who wrote it down and was later ordered to read it to her at Tyburn. See Henry Goodcole, *The Wonderfull Discouerie of Elizabeth Sawyer a Witch, late of Edmonton, Her Conuiction and Condemnation and Death* (London, 1621).

9 Reproduced in Marks, *Tyburn Tree*, between pp. 166 and 167.

10 Lacey Balwin Smith, "English Treason Trials and Confessions in the Sixteenth Century," *Journal of the History of Ideas* 15 (1954), p. 483.

11 For examples see Smith, "English Treason Trials," *passim*; Faller, *Turned to Account*, pp. 286–8; Marks, *Tyburn Tree*, pp. 155, 163–4.

12 Marks, *Tyburn Tree*, p. 172.

13 Henry Goodcole, *A True Declaration of the Happy Conversion, Contribution and Christian Preparation of Francis Robinson, Gentleman* (London, 1618), sig. A3; hereafter page references are cited in the text.

14 Goodcole, *The Wonderfull Discouerie of Elizabeth Sawyer*, sig. B3ᵛ.
15 Ibid., sig. A3ᵛ. According to Davis, *Factual Fictions*, p. 56, criminal behavior comprises the single largest subject-matter category of ballads in the Stationers' Register – 115 in all: fifty about murders, and sixty-five about executions. The next largest subject-matter category is Queen Elizabeth, with fifty-four ballads about her.
16 Harris, "Trials and Criminal Biographies," p. 16.
17 See ibid., pp. 6–15, for a brief description of this series. Goodcole had issued a predecessor of the *Proceedings*, in addition to his *Accounts*, entitled, *Londons Cry: Ascended to God, and Entered into the Hearts, and Eares of Men for Reuenge of Bloodshedders, Burglaires, and Vagabounds. Manifested the Last Sessions, Holden at Iustice Hall in the Old Baily the 9.10.11.12. of December, Ann Dom. 1619. Likewise Herein is Related, the Courts Legall Proceedings, against the Malefactors that were Executed at Tiburne and about London, and the Chiefest Offenders, There Offences and Confessions at Large Expressed* (London, 1620); similar printed accounts by anonymous hands survive for earlier trials.
18 Samuel Smith, *The Character of a Weaned Christian: or, The Evangelical Art of Promoting Self-denial* (London, 1675); for his early crime texts see, for example, Samuel Smith, *An Account of the Behaviour of the Fourteen Late Popish Malefactors, whils't in Newgate. And Their Discourse with the Ordinary. . . . Also, a Confutation of Their Appeals, Courage, and Cheerfulness at Execution* (London, 1679) – printed by Parkhurst, during Dunton's apprenticeship, incidentally; and *The Behaviour and Execution of Robert Green and Lawrence Hill, Who Suffered at Tyburn on Friday, February 21, 1678/9, with an Account of their Lives, Conditions, Deportment after Sentence, Discourses with Mr. Ordinary, and Other Most Remarkable Circumstances* (London, 1679); this was not written by Smith, but contains his imprimatur on its title-page, thus, "*Having at the Publisher's Request perused this Sheet, I do certifie, That the Discourses betwixt me and the Prisoners, and other matters of Fact therein, are truly related.*"
19 In an attempt to avoid payment of the Stamp Tax of 1712 on newspapers, it went from a single-folio broadsheet to six small folio pages, to allow its classification as a pamphlet. It reverted back to the single-leaf format in 1725, when the loophole in the law was closed. In 1730, for the first time, the *Account* was deliberately designed to be bound together with the *Proceedings*, which was then a quarto pamphlet of between twenty and twenty-eight pages, retailing for 6d. See Harris, "Trials and Criminal Biographies," pp. 9–10, 17.
20 Samuel Smith, *The Behaviour of Edward Kirk, After his Condemnation for Murdering His Wife; with the Advice and Prayers which he left with the Ordinary, desiring him to Publish the same for Reclaiming of Vicious Youth* (London, 1684), p. 1.
21 *Account*, 21 Apr. 1686, p. 1.
22 Marks, *Tyburn Tree*, p. 145.
23 Sir Leon Radzinowitz, *A History of English Criminal Law and its Administration from 1750*, 4 vols (New York: Macmillan, 1948), vol. I, p. 175 n. 45. By this time the population of metropolitan London was approaching a million people.
24 Smith, *Behaviour of Edward Kirk*, p. 1.

25 See Sharpe, "'Last Dying Speeches'," for the Foucauldian view, and Thomas Laqueur, "Crowds, Carnival and the State in English Executions, 1604–1868," in A. L. Beier, D. Cannadine and J. Rosenheim, eds, *The First Modern Society* (Cambridge: Cambridge University Press, 1989), pp. 305–56, for its antithesis.

26 See Lake, "Deeds against Nature."

27 Christopher Love, *The Penitent Pardoned* (London, 1657), p. "22" (the text is oddly paginated; the sequence runs as follows: 1–24, 19, 18, 19, 18, 23, 22 – this last is the page 22 I cite).

28 *The Execution of William Ireland and John Grove. . . . With their Carriage and Behaviour* (London, 1679), p. 6.

29 *Account*, 10 Mar. 1697, verso.

30 *Account*, 17 Jan. 1697, verso.

31 *Account*, 25 Sept. 1696, verso.

32 The following is a list of examples, by no means exhaustive, uncovered at the Huntington and the Clark libraries: [J. Ashton], *A Copy of Mr. Ashton's Paper, Delivered to the Sheriff at the Place of Execution, January 28. 1690/ 1* (London, 1691); [Robert Frances], *The Dying-Speech of Robert Frances of Grays-Inn, Esq; July 24, 1685. Delivered by His Own Hand to the Ordinary, at the Place of Execution, Desiring the Same Might be Published* (London, 1685); [George Norton], *The True Confession of Mr. George Norton, Concerning the Murther of Mr. Harris the Dancing Master, on the 11th of June last. Taken Out of his Own Papers, Delivered by Him to Mrs. Mary Edwards, before He Took the Fatal Draught of Poyson, on the 8th of August, of which He Died the Following Day, which was Appointed for His Execution at Tyburn* (London, 1699); [Roger Lowen], *A Paper Containing the Last Words of Mr. Roger Lowen, by him Written in German, and Deliver'd to the Ordinary of Newgate, at the Place of his Execution at Turnham Green the 25th of October, 1706. And now Faithfully Translated and Set forth . . . for Publick Satisfaction* (London, 1706); [Henry Harrison], *The Last Dying Words of Henry Harrison* (London, 1692); [id.], *The Last Words of a Dying Penitent* (London, 1692); [id.], *A True Copy of a Letter, Written by Henry Harrison* (London, 1692); [Margaret Martell], *A True Copy of the Paper Delivered by Margaret Martel* (London, 1697); [id.], *A True Translation of a Paper . . . Delivered by Margaret Martel* (London, 1697); [William Ivy], *The Penitent Murderer: or, An Exact and True Relation taken from the Mouth of Mr. William Ivy (lately Executed) Concerning the Murder by Him Committed upon the Body of William Pew . . . With his Confession of the Whole Fact, and his Contrition for the Same; as It was Delivered From his own Mouth to a Particular Friend, and by him Published, to Prevent all False Reports* (London, 1673); [Edward Kirk], *The Sufferers Legacy to Surviving Sinners: Or Edmund Kirk's Dying Advice to Young Men, Wrote by His Own Hand in Newgate, and Delivered to His Friend with a Desire that the Same Might Be Published* (London, 1684); [id.], *A True Paper Delivered by Edward Kirk* (London, 1684).

33 Nathaniel, Butler, *Blood Washed Away by Tears of Repentance: Being an Exact Relation of the Cause and Manner of that Horrid Murther Committed on the Person of John Knight . . . by Nathaniel Butler . . . Written with his Owne Hand* (London, 1657).

34 Ibid., sig. a. The unauthorized biography might be *A True Description of the Parentage, Education, Life and Death of Na. Butler, Apprentice to Mr. Gooday, Drawer of Cloth in Carter Lane, Aug. 6 1657* (London, 1657).

35 *A Full and the Truest Narrative of the Most Horrid, Barbarous and Unparallelled Murder, Committed on the Person of John Knight* [London, 1657], sig. aᵛ.

36 In his diary for 21 Jan. 1664, Samuel Pepys wrote of hearing at the coffee-house of the last speech of Col. James Turner, interpreted by its auditors as an attempt to delay the inevitable: "Turner's discourse on the Cart, which was chiefly to clear himself of all things laid to his charge but this fault for which he now suffers, which he confesses. He deplored the condition of his family. But his chief design was to lengthen time, believing still a reprieve would come, though the Sheriffe advised him to expect no such thing, for the King resolved to grant none" (Robert Latham and William Matthews, eds, *The Diary of Samuel Pepys*, 11 vols (Berkeley and Los Angeles: University of California Press, 1970–83), vol. V, pp. 23–4).

37 *The Wonders of Free-Grace: or a Compleat History of all the Remarkable Penitents that have been executed at Tyburn, and Elsewhere, for these last Thirty Years* (London, 1690), p. 48. Cf. Richard Foulkes, *An Alarme For Sinners: Containing the Confession, Prayers, Letters, and Last Words of Richard Foulkes. . . . Published from the Original, Written with His Own Hand, during his Reprieve, and Sent by Him at his Death to Doctor Lloyd, Dean of Bangor* (London, 1679).

38 *The Wonders of Free-Grace*, p. 71. Cf. [Margaret Clark], *A Warning for Servants: and a Caution to Protestants* (London, 1680), esp. pp. 17–23; and *The True Confession of Margaret Clark, Who Consented to the Burning of Her Masters Mr. Peter Delanoy's House in Southwark. Delivered in Prison to Many Witnesses a Little Before Her Death. And Confirmed by Her Self at the Place of Execution, by Answering All Questions then Put to Her by the Reverend and Worthy Divine, Dr. Martin, Now Minister at S. Saviours Southwark. Printed for General Satisfaction* (London, 1680).

39 This is evident in the chronological bibliography provided by Faller in *Turned to Account*, esp. pp. 299ff.

40 Quoted in Linebaugh, "The Ordinary of Newgate," p. 254.

41 Ibid., p. 255.

42 [Daniel Defoe], *The History of the Press-Yard* (London, 1717), pp. 49, 52–3.

43 *Dictionary of National Biography*, s.v. Lorrain, Paul; Linebaugh, "The Ordinary of Newgate," p. 250.

44 This ad, for example, "*Whereas there formerly have been, and still are, several false Accounts in Print, in relation to the Condemned Prisoners; and particularly this very Session, which is utterly False: The Ordinary thinks it necessary to acquaint the World (to prevent the like for the Future) That no true Account can be given of the Condemned Prisoners Behaviour, Confession, and Last Dying Speeches, which is not Attested under his own Hand,*" appeared in the following issues of the *Account*: 6 Nov. 1695; 13 Dec. 1695; 20 Mar. 1696; 4 May 1696; 21 Dec. 1692 (a slightly different version).

45 Thomas Gent, *The Life of Mr. Thomas Gent, Printer, of York* (London, 1832), pp. 101–4, 140–1.

46 Linebaugh, "The Ordinary of Newgate," p. 259.
47 Harris, "Trials and Criminal Biographies," pp. 22–3.
48 Philip Rawlings, *Drunks, Whores and Idle Apprentices: Criminal Biographies of the Eighteenth Century* (London and New York: Routledge, 1992), pp. 2, 7.
49 Quoted in Radzinowitz, *History of English Criminal Law*, vol. I, p. 181 n. 63; see also ibid., n. 64.
50 Editions tallied by Rawlings, *Drunks, Whores and Idle Apprentices*, p. 2.
51 *The History of the Remarkable Life of John Sheppard* (London, 1724), pp. 27–8.
52 *A Narrative Of all the Robberies, Escapes, &c. Of John Sheppard* (London, 1724). This work is attributed to Daniel Defoe, though the title-page states that it was "Written by himself during his Confinement in the Middle Stone-Room, after his being retaken in Drury-Lane" and "Published at the particular Request of the Prisoner." Numerous portraits of Sheppard can be found in reissues of criminal lives; they have been discussed recently by Marcia Pointon, *Hanging the Head: Portraiture and Social Formation in Eighteenth-Century England* (New Haven and London: Yale University Press, 1993), pp. 89–90.
53 Quoted in Christopher Hibbert, *The Road to Tyburn: The Story of Jack Sheppard and The Eighteenth-Century London Underworld* (Cleveland and New York: World, 1957), pp. 221–2. For a full description of the event in the eighteenth century see Radzinowitz, *History of English Criminal Law*, vol. I, pp. 165–205.
54 Henry Fielding, *An Enquiry into the Causes of the Late Increase of Robbers, &c. with some Proposals for Remedying this Growing Evil* (1751); repr. in William E. Henly, ed., *The Complete Works of Henry Fielding*, 16 vols (New York: Barnes and Noble, 1967), vol. XIII, p. 120–1.
55 Henry Fielding, *The History of the Life of the Late Jonathan Wild*, in his *Miscellanies*, vol. III (London, 1743). For Walpole and Boswell see Rawlings, *Drunks, Whores and Ide Apprentices*, p. 4.
56 *Rambler*, No. 60.
57 [Daniel Defoe], *The History and Remarkable Life of the Truly Honourable Col. Jacque, Commonly Call'd Col. Jack* (London, 1723), p. 398
58 For a partial bibliography see Gerald Howson, *Thief-Taker General: The Rise and Fall of Jonathan Wild* (New York: St Martin's Press, 1970), pp. 324–5.
59 For a coded discussion of sources see Alexander Smith, *A Compleat History of the Lives and Robberies of the most Notorious Highway-Men, Foot-Pads, Shop-Lifts, and Cheats, of both Sexes, in and about London and Westminster, and all Parts of Great Britain, for above an Hundred Years past, continu'd to the present Time*, 5th edn, 2 vols (London, 1719), vol. I, pp. iv–viii.
60 London, 1734; page references are cited in the text. Wiles, *Serial Publication in England*, pp. 131–2, describes this text as a combination of Alexander Smith's *General History* (1st pub. 1714) and Charles Johnson's *Genuine Account of the . . . most Notorious Pyrates* (London, 1724). The latter work has been ascribed to Defoe, writing under the "Johnson" pseudonym. Defoe died in 1730, so he is not the "Johnson" of the *General History*.
61 See Linebaugh, "The Ordinary of Newgate," pp. 260–9.

62 All of whom, coincidentally, wrote diaries or left memoirs of their lives. For a discussion of the vogue for such collections in the eighteenth century, see Pointon, *Hanging the Head*, ch. 2.

63 George Fox's *Journal* lacked such an image because the Quakers regarded such representations as blasphemous.

64 However, Pepys's print collection included images of eight executed male-factors and one pirate; see John Charrington, *A Catalogue of the Engraved Portraits in the Library of Samuel Pepys* (Cambridge: Cambridge University Press, 1936). Certainly by the end of the eighteenth century criminal prints were collected by gentlemen to fill out the bottom end of their hierarchically organized catalogues of portraits, as described in Pointon, *Hanging the Head*, pp. 91–4.

65 For further information, see Wiles, *Serial Publication*, p. 293.

66 At least eight different serially published compilations of criminal biographies appeared in Britain before 1750, besides Johnson's 1734 text; cf. the items in the bibliography of Wiles, *Serial Publication*, pp. 290, 293, 294, 322, 331, 332–3, 352–3, 355.

67 Keith Maslen, "Printing for the Author: From the Bowyer Printing Ledgers, 1710–1775," *The Library*, 5th ser., 27 (1972), p. 304.

68 Teresia Constantia Phillips, *An Apology for the Conduct of Mrs. Teresia Constantia Phillips*, 3 vols ([London], 1748–9), vol. II, p. 90; vol. I, pp. 270–1. Hereafter page references are cited in the text.

69 *General Advertiser*, 13 Apr. 1748. It was repeated on the 14th, 16th, 19th, 20th, 21st, and 22nd. Beginning with the ad on the 20th, the second number was announced. Ads for subsequent numbers continued to appear throughout the year.

70 Among such items are, *A Defence of the Character of a Noble Lord, from the Scandalous Aspersions Contained in a Malicious Apology. In a Letter to the supposed Authoress* (London, 1748); *A Familiar Epistle to the Celebrated Mrs. Con. Phillips, on her Apology*, n.p., n.d.; Henry Dennis, *An Answer to the Anonymous Author of a Familiar Epistle to Mrs. Con. Phillips* (London, 1749); Teresia Constantia Phillips, *A Letter humbly addressed to the Right Honourable, the Earl of Chesterfield* (London, 1750); *A Dialogue in the Shades Below: Manag'd by Mrs. Phill—ps, Mrs. Pilk—nton, Dean Swift, Galilaeo, Lais and the Courtezan, and several other persons of Taste and Distinction. Together with the Trial and Sentence of Mrs. Phill—ps and Mrs. Pilk—nton* (London, n.d.); *The Parallel; or Pilkington and Phillips Compared. Being Remarks upon the Memoirs of those two celebrated Writers* (London, 1748). The *General Advertiser* for 9 June 1748 carried an advertisement for a book entitled *A Genuine Copy of the Tryal of Tho. Grimes, Esq; alias Lord C——, for a barbarous and inhuman Rape, committed on the body of Miss T.C.P. a young Girl of Thirteen Years of Age. On a special Commission of Oyer and terminer, held at the Old Court House, now a B—o at Ch—r—g C—ss. To which is annexed, The Ordinary's Account of the Words and Confession, delivered to the Sheriff before he was to have been turn'd off.*

71 *A familiar Epistle to the Celebrated Mrs. Phillips*, p. 9.

72 Dennis, *An Answer to the Anonymous Author*, pp. 4, 5, 7.

73 *A Familiar Epistle to the Celebrated Mrs. Phillips*, pp. 21–2; *The General*

Advertiser, 21 July 1748; Phillips, *Apology*, vol. II, p. 244; vol. I, sig. *ᵛ; Dennis, *An Answer to the Anonymous Author*, p. 8.

74 *The Gentleman's Magazine* 33 (1766), p. 83.

75 Laetitia Pilkington, *Memoirs of Mrs. Laetitia Pilkington, Wife to the Rev. Matthew Pilkington. Written by Herself*, 2 vols (London, 1749); vol. III of this work appeared posthumously, edited by her son, John Carteret Pilkington, as *The Third and Last Volume of the Memoirs of Mrs Laetitia Pilkington, Written by Herself* (London, 1754). The quotation is from vol. III, p. 33; hereafter page references are cited in the text.

76 On influence see also *A Dialogue in the Shades Below* and *The Parallel*, cited in n. 70 above, which compare the two texts.

77 For a bibliography, see Laetitia Pilkington, *The Memoirs of Mrs. Letitia Pilkington 1712–1750, Written by Herself*, ed. Iris Barry (London: Geo. Routledge & Sons, 1928), pp. 468–70.

78 Charlotte Charke, *A Narrative of the Life of Mrs. Charlotte Charke*, 2nd edn (1755; facsimile edn, Gainesville: Scholar's Facsimiles & Reprints, 1969), pp. iv, 13. Hereafter page references are cited in the text.

79 Advertisement in the *Bristol Weekly Intelligencer*, Mar. 1755, quoted in Fidelis Morgan, *The Well-Known Troublemaker: A Life of Charlotte Charke* (London and Boston: Faber and Faber, 1988), pp. 182–3. Facsimiles of the title-page and frontispiece of the first edition may be found between pp. 13 and 14 of Charke's text in the facsimile edition of the *Narrative*.

80 Whyte's anecdote is printed in Morgan, *Troublemaker*, pp. 181–2.

81 Felicity A. Nussbaum, *The Autobiographical Subject: Gender and Ideology in Eighteenth-Century England* (Baltimore and London: The Johns Hopkins University Press, 1989), p. 190.

Epilogue: "The Author . . . Our Hero"

1 Simon Mason, *A Narrative of the Life and Distresses of Simon Mason, Apothecary* (Birmingham, [1754]), pp. ii–iii.

2 James Houstoun, *The Works of James Houstoun, M.D. Containing Memoirs of his Life and Travels in Asia, Africa, America, and Most Parts of Europe. From the Year 1690, to the Present Time* (London, 1753), p. 8.

3 [Oldys et al., eds], *Biographia Britannica*, vol. I, p. xii.

4 Ibid.

5 Robert Scholes, "Narration and Narrativity in Film and Fiction," in his *Semiotics and Interpretation* (New Haven and London: Yale University Press, 1982), pp. 60–1.

6 *Gentleman's Magazine* 62 (Dec. 1791), p. 1137.

7 *English Review* 18 (July 1791), p. 375.

8 Peter Pindar, *Ode to the Hero of Finsbury Square; Congratulatory on his Late Marriage, and Illustrative of his Genius as his own Biographer* (London, 1795), p. 5; hereafter page references are cited in the text.

9 Allan Macleod, *Lackington's Confessions Rendered into Narrative. To which are added Observations on the Bad Consequence of Educating*

Daughters at Boarding-Schools (London, 1804), p. 138. An American edition of Lackington's version was published in 1806.

10 James Lackington, *The Confessions of J. Lackington, Late Bookseller at the Temple of the Muses, in a Series of Letters to a Friend. To Which are added, Two Letters on the Bad Consequences of Having Daughters Educated at Boarding-Schools* (London, 1804), p. 138; hereafter page references are cited in the text.

11 Unpaginated advertisement bound in at the front of the book; it survives in random copies of the *Memoirs* and other works in the series.

References

Primary Sources

Manuscripts

British Library:
  Add. MS 27351–5. Diary of Mary Rich, the Countess of Warwick.
  Add. MS 27356. Occasional Meditations of Mary Rich.
  Add. MS 27357. Some Specialties in the Life of M. Warwicke.

Dr. Williams's Library, London:
  MS 12.78. Papers of Thomas Jollie.
  MS 24.7. Notebook of Owen Stockton 1665–80.
  MS 24.8. Occasional Reflections of Mrs. Owen Stockton.
  MS 28.4. Diary of Elias Pledger 1665–1725.
  Baxter MS 61.13. Diary of Richard Rogers 1587–90.

Friends' House Library, London:
  Swarthmore MS vols I–III. Letters of Early Friends.
  Meeting for Sufferings Minute Book, vols I–X, 1675–95.
  Morning Meeting Minute Book, vols I and II, 1673–94.
  Yearly Meeting Minute Book, vol. I, 1672–93.

Sidney Sussex College Library, Cambridge:
  MS 45. Diary of Samuel Ward 1595–1625.

Serials

General Advertiser. April–August 1748.
The Night-Walker: or, Evening Rambles in Search after Lewd Women, with the Conferences held with them, etc. September 1696–April 1697.

The Proceedings on the Kings Commission of the Peace Oyer and Terminer, and Gaol-delivery at Newgate, held for the City and County of Middlesex, at Justice Hall, in the Old Bailey. Miscellaneous numbers, 1683–1700.

The True Account of the Behaviour, and Confession of the Criminals . . . Executed at Tyburn; later *The Ordinary of Newgate, His Account of the Behaviour, Confession, and Dying Words of the Malefactors who were Executed at Tyburn.* Miscellaneous numbers, 1684–1700.

Printed Books

[Alleine, Theodosia, et al.]. *The Life and Death of Mr. Joseph Alleine.* London, 1672.

Ambrose, Isaac. *Media: The Middle Things, in Reference to the First and Last Things: or, the Means, Duties, Ordinances, Both Secret, Private, and Publike, for Continuance and Increase of a Godly Life.* 2nd edn. London, 1652.

[Ashton, J.]. *A Copy of Mr. Ashton's Paper, Delivered to the Sheriff at the Place of Execution, January 28. 1690/1.* London, 1691.

Axon, Ernest, ed. *Oliver Heywood's Life of John Angier . . . also Samuel Angier's Diary.* Chetham Society Publications, new ser, XCVII. Manchester, 1937.

Baxter, Richard. *A Christian Directory: Or, A Summ of Practical Theologie, and Cases of Conscience.* London, 1673.

——. *A Breviate of the Life of Margaret, The Daughter of Francis Charlton . . . and Wife of Richard Baxter.* London, 1681.

——. *The Last Work of a Believer . . . Prepared for Mary . . . Hanmer . . . [and] at the Desire of Her Daughter, before Her Death, Reprinted.* London, 1682.

Beadle, John. *The Journal or Diary of a Thankful Christian.* London, 1656.

Beck, John. *A Certain and True Relation of the Heavenly Enjoyments and Living Testimonies of God's Love . . . Declared upon the Dying-Bed of Sarah, the Wife of John Beck.* [London], 1680.

Becon, Thomas. *The sycke mannes salue.* London, 1561.

The Behaviour and Execution of Robert Green and Lawrence Hill, Who Suffered at Tyburn on Friday, February 21, 1678/9, with an Account of their Lives, Conditions, Deportment after Sentence, Discourses with Mr. Ordinary, and Other Most Remarkable Circumstances. London, 1679.

Besse, Joseph. *An Abstract of the Sufferings of the People Called Quakers for the Testimony of Good Conscience . . . Taken from Original Records, and other Authentic Accounts . . . to the Year 1666.* 3 vols London, 1733–8.

——. *A Collection of the Sufferings of the People Called Quakers . . . from . . . 1650 to the Time . . . of the Act of Toleration.* 2 vols. London, 1753.

The Bloody Assizes: or, a Compleat History of the Life of George Lord Jefferies, from his Birth to this present Time . . . Faithfully Collected by several West-Countrey Gentlemen, who were both eye and Ear-witnesses to all the Matter of Fact. London, 1689.

Briggs, Thomas. *An Account of some of the Travels and Sufferings of . . . Thomas Briggs.* [London], 1685.

Bruce, John, ed. *Diary of John Manningham, of the Middle Temple, and of Bradbourne, Kent, Barrister-at-Law, 1602–1603.* Camden Society Publications XCIX. London, 1868.

Bugg, Francis. *The Pilgrim's Progress from Quakerism to Christianity*. London, 1698.

Bunyan, John. *Grace Abounding to the Chief of Sinners*. Roger Sharrock, ed. Oxford: Clarendon Press, 1962.

Burnyeat, John. *The Truth Exalted in the Writings of . . . John Burnyeat, Collected Into this Ensuing Volume as a Memorial to his Faithful Labours in and for the Truth*. London, 1691.

Burrough, Edward. *Something in Answer to a Book Called Choice Experiences, Given forth by One J. Tvrner*. [London], 1654.

——. "A Testimony Concerning the Beginning of the Work of the Lord, and the First Publication of Truth, In this City of London [1662]." In *Letters, &c., of Early Friends; Illustrative of the History of the Society, From Nearly its Origin, to About the Time of George Fox's Decease,* John Barclay, ed., 287–310. London: Harvey and Darton, 1841.

——. *A True Description of my Manner of Life, Of what I have been in My Profession of Religion unto this very Day: And What I am at Present, by the Grace of God*. London, 1663.

Butler, Nathaniel. *Blood Washed Away by Tears of Repentance Being an Exact Relation of the Cause and Manner of that Horrid Murther Committee on the Person of John Knight . . . by Nathaniel Butler . . . Written with his Owne Hand*. London, 1657.

Calamy, Edmund. *An Abridgement of Mr. Baxter's History of his Life and Times*. London, 1702; 2nd edn, 2 vols, London, 1713.

Caton, William. *A Journal of the Life of . . . Will. Caton. Written by his own Hand*. London, 1689.

Charke, Charlotte. *A Narrative of the Life of Mrs. Charlotte Charke . . . Written by Herself*. 2nd edn. London, 1755; facsimile reprint, Gainesville: Scholar's Facsimiles & Reprints, 1969.

Chorlton, John. *The Glorious Reward of Faithful Ministers Declared and Improved*. London, 1696.

[Clark, Margaret]. *A Warning for Servants: and a Caution to Protestants. Or, the Case of Margaret Clark, lately Executed for Firing her Masters House in Southwark*. London, 1680.

——. *The True Confession of Margaret Clark, Who Consented to the Burning of Her Masters Mr. Peter Delanoy's House in Southwark. Delivered in Prison to Many Witnesses a Little Before Her Death. And confirmed by Her Self at the Place of Execution, by Answering All Questions then Put to Her by the Reverend and Worthy Divine, Dr. Martin, Now Minister at St Saviours Southwark. Printed for General Satisification*. London, 1680.

Clarke, Samuel. *The Lives of Sundry Eminent Persons in this Later Age*. London, 1683.

Coverdale, Miles. *Certain Most Godly, Fruitful, and Comfortable Letters of such true saints and holy Martyrs of God . . . written in the time of their affliction and cruel punishment*. London, 1564.

[Crashaw, Thomas]. *The Honovr of Vertve. Or The Monument Erected by the Sorrowful Husband, and the Epitaphes Annexed by Learned and Worthy Men, to the Immortal Memory of that Worthy Gentle-woman Mrs. Elizabeth Crashaw*. [London, 1620].

Crisp, Stephen. *A Memorable Account of the Christian Experiences, Gospel Labours, Travels, and Sufferings of . . . Stephen Crisp*. London, 1694.

Croker, T. C., ed. *Autobiography of Mary Countess Warwick*. London: Percy Society, 1848.

[Dangerfield, Thomas]. *Mr. Dangerfields Particular Narrative of the late Popish Design to Charge those of the Presbyterian Party with a Pretended Conspiracy against his Majesties Person, and Government*. London, 1679.

——. *Dangerfield's Memoires, Digested into Adventures, Receits, and Expenses. By his Own Hand*. London, 1685.

Davies, G., ed. *Memoirs of the Family of Guise of Elmore, Gloucestershire*. Camden Society Publications, 3rd ser., XXVIII. London, 1917.

de Beauvoir, Simone. *Memoirs of a Dutiful Daughter*. James Kirkup, trans. Cleveland and New York: World Publishing Company, 1959.

A Defence of the Character of a Noble Lord, from the Scandalous Aspersions Contained in a Malicious Apology. In a Letter to the Supposed Authoress. London, 1748.

[Defoe, Daniel]. *Reformation of Manners, a Satyr. Vae Vobis Hypocrite*. [London], 1702.

——. *The History of the Press-Yard*. London, 1717.

——. *The Life and Strange Surprizing Adventures of Robinson Crusoe, of York, Mariner*. London, 1719.

——. *The History and Remarkable Life of the Truly Honourable ... Col. Jacque, Commonly Call'd Col. Jack*. London, 1723.

Dennis, Henry. *An Answer to the Anonymous Author of a Familiar Epistle to Mrs. Con. Phillips*. London, 1749.

Dering, Heneage. "Autobiographical Memoranda of Heneage Dering Dean of Ripon." In *Yorkshire Diaries and Autobiographies in the Seventeenth and Eighteenth Centuries*, vol. 1, Charles Jackson, ed., Surtees Society Publications LXV, 333–50. Durham, 1877.

A Dialogue in the Shades Below: Manag'd by Mrs. Phill—ps, Mrs. Pilk—nton, Dean Swift, Galilaeo, Lais and the Courtezan, and several other persons of Taste and Distinction. Together with the Trial and Sentence of Mrs. Phill—ps and Mrs. Pilk—nton. London, n.d.

Drake, Peter. *The Memoirs of Capt. Peter Drake*. Dublin, 1755.

Duncon, John. *The Holy Life and Death of the Lady Letice, Vi-Countess Falkland*. 3rd edn. London, 1653.

[Dunton, John]. *The Mourning-Ring, In Memory of Your Departed Friend, ... Recommended as Proper to Be Given at Funerals*. 2nd edn. London, 1692.

——. *The Life and Errors of John Dunton Late Citizen of London; Written by Himself in Solitude*. London, 1705.

——. *Dunton's Whipping-Post: Or, a Satyr upon Everybody*. London, 1706.

A Dyurnall for deuoute soules to ordre them selfe thereafter. [London], n.d.

[Ellwood, Thomas, et al., eds.] *A Journal or Historical Account of the Life, Travels, Sufferings, Christian Experiences and Labour of Love in the Work of the Ministry, of ... George Fox*. London, 1694.

——. *A Collection of Many Select and Christian Epistles, Letters and Testimonies, Written on Sundry Occasions, by ... George Fox*. London, 1698.

Epistles from the Yearly Meeting of Friends ... 1681–1817. London, 1818.

Evans, Katharine, and Chevers, Sarah. *This is a Short Relation of the Cruel Sufferings (For the Truths Sake) of Katharine Evans and Sarah Chevers in the Inquisition in the Isle of Malta*. London, 1662.

The Execution of William Ireland and John Grove. . . . *With their Carriage and Behaviour.* London, 1679.

A Familiar Epistle to the Celebrated Mrs. Con. Phillips, on her Apology. By a Gentleman of the Inner Temple. n.p., n.d.

Featherstone, Sarah, and Browne, Thomas. *Living Testimonies Concerning the Death of the Righteouss, or, The blessed End of Joseph Featherstone and Sarah his Daughter.* [London], 1689.

[Field, John, ed.] *A Collection of the Christian Writings, Labours, Travels, and Sufferings of . . . Roger Haydock. To which is added, an Account of his Death and Burial.* London, 1700.

Fielding, Henry. *The History of the Life of the Late Jonathan Wild.* In his *Miscellanies,* vol. III. London, 1743.

——. *An Enquiry into the Causes of the Late Increase of Robbers, &c. with some Proposals for Remedying this Growing Evil* (1751). Repr. in *The Complete Works of Henry Fielding,* William E. Henly, ed., vol. XIII, 6–129. New York: Barnes and Noble, 1967.

Fishwick, Henry, ed. *The Note Book of the Rev. Thomas Jolly 1671–1693.* Chetham Society Publications, new ser., XXXIII. Manchester, 1895.

Foulkes, Richard. *An Alarme For Sinners: Containing the Confession, Prayers, Letters, and Last Words of Richard Foulkes . . . Published from the Original, Written with His Own Hand, during his reprieve, and Sent by Him at his Death to Doctor Lloyd, Dean of Bangor.* London, 1679.

Foxe, John. *Acts and Monuments.* London, 1563.

[Frances, Robert]. *The Dying-Speech of Robert Frances of Grays-Inn, Esq; July 24, 1685. Delivered by His Own to the Ordinary, at the Place of Execution, Desiring the Same Might be Published.* London, 1685.

Fretwell, James. "A Family History Begun by James Fretwell." In *Yorkshire Diaries and Autobiographies in the Seventeenth and Eighteenth Centuries,* vol. 1, Charles Jackson, ed., Surtees Society Publications LXV, 163–243. Durham, 1877.

A Full and the Truest Narrative of the Most Horrid, Barbarous and Unparallelled Murder, Committed on the Person of John Knight. [London, 1657].

Gale, Theophilus. *The Life and Death of Thomas Tregosse.* London, 1671.

——. *The Life and Death of Mr. John Rowe of Crediton in Devon.* London, 1673.

Gay, John. *Poetry and Prose.* Vinton A. Dearing, ed. 2 vols. Oxford, 1974.

Gent, Thomas. *The Life of Mr. Thomas Gent, Printer, of York.* London, 1832.

Goodcole, Henry. *A True Declaration of the Happy Conversion, Contrition, and Christian Preparation of Francis Robinson, Gentleman.* London, 1618.

——. *Londons Cry: Ascended to God, and Entered into the Hearts, and Ears of Men for Reuenge of Bloodshedders, Burglaires, and Vagabounds Manifested the Last Sessions, Holden at Justice Hall in the Old Baily the 9.10.11.12. of December, Ann Dom. 1619. Likewise Herein is Related, the Courts Legall Proceedings, against the Malefactors that were Executed at Tiburne and about London, and the Chiefest Offenders, There Offences and Confessions at Large Expressed.* London, 1620.

——. *The Wonderfull Discouerie of Elizabeth Sawyer a Witch, late of Edmonton, Her Conuiction and Condemnation and Death.* London, 1621.

Gray, John M., ed. *Memoirs of the Life of Sir John Clerk.* London, 1895.

Green, Thomas. *A Declaration to the World, of My Travel and Journey out of*

Aegypt into Canaan Through the Wilderness, & Through the Red-Sea, from under Pharaoh, and Now Hath a Sure Habitation in the Lord, Where Rest and Peace is Known. London, 1659.

Halhead, Myles. *A Book of some of the Sufferings and Passages of Myles Halhead*. London, 1690.

Hall, Joseph. *The Arte of Divine Meditation: Profitable for all Christians to knowe and practise*. London, 1606.

——. *Occasional Meditations*. 3rd edn. London, 1633.

Halliwell, James Orchard, ed. *The Autobiography and Correspondence of Sir Simonds D'Ewes*. 2 vols. London: Richard Bently, 1845.

Harrison, G. B., ed. *Advice to His Son by Henry Percy Ninth Earl of Northumberland*. London: Ernest Benn Limited, 1930.

[Harrison, Henry]. *A True Copy of a Letter, Written by Henry Harrison*. London, 1692.

——. *The Last Dying Words of Henry Harrison*. London, 1692.

——. *The Last Words of a Dying Penitent*. London, 1692.

Harrison, William, and Leygh, William. *Deaths Advantage Little Regarded, and the Soules Solace Against Sorrow*. 2nd edn. London, 1602.

[Henry, Matthew]. *An Account of the Life and Death of Mr. Philip Henry*. 2nd edn. London, 1699.

[Heywood, Oliver]. *A Narrative of the Holy Life, and Happy Death of . . . Mr. John Angier*. London, 1685.

Heywood, Thomas, ed. *The Diary of the Rev. Henry Newcome, from September 30, 1661, to September 29, 1663*. Chetham Society Publications XVIII. Manchester, 1849.

Hinde, William. *A Faithfull Remonstrance of the Holy Life and Happy Death, of John Bruen*. London, 1641.

The History of the Remarkable Life of John Sheppard. London, 1724.

Houstoun, James. *The Works of James Houstoun, M.D. Containing Memoirs of his Life and Travels in Asia, Africa, America, and Most Parts of Europe. From the Year 1690, to the Present Time*. London, 1753.

Howgill, Francis, et al. *A Testimony concerning the Life, Death, Trials, Travels and Labours Of Edward Burroughs*. London, 1662.

Hunter, Joseph, ed. *The Diary of Ralph Thoresby*. 2 vols. London, 1830.

Hutchinson, Lucy. *Memoirs of the Life of Colonel Hutchinson*. James Sutherland, ed. London: Oxford University Press, 1973.

Hyde, Edward. *The History of the Rebellion and Civil Wars in England*. 7 vols. Oxford: Oxford University Press, 1839–40.

[Ivy, William]. *The Penitent Murderer; or, An Exact and True Relation taken from the Mouth of Mr. William Ivy (lately Executed) Concerning the Murder by Him Committed upon the Body of William Pew . . . With his Confession of the Whole Fact, and his Contrition for the Same, as It was Delivered From his own Mouth to a Particular Friend, and by him Published, to Prevent all False Reports*. London, 1673.

Jackson, Charles, ed. *The Autobiography of Alice Thornton*. Surtees Society Publications LXII. Durham, 1875.

Johnson, Charles. *A General History of All the Lives and Adventures of the Most Famous Highwaymen, Murderers, Street-Robbers, &c. To which is added, A Genuine Account of the Voyages and Plunders of the Most Notorious Pyrates*. London, 1734.

[Kirk, Edward]. *A True Paper Delivered by Edward Kirk.* London, 1684.

——. *The Sufferers Legacy to Surviving Sinners; Or Edmund Kirk's Dying Advice to Young Men, Wrote by His Own Hand in Newgate, and Delivered to His Friend with a Desire that the Same Might Be Published.* London, 1684.

Lackington, James. *Memoirs of the First Forty-Five Years of the Life of James Lackington, the Present Bookseller in Chiswell-street, Moorfields, London.* London, [1791].

——. *The Confessions of J. Lackington, Late Bookseller at the Temple of the Muses, in a Series of Letters to a Friend To Which are added, Two Letters on the Bad Consequences of Having Daughters Educated at Boarding Schools.* London, 1804.

Latham, Robert, and Mathews, William, eds. *The Diary of Samuel Pepys.* 11 vols. Berkeley and Los Angeles: University of California Press, 1970–83.

Lee, Matthew Henry, ed. *Diaries and Letters of Philip Henry of Broad Oak, Flintshire 1631–1696.* London: Kegan Paul, Trench & Co., 1882.

Lee, Sidney L., ed. *The Autobiography of Edward, Lord Herbert of Cherbury.* London: John C. Nimmo, 1886.

Ley, John. *A Pattern of Pietie. Or the Religious Life and Death of that Grave and Gracious Matron Mrs. Jane Ratcliffe.* London, 1640.

The Life & Death of Stephen Marshal, Minister of the Gospel at Finchingfield in Essex. London, 1680.

The Life and Death of Mr. Vavasor Powell, That Faithful Minister and Confessor of Jesus Christ. Wherein His Eminent Conversion, Laborious, Successful Ministry, Excellent Conversation, Confession of Faith, Worthy Sayings, and other Remarkable Passages, in his Life, and at his Death, are faithfully Recorded for Publick Benefit. With some Elogies and Epitaphs by His Friends. London, 1671.

The Life and Death of Ralph Wallis the Cobler of Glocester: Together with some inquiring into the Mystery of Conventicleism. London, 1670.

The Living Words of a Dying Child, Being a True Relation of some part of his Words that came forth, and were spoken by Joseph Briggins on his Death-bed. [London], 1675.

Lomas, S. C., ed. "The Memoirs of Sir George Courthorp 1616–85." *Camden Miscellany XI,* Camden Society Publications, 3rd ser., XIII, 93–157. London, 1907.

Love, Christopher. *The Penitent Pardoned. A Treatise: Wherein is Handled the Duty of Confession of Sin, and the Priviledge of the Pardon of Sin.* London, 1657.

[Lowen, Roger]. *A Paper Containing the Last Words of Mr. Roger Lowen by him Writted in German, and Deliver'd to the Ordinary of Newgate, at the Place of his Execution at Turnham Green by the 25th of October, 1706. And now Faithfully Translated and Set forth . . . for Publick Satisfaction.* London, 1706.

Lydgate, John. *The Fall of Princes.* Henry Bergen, ed. 4 vols. Washington: Carnegie Institution, 1923.

Macfarlane, Alan, ed. *The Diary of Ralph Josselin, 1616–1683.* British Academy Records of Social and Economic History, new ser., III. London, 1976.

Macleod, Allan, *Lackington's Confessions Rendered into Narrative To which are added Observations on the Bad Consequence of Educating Daughters at Boarding-Schools.* London, 1804.

[Martell, Margaret]. *A True Copy of the Paper Delivered by Margaret Martel.* London, 1697.

——. *A True Translation of a Paper . . . Delivered by Margaret Martel.* London, 1697.

Mason, Simon. *A Narrative of the Life and Distresses of Simon Mason, Apothecary.* Birmingham, [1754].

Mayo, Richard. *The Life and Death of Edmund Staunton D.D.* London, 1673.

M'Crie, Thomas, ed. *The Life of Mr. Robert Blair.* Edinburgh: Wodrow Society, 1848.

Meads, Dorothy M., ed. *Diary of Lady Margaret Hoby 1599–1605.* London: Routledge & Sons, 1930.

Melville, James. *Memoirs of His Own Life by Sir James Melville.* Bannatyne Club Publications XVII. London, 1827.

Memoir of Lady Warwick: Also her Diary from A.D. 1666 to 1672. London, 1847.

Morehouse, H. J., ed. "A Dyurnall, or Catalogue of All My Accions and Expences from the 1st of January, 1646[/7] – Adam Eyre." In *Yorkshire Diaries and Autobiographies in the Seventeenth and Eighteenth Centuries,* vol. 1, Charles Jackson, ed., Surtees Society Publications LXV, 1–118. Durham, 1877.

Morland, Stephen C., ed. *The Somersetshire Quarterly Meeting of the Society of Friends 1668–1699.* Somerset Record Society Publications LXXV. n.p., 1978.

A Myrroure for Magistrates. Lily B. Campbell, ed. 1938. Repr. New York: Barnes and Noble, 1960.

A Narrative Of all the Robberies, Escapes, &c. Of John Sheppard. London, 1724.

[Newcome, Henry]. *A Faithful Narrative of the Life and Death of That Holy and Laborious Preacher Mr. John Machin.* London, 1671.

Nicolls, Ferdinando. *The Life and Death of Mr. Ignatius Jurdain, One of the Aldermen of the City of Exeter.* London, 1654.

[Nixon, Anthony]. *Londons Dove: or A Memorial of the Life and Death of Maister Robert Dove, Citizen and Marchant-Taylor of London and of his Several Almsdeeds and Large Bountie to the Poore, in His Life Time.* London, 1612.

[Norton, George]. *The True Confession of Mr. George Norton Concerning the Murther of Mr. Harris the Dancing Master, on the 11th June Last. Taken Out of his Own Papers, Delivered by Him to Mrs. Mary Edwards, before He Took the Fatal Draught of Poyson, on the 8th of August, of which He Died the Following Day, which was appointed for His Execution at Tyburn.* London, 1699.

[Oldys, William, et al., eds]. *Biographia Britannica; or the Lives of the most Eminent Persons who have flourished in Great Britain and Ireland, from the earliest Ages to the Present Times.* 7 vols. London, 1747–66.

The Parallel; or Pilkington and Phillips Compared. Being Remarks upon the Memoirs of those two celebrated Writers. London, 1748.

Parkinson, Richard, ed. *The Autobiography of Henry Newcome.* 2 vols. Chetham Society Publications XXVI and XXVII. London, 1852.

Petto, Samuel. *The Voice of the Spirit. Or an Essay towards a Discoverie of the witnessings of the Spirit.* London, 1654.

Phillips, Teresia Constantia. *An Apology for the Conduct of Mrs. Teresia Constantia Phillips.* 3 vols. [London], 1748-9.

——. *A Letter humbly addressed to the Right Honourable, the Earl of Chesterfield.* London, 1750.

Pilkington, John Carteret. *The Real Story of John Carteret Pilkington.* London, 1760.

Pilkington, Laetitia. *Memoirs of Mrs. Letitia Pilkington, Wife to the Rev. Matthew Pilkington. Written by Herself.* 3 vols. London, 1749–54.

Pindar, Peter. *Ode to the Hero of Finsbury Square; Congratulatory on his Late Marriage, and Illustrative of his Genius as his own Biographer.* London, 1795.

The Popish Champion: or, a Compleat History of the Life and Military Actions of Richard Earl of Tyrconnel, Generalissimo of all the Irish Forces Now in Arms. London, 1689.

Priestley, Jonathan. "Some Memoirs Concerning the Family of the Priestleys, Written at the Request of a Friend, by Jonathan Priestley, Anno Domini 1696, Aetatis Suae 63." In *Yorkshire Diaries and Autobiographies in the Seventeenth and Eighteenth Centuries*, vol. 2, Charles Jackson, ed., Surtees Society Publications LXXVII, 1–41. Durham, 1886.

Rix, S. Wilton, ed. *The Diary and Autobiography of Edmund Bohun.* Beccles: private printing, 1853.

Rogers, John. *Ohel or Beth-shemesh. A Tabernacle for the Sun: or Irenicum Evangelicum. An Idea of Church-Discipline, in the Theorick and Practick Parts.* London, 1653.

Rogers, Richard. *Seven Treatises, Containing Svch Direction as is Gathered Ovt of the Holie Scriptvres, Leading and Guiding to True Happines, Both in this Life, and in the Life to Come: and May be Called the Practise of Christianitie.* London, 1603.

Rogers, Timothy. *The Character of a Good Woman, Both in a Single and Marry'd State. In a Funeral Discourse . . . Occasioned by the Decease of Mrs. Elizabeth Dunton . . . With an Account of Her Life and Death; And Part of the Diary Writ With Her Own Hand.* London, 1697.

Rutt, John Towill, ed. *An Historical Account of My Own Life, with Some Reflections on the Times I Have Lived in. By Edmund Calamy.* 2 vols. London, 1829.

Samble, Richard. *A Handful after the Harvest-Man: or, a Loving Salutation to Sion's Mourners, being a Collection of several Epistles & Testimonies of . . . Richard Samble.* London, 1684.

Scott, George. *The Memoires of Sir James Melvil of Hal-Hill.* London, 1683.

Shaw, John. "The Life of Master John Shaw." In *Yorkshire Diaries and Autobiographies in the Seventeenth and Eighteenth Centuries*, vol. 1, Charles Jackson, ed., Surtees Society Publications LXV, 121–62. Durham, 1877.

Smith, Alexander. *A Compleat History of the Lives and Robberies of the most Notorious Highway-Men, Foot-Pads, Shop-Lifts, and Cheats, of both Sexes, in and about London and Westminster, and all Parts of Great Britain, for above an Hundred Years past, continu'd to the present Time.* 5th edn. 2 vols. London, 1719.

Smith, Samuel. *An Account of the Behaviour of the fourteen late popish Malefactors, whils't in Newgate And Their Discourse with the Ordinary . . . Also, a Confutation of Their Appeals, Courage, and Cheerfulness at Execution.* London, 1679.

——. *The Behaviour of Edward Kirk, After his Condemnation for Murdering His Wife; with the Advice and Prayers which he left with the Ordinary, desiring him to Publish the same for Reclaiming of Vicious Youth.* London, 1684.

——. *The Character of a Weaned Christian: or, The Evangelical Art of Promoting Self-denial.* London, 1675.

Some Remarkable Passages in the Holy Life and Death of the Late Reverend Mr. Edmund Trench; Most of them Drawn Out of His Own Diary. London, 1693.

Stafford, Anthony. *The Femall Glory: or, The Life, and Death of Our Blessed Lady, the Holy Virgin Mary.* London, 1635.

——. *Honour and Vertue, Triumphing over the Grave. Exemplified in a Faire Devout Life, and Death, Adorned with the Surviving Perfections of Edward Lord Stafford, Lately Deceased; the Last Baron of that Illustrious Family: Which Honour in Him Ended with as Great Lustre as the Sunne Sets within a Serene Sky.* London, 1640.

Staunton, Edmund. *A Sermon Preacht at Great Milton in the County of Oxford: Decemb: 9. 1654. At the Funerall of that Eminent Servant of Jesus Christ Mrs. Elizabeth Wilkinson Late Wife to Dr. Henry Wilkinson Principall of Magdalen Hall: Whereunto is Added a Narrative of Her Godly Life and Death.* Oxford, 1659.

Stubbes, Philip. *A Christal Glasse for Christian Women Containing, a most excellent Discourse, of the Godly life and Christian death of Mistresse Katherine Stubbes.* London, 1591.

Sylvester, Matthew, ed. *Reliquiae Baxterianae: or, Mr. Richard Baxter's Narrative of the Most Memorable Passages of his Life and Times.* London, 1696.

Taylor, Jeremy. *Holy Living and Holy Dying.* P. G. Stanwood, ed. 2 vols. Oxford: Clarendon Press, 1989.

Threnodia in Obitvm D. Edovardi Lewkenor Equitus, & D. Svsannae Coniugus Charibimae. Funerall Verses Upon the Death of the Right Worshipful Sir Edward Levvkenor Knight, and Madame Svsan his Lady. London, 1606.

T[ownsend], T[heophila]. *A Testimony concerning the Life and Death of Jane Whitehead.* London, 1676.

Trosse, George. *The Life of the Reverend Mr. George Trosse Written By Himself, and Published Posthumously According to his Order in 1714.* A. W. Brink, ed. Montreal and London: McGill-Queens University Press, 1974.

Turner, J[ane]. *Choice Experiences of the Kind Dealings of God before, in, and after Conversion; Laid Down in Six General Heads. Together with some Brief Observations upon the Same.* London, 1653.

Turner, J. H., ed. *The Autobiography, Diaries, Anecdote and Event Books of the Rev. Oliver Heywood.* 4 vols. Brighouse, 1882–5.

Vint, J. W., ed. *The Whole Works of the Rev. Oliver Heywood.* 5 vols. Idle, 1825–27.

Wadsworth, Thomas. *Wadsworth's Remains: Being a Collection of Some Few Meditations With Respect to the Lords Supper. . . . With a Preface Containing Several Remarkables of His Holy Life and Death, From His Own Note-book, and Those That Knew Him Best.* London, 1680.

Walker, Anthony. *Eyphka, Eyphka, The Virtuous Woman Found Her Loss Bewailed and Character Exemplified in a Sermon Preached at Felsted in Essex, April, 30, 1678 . . . . With so Large Additions as May be Stiled the Life of that Noble Lady. To Which Are Annexed Some of Her Ladyships Pious and Useful Meditations.* London, 1678.

——. *The Holy Life of Mrs. Elizabeth Walker*, London, 1690.

[Walker, Henry]. *Spirituall Experiences, Of Sundry Beleevers. Held forth by Them at Severall Solemne Meetings, and Conferences to that End.* 2nd edn. London, 1653.

Wesley, Samuel. *A Sermon Concerning Reformation of Manners, Preach'd . . . To one of the Religious Societies.* London, 1698.

[Whitehead, George, ed.] *A Seasonable Account of the Christian Testimony and Heavenly Expressions of Tudor Brain upon his Death Bed.* London, 1698.

Whitehead, John. *A discourse delivered at the New Chapel in the City-Road, on the ninth of March 1791, At the Funeral of the Rev. Mr. John Wesley.* 4th edn. London, 1791.

Whitford, Richard, *The Folowynge of Cryste.* Edward J. Klein, ed. New York and London: Harper & Brothers, 1941.

W[hiting], J[ohn]. *A Catalogue of Friends Books; Written by many of the People, Called Quakers, from the Beginning or First Appearance of the said People.* London, 1708.

——. *Persecution Expos'd, in some Memoirs relating to the Sufferings of John Whiting, and many others of the People called Quakers.* London, 1715.

[Whitrow, Joan]. *The Work of God in a Dying Maid, being a short Account of the Dealings of the Lord with one Susanna Whitrow.* London, 1677.

Wilkinson, Tate. *Memoirs of His Own Life, By Tate Wilkinson, Patentee of the Theatres-Royal, York and Hull.* 4 vols. York, 1790.

Wilson, Arthur. "Observations of God's Providence, in the Tract of My Life." In *Desiderata Curiosa*, F. Peck, ed., 2 vols, II, book XII, no. v, 6–35. London, 1735.

The Wonders of Free-Grace: or a Compleat History of all the Remarkable Penitents that have been executed at Tyburn, and Elsewhere, for these last Thirty Years. London, 1690.

[Woodcock, Thomas]. *An Account of Some Remarkable Passages in the Life of a Private Gentleman [. . .] Left Under His Own Hand, To Be Communicated to the Publick after his Decease.* 2nd edn. London, 1711.

[Woodward, Josiah]. *An Account of the Societies for Reformation of Manners. In London and Westminster, and other Parts of the Kingdom. With a Persuasive to Persons of all Ranks to be Zealous and Diligent in Promoting the Execution of the Laws against Prophane-ness and Debauchery, for the Effecting a National Reformation.* London, 1699.

——. *Fair Warnings to a Careless World, or the Serious Practice of Religion Recommended by the Admonitions of Dying Men.* London, 1707.

Secondary Sources

Andrews, Evangeline, and Andrews, Charles, eds. *Jonathan Dickinson's Journal or, God's Protecting Providence.* New Haven: Yale University Press, 1945.

Bahlman, Dudley W. R. *The Moral Revolution of 1688.* New Haven: Yale University Press, 1957.

Barron, Caroline M. "Richard Whittington: The Man behind the Myth." In

Studies in London History, A. E. J. Hollander and William Kellaway, eds, 195–248. London: Hodder and Stoughton, 1969.

Barthes, Roland. "Introduction to the Structural Analysis of Narratives." In Roland Barthes, *Image – Music – Text*, Stephen Heath, ed. and trans., 79–124. New York: Noonday, 1977.

——. "The Death of the Author." In Roland Barthes, *Image – Music – Text*, Stephen Heath, ed. and trans., 142–8. New York: Noonday, 1977.

——. "The Discourse of History." Stephen Bann, trans. In *Comparative Criticism: A Yearbook*, E. S. Shaffer, ed., vol. III (1981), 3–20.

Bauman, Richard. *Let Your Words Be Few: Symbolism of Speaking and Silence among Seventeenth-Century Quakers*. Cambridge: Cambridge University Press, 1983.

Beaty, Nancy Lee. *The Craft of Dying: A Study in the Literary Tradition of the Ars Moriendi in England*. New Haven and London: Yale University Press, 1970.

Belanger, Terry. "Publishers and Writers in Eighteenth-Century England." In *Books and their Readers in Eighteenth-Century England*, Isabel Rivers, ed., 5–25. Leicester: Leicester University Press, 1982.

Bender, John, and Wellbery, David E., eds. *Chronotypes: The Construction of Time*. Stanford: Stanford University Press, 1991.

Benveniste, Emile. *Problems in General Linguistics*. Mary Elizabeth Meek, trans. Coral Gables: University of Miami Press, 1971.

Bolgar, R. R. *The Classical Heritage and its Beneficiaries*. Cambridge: Cambridge University Press, 1963.

Bourdieu, Pierre. *The Field of Cultural Production*. Randal Johnson, ed. and introd. New York: Columbia University Press, 1993.

Brooks, Peter. *Reading for the Plot: Design and Intention in Narrative*. New York: Vintage, 1985.

Bruss, Elizabeth W. *Autobiographical Acts: The Changing Situation of a Literary Genre*. Baltimore and London: The Johns Hopkins University Press, 1976.

——. "Eye for I: Making and Unmaking Autobiography in Film." In *Autobiography: Essays Theoretical and Critical*, James Olney, ed., 296–320. Princeton: Princeton University Press, 1980.

Buck, John Dawson Carl. "The Motives of Puffing: John Newbery's Advertisements 1742–1767." *Studies in Bibliography* 30 (1977), 196–210.

Burckhardt, Jacob. *The Civilization of the Renaissance in Italy*. S. G. C. Middlemore, trans. 2 vols. New York: Harper & Row, 1958.

Caldwell, Patricia. *The Puritan Conversion Narrative: The Beginnings of an American Expression*. Cambridge: Cambridge University Press, 1983.

Capp, Bernard. *English Almanacs 1500–1800: Astrology and the Popular Press*. Ithaca: Cornell University Press, 1979.

Carrithers, Michael, Collins, Steven and Lukes, Steven, eds. *The Category of the Person*. Cambridge: Cambridge University Press, 1985.

Charrington, John. *A Catalogue of the Engraved Portraits in the Library of Samuel Pepys*. Cambridge: Cambridge University Press, 1936.

Chartier, Roger, ed. *Passions of the Renaissance*. Arthur Goldhammer, trans. vol. III of *A History of Private Life*. Cambridge, MA, and London: Belknap Press, 1989.

——. *The Order of Books: Readers, Authors, and Libraries in Europe between the Fourteenth and Eighteenth Centuries*. Lydia G. Cochrane, trans. Stanford: Stanford University Press, 1994.

Cliffe, J. T. *The Puritan Gentry: The Great Puritan Families of Early Stuart England*. London: Routledge & Kegan Paul, 1984.

——. *The Puritan Gentry Besieged, 1650–1700*. London and New York: Routledge, 1993.

Coleman, D. C. *The British Paper Industry 1495–1860: A Study in Industrial Growth*. Oxford: Clarendon Press, 1958.

Collinson, Patrick. "The English Conventicle." In *Voluntary Religion*, W. J. Shiels and Diana Wood, eds, 223–59. Studies in Church History, vol. 23. n.p.: Blackwell, 1986.

Cope, Jackson I. "Seventeenth-Century Quaker Style." In *Seventeenth-Century Prose: Modern Essays in Criticism*, Stanley E. Fish, ed., 200–35. New York: Oxford University Press, 1971.

Cragg, Gerald R. *Puritanism in the Period of the Great Persecution 1660–1688*. Cambridge: Cambridge University Press, 1957.

Cressy, David. *Literacy and the Social Order: Reading and Writing in Tudor and Stuart England*. Cambridge: Cambridge University Press, 1980.

——. "Levels of Illiteracy in England, 1530–1730." In *Literacy and Social Development in the West: A Reader*, Harvey J. Graff, ed., 105–24. Cambridge: Cambridge University Press, 1981.

Crites, Stephen. "Storytime: Recollecting the Past and Projecting the Future." In *Narrative Psychology: The Storied Nature of Human Conduct*, Theodore J. Sarbin, ed., 152–73. New York: Praeger, 1986.

Cumbers, Frank. *The Book Room: The Story of the Methodist Publishing House and Epworth Press*. London: The Epworth Press, 1956.

Curtis, T. C., and Speck, W. A. "The Societies for the Reformation of Manners: A Case Study in the Theory and Practice of Moral Reform." *Literature and History* 3 (1976), 45–64.

Darnton, Robert. *The Great Cat Massacre and Other Episodes in French Cultural History*. New York: Vintage Books, 1985.

Davis, Lennard J. *Factual Fictions: The Origins of the English Novel*. New York: Columbia University Press, 1983.

Day, Robert Adams. "John Dunton and William Bentley: Brothers Under the Skin." In *Studies in Eighteenth-Century Culture* 16, O. M. Brack, Jr., ed., 125–38. Madison: University of Wisconsin Press, 1986.

Dumont, Louis. *Essays on Individualism: Modern Ideology in Anthropological Perspective*. Chicago and London: University of Chicago Press, 1986.

Elias, Norbert. *The History of Manners*. Edmund Jephcott, trans. Vol. I of *The Civilizing Process*. New York: Pantheon, 1976.

——. *Power & Civility*. Edmund Jephcott, trans. Vol. II of *The Civilizing Process*. New York: Pantheon, 1982.

——. *The Society of Individuals*. Edmund Jephcott, trans. Michael Schröter, ed. Oxford: Blackwell, 1991.

Faller, Lincoln B. "In Contrast to Defoe: The Rev. Paul Lorrain, Historian of Crime." *Huntington Library Quarterly* 39 (1976), 59–78.

——. *Turned to Account: The Form and Functions of Criminal Biography in Late Seventeenth- and Early Eighteenth-Century England*. Cambridge: Cambridge University Press, 1987.

Feather, John. *A History of British Publishing*. London: Croom Helm, 1988.

——. "From Rights in Copies to Copyright: The Recognition of Authors' Rights in English Law and Practice in the Sixteenth and Seventeenth Centuries." In

The Construction of Authorship: Textual Appropriation in Law and Literature, Martha Woodmansee and Peter Jaszi, eds, 191–209. Durham and London: Duke University Press, 1994.

Folkenflik, Robert. "Introduction: The Institution of Autobiography." In *The Culture of Autobiography: Constructions of Self-Representation*, Robert Folkenflik, ed., 1–20. Stanford: Stanford University Press, 1993.

Foucault, Michel. "What is an Author?" Josué V. Harari, trans. In *Textual Strategies: Perspectives in Post-Structuralist Criticism*, Josué V. Harari, ed., 141–60. Ithaca: Cornell University Press, 1979.

Fox-Genovese, Elizabeth. *Feminism Without Illusions: A Critique of Individualism*. Chapel Hill and London: University of North Carolina Press, 1991.

Gallagher, Catherine. *Nobody's Story: The Vanishing Acts of Women Writers in the Marketplace, 1670–1820*. Berkeley and Los Angeles: University of California Press, 1994.

Gaskell, Philip. *A New Introduction to Bibliography*. Oxford and New York: Oxford University Press, 1972.

Geertz, Clifford. "'From the Native's Point of View': On the Nature of Anthropological Understanding." In *Culture Theory: Essays on Mind, Self, and Emotion*, Richard A. Shweder and Robert A. LeVine, eds, 123–36. Cambridge: Cambridge University Press, 1984.

Gergen, Kenneth J., and Gergen, Mary M. "Narratives of the Self." In *Studies in Social Identity*, K. Scheibe and T. Sarbin, eds, 254–73. New York: Praeger, 1983.

Giddens, Anthony. *The Consequences of Modernity*. Stanford: Stanford University Press, 1990.

——. *Modernity and Self-Identity: Self and Society in the Late Modern Age*. Stanford: Stanford University Press, 1991.

Girouard, Mark. *Life in the English Country House: A Social and Architectural History*. Harmondsworth: Penguin, 1980.

Gittings, Clare. *Death, Burial and the Individual in Early Modern England*. London, 1984.

Goffman, Erving. *The Presentation of Self in Everyday Life*. Garden City, NY: Doubleday and Company, 1959.

Greene, Thomas M. *The Light of Troy: Imitation and Discovery in Renaissance Poetry*. New Haven: Yale University Press, 1982.

Gunn, Janet Varner. *Autobiography: Toward a Poetics of Experience*. Philadelphia: University of Pennsylvania Press, 1982.

Gusdorf, Georges. "Conditions and Limits of Autobiography." James Olney, trans. In *Autobiography: Essays Theoretical and Critical*, James Olney, ed., 28–48. Princeton: Princeton University Press, 1980.

Hall, David J. "'The Fiery Tryal of their Infallible Examination': Self-Control in the Regulation of Quaker Publishing in England from the 1670s to the mid 19th Century." In *Censorship & the Control of Print in England and France 1600–1910*, Robin Myers and Michael Harris, eds, 59–86. Winchester: St Paul's Bibliographies, 1992.

Haller, William. *The Rise of Puritanism*. Harper Torchbook edn. New York: Harper & Row, 1957.

——. *Foxe's Book of Martyrs and the Elect Nation*. London: Jonathan Cape, 1963.

Hampton, Timothy. *Writing From History: The Rhetoric of Exemplarity in Renaissance Literature*. Ithaca and London: Cornell University Press, 1990.

Harris, Michael. "Trials and Criminal Biographies: A Case Study in Distribution." In *Sale and Distribution of Books from 1700*, Robin Myers and Michael Harris, eds, 1–36. Oxford: Oxford Polytechnic Press, 1982.

Heller, Thomas C., Sosna, Morton, and Wellbery, David E., eds. *Reconstructing Individualism: Autonomy, Individuality, and the Self in Western Thought.* Stanford: Stanford University Press, 1986.

Hetet, John. "A Literary Underground in Restoration England: Printers and Dissenters in the Context of Constraints 1660–1689." Ph.D. thesis. University of Cambridge, 1987.

Hibbert, Christopher. *The Road to Tyburn: The Story of Jack Sheppard and The Eighteenth-Century London Underworld.* Cleveland and New York: World, 1957.

Hill, Christopher. *Society and Puritanism in Pre-Revolutionary England.* London: Martin Secker & Warburg Ltd, 1964.

Holland, Norman N. "Unity Identity Text Self." In *Reader-Response Criticism: From Foundation to Post-Structuralism*, Jane P. Tompkins, ed., 118–33. Baltimore and London: The Johns Hopkins University Press, 1980.

Horle, Craig W. *The Quakers and the English Legal System 1660–1688.* Philadelphia: University of Pennsylvania Press, 1988.

Houlbrooke, Ralph. "Death, Church, and Family in England between the Late Fifteenth and the Early Eighteenth Centuries." In *Death, Ritual and Bereavement*, Ralph Houlbrooke, ed., 25–42. London and New York: Routledge, 1989.

Howson, Gerald. *Thief-Taker General: The Rise and Fall of Jonathan Wild.* New York: St Martin's Press, 1970.

Hunter, G. K. "The Marking of Sententiae in Elizabethan Printed Plays, Poems and Romances." *The Library*, 5th ser., 6 (1951), 171–8.

Hunter, J. Paul. "The Insistent I." *Novel* 13 (1979), 19–37.

———. *Before Novels: The Cultural Contexts of Eighteenth-Century English Fiction.* New York and London: W. W. Norton, 1990.

Huntley, Frank Livingstone. *Bishop Joseph Hall and Protestant Meditation in Seventeenth-Century England.* Binghamton, NY: Center for Medieval and Early Renaissance Studies, 1981.

Iser, Wolfgang. *Prospecting: From Reader Response to Literary Anthropology.* Baltimore and London: The Johns Hopkins University Press, 1989.

Ivy, G. S. "The Bibliography of the Manuscript-Book." In *The English Library Before 1700*, Francis Wormald and C. E. Wright, eds, 32–65. London: Athlone Press, 1958.

Jardine, Lisa. *Erasmus, Man of Letters: The Construction of Charisma in Print.* Princeton: Princeton University Press, 1993.

———, and Grafton, Anthony. "'Studied for Action': How Gabriel Harvey Read His Livy." *Past and Present* 129 (1990), 30–78.

Keeble, Neil. *The Literary Culture of Nonconformity in Later Seventeenth-Century England.* Leicester: Leicester University Press, 1987.

Kermode, Frank. *The Sense of an Ending: Studies in the Theory of Fiction.* New York: Oxford University Press, 1967.

Kernan, Alvin. *Samuel Johnson & the Impact of Print.* Princeton: Princeton University Press, 1987.

Knappen, M. M. *Two Elizabethan Puritan Diaries by Richard Rogers and Samuel Ward.* Chicago: American Society of Church History, 1933.

Knight, Charles. *Shadows of the Old Booksellers*. London: Bell and Daldy, 1865.

Knott, John R. *Discourses of Martyrdom in English Literature, 1563–1694*. Cambridge: Cambridge University Press, 1993.

Lake, Peter. "Deeds against Nature: Cheap Print, Protestantism and Murder in Early Seventeenth-Century England." In *Culture and Politics in Early Stuart England*, Kevin Sharpe and Peter Lake, eds, 257–83. Stanford: Stanford University Press, 1993.

Landon, Richard D. "Small Profits do Great Things: James Lackington and Eighteenth-Century Bookselling." *Studies in Eighteenth-Century Culture* 5 (1976), 387–99.

Lang, Candace. "Autobiography in the Aftermath of Romanticism." *diacritics* 12 (Winter 1982), 2–16.

Laqueur, Thomas. "Crowds, Carnival and the State in English Executions, 1604–1868." In *The First Modern Society*, A. L. Beier, D. Cannadine and J. Rosenheim, eds, 305–56. Cambridge: Cambridge University Press, 1989.

Lejeune, Philippe. "The Autobiography of Those Who Do Not Write." In Philippe Lejeune, *On Autobiography*, Katherine Leary, trans., Paul John Eakin, ed., 185–215. Minneapolis: University of Minnesota Press, 1989.

——. "Teaching People to Write Their Life Story." In Philippe Lejeune, *On Autobiography*, 216–31.

Linebaugh, Peter. "The Ordinary of Newgate and his *Account*." In *Crime in England 1550–1800*, J. S. Cockburn, ed., 246–69. Princeton: Princeton University Press, 1977.

——. *The London Hanged: Crime and Civil Society in the Eighteenth Century*. Cambridge: Cambridge University Press, 1992.

Lloyd, Arnold. *Quaker Social History 1669–1738*. London: Longmans, Green & Co., 1950.

Loesberg, Jonathan. "Autobiography as Genre, Act of Consciousness, Text." *Prose Studies* 4 (1981), 169–85.

Love, Harold. "Preacher and Publisher: Oliver Heywood and Thomas Parkhurst." *Studies in Bibliography* 31 (1978), 227–35.

Lukes, Steven. *Individualism*. Oxford: Blackwell, 1973.

Lyons, John D. *Exemplum: The Rhetoric of Example in Early Modern France and Italy*. Princeton: Princeton University Press, 1989.

Macfarlane, Alan. *The Origins of English Individualism: The Family, Property and Social Transition*. Oxford: Blackwell, 1978.

——. *The Culture of Capitalism*. Oxford and Cambridge, MA: Blackwell, 1987.

MacIntyre, Alasdair. *After Virtue: A Study in Moral Theory*. 2nd edn. Notre Dame, IN: Notre Dame University Press, 1984.

Macpherson, C. B. *The Political Theory of Possessive Individualism: Hobbes to Locke*. Oxford: Oxford University Press, 1962.

Marks, Alfred. *Tyburn Tree: Its History and Annals*. London: Brown, Langham & Co., n.d.

Martz, Louis B. *The Poetry of Meditation: A Study in English Religious Literature of the Seventeenth Century*. Revised edn. New Haven and London: Yale University Press, 1962.

Maslen, Keith. "Printing for the Author: From the Bowyer Printing Ledgers, 1710–1775." *The Library*, 5th ser., 27 (1972), 302–9.

McEwen, Gilbert D. *The Oracle of the Coffee House: John Dunton's* Athenian Mercury. San Marino, CA: Huntington Library, 1972.

McKenzie, D. F. "Typography and Meaning: The Case of William Congreve." In *Buch and Buchhandel in Europa im achtzehnten Jahrhundert*, Giles Barber and Bernhard Fabian, eds, 81–125. Hamburg: Dr Ernst Hauswell & Co., 1981.

McKeon, Michael. *The Origins of the English Novel 1600–1740*. Baltimore and London: The Johns Hopkins University Press, 1987.

Mink, Louis O. "Narrative Form as a Cognitive Instrument." In *The Writing of History: Literary Form and Historical Understanding*, Robert H. Canary and Henry Kozicki, eds, 129–49. Madison: University of Wisconsin Press, 1978.

Misch, Georg. *A History of Autobiography in Antiquity*. E. W. Dickes, trans. 2 vols. 1907. Repr. London: Routledge & Kegan Paul Ltd, 1950.

Moore, C. A. "John Dunton: Pietist and Impostor." *Studies in Philology* 22 (1925), 467–99.

Morgan, Fidelis. *The Well-Known Troublemaker: A Life of Charlotte Charke*. London and Boston: Faber and Faber, 1988.

Morgan, John. *Godly Learning: Puritan Attitudes towards Reason, Learning and Education, 1560–1640*. Cambridge: Cambridge University Press, 1986.

Mortimer, Russell S. "The First Century of Quaker Printers." *Journal of the Friends Historical Society* 40 (1948), 37–49.

Nehamas, Alexander J. "Writer, Work, Text, Author." In *Literature and the Question of Philosophy*, Anthony J. Cascardi, ed., 265–91. Baltimore and London: The Johns Hopkins University Press, 1987.

Nietzsche, Friedrich. *The Will to Power*. Walter Kaufmann and R. J. Hollingdale, trans. Walter Kaufman, ed. New York: Vintage, 1967.

Nussbaum, Felicity A. *The Autobiographical Subject: Gender and Ideology in Eighteenth-Century England*. Baltimore and London: The Johns Hopkins University Press, 1989.

O'Connor, Mary Catherine. *The Art of Dying Well: The Development of the Ars Moriendi*. New York: Columbia University Press, 1942.

O'Malley, Thomas P. "The Press and Quakerism 1653–1659." *Journal of the Friends Historical Society* 54 (1979), 169–84.

——. "'Defying the Powers and Tempering the Spirit.' A Review of Quaker Control Over Their Publications 1672–1689." *Journal of Ecclesiastical History* 33 (1982), 72–88.

Ong, Walter. *Orality and Literacy: The Technologizing of the Word*. London and New York: Methuen, 1982.

——. "Writing as a Technology that Restructures Thought." In *The Written Word: Literacy in Transition*, Gerd Baumann, ed., 23–50. Oxford: Clarendon Press, 1986.

Parks, Stephen. *John Dunton and the English Book Trade: A Study of his Career with a Checklist of his Publications*. New York and London: Garland Publishing, 1976.

Pascal, Roy. *Design and Truth in Autobiography*. Cambridge: Harvard University Press, 1960.

Penney, Norman. "George Fox's Writings and the Morning Meeting." *Friends' Quarterly Examiner* 36 (1902), 63–72.

——. "Our Recording Clerks." *Journal of the Friends Historical Society* 1 (1903–4), 12–22.

Peters, Julie Stone. *Congreve, the Drama, and the Printed Word*. Stanford: Stanford University Press, 1990.

Pilkington, Laetitia. *The Memoirs of Mrs. Letitia Pilkington 1712–1750, Written by Herself*. Iris Barry, ed. London: Geo. Routledge & Sons, 1928.

Pointon, Marcia. *Hanging the Head: Portraiture and Social Formation in Eighteenth-Century England*. New Haven and London: Yale University Press, 1993.

Pollock, Linda. *With Faith and Physic: The Life of a Tudor Gentlewoman Lady Grace Mildmay 1552–1620*. London: Collins & Brown, 1993.

Portus, Garnet V. *Caritas Anglicana or, An Historical Inquiry into those Religious and Philanthropical Societies that Flourished in England Between the Years 1678 and 1740*. London: A. R. Mowbray & Co., 1912.

Radzinowitz, Leon. *A History of English Criminal Law and its Administration from 1750*. 4 vols. New York: Macmillan, 1948.

Rawlings, Philip. *Drunks, Whores and Idle Apprentices: Criminal Biographies of the Eighteenth Century*. London and New York: Routledge, 1992.

Richetti, John. *Popular Fiction Before Richardson: Narrative Patterns 1700–1739*. Oxford: Clarendon Press, 1969.

Ricœur, Paul. *Hermeneutics and the Human Sciences*. John B. Thompson, ed. and trans. Cambridge and Paris: Cambridge University Press and Editions de la Maison des Sciences de l'Homme, 1981.

——. "Narrative Time." In *On Narrative*, W. J. T. Mitchell, ed., 165–86. Chicago: University of Chicago Press, 1981.

——. *Time and Narrative*. Kathleen McLaughlin and David Pellauer, trans. 3 vols. Chicago and London: University of Chicago Press, 1984.

——. "Life: A Story in Search of a Narrator." In *A Ricœur Reader: Reflection and Imagination*, Mario J. Valdés, ed., 425–37. Toronto and Buffalo: University of Toronto Press, 1991.

Rose, Mark. *Authors and Owners: The Invention of Copyright*. Cambridge and London: Harvard University Press, 1993.

Ross, Isabel. *Margaret Fell: Mother of Quakerism*. 2nd edn. York: William Sessions Book Trust, 1984.

Ross, Marlon B. "Authority and Authenticity: Scribbling Authors and the Genius of Print in Eighteenth-Century England." In *The Construction of Authorship: Textual Appropriation in Law and Literature*, Martha Woodmansee and Peter Jaszi, eds, 231–57. Durham and London: Duke University Press, 1994.

Runyon, David. "Types of Quaker Writings by Year – 1650–1699." In *Early Quaker Writings 1650–1700*, Hugh Barbour and Arthur O. Roberts, eds, 567–76. Grand Rapids: William B. Eerdmans Publishing Co., 1973.

Saunders, David, and Hunter, Ian. "Lessons from the 'Literatory': How to Historicise Authorship." *Critical Inquiry* 17 (1991), 479–509.

Scholes, Robert. "Language, Narrative, Anti-Narrative." In *On Narrative*, W. J. T. Mitchell, ed., 200–8. Chicago: University of Chicago Press, 1981.

——. "Narration and Narrativity in Fiction and Film." In Robert Scholes, *Semiotics and Interpretation*, 57–72. New Haven and London: Yale University Press, 1982.

Seaver, Paul S. *Wallington's World: A Puritan Artisan in Seventeenth-Century London*. Stanford: Stanford University Press, 1985.

Shanahan, Daniel. *Toward a Genealogy of Individualism*. Amherst: University of Massachusetts Press, 1992.

Sharpe, J. A. "'Last Dying Speeches': Religion, Ideology and Public Execution in Seventeenth-Century England." *Past and Present* 107 (1985), 144–67.

Sheehan, W. J. "Finding Solace in Eighteenth-Century Newgate." In *Crime in England 1550–1800*, J. S. Cockburn, ed., 229–45. Princeton: Princeton University Press, 1977.

Shevelow, Kathryn. *Women and Print Culture: The Construction of Femininity in the Early Periodical.* London and New York: Routledge, 1989.

Shumaker, Wayne. *English Autobiography: Its Emergence, Materials, and Form.* Berkeley and Los Angeles: University of California Press, 1954.

Silverman, Kaja. *The Subject of Semiotics.* Oxford and New York: Oxford University Press, 1983.

Simon, Joan. *Education and Society in Tudor England.* Cambridge: Cambridge University Press, 1966.

Smith, Charlotte Fell. *Mary Rich, Countess of Warwick (1625–1678): Her Family & Friends.* London: Longmans, Green & Co., 1901.

Smith, Joseph. *A Descriptive Catalogue of Friends' Books.* 2 vols. London, 1867.

Smith, Lacey Balwin. "English Treason Trials and Confessions in the Sixteenth Century." *Journal of the History of Ideas* 15 (1954), 471–98.

Smith, Nigel. *Perfection Proclaimed: Language and Literature in English Radical Religion 1640–60.* Oxford: Clarendon Press, 1989.

Spacks, Patricia Meyer. *Imagining a Self: Autobiography and Novel in Eighteenth-Century England.* Cambridge and London: Harvard University Press, 1976.

——. *Desire and Truth: Functions of Plot in Eighteenth-Century English Novels.* Chicago and London: University of Chicago Press, 1990.

Sprinker, Michael. "Fictions of the Self: The End of Autobiography." In *Autobiography: Essays Theoretical and Critical*, James Olney, ed., 321–42. Princeton: Princeton University Press, 1989.

Spufford, Margaret. "First Steps in Literacy: The Reading and Writing Experiences of the Humblest Seventeenth-Century Spiritual Autobiographers." *Social History* 4 (1979), 407–35.

Spurr, John. *The Restoration Church of England, 1646–1689.* New Haven and London: Yale University Press, 1991.

Starobinski, Jean. "The Style of Autobiography." Seymour Chatman, trans. In *Autobiography: Essays Theoretical and Critical*, James Olney, ed., 73–83. Princeton: Princeton University Press, 1980.

Starr, George. "From Casuistry to Fiction: the Importance of the *Athenian Mercury*." *Journal of the History of Ideas* 28 (1967), 17–32.

——. *Defoe and Casuistry.* Princeton: Princeton University Press, 1971.

Stevenson, Laura Caroline. *Praise and Paradox: Merchants and Craftsmen in Elizabethan Popular Literature.* Cambridge: Cambridge University Press, 1984.

Stone, Lawrence. *The Crisis of the Aristocracy 1558–1641.* Oxford: Clarendon Press, 1965.

——. *The Family, Sex and Marriage in England 1500–1800.* New York: Harper & Row, 1977.

Suleiman, Susan R., and Crosman, Inge, eds. *The Reader in the Text: Essays on Audience and Interpretation.* Princeton: Princeton University Press, 1980.

Tawney, R. H. *The Agrarian Problem in the Sixteenth Century.* London: Longmans, Green & Co., 1912.

——. *Religion and Rise of Capitalism*. 1926. Repr. Harmondsworth: Pelican, 1938.

Taylor, Charles. "The Concept of a Person." In Charles Taylor, *Human Agency and Language: Philosophical Papers*, vol. I, 97–114. Cambridge: Cambridge University Press, 1985.

——. *Sources of the Self: The Making of the Modern Identity*. Cambridge: Harvard University Press, 1989.

Todd, Margo. "The Samuel Ward Papers at Sidney Sussex College, Cambridge." *Transactions of the Cambridge Bibliographical Society* 7 (1985), 582–92.

——. *Christian Humanism and the Puritan Social Order*. Cambridge: Cambridge University Press, 1987.

——. "Puritan Self-Fashioning: The Diary of Samuel Ward." *Journal of British Studies* 31 (1992), 236–64.

Tompkins, Jane P., ed. *Reader-Response Criticism: From Formalism to Post-Structuralism*. Baltimore and London: The Johns Hopkins University Press, 1980.

Ullman, Walter. *The Individual and Society in the Middle Ages*. Baltimore: The Johns Hopkins University Press, 1966.

Vann, Richard T. *The Social Development of English Quakerism 1655–1755*. Cambridge, MA: Harvard University Press, 1969.

Vickers, Brian. *Francis Bacon and Renaissance Prose*. Cambridge: Cambridge University Press, 1968.

Watkins, Owen C. *The Puritan Experience*. London: Routledge & Kegan Paul, 1972.

Watson, Foster. *The English Grammar Schools to 1660: Their Curriculum and Practice*. Cambridge: Cambridge University Press, 1908.

Watt, Ian. *The Rise of the Novel: Studies in Defoe, Richardson and Fielding*. Berkeley and Los Angeles: University of California Press, 1957.

Watt, Tessa. *Cheap Print and Popular Piety, 1550–1640*. Cambridge: Cambridge University Press, 1991.

Watts, Michael R. *The Dissenters from the Reformation to the French Revolution*. Oxford: Clarendon Press, 1978.

Weber, Max. *The Protestant Ethic and the Spirit of Capitalism*. Talcott Parsons, trans. New York: Charles Scribner's Sons, 1958.

Weintraub, Karl J. "Autobiography and Historical Consciousness." *Critical Inquiry* 1 (1975), 821–48.

White, Hayden. *The Content of the Form: Narrative Discourse and Historical Representation*. Baltimore and London: The Johns Hopkins University Press, 1987.

White, Helen C. *English Devotional Literature [Prose] 1600–1640*. University of Wisconsin Studies in Language and Literature, no. 29. Madison: University of Wisconsin Press, 1931.

——. *The Tudor Books of Private Devotion*. Madison: University of Wisconsin Press, 1951.

Wiles, Roy M. *Serial Publication in England Before 1750*. Cambridge: Cambridge University Press, 1957.

Williams, Raymond. *Keywords: A Vocabulary of Culture and Society*. Revised edn. New York: Oxford University Press, 1983.

Wong, Hertha. *Sending My Heart Back Across the Years: Tradition and*

Innovation in Native American Autobiography. New York and Oxford: Oxford University Press, 1992.

Woodmansee, Martha. "The Genius and the Copyright: Economic and Legal Conditions of the Emergence of the 'Author'." *Eighteenth-Century Studies* 17 (1984), 405–48.

Worth, R. N. "Notes from Two Plymouth Diaries." *The Antiquary* 13 (1886), 242–4.

Wright, C. E. "The Dispersal of the Libraries in the Sixteenth Century." In *The English Library before 1700*, Francis Wormald and C. E. Wright, eds, 148–75. London: Athlone Press, 1958.

Wright, Louis B. *Middle-Class Culture in Elizabethan England.* Chapel Hill: University of North Carolina Press, 1935.

——. ed. *Advice to a Son: The Precepts of Lord Burghley, Sir Walter Ralegh, and Francis Osborne.* Ithaca: Cornell University Press, 1962.

Wright, Luella M. *The Literary Life of the Early Friends 1650–1725.* New York: Cambridge University Press, 1932.

Wunderli, Richard, and Broce, Gerald. "The Final Moment before Death in Early Modern England." *Sixteenth-Century Journal* 20 (1989), 259–75.

Index

Vickers, Brian, 73
Vivès, Juan Luis, 82
Voltaire, 41

Walker, Ann, 83
Walker, Anthony, 68–9, 115
Walker, Henry: *Spiritual Experiences*, 117n. 56
Walpole, Horace, 180
Ward, Samuel, 84–6, 88, 90, 95, 99
Watt, Ian, 26, 31
Weber, Max, 16, 23
Weintraub, Karl, 23
Wesley, John, 3–5, 40, 41, 46, 143; publishing activity, 4; *Journal*, 50, 51
Wesley, Samuel, 152
White, Hayden, 36
Whitehead, George, 4n. 2, 105n. 18

Whitehead, Jane, 129
Whitfield, George, 143; *Journal*, 51
Whitrow, Joan, 129
Whittington, Dick, 39
Whole Duty of Man, 155
Whyte, Samuel, 198
Wilkinson, Elizabeth, 68, 83
Wilkinson, Tate, 42–3
William & Mary, 151, 152, 172
Wilson, Arthur, 113n. 48
Woodward, Josiah, 104n. 13
Wright, henry: *First Part of the Disquisition of Truth*, 65
Wright, John, 63
writing, 44–5, 69–70, 72–7, 115. *See also* autobiography, manuscript; diary
Wyer, Robert, 77

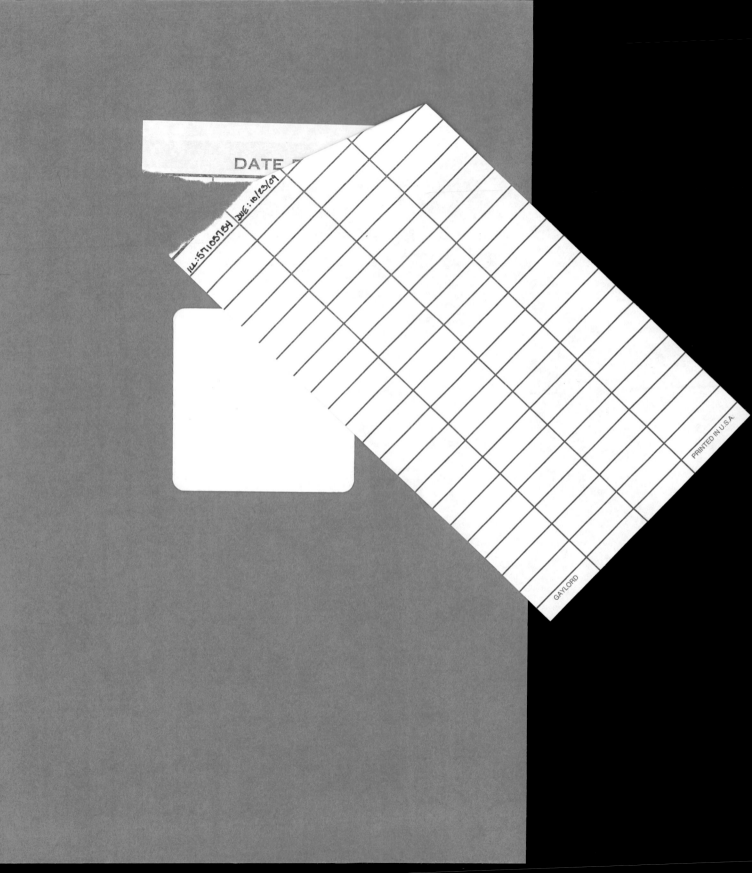